Edna Carew has forged a reputation over the past twenty years as a first-rate communicator who can whittle down complex concepts into plain, intelligible language. Formerly a specialist writer with *The Australian Financial Review*, she is the author of more than a dozen books on various aspects of finance, business and banking. Her best-sellers include the *Fast Money* and *Language of Money* series, *Paul Keating, Prime Minister* and *Westpac, the bank that broke the bank*.

'Fast Money 4 *builds on earlier versions of this indispensable reference book to provide a definitive, comprehensive, accessible guide to the Australian financial markets. The book contains a mine of information, making it essential reading for students of finance and banking, for those seeking employment in the markets as well as for investors keen to understand how these markets operate.'*

Professor Tom Valentine
Professor of Banking and Finance, University of Western Sydney

'Fast Money 4 *provides an excellent description and explanation of the key factors driving capital and financial markets in today's rapidly changing financial world . . . It also contains a succinct but thorough analysis of the key participants and latest developments in the capital markets. Despite the complexity of the issues, Edna Carew's easy-to-read style makes* Fast Money 4 *a "must read" for students—and also a useful "reminder" text even for professional market participants.'*

Wayne Lonergan
Partner, Corporate Finance, PricewaterhouseCoopers
and National President, Securities Institute of Australia

Also by Edna Carew

FAST MONEY 4

The bestselling guide to Australia's financial markets

EDNA CAREW

ALLEN & UNWIN

First published in 1998 by
Allen & Unwin
9 Atchison Street
St Leonards NSW 1590
Australia
Phone: (61 2) 8425 0100
Fax: (61 2) 9906 2218
E-mail: frontdesk@allen-unwin.com.au
Web: http://www.allen-unwin.com.au

National Library of Australia
Cataloguing-in-Publication entry:

Carew, Edna, 1949– .
  Fast money 4: the bestselling guide to Australia's financial
  markets.

  Includes index.
  ISBN 1 86448 994 4.

  1. Money market—Australia. I. Title. II. Title: Fast money four.

332.10994

Set in 10/11pt Times by DOCUPRO, Sydney
Printed and bound by Griffin Press, Adelaide

10 9 8 7 6 5 4 3 2 1

Contents

Tables and figures

Abbreviations

ABA	Australian Bankers' Association
ACCC	Australian Competition and Consumer Commission
AFIC	Australian Financial Institutions Commission
AFMA	Australian Financial Markets Association
AMBA	Australian Merchant Bankers' Association
APCA	Australian Payments Clearing Association
APRA	Australian Prudential Regulation Authority
ASC	Australian Securities Commission
ASIC	Australian Securities and Investment Commission
ASX	Australian Stock Exchange
ASXD	Australian Stock Exchange Derivatives (division)
ATMs	automatic teller machines
ATOA	Australian Treasury Operations Association
BBSW	bank-bill reference rate
BIS	Bank for International Settlements
CD	certificate of deposit
CHESS	Clearing House Electronic Subregister System
CLO	collateralised loan obligation
CLSS	Continuous Linked Settlement Services
CMO	collateralised mortgage obligation
COMEX	New York Commodity Exchange
CTAs	Commodity Trading Advisers
DTB	Deutsche Terminbörse
ECU	European Currency Unit
EFP	Exchange for Physical
EMU	European Monetary Union
ESA	exchange-settlement account
ES funds	exchange-settlement funds
ETO	exchange-traded option

Fannie Mae	Federal National Mortgage Association
FRA	forward-rate agreement
FSAC	Financial Sector Advisory Council
FX	foreign-exchange
Ginnie Mae	Government National Mortgage Association
IBSA	International Banks and Securities Association
ICCH	International Commodities Clearing House
ICONs	Initial Corporate Obligation Notes
IMF	International Monetary Fund
ISFs	individual share futures
ITA	Infrastructure Trust of Australia
LEPO	low-exercise-price option
LIFFE	London International Financial Futures Exchange
LOCAM	Large Order Call Automated Market
MTN	medium-term note
NCD	negotiable certificate of deposit
NCDs	non-callable deposits
NEM	National Electricity Market
NSW TCorp	New South Wales Treasury Corporation
NYMEX	New York Mercantile Exchange
NZFOE	New Zealand Futures and Options Exchange
OCH	Options Clearing House
OTC	over-the-counter
PAR	prime assets ratio
QTC	Queensland Treasury Corporation
RBA	Reserve Bank of Australia
RITS	Reserve Bank Information and Transfer System
RTGS	real-time gross settlement
SAFA	South Australian Government Financing Authority
SEATS	Stock Exchange Automated Trading System
SEC	Securities and Exchange Commission
SFE	Sydney Futures Exchange
SFECH	Sydney Futures Exchange Clearing House
SIMEX	Singapore International Monetary Exchange
SPI	share-price index
SPV	special-purpose vehicle
SWIFT	Society for Worldwide Interbank Financial Telecommunications
SYCOM	Sydney Computerised Market
TCV	Treasury Corporation Victoria
TIFFE	Tokyo International Financial Futures Exchange
TIMS	Theoretical Intermarket Margining System
TPC	Trade Practices Commission
TWI	trade-weighted index
WTI	West Texas Intermediate

Acknowledgements

In a career spanning twenty years of writing about financial markets it is impossible to nominate every individual who has contributed, in varying degrees along the way, to one's body of knowledge. Those who specifically helped with earlier versions of *Fast Money* feature in those editions, and their contributions remain as building blocks in this new text.

Fast Money was conceived in 1981, more or less by accident. A chance conversation between Geraldine Walsh and publisher John Iremonger led to a lunch at which Iremonger intended to ask me to write a book about sex therapists. I came away with a commission to write a book about the money markets in Australia. As a specialist writer with *The Australian Financial Review* (having been recruited some years earlier by its editor, Max Walsh) I was well-placed to shed some light on the complexities of Australia's expanding financial sector.

The first edition of *Fast Money* was rapidly overtaken by sweeping changes which led to *Fast Money 2*'s appearance in 1985, and subsequently *Fast Money 3*. *Fast Money 4* should have made its entry before now but was deliberately delayed until the dust might settle after the Wallis inquiry into the financial system. As any observer of financial markets knows, however, the dust never does settle and an author, ultimately, has to surrender a book for publication.

I had no thought, when putting together that first *Fast Money* in the early 1980s, that I would be updating the text so many years later. But I do recall a comment by Jillian Broadbent, then a rising executive at Bankers Trust and now a member of the Reserve Bank board, that I would find myself in a similar position to the noted economist Paul Samuelson, constantly updating the work. I was gratified at her analogy but sceptical of her optimism that *Fast Money* had such a bright future. She was more right than wrong, although sales of *Fast Money*, regrettably, could not be said to match those of Samuelson's landmark textbook on economics. But the book has been sufficiently widely used to justify frequent revisions. Several of those interviewed for this latest edition remarked that they had used the first *Fast Money* in their studies. It is gratifying to know that the book genuinely serves a purpose, filling the gap I had encountered when, as a newcomer to both Australia and to the financial markets, I had sought something helpful to read. Finding nothing, I eventually wrote my own guide.

Many people helped fashion *Fast Money 4* into a comprehensive text covering the latest developments and innovations. I particularly thank those who took the time to read chapters and, despite pressured work schedules of their own, enthusiastically offered comments and advice. I am especially indebted to Frank Campbell and his staff in domestic markets at the Reserve Bank—John Hoare, Darryl Ross, Colleen Anderson, Bob Perry. Thanks also to Bob Rankin and Darren Flood in the RBA's international department and to those who provided assistance on various technical aspects relating to regulatory changes: John Veale, Les Phelps and Les Austin.

Elsewhere in the markets, I thank the following for their generous contributions in reading and commenting on drafts: Paul Robertson, Geoff Bowmer, Paul Bide, Stephen Chambers, Glenn McDowell, Richard Mason, Lou Ghirardello, Steve Knight, Tony Gill, Nancy Fox, Bruce Arnold, Phil Hatten, David Finnimore, Andrew Moylan, Chum Darvall, Richard Bennett, Paul Ritchie, Steven Mater, James Watts.

Others who helped with information, responded promptly and willingly to queries and calls to check facts include: Les Hosking and staff at the Sydney Futures Exchange, particularly Tony Dreise, Brett Stevenson, Grant Hinrichsen; at the Australian Stock Exchange: Paul Pinnock, Tony Hunter and Colin Scully; at AFMA Ken Farrow and John Rappell; IBSA's Robert Webster and Austraclear's John Hall; John Bills at the Australian Finance Conference; and elsewhere Peter Anderson, Russell Armstrong, Jonathan Batten, Richard Bennett, Tony Berriman, Bob Biven, Jason Cavanagh, David Chin, Lyn Cobley, Paul Cordeiro, Michael Dontschuk, Andre Franco, Peter Gow, Phil Gray, Lorraine Grove, Randell Heyman, Ian Kay, Steve Kennedy, Mark Langsworth, Peter Mack, Janet Marsh, Terry Maxted, Greg Medcraft, Greg Mizon, Tom Murphy, Mike Norton, Tony Pearson, Debra Robertson, Anthony Robson, Peter Sheahan, Craig Shapiro, Jonathan Stebbins, Mike Stinson, Peter Taplin, Els Termaat, Graham Timms, Geoff Tompsett,

Ian Town, Nea Williamson, Simon Wright, David Zobel and, for their general assistance, Erin Cockerton and Jacqui Wise.

The tyranny of distance was mitigated by Sheila Ferguson's willingness to undertake some footwork and I thank her for her assistance with chapter 16, and those she spoke with who include some of those mentioned above as well as: Chris Bell, Phil Boyle, Dick Bryant, Steve Davidson, Michael Dodds, Harry Hull, Graeme Johnson, Jerry McCready, John Pilkington, John Stocks, Nick Volontakis, Andrew Wardle.

My appreciation to the many others who over the years have responded readily and good-naturedly to requests for information and guidance.

As ever, John Hoffmann's editing skills reinforced clarity and polish. And Holly the border collie still helps to keep a sedentary writer in an acceptable state of fitness.

Introduction

W hen I set out in 1982 to write the first *Fast Money*, the arcane
subject matter, the operations of Australia's money markets—the
term 'financial markets' was not yet even born—was of little interest
to the average Australian. When queried about what I was writing,
I'd say 'a book about the money markets' and the response inevitably was: you mean the sharemarkets? Now, in the late 1990s,
many developments have combined to bring together the financial
markets and the average investor (a development in itself: people
no longer 'save', they 'invest').

As the twentieth century nears its close, changing demographics
have brought financial markets a far higher—and more relevant—
profile than they enjoyed in previous decades, thanks to the
mounting importance assigned to the need for individuals to plan
for their retirement. As the baby-boomers approach their senior
years, and improved medical knowledge and general health and
fitness contribute to increased longevity, more and more attention
is focused on savings and investment strategies to underpin an
enjoyable and financially secure old age.

These trends, combined with the compulsory nature of superannuation, have shed an unprecedented spotlight on financial
markets as investors of varying means turn to the traditional asset
classes of cash, shares, fixed interest (or fixed income) and property
to try to maximise their wealth. The exotic world of high finance
is now of interest to all. And the retail investor is increasingly
important for the wholesale as well as the retail financial markets.
At the same time, a wave of privatisations has brought mounting
numbers of Australians to the sharemarket, and has involved invest-

ment banking skills and sophisticated structured finance techniques in what were previously government-funded infrastructure projects.

The average Australian has become familiar with not just the sharemarket but also with fixed interest, foreign exchange, unit trusts and so forth. The daily financial press routinely pours out articles on how best to invest, how to plan for retirement, how to make the most of low inflation and a booming stockmarket. Television programs beam the doctrines of sage investment into living rooms across Australia. The appetite for information about investment seems to be insatiable. Bookstores devote shelves to finance and investment, where once that rated a small corner—which was stacked mostly with expensive tomes from the US. Smart investment has become a national obsession.

Blame it on the baby-boomers, the 'me' generation now in its forties and fifties, which never did anything by halves; in its ebullient way, it believed it had discovered sex and drugs as no-one had before and now confronts retirement with unprecedented energy, planning and enthusiasm. Blame it on the federal government which, faced with a demographic force signalling an upsurge in grey heads, brought in compulsory superannuation as it became clear that the public purse, supported in future years by a workforce that, proportionately, was declining compared with the rest of the population, could no longer support a generous pension system. Blame it on financial deregulation (it got blamed for most of the flaws of the 1980s) which blew apart the cosy banking cartel that so well served the elite it chose to cater for and only now, so many years after its birth, is winning some credit for seeing consumers served in a low-interest-rate and low-inflation environment by a wider range of products and institutions. Blame it on technology which, along with deregulation and internationalisation, has brought down barriers between countries. Without advances in communications there would be no globalisation of markets, nor would that be possible without deregulation. The upshot is that the Australian investor, or the US or UK or German, Swiss, Japanese or Singaporean investor, is no longer shackled by national boundaries. Fund managers straddle the globe, and the pot they manage gets bigger every year. And investors increasingly want to know what is happening to their bit of the pot. So while earlier versions of *Fast Money* chiefly served those studying or working in the financial markets, *Fast Money 4* speaks to a far wider audience which includes not just students of the markets and those who work in them but the great mass of ordinary Australians who, directly or indirectly, to a small or large extent, look to those markets to help them accumulate and maximise financial resources.

The financial markets, once infamous for trading for trading's sake, have been legitimised as a meaningful sector of the economy.

And the need to understand what drives them and how they work has never been more widely felt. *Fast Money 4* has been written to help satisfy that need.

Calendar of main economic and financial events: 1936–98

1936–37

Report of the Royal Commission into Money and Banking.

1939

April   Robert Gordon Menzies elected prime minister of a conservative coalition government.

August   The commonwealth took control of foreign exchange transactions.

September   Outbreak of the Second World War.

1941

October   War-time banking regulations announced.
             Yokohama Specie Bank Ltd ceased operating in Sydney.
             John Curtin elected prime minister of Labor government.

1942

February   The Commonwealth Bank was granted special powers to fix maximum interest rates.

July   The Bank of China began operating in Sydney.

1944

July   Forty-four nations met at the Bretton Woods Conference in New Hampshire, US, to establish a new international monetary system. The International Monetary Fund and

1

the International Bank for Reconstruction and World Development (World Bank) were formed.

1945

May   VE (Victory in Europe) Day.

July   Joseph Chifley was appointed prime minister following the death of John Curtin.

August   End of the Second World War.
           The Banking Act (regulating banking) and the Commonwealth Bank Act (reorganising the Commonwealth Bank) were passed.

1946

June   The Commonwealth Insurance Commissioner was appointed, under the Life Insurance Act, 1945, to supervise activities of life offices.

1947

May   Australia was approved as a member of the International Monetary Fund (IMF) and of the World Bank.

October   The Banking Bill to nationalise the trading banks was introduced into the House of Representatives. Following action in the High Court and Privy Council, the legislation was invalidated.

1949

December   The Chifley government was defeated and Menzies was re-elected prime minister of a Liberal/Country Party government.

1953

December   The Commonwealth Trading Bank began operating—previously it had been the general banking division of the Commonwealth Bank.

1956

February   The LGS (liquid assets and government securities) convention for the trading banks was established.

1958

October   The first issue of Special Bonds was made.

1959

February   The official short-term money market was established. A committee was set up to examine the introduction of decimal currency (it reported in favour in August 1960).

April   Assent was given to the Reserve Bank Act, the Commonwealth Act, the Banking Act and the Banking (Transitional Provisions) Act. These Acts became operative on 14 January 1960. The central banking functions of the Commonwealth Bank passed to the newly-constituted Reserve Bank.

November   The first issue was made of seasonal treasury notes; the notes were issued from November until April.

1960

January   The first Australian futures market opened, trading in greasy wool at the Sydney Greasy Wool Futures Exchange.
The trading banks' 'special deposits' were replaced with statutory reserve deposits (SRDs).

1961

The Organisation for Economic Cooperation and Development was formed, headquartered in Paris.

1962

July   13-week treasury notes became continuously available.

1963

November   Savings banks were allowed to offer personal loans.

1964

August   The major trading banks established the Australian Banks' Export Refinance Corporation.

1965

January   The infant commercial bill market received official

3

recognition when the Reserve Bank allowed the authorised money market dealers to trade in bills of exchange.

May   Guidelines were introduced on capital raisings in Australia by companies controlled overseas. This was a response to UK and US measures to restrict capital outflow.

November   The Housing Loans Insurance Corporation began operating in all states.
The Vernon Committee reported after examining postwar development in Australia.

During the year the Reserve Bank lifted qualitative guidelines on bank lending and no longer told the banks to whom they could lend.

1966

January   Prime minister Menzies retired and was succeeded by Harold Holt.

February   Decimal currency was adopted in Australia, with one Australian dollar equal to $US1.20 and one pound sterling equal to $A2.50.

September The trading banks began to provide unsecured personal loans, at a set maximum amount and for a set term.

1967

March   The trading banks were allowed to offer secured personal loans; previous controls on maximum terms and amounts were abandoned.

July   The trading banks were given approval to lend short-term mortgages and bridging loans.
New Zealand introduced decimal currency, with one $NZ equal to $US1.39045.

November   The Australian Resources Development Bank was launched.
The 26-week treasury note was introduced.

1968

May   The trading banks were allowed to handle lease finance.

1969

May — Trading banks were allowed to issue certificates of deposit.

December — Savings bank investment accounts were introduced.

1970

May — The terms of the Banks (Shareholdings) Act applied from this time: the Act was proclaimed in 1972 and limited the maximum individual shareholding to less than 10 per cent of a bank's capital.

1971

February — The UK introduced decimal currency, with one pound equal to 100 new pence and $US2.40.

June — The Australian Industry Development Corporation began operating.
Australia joined the OECD.

August — The US suspended convertibility of the $US into gold, a move that set the scene for the collapse of the Bretton Woods system of fixed exchange rates.
In Australia the trading banks were allowed to deal as principals with the Reserve Bank in foreign exchange and to set their own charges on forward cover.

September — The Reserve Bank introduced surveillance of capital transactions bringing more than $A250 000 into Australia.

December — The Smithsonian realignment of international currency parities was introduced.
Australia and New Zealand currencies became linked to the $US instead of to sterling.

1972

June — The UK floated sterling.

July — The Reserve Bank started to quote forward rates as premium/discount against the spot $US rate instead of fixed charges. Limits were imposed on the amount of forward cover allowed to the banks each day and banks were not allowed to deal forward with non-residents.

5

September   Controls were introduced on capital flowing into Australia, in the form of an embargo on borrowings which were repayable in less than two years.
The guidelines on overseas companies borrowing in Australia (introduced May 1965) were removed.

November   The Bank of China's banking authority was surrendered.
The Sydney Greasy Wool Futures Exchange changed its name to the Sydney Futures Exchange, to reflect a broader range of commodities traded.

December   Australia revalued its dollar by 7.05 per cent to equal $US1.2750.
Controls on funds flowing into Australia were tightened and a variable deposit requirement (VDR) introduced on overseas borrowings. Under the VDR, 25 per cent of funds borrowed from overseas had to be lodged in Australian currency with the Reserve Bank as an interest-free deposit until the borrowing was repaid.
A Labor government won federal election; Gough Whitlam was elected prime minister.

1973

February   Controls on capital inflow to Australia were further tightened.
Heavy speculation on the $US forced foreign exchange markets to close on 12 and 13 February.
The $US was devalued 10 per cent against gold to a gold price of $US42.22 per ounce.
The lira and the yen were floated.

March   Further speculation against the $US caused foreign exchange markets to close from 2 to 19 March; banks could deal but central banks could not intervene. The Reserve Bank of Australia restricted dealings in $US, both spot and forward.
European joint float markets formally reopened, with six EEC countries (Belgium, Luxembourg, Denmark, France, Germany, Netherlands) operating a joint float against the $US.

September   The interest-rate ceiling on certificates of deposit was abolished. The $A was revalued by 5 per cent to a midrate of $US1.4875.

October   The VDR was increased to $33\frac{1}{3}$ per cent.

1974

January   Controls over capital outflows from the US were abolished.

June   The IMF announced guidelines for floating currencies and new Special Drawing Rights were established.
               The Reserve Bank of Australia introduced a 'seven-day rule' which meant traders using the banks' official forward market had to take out cover against exchange rate movements within seven days of incurring the risk.
               The VDR was reduced to 25 per cent.

July   The Rae Committee (Select Committee on Securities and Exchange) tabled a five-volume report on the securities industries and trading practices.

August   The Financial Corporations Act became operative. Part IV of the Act, which provides for the regulation of non-bank financial institutions, was not proclaimed.
               The VDR was reduced to 5 per cent.

September   The $A was devalued by 12 per cent against the $US. The fixed link to the $US was replaced with a link to a trade-weighted basket of currencies.

October   Bankcard was launched.

November   Restrictions were relaxed on foreign capital inflow to Australia and the VDR lifted.

1975

November   Prime minister Gough Whitlam was sacked by the governor-general and Malcolm Fraser became prime minister of a Liberal/Country Party government.

December   US citizens were allowed to buy and sell gold for the first time since 1933.

1976

January   Australian Savings Bonds were introduced to replace Special Bonds.
               Australian residents were allowed to buy and sell gold.

February   The Australian options market started trading.
               A monetary 'target' was announced and subsequently given each year in the treasurer's budget speech.

7

April	The treasurer announced the Australian government's new foreign investment policy.
May	The Reserve Bank discontinued quoting interbank spot and forward sterling rates.
November	The $A was devalued by 17.5 per cent and a 'flexible peg' system of exchange-rate management was introduced. The responsibility for the day-to-day management of the exchange rate was given to the governor of the Reserve Bank, the secretary of the Treasury and the secretary of the Department of Prime Minister and Cabinet.

1977

January	Australia restricted the inflow of funds from abroad. The embargo was increased to cover overseas borrowings repayable within two years and the variable deposit requirement on overseas borrowings was revived at 25 per cent. Controls were introduced on the timing of payments and receipts.
July	The Australian variable deposit requirement was suspended and the embargo relaxed to apply to overseas borrowings repayable within six months.

During the year the promissory note market grew significantly.

1978

April	Gold futures began trading on the Sydney Futures Exchange.
June	Some relaxation occurred in the Australian government's foreign investment policy. The embargo on overseas borrowings repayable within six months was suspended.
September	The Primary Industry Bank of Australia was established.

1979

January	The Committee of Inquiry into the Australian Financial System (Campbell Committee) was established.
March	The European Monetary System (EMS) replaced the 'snake' or joint European currency float.
May	Difficulties of the Adelaide-based financier Finance

Corporation of Australia came to light. The Reserve Bank and major trading banks moved to rescue its banking parent, the Bank of Adelaide.

June   The trading banks entered the currency hedge market.

October   Interest-rate futures began trading on the Sydney Futures Exchange (bank bill futures contract).
The ANZ Bank's takeover of the Bank of Adelaide was approved.
The UK abolished remaining exchange controls.

December   Australia introduced a tender system for selling treasury notes.
Australia's National Companies and Securities Commission was established.

1980

February   The government endorsed a private-industry-based scheme to cover the insurance of building society deposits.

March   Regulations were relaxed on portfolio investments overseas by Australian residents. Limits were increased on equity and real-estate investments.

April   A tap system for selling Australian government (treasury) bonds was introduced, replacing the previous pattern of periodic loans.

May   The maximum shareholding that a bank could hold in a merchant bank was lifted from 33.3 per cent to 60 per cent.

June   Loan Council announced new marketing arrangements for semi-government securities and replaced maximum underwriting commissions with a scale of fees.

July   Surveillance of capital inflow to Australia eased so that delays on inflows were reduced.

December   Interest-rate ceilings were removed from bank deposits.

1981

February   A new bank, the Australian Bank Ltd, was established.

June   The treasurer consented to the mergers of the Bank of New South Wales with the Commercial Bank of Australia,

	and the National Bank of Australasia with the Commercial Banking Company of Sydney Ltd.
July	All restrictions were removed from Australian investment overseas in equities and real estate. The Rural Bank of NSW was reconstituted as the State Bank of NSW.
August	Trading banks were permitted to issue certificates of deposit for a minimum period of 30 days (previously three months).
November	The final report of the Committee of Inquiry into the Australian Financial System (Campbell Committee) was tabled in the House of Representatives.

1982

February	Loan Council announced an examination of its role and of the possibility of selling treasury bonds through a tender system, raising implications for the marketing of semi-government securities.
March	The treasurer announced a number of measures giving banks and savings banks greater flexibility in fundraising.
June	The authorised dealers were allowed greater flexibility regarding the 30 per cent of their assets not held in government securities. The Reserve Bank announced the removal of restrictions on bank lending (quantitative controls). A system for selling treasury bonds by tender was approved. Approval was also given for the states to establish 'central borrowing authorities' to raise funds on behalf of the smaller authorities.
August	The annual budget introduced a bank account debits (BAD) tax. Savings bank regulations were amended to allow savings banks more flexibility.
December	Foreign shareholders rearranging their existing holdings in Australian merchant banks could do so without having to find Australian buyers provided the rearrangement did not result in a decrease in Australian equity.

1983

January   The treasurer announced the government's decision to allow entry of ten new banks, including foreign banks. Applications were to be submitted by 31 May.
Financial institutions duty (FID) was introduced in New South Wales and Victoria (other states followed).
The Reserve Bank announced that all foreign-exchange dealings between itself and the trading banks would be for two days' value, ie, for delivery and settlement two business days after the transaction was written.

February   The deadline for new bank applications was extended to 30 June.
Share-price index futures began trading on the Sydney Futures Exchange.

March   The Australian Labor Party won federal office.
Australia's dollar was devalued by 10 per cent.

May   The treasurer announced the formation of a group to review the Australian financial system and the findings of the Campbell Committee, in the light of the Labor government's economic and social objectives. The question of new banks was shelved pending the outcome of the review.

July   Loan Council lifted controls from the large semi-government authorities.

August   A proposed Cheques Act was announced. Regulation of the futures industry was proposed.

October   Significant changes were announced to Australia's foreign-exchange arrangements; the Reserve Bank withdrew from the forward market, banks won increased flexibility to hold foreign-currency balances and to quote their own rates to customers, and the Reserve Bank was to announce the $A/$US midrate at the end of the trading day instead of at 9.30 am.

November   Legislation outlining the merger between the State Bank of South Australia and the Savings Bank of South Australia was introduced in the South Australian parliament.

December   The Australian dollar was floated and most exchange controls abolished. The Reserve Bank no longer announced a daily $A/$US midrate or trade-weighted index. Banks no longer had to settle their foreign exchange positions with the Reserve Bank at the end of the day. The RBA stated it would not intervene in foreign-exchange markets except to test market conditions and to smooth very large flows.

1984

February   The Martin Review Group's report on the Australian financial system was released. The report endorsed continued deregulation and entry of new, including foreign, banks.
The two-year treasury bond futures contract was introduced on the Sydney Futures Exchange.

March   The ALP caucus supported the suggestion of expanding the number of operators in foreign exchange and lifting controls on the maturities of bank deposits.

April   Australian stock exchanges were deregulated. Brokers' commission rates became negotiable and broking firms were allowed to incorporate. Several banks and merchant banks formed partnerships with broking firms.
The federal government approved a proposal from the merchant bank Hill Samuel Australia Ltd to form a new bank, to be called the Macquarie Bank Ltd.
The treasurer formally called for applications from non-bank financial institutions interested in becoming an authorised dealer in foreign exchange.

May   The Reserve Bank announced that banks could include loans to authorised dealers in their liquid assets and government securities (LGS) ratio.
The Reserve Bank foreshadowed a move to expand the range of bond-traders with whom it dealt directly.

June   The treasurer announced that 40 non-bank financial institutions were to be granted authority to trade in foreign exchange.
The Commonwealth Bank was restructured and its capital increased.

July   The Australian Payments System Council was established, under Reserve Bank chairmanship, to examine the basis of access for new participants to the banks' cheque payments system.
The ALP federal conference gave its approval to limited foreign-bank entry.

Commonwealth payments to the states became payable weekly on Tuesdays, instead of on the first and fifteenth of each month.

August   The fourteen-day rule applying to trading bank deposits was lifted, enabling banks to pay interest on deposits taken for less than fourteen days and to pay interest on cheque accounts.

The Reserve Bank announced the introduction of repurchase agreements (repos) in commonwealth government securities between itself and the authorised money-market dealers.

September The federal government invited applications for bank licences and outlined the conditions on which licences would be granted. Applications were to be lodged by 23 November. It also confirmed the Bank of China's licence to operate in Australia would be reinstated.

The treasurer announced a moratorium on existing foreign-investment guidelines applying to foreign ownership of merchant banks so that shareholdings could be logically restructured; and an increase from 10 to 15 per cent in the maximum individual shareholding in an Australian bank.

The government abolished the 30/20 rule which allowed tax concessions to life offices and pension funds provided they held at least 30 per cent of their assets in public securities, two-thirds of that in commonwealth government securities.

November The Reserve Bank confirmed the establishment of a group of reporting bond-dealers who would have direct access to the central bank when trading in commonwealth government securities of more than one year to maturity.

Forty-two applications for bank licences were lodged with the federal government.

December The ten-year treasury bond futures contract was introduced on the Sydney Futures Exchange.

The treasurer announced changes to the tax treatment of zero-coupon bonds and other securities which offered a chance to delay interest payments and therefore defer tax. Tax would now be paid on the interest accrued each year.

The Reserve Bank announced a list of 21 reporting bond-dealers.

The ceiling on foreign ownership of an Australian sharebroking firm was lifted to 50 per cent (previously 14.99 per cent).

1985

January
Some restrictions relating to foreign investment in Australian securities were lifted. This allowed foreign government agencies whose operations are similar to those of private sector companies, and foreign banks other than central banks, to invest in Australian securities.

The treasurer announced that targeting M3 in the projected 8 to 10 per cent range had been abandoned for 1984/85. Monetary measures remained under review.

Sterling came under downward pressure, resulting in the Bank of England's decision to reactivate—for one day and at 12 per cent—its minimum lending rate (MLR) which had been suspended since August 1981.

February
The NSW Building Society announced its plans to convert to savings bank status.

The National Australia Bank and the United Permanent Building Society announced their agreement allowing United Permanent access to the cheque-clearing system through the NAB. Customers of United Permanent were offered cheque-account facilities and access to the NAB's Australia-wide network of automatic teller machines.

The treasurer announced the government's approval for the establishment of sixteen foreign trading banks.

March
The Macquarie Bank Ltd (formerly the merchant bank Hill Samuel Australia Ltd) began trading.

The Reserve Bank established the Foreign Exchange Market Consultative Group as a forum for discussing issues and standards in the foreign-exchange markets.

Japan's Ministry of Finance relaxed the conditions on eligibility for non-resident issues of euro yen bonds.

April
The remaining ceilings on bank interest rates were removed, with the exception of those on loans of less than $100 000 for owner-occupied housing.

May
The prime assets ratio (PAR) replaced the LGS convention, with 12 per cent of each bank's total liabilities in $A (excluding shareholders' funds) within Australia, to

be held in prime assets, these being notes and coin, balances with the Reserve Bank, treasury notes and other commonwealth government securities, and loans to authorised dealers secured against government securities. Funds in statutory reserve deposits (SRDs) up to 3 per cent of total deposits counted towards PAR.

June   The Ministry of Finance allowed non-Japanese borrowers in the euro yen market to issue floating-rate notes and deep-discount and zero-coupon bonds, and bonds with currency-conversion and dual-currency features.

The Group of Ten met in Tokyo and agreed that the present exchange-rate system provided essential flexibility in a difficult global environment and that a return to a system of fixed parities was unrealistic. However, further action to provide greater stability was desirable and it was essential to maintain sound domestic policies and cooperation among major countries. The meeting examined a proposal to introduce exchange-rate target zones.

The NSW Building Society became the Advance Bank Australia.

The Australian Financial Markets Screen Dealers' Association members agreed on regulation of the forward market in bank bills.

July   The federal government offered its first tender of capital-indexed bonds.

September   Plaza Agreement was reached by the Group of Five in New York's Plaza Hotel. The G–5 (France, West Germany, Japan, the UK and the US) agreed that large external imbalances posed a potential threat, eg, the deterioration in the US's external position and the contribution of the US's current account deficit to the rising wave of support for protectionism. It was agreed that exchange rates would more closely reflect economic conditions and that the aim should be an orderly appreciation of the main non-dollar currencies against the $US. The G–5 professed themselves willing to cooperate to encourage this.

Chase AMP Bank became the first of the new foreign banks to open in Australia.

October   The Tokyo stock exchange launched trading in financial futures.

15

Lloyds Bank NZA became the second foreign bank to open in Australia.

November   Barclays Bank Australia and Bank of Tokyo Australia began operating.

December   France eased exchange controls, allowing companies to use foreign currency options and transact interest-rate swaps.
Citibank Australia and IBJ Australia Bank began operating.
The Bank of China opened for business in Australia after a thirteen-year absence.

1986

January   The US began futures trading in ECU contracts.
Australian Resources Development Bank to be wound down.
Mitsubishi Bank Australia opened its doors.

February   Huge speculation against the Irish pound resulted in higher interest rates to protect the currency.
The Paris financial futures market opened—*Marché à Terme d'Instruments Financiers (MATIF)*.
Deutsche Bank Australia, Hong Kong Bank Australia, NatWest Australia and Bankers Trust Australia opened for business.

April   The interest-rate ceiling for new housing loans was removed. Existing home loans remained subject to the existing maximum rate of 13.5 per cent.
Bank of France intervention in the exchange rate was suspended, and foreign exchange markets closed by all central banks in the European Monetary System. Ministers and central bank governors agreed on the ninth realignment of parities within the EMS.
Standard Chartered Bank Australia opened its doors.
The Reserve Bank announced it would use external auditors to help in bank supervision.
The Rural Credits Department of the Reserve Bank was to be phased out.

May   Bank of America Australia and Bank of Singapore Australia began operating.

June   Japan's Ministry of Finance allowed foreign commercial banks to issue euro-yen bonds.

August   In measures aimed at stemming the rise of the yen against the $US, the Ministry of Finance eased restrictions on overseas yen loans by insurance companies, and lifted the annual ceiling on foreign lending to 10 per cent of annual increase in total assets.
The Reserve Bank eased some restrictions on official money-market dealers, giving them greater scope to use futures markets and additional freedom when buying and selling securities under repurchase agreements. Foreign-ownership ceiling lifted from 25 to 50 per cent.
Bank of America Australia abandoned plans for retail banking.
Statutory reserve deposits to be phased out.

September   In a move to boost currency reserves, the Bank of England, on behalf of UK Treasury, launched a $US4 billion ten-year floating-rate note, the largest issue yet made by a single borrower on the eurobond market.
Again anxious to stem the yen's rise against the $US, Japan removed the ceiling on life assurance funds which the Ministry of Posts and Telecommunications could invest in foreign currency securities.

October   United Permanent Building Society and National Mutual Royal Bank to merge.
Westpac Banking Corporation to enter life insurance.
Perth Building Society and Victoria's Hotham Permanent Building Society to merge and form the Challenge Bank Ltd.

November   The EEC endorsed the first stage of a two-phase plan for full liberalisation of capital movements within the community by the end of 1992.

December   Japan opened a new Tokyo offshore banking centre with 181 licensed domestic and foreign institutions.
Westpac bought a US primary dealer, William E. Pollock.

1987

January   The Reserve Bank announced that banks would be required to notify the central bank of any exceptionally large exposures they were considering.

February   Louvre Accord was agreed by the Group of Seven (except Italy)—the group met within the framework of the Tokyo Economic Declaration, agreed currencies

17

were within a range broadly consistent with underlying economic fundamentals and agreed to cooperate closely to foster stability in exchange rates around prevailing levels.

April   The reserve asset ratio for savings banks was reduced to 13 per cent.

Ministers and governors of the Group of Seven agreed that exchange rates were broadly consistent with economic fundamentals and reaffirmed the basic policy intentions outlined at the Louvre meeting (February 1987).

The US's Commodities Futures Trading Commission (CFTC) approved a request from the Chicago Board of Trade to launch a night trading session, the first on a US exchange, in futures and options.

In a move designed to encourage the development of offshore banking units, the Australian government announced that interest payments on $A-denominated loans made by offshore banks would be free from interest withholding tax.

July   The Single European Act came into effect, providing for the establishment, by the end of 1992, of a market characterised by the free circulation of people, goods, services and capital, by closer cooperation in economic, monetary and social policy and by the recognition of EEC authority in environmental matters.

The Federal Reserve Bank of New York extended access to its foreign-exchange desk (previously limited to about a dozen commercial banks) to several currency brokers, initially only to gather market information but leaving open the possibility of using the brokers in its foreign exchange market intervention.

The Bank of England published a 'grey paper' establishing a new regulatory regime for the wholesale financial markets including a list of institutions to be supervised by the Bank of England, and, for the first time, sterling, foreign-exchange and bullion markets.

The Australian Labor Party was re-elected to a third term under prime minister R.J. Hawke and treasurer Paul Keating.

Queensland's largest building society, Metropolitan Permanent, announced plans to convert to a savings bank and a public company.

August   The Tasmania Bank was created by a merger between
             the Launceston Bank for Savings and the Tasmanian
             Permanent Building Society.

September   G–7 finance ministers and central bank governors com-
             mitted themselves to taking further action as necessary
             to achieve the goals set out in the Louvre Accord of
             February 1987.
             The US Treasury secretary, at the annual IMF/World
             Bank meeting, proposed using a basket of commodities
             including gold as an additional indicator in the G–7's
             coordination process, to provide an 'anchor' to coordi-
             nated floating.
             The Reserve Bank of Australia prohibited individual
             foreign-exchange traders from dealing on their own
             account.

October   Japan allowed all foreign banks to participate in gov-
             ernment bond underwriting syndicates (previously only
             foreign banks which had operated in Japan for five
             years could participate).
             World stockmarket crash produced panic selling. The
             US and West German authorities reaffirmed their com-
             mitment to currency stability.
             Under a new ruling of the Accounting Standards Review
             Board, Australian companies would have to account for
             all foreign-exchange losses in the year they are
             incurred.

December   Finance ministers and central bank governors of the
             G–7 issued a statement which reaffirmed basic eco-
             nomic policy objectives agreed in the Louvre Accord
             and agreed to continue coordination efforts in 1988.
             The Commonwealth Bank's monopoly on school bank-
             ing ended after 57 years.

1988

January   Australian Savings Bonds were suspended and treasury
             bonds to be issued in multiples of $1000.

February   The Sydney Futures Exchange began trading an $A
             contract.

April   The Association of International Bond Dealers gained
             the status of a 'designated foreign exchange' whereby
             securities traded by its members could also be traded

at the London exchange. Members would be monitored by the AIDB rather than UK authorities.

The Bank of England presented regulations affecting brokers in wholesale sterling, foreign exchange and bullion markets. Brokers, even if only name-passers and not accepting risks, would have to meet minimum capital standards, although these would be lowered if certain risks were covered by insurance.

A three-year treasury bond contract was approved for the Sydney Futures Exchange.

June   The EEC council of finance ministers endorsed a directive giving eight member states until 1 July 1990 to fully liberalise capital movements within the EEC. Greece, Ireland, Portugal and Spain were given until the end of 1992.

The US Securities and Exchange Commission (SEC) invited comment by mid-September on proposals to overhaul, for the first time in 24 years, rules on securities offerings outside the US, based on a new approach which recognised the primacy of the laws of the country in which a market is located.

August   The Reserve Bank issued guidelines for a risk-based measurement of banks' capital adequacy, broadly consistent with the proposal developed by the Bank for International Settlements.

The treasurer announced the abolition of the SRD requirement for trading banks and the removal of the distinction between trading and savings banks.

The UK issued treasury bills in ECUs through the Bank of England.

The London International Financial Futures Exchange (LIFFE) re-examined a plan to introduce a futures contract based on ECU deposit rates.

September The SRD ratio was reduced to zero and the funds in SRD accounts transferred to *non-callable deposits* (NCDs).

Prime Assets Ratio (PAR) was reduced from 12 to 10 per cent and Banking (Savings Banks) Regulations amended to allow PAR to replace the savings banks' reserve asset ratio (RAR).

Victoria's RESI building society announced its conversion to the Bank of Melbourne.

November The US Commodities Futures Trading Commission

allowed non-US members of the Sydney Futures Exchange (the first foreign exchange) to sell and advertise most futures and options contracts in the US, without registration.

The Perth-based financier Rothwells Ltd collapsed.

December The US Federal Reserve Board announced that US banks would be able to accept foreign-currency deposits.

1989

January The State Bank of Victoria took control of the Australian Bank Ltd.

February Tax file numbers were introduced.

March Home loan interest rates hit 18 per cent.

May The first fixed-rate home loan packages were introduced in Australia.

The Reserve Bank withdrew the accreditation of the authorised dealer First Federation Discount Company Ltd following the collapse of its parent, Spedley Holdings Ltd.

July A new governor was appointed to the Reserve Bank: Bernie Fraser, formerly secretary of the treasury, replaced R.A. (Bob) Johnston, who retired after seven years as RBA governor.

August The federal government announced its Retirement Income Policy.

Moody's Investors Service downgraded Australia's long-term credit-rating from Aa1 to Aa2.

September The Reserve Bank announced that the interest rate paid on non-callable deposits would be set monthly at 5 percentage points below the average yield at tender in the previous month's thirteen-week treasury notes.

November A London court ruled that the borough of Hammersmith & Fulham, which had entered into several hundred swap transactions, ostensibly to hedge but in reality as a punt on interest rates, was not empowered to enter into capital market transactions and that its entry into such transactions with a view to profit was unreasonable and unlawful.

Fall of Berlin Wall

Sydney Futures Exchange launched SYCOM (Sydney Computerised Overnight Market), the world's first after-hours electronic trading system, which enabled electronic after-hours trading of the exchange's contracts.

December   Changes to the Banking Act removed the distinction between trading and savings banks and gave legislative backing to the Reserve Bank's powers in bank supervision.

1990

January   The Reserve Bank reduced cash rates by one percentage point to around 17 per cent.

February   The Reserve Bank eased cash rates by 0.5 percentage points to around 16.5 per cent.
Changes were made to the ownership guidelines covering authorised dealers in the short-term money market aimed at strengthening the degree of ownership support; a dealer could be owned by a single entity, provided it met Reserve Bank standards, and the limit of 50 per cent foreign ownership was removed. The dealers were also given additional flexibility to use futures and options.

March   The ANZ and National Mutual announced plans to merge to create a mega financial institution. The plan was subsequently blocked by the federal government.
Federal election: Labor won a record fourth term.

April   The Reserve Bank reduced cash rates by 1.5 percentage points to a range of 15–15.5 per cent.
Paul Keating was appointed deputy prime minister, John Hewson leader of the opposition.

May   PAR was reduced to 6 per cent.

July   Two new authorised dealer companies were approved, Rothschild Australia Discount Limited and Schroders Australia Discount Limited.
The governor of the Reserve Bank, Bernie Fraser, scotched rumours about the stability of the Bank of Melbourne.

August   The Reserve Bank reduced cash rates by one percentage point.

September   Authorised money-market dealer Short Term Holdings Ltd acquired all the issued capital of authorised dealer BNY Discount Ltd, with the name of the new entity to be Short Term Discount Ltd. Short Term Acceptances Ltd was phased out.

The Reserve Bank announced changes to banks' holdings of other banks' capital instruments: for the purposes of assessing capital adequacy, a bank's holdings of other banks' capital instruments (as shown in its books) would be deducted from the investing bank's total capital and assets. The new requirement would take effect from 30 September 1991 to allow time for adjustment.

October   The governor of the RBA, Bernie Fraser, issued a statement supporting Metway Bank Ltd, noting it was a sound bank and that 'rumours concerning its stability have no substance'.

The Reserve Bank reduced cash rates by one percentage point to around 13 per cent.

In the annual review of the trade-weighted index, the United Arab Emirates dirham was added to the basket. The weights of Japan and the UK increased slightly while those of the US, New Zealand and Germany's deutschmark declined.

November   State Bank of Victoria collapsed and was subsequently taken over by the Commonwealth Bank.

December   The Reserve Bank again eased interest rates by one percentage point to around 12 per cent.

1991

January   Gulf War began and ended.

Australia's new Corporations Law started to operate.

March   Lippo Finance Australia Ltd, a wholly-owned subsidiary of PT Lippo Bank, Indonesia, was granted an authority to deal in foreign exchange.

April   The UK's House of Lords ruled that all swap market transactions entered into by a London borough council were illegal, which left some 80 banks owed hundreds of millions of pounds by 131 local councils.

The RBA eased monetary policy, reducing cash rates by about half a percentage point to around 11.5 per cent. NDC Securities Ltd chose to cease operating as an authorised short-term money-market dealer, leaving eight authorised dealers.

May   The RBA lowered interest rates by one percentage point to around 10.5 per cent.

June   Toyo Trust Australian Ltd, a wholly-owned subsidiary of The Toyo Trust and Banking Company Limited, Japan, was issued an authority to deal in foreign exchange.

Paul Keating, having launched an unsuccessful challenge against prime minister Bob Hawke, resigned as federal treasurer and joined the backbenches.

July   International closure by bank supervisors of the $20 billion Bank of Credit and Commerce International (aka Bank of Crooks and Criminals International) following an auditor's investigation, commissioned by the Bank of England, which provided proof of fraudulent dealings.

August   The Reserve Bank Information and Transfer System (RITS), a simultaneous electronic transfer and settlement system for commonwealth government bonds, began operating.

The Reserve Bank issued amendments, in line with international practice, to the guidelines on capital adequacy. Under guidelines released in August 1988, banks were allowed to include general provisions for doubtful debts as part of Tier 2 capital; from September 1993 general provisions would be excluded from Tier 2 capital and were to count as no more than 1.25 per cent (previously 1.5 per cent) of risk-weighted assets.

Boris Yeltsin took charge in Russia.

September   Reserve Bank activity in the domestic money market reduced the cash rate by one percentage point to around 9.5 per cent.

October   The Reserve Bank revised the weights used for currencies in the trade-weighted index for the $A, with the weighting of the yen, the largest in the basket, increasing while that of the $US, the second largest, fell, as did the UK's sterling (third largest) and the $NZ (fourth largest). The weightings for the South Korean won (fifth largest), the deutschmark and Singapore dollar increased.

The RBA completed a review of the treatment of future income-tax benefits for capital adequacy purposes, stating that future income-tax benefits did not fully satisfy the tests required for inclusion in capital and should therefore be deducted from Tier 1 capital (and assets) when calculating minimum capital ratios.

November   The RBA eased interest rates by about one percentage point, to around 8.5 per cent.
The federal treasurer announced the introduction of a new five-week treasury note to be issued through the regular, usually weekly, tenders in addition to the existing thirteen and twenty-six-week notes. The new notes would add to the government's flexibility in managing cash balances.
Warrants were listed on ASX.

December   Paul Keating successfully challenged Bob Hawke to become prime minister.
Credit Suisse Bullion Pacific Ltd, a wholly-owned subsidiary of Credit Suisse, was granted authority to deal in foreign exchange.
The Sydney Futures Exchange established new clearing arrangements under a wholly-owned subsidiary, Sydney Futures Exchange Clearing House (SFECH).

1992

January   The Reserve Bank reduced interest rates by about one percentage point to around 7.5 per cent, so that cash rates had been more than halved from 18 per cent two years earlier.

February   Foreign banks were to be allowed to establish branches as well as subsidiaries in Australia, subject to compliance with Reserve Bank prudential arrangements.
The governor of the Reserve Bank, Bernie Fraser, issued a statement in support of the R&I Bank of Western Australia, saying that rumours concerning its viability were totally lacking in substance and pointing out that the R&I Bank was subject to Reserve Bank prudential supervision.
Authorised money-market dealer FBA (Discount) Ltd changed its name to CS First Boston Australia Discount Ltd.
The RBA prepared guidelines on the treatment, for capital-adequacy purposes, of arrangements under which banks securitise or otherwise transfer loans from their balance sheet, with the effect that a bank is

relieved of the need to hold capital in support of assets which it sells or securitises only when the sale is 'clean and final'.

The RBA issued guidelines on banks' involvement in fund management to the effect that banks' fund management activities be kept separate from the bank so that the bank is not affected by changes in the fortunes of its managed funds. In particular, a bank should be under no general or implied obligation to support its managed funds, and this has to be expressly acknowledged by all investors in such funds. Banks which cannot demonstrate a clear separation will be required to hold capital in support of those funds.

April   John Phillips, for the previous five years deputy governor of the Reserve Bank, retired after a long career at the forefront of central banking.

All States and Short-Term groups merged their money-market operations, with All-States Discount Ltd ceasing to operate, so that the number of authorised dealers was reduced to seven.

May   Reserve Bank activity in the domestic money market reduced the overnight cash rate by one percentage point to around 6.5 per cent.

June   The federal government released its Security in Retirement Policy, including an increase in the superannuation preservation age to 60 by 2025, the endorsement of allocated pensions and a flat 15 per cent rebate on annuities and pensions from 1 July 1994.

July   Compulsory employer-provided superannuation for almost all employees began, set at 4 per cent of wages (3 per cent for small businesses), growing to 9 per cent by 2002.

The RBA reduced overnight interest rates by a further 0.75 percentage points to around 5.75 per cent.

The RBA announced that instead of dealing with a select group of reporting bond dealers it will deal with any counterparty which is a member of RITS whose members stood at more than 50. Lists of reporting bond dealers were no longer published.

The Australian Financial Institutions Commission (AFIC) was formed as a regulatory body supervising non-bank financial institutions, mainly building societies and credit unions, in the same way that the Reserve Bank oversees banks.

September   Upheaval in European financial markets: Britain's pound sterling was in freefall, the Italian lira under intense pressure and both temporarily out of the European Monetary System. Interest rates were also in the spotlight with the UK making four adjustments in 36 hours and Sweden pegging short-term interest rates at 500 per cent as it tried to protect the krona against speculation. Germany's deutschmark was the strongest currency in Europe, and the $US was benefiting as a 'safe haven'.

October   The RBA revised the weights used for currencies in the trade-weighted index (TWI) to reflect a continued rise in trade with Asia despite a small fall in Japan's share of Australian trade. Asian trading partners accounted for about 55 per cent of the trade weights, up from 52 per cent in 1991.
The $A hit a five-year low of 69.55 US cents.

November   Australian Gilt Securities was granted an authorised dealership, taking the number of authorised dealers back to eight.

December   The New Zealand Futures and Options Exchange became a subsidiary of the Sydney Futures Exchange.

1993

January   Australian Securities Commission issued a discussion paper calling for submissions on issues raised by activities in over-the-counter derivatives markets.

February   First issue of infrastructure bonds.
The foreign exchange markets' Consultative Group was disbanded. The group had been formed by the Reserve Bank in the wake of the $A float in 1983 and had helped in the evolution of the foreign-exchange market. The Australian Forex Association now agreed to become the main industry body through which the RBA would consult foreign-exchange market operators.

March   The Reserve Bank reduced overnight interest rates by 0.5 percentage points to around 5.25 per cent.
Labor under Paul Keating won the federal election,

securing a fifth consecutive term in office for the ALP which had held government since 1983.

April   The Reserve Bank relaxed its rule regarding bank ownership of an authorised dealer. Under certain circumstances, it would allow a bank to own up to 75 per cent equity in an authorised dealer (an increase from 12.5 per cent). The change was brought in to widen the scope for financial institutions with substantial capital and relevant experience to participate in the authorised (official) short-term money market.

May   Overseas Union Bank Ltd was granted an authority to operate as a branch in Australia.

June   Interest rates on banks' non-callable deposits (NCDs) were increased on the understanding that the banks would use the resulting benefit for lending to small and medium-sized business. Instead of being paid an interest rate set at 5 percentage points below the average yield at tender of thirteen-week treasury notes, banks would be paid an interest rate on NCDs equal to the rate on thirteen-week treasury notes.

A small business advisory panel was established, chaired by the governor of the Reserve Bank.

July   Group of Thirty (G–30) Washington-based international private-sector study group released its report, *Derivatives: Practices and Principles*. This recommended guidelines which became accepted as industry practice.

Australian Securities Commission issued a draft report on over-the-counter derivatives markets and an exposure draft of a policy statement on exempt futures markets.

The RBA changed the time at which it offered rediscount facilities on treasury notes from 9.30 am to 8.30 am in line with new interbank settlement arrangements which required banks to have their exchange-settlement accounts with the RBA in credit by 9 am. Occasionally it might be necessary for a bank to rediscount treasury notes before 9 am to achieve that. The RBA also dropped its practice of making a daily announcement of a rediscount rate for treasury notes but would quote a rate at which it was prepared to buy notes under the rediscount facility.

SBC Dominguez Barry Ltd was granted authority to

operate as a short-term money-market dealer, taking the number of authorised dealers to nine.

The RBA reduced overnight interest rates by 0.5 per cent to 4.75 per cent in response to evidence of continued slow growth and low inflation.

August   The European Monetary System suffered a further crisis which was resolved by widening the bands within which most members' currencies were allowed to fluctuate to 15 per cent either side of their midrate.

September The $A plunged to a new low of 47.1 on the trade-weighted index.

October Members of RITS became able to submit bids electron-ically through RITS for all offers at tender of commonwealth government securities.

The softer commodity prices pushed the $A to 64.10 US cents.

The RBA revised the weights used for the trade-weighted index (TWI) for the $A. Weights for Japan and the US remained the largest. The importance of Asian countries other than Japan continued to increase with these countries accounting for 32 per cent of the index, up from 30 per cent in 1992 and 24 per cent in 1988.

The Sydney Futures Exchange reduced the size of its share-price index (SPI) futures contract from a value of $100 times to $25 times the All-Ordinaries index.

November Australian Securities Commission adopted policy 70 (exempt futures market) and called for applications under that policy to be made by 31 January 1994. Forty applications were received.

The Sydney Futures Exchange launched overnight options on three-year and ten-year treasury (common-wealth) bonds, becoming the first exchange to offer overnight options on treasury bonds.

The Australian Bankers' Association released a Code of Banking Practice.

December Merrill Lynch International (Australia) Ltd was granted an authority to operate as a money-market dealer, taking the number of authorised dealers to ten.

The RBA announced new guidelines for banks when classifying and reporting problem loans and other impaired assets to achieve increased consistency in treat-ment of such loans and enable meaningful comparisons.

> A 50 per cent risk-weighting was to apply to bank loans secured by mortgage over residential property, irrespective of whether the property was owned by the borrower. This approach was consistent with the BIS capital adequacy framework and in line with practice elsewhere including in the UK and US.

During 1993 the Maastricht Treaty created a redesigned European economic union, which added two elements to the European community, a common foreign policy and cross-border cooperation in justice and police matters.

1994

January	The Sydney Futures Exchange extended the trading hours of SYCOM by two hours to a 6 am close.
February	The Reserve Bank was reviewing the 1992 guidelines regarding banks' involvement in fund management. The US Federal Reserve tightened interest rates, sparking a worldwide sell-off in bonds. Metallgesellschaft Corporation, US subsidiary of the giant German metals and mining group Metallgesellschaft AG, revealed losses of $US1.8 billion ($A2.5 billion) through oil futures and options.
March	The Sydney Futures Exchange listed overnight options on its share-price index futures contract.
April	Two US companies, Procter & Gamble and Gibson Greetings, reported losses stemming from derivatives transactions: $US157 million by Procter & Gamble and $US23 million by Gibson Greetings.
May	Australian Securities Commission's final report on over-the-counter derivatives markets was released. Rabo Australia Ltd, a wholly-owned subsidiary of Rabobank Nederland, was granted an authority to deal in foreign exchange. The Sydney Futures Exchange launched individual share futures (ISF) contracts on BHP, National Australia Bank and News Corporation.
July	Changes were made to the maximum level of tax-deductible superannuation contributions—now based on age rather than on a combination of income and age. Indexed Reasonable Benefit Limits were introduced—starting at $400 000 for a lump sum and $800 000 if at least half

the payment was taken as a complying annuity. Changes were made to the tax treatment of annuities and allocated pensions.

Bank of America, Deutsche Bank and NBD Bank were granted authority to operate as branches in Australia.

State Bank of New South Wales was granted a banking authority under the Banking Act 1959.

Bank of South Australia Ltd, which took over the core operations of the State Bank of SA, was defined as a 'bank' under the Banking Act.

August   The RBA tightened monetary policy, raising cash rates by 0.75 per cent to 5.5 per cent. The increase, the first in five years, was deemed necessary to help sustain non-inflationary growth.

ASXD announced share ratio contracts.

September   The Sydney Futures Exchange listed a further four individual share futures, on the shares of MIM, Western Mining Corporation, BTR Nylex and Westpac Banking Corporation.

October   The RBA revised the weights used for currencies in the trade-weighted index (TWI) for the $A. Japan and the US remained the most important countries in the index. The weight for New Zealand, third largest, increased. Asian countries excluding Japan accounted for 32 per cent of the index.

Following consultation with the banks, the RBA issued new guidelines relating to the composition of bank boards.

Fay, Richwhite Australia Ltd announced it was divesting its ownership of the authorised money-market dealers F.R. Australian Discount Ltd, leaving nine authorised money-market dealers.

Following its October board meeting, the Reserve Bank lifted cash rates by one percentage point to 6.5 per cent to avoid an overheating of the economy and to prolong sustainable growth in production and employment.

The RBA announced changes to the rediscount facility for treasury notes with up to 90 days to maturity. The effect was to cap the rediscount penalty rather than have the penalty increase with the residual maturity of the notes.

November   The Sydney Futures Exchange further extended SYCOM's trading hours to a 7 am close, providing nearly 21 hours of trading.

December   The Reserve Bank was active in the market to lift the
            cash rate by one percentage point to around 7.5 per cent.
            This was because, despite a severe drought, the econ-
            omy was growing strongly.
            The Californian municipality Orange County filed for
            bankruptcy after a $US1.7 billion loss arising from a
            combination of a steep rise in interest rates and a highly
            leveraged investment strategy involving derivatives in
            the form of 'inverse floaters', notes paying the holder
            a floating rate that increases as interest rates fall.

During 1994 returns from sharemarkets and fixed-income markets
in Australia and internationally dropped by between 5 and 10 per
cent.

1995

January   The Reserve Bank issued a new prudential statement to
            banks covering a number of issues relating to asset
            quality, such as how banks should recognise and report
            impaired assets, value security and determine the level
            of provisions; how they should have in place credit-risk
            grading systems to help assess asset quality and credit
            exposures.

February   Collapse of Barings PLC, 233-year-old British merchant
            bank, following unsustainable losses of around $US1.5
            billion ($A2 billion) relating to futures trading by its
            Singapore office on Japanese and Singaporean futures
            exchanges. The demise prompted a worldwide review
            by banks of their risk-management systems, particularly
            as they related to derivative products such as futures
            and options. Barings business was taken over by the
            giant Dutch group ING.
            The Sydney Futures Exchange listed individual share
            futures on BTR Nylex, MIM Holdings, Westpac Bank-
            ing Corporation and Western Mining on SYCOM.
            Mexican debt and currency crisis, collapse of the peso.
            The $US slid to its lowest level in two years, hitting
            1.437 against the deutschmark; the $A went into a
            freefall, partly as one of the 'dollar bloc' and also
            because hedge and commodity fund activity sent prices
            down.
            Colonial Mutual Discount Company Ltd announced it
            would cease trading as an authorised dealer. The deci-
            sion followed the acquisition by its parent, Colonial

Mutual Life Assurance Society Ltd, of the State Bank of NSW and was taken to avoid breaching Reserve Bank rules covering ownership of an authorised dealer. CMD, previously Delfin Discount Company Ltd, had been an authorised dealer since the official money market began in 1959.

March   Currency crisis continued, with the $US and $A dropping to fresh lows against the yen and deutschmark. The $US fell to a post-1945 low of 88.01 yen and 1.3450 deutschmarks, the $A sank to a record low of 63.73 yen and 0.9938 deutschmarks.

SBC (Sydney) Ltd, wholly-owned subsidiary of Swiss Bank Corporation, was granted an authority to deal in foreign exchange.

The Sydney Futures Exchange listed a further three individual share futures, on the shares of CRA Ltd, Fosters Brewing Group and ANZ Bank, with ANZ and CRA also listed on SYCOM.

The Sydney Futures Exchange reintroduced a deliverable wool futures contract based on 21-micron merino fleece wool.

ASXD began trading low-exercise-price options (LEPOs).

April   Turmoil in international currency markets continued with the $A equal to 62 yen, a depreciation of 62 per cent over a decade of which almost one-third had taken place in the first three months of 1995. During the month it hit new lows of 59.16 yen and the $US dropped to 79.75 yen.

The Reserve Bank issued two discussion papers presenting the case for a move to real-time gross settlement and how this could be achieved. This followed discussions between the RBA and the Australian Payments Clearing Association regarding ways to reduce credit risks in interbank payments and keep pace with international best practice in payments systems.

The Sydney Futures Exchange doubled the size of its bank-accepted bill futures contract to $1 million.

May   The Reserve Bank announced it would reduce the interest rate paid on banks' non-callable deposits held with it. From July, the interest rate would be set at 5 percentage points below the average yield at tender of thirteen-week treasury notes which took the rate back to the formula used between 1989 and 1993.

The Sydney Futures Exchange celebrated its 35th anniversary.

June   Australia's current account deficit, which peaked at $2.9 billion in May, brought further weakness to the $A which traded at 71 US cents, down from 77.5 cents six months earlier and holding under one deutschmark, around 0.98 compared with 1.2000 six months previously.

July   Westpac launched a takeover offer for Challenge Bank in WA.

August   The $A recovered to 74 US cents, 72 yen and 1.0800 deutschmarks.

Following a merger between SBC Australia Ltd and Potter Warburg Pty Ltd, the company owned two subsidiaries operating as authorised dealers, SBC Australia Discount Ltd and Potter Warburg Discount Ltd, which was a breach of Reserve Bank rules. Potter Warburg ceased trading, with authorised dealer activities concentrated in SBC Australia Discount Ltd which went on to trade as SBC Warburg Australia Discount Ltd. The move took the number of authorised dealers to seven.

The Reserve Bank released draft business specifications on real-time gross settlement.

September   The Sydney Futures Exchange established a trading link with the giant New York Mercantile Exchange (NYMEX) enabling SFE members to trade the NYMEX's popular commodity contracts, particularly the West Texas Intermediate (WTI) crude oil contract. Fosters Brewing share futures were listed on SYCOM; BTR Nylex share futures were delisted.

Weights in the trade-weighted index were revised, with the Philippines peso replacing the United Arab Emirates dirham in the list of 24 currencies. The shares of Japan and the US declined further while the rapidly growing Asian countries, other than Japan, continued to increase in importance to 33 per cent of the index (32 per cent a year earlier). New Zealand's weight also rose slightly.

October   The Reserve Bank issued revised prudential guidelines covering bank involvement in fund management and securitisation. These emphasised disclosure and other moves to ensure investors understand they have no claims, beyond any explicit legal entitlements, against banks if investments performed badly, lessened constraints on banking groups' ability to provide services such as credit enhancement, liquidity support and underwriting to fund management and securitisation schemes and more clearly specified capital requirements associated with the provision of services by banking groups to fund management and securitisation schemes. Banks were to operate effective systems and identify and control risks associated with fund management and securitisation.

The Sydney Futures Exchange added diversified manufacturer Pacific Dunlop Ltd to its list of share futures; this followed the delisting of BTR share futures and maintained the list at ten.

November   ACCC (Australian Competition and Consumer Commisson) was formed by a merger of the Trade Practices Commission and the Prices Surveillance Authority.

December   The Reserve Bank indicated it would relax its policy on equity investments by banks to facilitate banks making equity investments in, as well as lending to, their business customers. This was a departure from prevailing policy where, except in one-off 'work-out' situations, banks were discouraged from taking significant equity investments in non-financial businesses. To avoid potential conflict of interest and concentration of risk, individual investments were limited to a fraction of a bank's Tier 1 capital, although larger investments would be considered under special circumstances.

1996

February   The Sydney Futures Exchange listed options on wool futures.

March   Federal election: after thirteen years in office, Labor lost to a Liberal–National Party opposition which formed government under John Howard. Kim Beazley became opposition leader.
SFE listed wheat futures and option contracts and deliverable share futures.

April   The Sydney Futures Exchange launched serial (short-dated) option contracts on three-year and ten-year commonwealth bonds and on share-price index futures. The SFE also listed, via an electronic trading link, COMEX gold, silver and copper futures.

May   The Reserve Bank announced successive steps for the introduction of real-time gross settlement, broadening the range of counterparties with which it would be prepared to deal in its domestic market operations from the authorised dealers to all members of RITS, paying interest on overnight balances in exchange settlement accounts of banks and of special service providers. The authorised dealers would be wound down and exchange settlement accounts become the outlet for banks' surplus funds. Balances in these accounts would count towards banks' prime assets.

Federal treasurer Peter Costello announced details of an inquiry into the Australian financial system, to be chaired by Stan Wallis, managing director of Amcor Ltd since 1977.

June   The Reserve Bank confirmed that, once real-time gross settlement was in place, banks would be able to use their prime assets to provide within-day liquidity, through repurchase agreements (repos) with the Reserve Bank.

July   Reflecting a view that the Australian economy could grow slightly more quickly without threatening a 2–3 per cent inflation target, the Reserve Bank board approved a cut in interest rates of 0.5 percentage points to around 7 per cent.

The Sydney Futures Exchange listed eight additional bank-accepted bill contract months, extending the bank-bill yield curve from three to five years.

Macquarie Bank Ltd listed on the Australian Stock Exchange.

August   Ian Macfarlane was confirmed as governor of the Reserve Bank, succeeding Bernie Fraser.

The authorised short-term money-market dealers, established in 1959, were abolished as part of a progressive reform of the settlement system for high-value payments (real-time gross settlement).

September   In the annual revision of the trade-weighted index, the shares of Japan and the US fell further while trading between Australia and the Asian region, excluding Japan, increased to 42 per cent.

November   With the inflation outlook improving there appeared to be increased scope for the economy to achieve a faster rate of growth and to this end the Reserve Bank was active in the market to bring down the cash rate by a further 0.5 percentage points to around 6.5 per cent.
The New Zealand Futures and Options Exchange listed an electricity futures contract.

December   The Reserve Bank brought down interest rates by a further 0.5 percentage points to around 6 per cent.

1997

January   Following a release by the Basle Committee on Banking Supervision, the Reserve Bank issued new guidelines covering prudential supervision with particular reference to banks' capital adequacy in respect of market risks. The new guidelines, to be fully implemented by the end of 1997, addressed the risk of losses for banks from fluctuations in interest and exchange rates, and equity and commodity prices. These would supplement existing capital adequacy requirements covering credit risk, that is, the risk that a borrower or other counterparty might not meet its obligations to a bank.

March   Final report of the Financial System Inquiry (Wallis committee) released.

May   Arrangements between the Reserve Bank and banks' external auditors, initiated in 1986, had been under a fresh review. Under the arrangements, the RBA received from each bank's external auditors an annual assurance that the information supplied by the bank to the central bank was reliable, that key management systems in the bank were effective and prudential requirements observed. Responsibility for providing the RBA with such assurances would now shift from external auditors to the chief executive and the board of each bank. External auditors retained their responsibilities to provide the RBA with assurances regarding each bank's observance of prudential regulations and reliability of the information provided by a bank to the RBA.
With inflationary expectations reducing, employment growth still dragging and economic growth unlikely to

fuel upward pressure on inflation, the cash rate was further eased to around 5.5 per cent.

Sustained speculation against the Thai baht was held back only by coordinated defence from the central banks of South-East Asia.

June   The Reserve Bank reviewed arrangements for its domestic markets operations and PAR in preparation for the introduction of real-time gross settlement and other changes in market conditions, including the declining supply of commonwealth bonds. The banks' PAR ratio was to be cut from 6 per cent of banks' liabilities (excluding capital) to 3 per cent and the range of eligible securities for PAR would be widened to include $A-denominated securities issued by state and territory governments. These securities would also be eligible for repos with the RBA.

The Stock Exchange of Thailand, which had been falling for three months, hit a record low.

July   The Reserve Bank announced that, following a review of the costs and benefits of holding a significant proportion of international reserves in gold, it had decided that the prevailing level of gold holdings was no longer justified and over the previous six months had gradually sold 167 tonnes of gold, reducing its holdings from 247 to 80 tonnes. The level of international reserves was maintained as the proceeds were immediately converted into foreign-exchange assets such as $US, yen and deutschmark government securities. The RBA's move followed earlier substantial sales by central banks in Austria, Belgium, Canada, the Netherlands, Portugal and South Africa.

Reflecting an improving outlook for Australia's medium-term inflation rate, with consequent hopes for faster economic growth and employment, the Reserve Bank announced it would act in the market to reduce the cash rate by 0.5 percentage points (50 basis points) to around 5 per cent.

A currency crisis erupted in Thailand, with the country calling in IMF assistance, announcing a managed float of the baht which fell 18 per cent in one day. Over the following week the Philippines peso and Malaysian ringgit came under attack and the Philippines central bank announced the peso would float, a move approved by the IMF. By late in the month a regional currency crisis was in full swing, with the ringgit at a three-year low and Dr Mahathir citing international speculators, especially US multi-billion-dollar hedge funds, as the culprits.

August Currency turmoil continued as South-East Asian share and currency markets were hit by panic selling in key regional markets of Hong Kong, Singapore, Indonesia, Thailand, Malaysia and the Philippines. The Australian All-Ordinaries index also fell. The currencies of Thailand, Indonesia and the Philippines fell to new lows against the $US; the Malaysian ringgit hit a 25-year low against the $US and even Singapore's dollar hit its lowest point in three years. The IMF reached an agreement with Thailand for a $US17.2 billion rescue package, including $1 billion from Australia.

September International credit-ratings agency Standard & Poor's downgraded Malaysia's long-term outlook to negative. Malaysia's ringgit, which had lost almost 28 per cent of its value against the $US since early July, hit a new low of 3.200, its lowest since the currency was officially floated in 1973. Indonesia's rupiah also recorded a new low of 3200 to the $US.

Indonesia, in an attempt to reduce its budget deficit, stopped issuing tax refunds; the value of the rupiah had sunk by 20 per cent over previous two months.

The $A, undermined by financial speculation about further interest-rate cuts and suggestions that the outlook for commodity exports was weakening, fell to a 27-month low of 71.73 US cents.

The federal government's specialist development financier, AIDC Ltd, was sold to Babcock & Brown and Union Bank of Switzerland.

The annual review of the trade-weighted index saw the United Arab Emirates' dirham returned to the basket. Japan's share of the TWI fell further, to 18 per cent but trade between Australia and other countries in Asia continued to grow, reaching 43 per cent.

The Bank of New Zealand, a subsidiary of National Australia Bank, ceased to be authorised as a bank.

The federal government released its response to the Wallis committee's findings: a new supervisory body, the Australian Prudential Regulation Authority, to be established to oversee all deposit-taking institutions; the

RBA to lose supervision of banks, retain monetary policy and responsibility for stability of the financial system and carry increased responsibility for the payments system.

October   World stockmarkets, already unnerved on the eve of the tenth anniversary of the 1987 global stockmarket collapse, were further unsettled by continuing turbulence in Asia where a currency crisis was gripping Thailand, Indonesia, Malaysia and the Philippines, fuelling concerns about the economic health of the region. Vietnam fell under the shadow of the crisis, with its central bank doubling its non-convertible currency's permitted trading band to 10 per cent either side of the official daily rate. By mid-month, the five-month long crisis had deepened, dragging the currencies of Malaysia, Taiwan and Singapore to new lows, the $A to a 28-month low of 70.95 US cents which reflected the view of overseas investors that Australia's economic growth would be dampened by the Asian turmoil. In the last week of the month disaster spilled over to Hong Kong as speculators decided that the $HK was overvalued; the sharemarket suffered its largest one-day fall, chaos reigned in other regional markets including Australia. Hong Kong shares fell by 14 per cent after the Hong Kong Monetary Authority raised interest rates to 300 per cent (from 6 per cent two days earlier) in a bid to defend the $HK's link to the $US. The Hong Kong sharemarket lost 30 per cent in four trading days. The $A fell to a 44-month low of 68.95 US cents following a plunge in the gold price; South Korea's won was battered to 930 and its sharemarket fell by 10 per cent. Sparked by events in Hong Kong, panic-selling infected Wall Street with the New York Stock Exchange recording its biggest one-day points fall which triggered the exchange's first automatic shutdown. Australia's All-Ordinaries index fell by 7 per cent, European markets were down by 9 per cent in what became tagged the sharemarket crash of 1997. Then, in a rapid recovery, the All-Ordinaries regained $22 billion in one day, after four days in which the market had lost $60 billion or 15 per cent; world sharemarkets bounced back but nervousness lingered. The $A recovered to 70.36 US cents. After a five-day rollercoaster ride investors around the world were confused and unsettled.

Dr H. C. (Nugget) Coombs, arguably the most influential public servant of the post-war period, first governor of the Reserve Bank, founding chairman of the Elizabethan Theatre Trust and of the Council for Aboriginal Affairs and Aboriginal rights activist, died at the age of 91.

The International Commercial Bank of China was authorised as a foreign bank.

The Reserve Bank issued revised entry criteria for foreign bank representative offices in Australia, requiring a foreign bank wishing to establish a representative office to obtain registration as a foreign company under the Corporations Law while foreign banks already operating a representative office had to register within twelve months.

The Sydney Futures Exchange announced an end to open-outcry floor trading and a move to full electronic trading on SYCOM by early 1999.

November   Nervousness in regional sharemarkets continued. Around the middle of the month, Hokkaido Takushoku Bank, one of Japan's biggest nationwide banks and one of its ten money-centre banks, collapsed. Concern about the stability of the Japanese banking system intensified, the country's stockmarket fell and the yen dropped to a five-year low of 126 to the $US. Fears increased when Japan's oldest and fourth-largest stockbroker, Yamaichi Securities, collapsed, bringing Japan its third financial institution failure in a month after stockbroker Sanyo Securities and Hokkaido Takushoku Bank. Then South Korea, Australia's second-largest export market, buckled under the weight of foreign debt; a rescue package was mounted, to which Australia contributed. US president Bill Clinton conceded that the Asian crisis was a global problem: East Asia had accounted for 40 per cent of total growth in the world economy with South Korea supplying 4 per cent of growth in 1996. Gold price fell below $US300 on the back of sales by world central banks and weaker commodity prices pulled the $A down to 67.95 US cents. The collapse of a second-tier bank in Japan, Tokuyo City Bank, because of non-performing loans in real-estate ventures, was the fourth failure in November. At an APEC summit in Vancouver, the finance ministers of the world's leading economies met to try to strengthen turbulent international monetary system.

The spectacularly successful $14.3 billion Telstra float saw one-third of Telstra sold by the federal government. Telstra shares went on to sell well in the US as American Depository Receipts. Telstra became the sixth-largest company on ASX by market capitalisation. ING Bank NV was authorised as a foreign branch bank.

The Bank of Melbourne was acquired by Westpac Banking Corporation.

December $A fell further, to 67.30 US cents, after the release of figures showing that the current account deficit had increased by 55 per cent to $4.6 billion in the September quarter and in October Australia's trade balance had shown a deficit for the first time in seven months. The Reserve Bank's index of commodity prices was also down. By mid-month the $A had hit a new four-year low of 64.60 US cents and was under 40 UK pence.

Asian markets remained weak and unsettled, the yen hit a new five-year-plus low of 131.38 to the $US and Indonesia's rupiah was at a new low of 5.700 against the $US, down 55 per cent since the start of the year. South Korea, gripped by financial panic amid fears of further corporate crises and loan defaults, had funds pumped in by the IMF and thirteen other countries. With the won down almost 70 per cent since the end of 1996, South Korea was forced by the IMF to float its currency, which prompted a flood of buying that pushed the won up by 16 per cent against the $US. The float ended the managed exchange rate system which had been in force since the won shifted from a fixed rate to the $US in 1954 at the end of the Korean war and was a clear shift from an era of protectionism to a new liberalisation. And in Japan, where the economy had grown a mere 1 per cent in the year to September, a new economic stimulus package was unveiled and income tax cuts introduced to raise spending.

Standard & Poor's downgraded resources giant BHP's credit-rating outlook from stable to negative because of a poor financial performance and difficult market conditions. BHP shares tumbled to $12.65; they had been $20 a year earlier.

The federal government released a paper, *Australia: a regional financial centre*, which included a number of initiatives of the former Keating government aimed at establishing Australia as a regional finance centre.

Toyo Trust & Banking Co Ltd ceased to have a representative office in Australia.

1998

January   The $A hit an eleven-year low of 63.19 US cents, pushed down by an eighteen-year low in the gold price of $US282, weak commodity prices and a worsening of the financial crisis in Asia with currencies at historic lows against the $US as investors rushed for a safe haven in the greenback. The $A was caught in the turmoil; the Reserve Bank intervened to support the $A above 63 US cents, the first time the central bank had been in the market since October 1993.

Peregrine Investments, formerly one of East Asia's most powerful financial houses, fell victim to the Asian debt market; a key trigger in its demise was funds lent to Steady Safe, an Indonesian transport business which borrowed in $US but earned its income in rupiah.

The All-Ordinaries fell on fears of the impact of the Asian meltdown on Australia; likewise, in the US, the Dow Jones fell as concerns grew that the slowdown in Asia would damage profits of US companies.

Under pressure from the IMF, Indonesia embraced a big economic package which hit some of President Suharto's favoured projects. Despite that, the Indonesian stockmarket fell and the rupiah weakened but recovered from an all-time low of 16 000 against the $US to 13 500.

Dresdner Bank AG was authorised as a branch of a foreign bank in Australia.

Reserve Bank guidelines covering capital requirements for market risk came into force; these followed recommendations of the Basle Committee on Banking Supervision and require banks to hold capital against the risk of loss from changes in currency and interest rates and equity and commodity prices.

Sydney Futures Exchange Clearing House increased its guarantee from $100 million to $150 million, following strong lift in SFE turnover, up 11.3 per cent in 1997.

March   Graeme Thompson, a deputy governor of the Reserve Bank, appointed chief executive of the Australian

Prudential Regulation Authority (APRA), with Professor Jeff Carmichael as chairman.

April The Reserve Bank announced changes to banks' liquidity management to replace the Prime Assets Ratio (PAR).

N.M. Rothschild & Sons (Australia) Ltd was authorised as a locally incorporated bank.

May On the eve of the annual budget, the $A fell to a 12-year low of 61.73 against $US, adversely affected by the political crisis in Indonesia.

Indonesia's president Suharto resigned after more than 30 years in office.

The federal government announced a budget surplus, proposed tax cuts and a goods and services tax.

June ABN AMRO secured a banking licence in Australia.

The $A was battered to a 12-year low of 58.26 US cents despite substantial RBA intervention to support it. The currency, dragged down by regional problems, a lower gold price and lower commodity prices, was testing its previous record low of 57.10 US cents, hit in July 1986. As a consequence of dramatic fall in the $A and subsequent uncertainty on interest rates, the SFE experienced its busiest trading in its 38-year history with a run of record-breaking sessions.

The AMP Bank Ltd made a spectacular debut when its shares listed on ASX with an opening price of $35.99 compared to an issue price of $16. AMP shares briefly hit $45, closed at $23 and subsequently dropped below $20.

Australian consumer sentiment slumped. Export earnings were down.

Japan was in its worst recession in 23 years, with the yen at an eight-year low to the $US at 144.53, which prompted concerted intervention by the central banks of the US and Japan to reverse its fall.

The Reserve Bank began operating real-time gross settlement.

Legislation was passed enabling APRA and ASIC to begin operating, and established a Payments System Board within the RBA.

1

Towards 2010

The 1990s have seen the Australian financial markets evolve and expand in ways that capitalised on the deregulatory reforms and technological advances of the 1980s to bring increased internationalisation and intensified competition. This, against a background of low inflation and low, more stable interest rates, has resulted in benefits for borrowers and consumers, particularly home-buyers and small business.

Challenge and change have been the hallmarks of at least the past two decades. Australia entered the 1990s with a larger, more vigorous and effective financial system than had been feasible in the pre-deregulation days of rigid controls that inhibited efficient allocation of funds. The 1980s were years of change and exceptional expansion in activities. But the 1980s themes of seemingly limitless growth, macho markets with big turnover which indulged in trading for trading's sake and were staffed, so the image went, by screen jockeys and cowboy traders, evaporated in the early 1990s under the weight of losses and a dismal recession, an experience shared by most major economies. Harsh lessons were endured along the way by market operators, regulators and the investing public.

Recovery followed, in time, and different attitudes developed as financial markets grew in maturity in every sense, with a determined focus on regulation and documentation of dealing, risk-management and control systems, behavioural standards and practices, servicing the customer, improving efficiencies and cutting costs. In the 1990s the markets, and their regulators, faced the challenge of bedding down the radical changes that had taken place.

But the relentless pursuit of efficiency and optimum trading conditions continued, in tandem with continued advances in technology that create their own demands and opportunities. The result is that the markets are open to—arguably often dominated by—international forces, as funds move freely between Australia and overseas. There is no longer rigid segmentation of groups into narrow specialties such as banking, savings, insurance, investment banking and so on; rather, major banking groups are diversified financial organisations offering the facilities of banking, investment, corporate advice and finance, insurance, fund management, stock-broking—the full gamut of financial services. Many foreign-owned investment banks opened as branches in Australia and became banks, taking the total number of banks in 1998 to 44. And the markets have expanded and developed in depth and sophistication.

Financial markets, which include sectors dealing in cash and securities such as notes and fixed-income bonds, foreign exchange, futures trading, over-the-counter swaps and options and securitisation, are customer-driven; management of risks has become paramount for professional market operators and customers alike.

The maturing of the markets in the 1990s can be mapped by a number of significant events and trends.

- Considerable merger activity and obscuring of earlier distinctions between financial specialists such as banks, investment banks and insurance companies led to the financial system being regarded as comprising *financial services providers*. While mergers in Australia involved large banks, regional banks and insurance companies, it did not extend to mergers between the major banks as occurred in the US and Europe.
- Intensified competition in financial markets continued, leading to a contraction in margins and prompting vigorous efforts to cut costs, which involved staff reductions and branch closures. At the same, the pervasive use of technology also intensified— itself, though, an increasingly significant component in costs. Financial institutions, notably banks, reduced cross-subsidies in some services, rationalised others and increasingly relied on fees and charges as a source of revenue.
- After the frenzy of the 1980s and losses of the early 1990s, high levels of profitability were again achieved, largely because of the significant emphasis placed on the management and control of risk and a sharpened focus on returns on capital on the part of all financial services providers.
- An increasingly strict prudential framework has been crafted, with banks' capital as its cornerstone, and a shift to coordinated supervision given expression in 1998 with the establishment of the Australian Prudential Regulation Authority.
- The deregulation of the 1980s saw the banks reverse an earlier

decline and increase their share of business at the expense of other financial institutions. An institutional change peculiar to Australia was the abolition, in 1996, of the authorised dealers, a group with which the Reserve Bank had carried out its market operations for almost 40 years; the demise of the dealers was part of a shift to a system of real-time gross settlement for high-value payments. As a consequence, the cash market was opened to greater competition.

- Globalisation of financial markets continued so that, despite time-zone differences, Australian markets are plugged into world markets around the clock. Several banks operate foreign-exchange dealings on a 24-hour cycle and the Sydney Futures Exchange trades for close to 24 hours through a combination of a day-trading session in Sydney and its after-hours system, SYCOM. Internationalisation is also reflected in the establishment of foreign bank branches in Australia, and in the acquisition by Australian banks and insurance companies of overseas operations. Following some adverse outcomes in the late 1980s, several Australian banks curtailed their offshore business, deciding instead that the capital required to support it could be more lucratively employed closer to home.

- Fund managers enjoy an increasingly higher profile, overseeing a growing volume of funds under management, reflecting legislative changes underpinning superannuation and the focus on the need to save for retirement which has considerably elevated the role of the retail investor.

- Internationally, Australian developments had parallels in major overseas markets, with mutual and pension funds growing enormously. A feature of the 1990s was the growth of hedge funds which drew considerable blame for stoking instability in foreign-exchange markets with their capacity to pounce opportunistically on a weak currency and drive it lower for their own profit motives. This occurred in 1992 with a number of European currencies, particularly sterling, in 1997 in Asia and in 1998 when they battered the $A to near-record lows.

- Overall, banking systems in English-speaking countries and in Scandinavia returned to health after the bad-debt experiences of the late 1980s and early 1990s. At the same time, though, problems in the Japanese banking system, as well as in several Asian economies, posed a lingering threat for the global economy.

- In Australia, the Reserve Bank adopted a more open approach to monetary policy management, establishing an inflation target and an operational target to implement policy in the form of a cash-rate target which it publicly announced. Having the central bank announce its target cash rate tended to reduce volatility in short-term interest rates. A much lower level of inflation brought the structure of interest rates down substantially from the levels of the 1980s.

- A contraction in government (commonwealth and state) borrowings and a series of privatisations led to a decline in the volume of securities they issued. As investors sought alternative outlets vigorous growth was fuelled in private-sector fixed-income paper such as mortgage-backed and asset-backed securities, corporate bonds and CPI-linked infrastructure bonds.

Regulatory developments

When financial deregulation was introduced and before sufficient time had elapsed for its benefits to flow through, there was a tendency to confuse a *deregulated* financial market with an *unregulated* market. The difference is important. Financial deregulation in Australia meant dismantling rules that artificially limited the range of financial services available to the community, placed arbitrary limits on interest rates, told banks how much they could lend and to whom, and separated different categories of financial intermediaries into defined fields of operation. Many of these rules and controls dated from the Second World War or earlier; not only did they no longer serve a useful function, they also constrained economic development. Deregulation did not extend to removing controls that served a prudential purpose—these were in fact increased and strengthened during the 1990s—nor did it absolve the Reserve Bank of any responsibility for the financial system.

The more detailed and formal rules applying to bank capital, which include a risk-weighting of banks' assets, are one move by the regulators to ensure the banking system, and by implication the financial system, is buttressed against excessive risks. The risk-weighted framework for capital adequacy was devised by the Bank for International Settlements' supervisors' committee, popularly known at the time as the Cooke Committee after its then chairman Peter Cooke, a former Bank of England official. The motive for these rules lay in a desire, born of the experience of earlier bank crises and third-world debt, and in the light of banks' increasingly varied operations, to ensure that banks supported *all* their activities—those on the balance sheet and those off—with an adequate amount of capital. To a large extent the move was a response to the increasing penetration by thinly capitalised Japanese banks in Europe and the US, and a wish to see banks operate internationally on equal footing. The rules have been adopted internationally, among the OECD countries, in the interests of convergence and harmony in an integrated financial world. This first step in globalising markets' approach to risk focused on credit risk (the risk that a loan might not be repaid), an initiative that was extended ten years later, in 1998, to market risk (the risk of losses arising from adverse movements in price).

In 1993 the Group of Thirty (G–30, a private-sector think tank) released a report on the growing market in derivatives which further cemented an already developing concept of risk-management, a need that was subsequently heightened by a series of derivatives-related disasters involving a number of high-profile companies, including the collapse of the UK bank, Barings PLC. As a consequence, throughout the second half of the 1990s banks upgraded their risk-management systems to measure and manage risk.

As part of a move to ensure that all financial institutions were adequately capitalised and supervised, in 1992 the Australian Financial Institutions Commission (AFIC) was established to lift standards of prudential supervision of building societies and credit unions. As ever, regulators have been trying to keep pace with an increasingly integrated financial system where the distinctions blurred as insurance companies and mortgage originators make inroads into home lending, fund managers offer products which are very similar to deposits and banks offer superannuation products such as retirement saving accounts (RSAs) on their own balance sheets. In response to the relentless momentum of change, and against a background of technological advances in electronic communications that continue to revolutionise how business is conducted, in 1996 the federal government commissioned an inquiry into the financial system. An outcome of the findings of the committee of inquiry (Wallis committee, headed by high-profile industrialist Stan Wallis) was further regulatory change, including the creation of the Australian Prudential Regulation Authority (APRA) to oversee all deposit-taking institutions and insurance and superannuation companies, an initiative that reflected the view that prudential supervision and regulation are best handled through an integrated approach which could cope with the rise in financial conglomerates.

Within the financial markets, the growing emphasis on self-regulation has had clear expression in the growth of the Australian Financial Markets Association (AFMA), the acknowledged representative body of the over-the-counter financial markets, whose work in devising a market code of conduct, standards of behaviour, strong framework of self-discipline and dealer accreditation examination has done much to lift the profile of the financial markets.

Privatisation

Throughout the 1990s commonwealth and state governments privatised a significant proportion of public-sector assets, either fully or partially transferring the ownership of public enterprises into private individual and institutional hands. This has occurred especially in three sectors: financial services (Commonwealth Bank, several state banks and insurance companies); transport and communications (Qantas and Telstra) and electricity and gas (sales of electricity generators and distributors). By the late 1990s Australia had one of the largest privatisation programs of the OECD countries, ranking after trailblazers such as the UK and New Zealand. The proceeds of privatisations have been used to reduce government debt. The privatisations, of which nearly half have involved floats, significantly increased the level of share ownership in Australia as many people became shareholders for the first time.

The rise of the financial conglomerate

On an institutional level, the markets underwent considerable rationalisation in the late 1990s, largely reflecting the consolidation and centralisation of counterparts overseas. Bank mergers among major world names were common in 1996 and 1997; for example, high-profile mergers in 1996 were those of the US giants Chase Manhattan and Chemical Bank, and two huge Japanese houses, Bank of Tokyo and Mitsubishi Bank. Also in the US, First Chicago merged with National Bank of Detroit (NBD Bank). In 1997 the two Swiss giants, Swiss Bank Corporation and Union Bank of Switzerland, merged. Other global operators reorganised in ways that nonetheless had significant impact on various markets: Citibank elected to close its interbank trading room in Frankfurt; Deutsche Bank centralised its operations in key centres around the world. In 1998 Citibank and Travelers created a $US700 billion giant. According to Rob Ferguson, managing director of Bankers Trust Australia Ltd, the key strategy driving many of these moves has been a 'need for financial institutions of all kinds to get closer to retail customers . . . they will do so by building an effective retail strategy'. Commenting on how the future will look, Ferguson said:

> So this is a remarkable paradox: the financial institutions of the future will be following the same path to success as the 'old-fashioned' banks of 40 years ago. Of course, these 'new' retail banks will operate in a very different environment and be much more sophisticated than their predecessors. They will offer a wider range of services and be subject to strong competition, both from

new industry innovators using the Internet and other technologies
that break down entry barriers . . .

The story of Australia's financial markets over the past half-century
has been one of evolution and development in response to changes
in the world's financial environment and in the domestic regulatory
climate. The changes of the 1990s, though, have been such that the
markets operate in a new era wrought not only by regulatory
changes but also by increasing sophistication in communications
and technology, and by a return in Australia to lower interest rates
on the back of low inflation. Financial reform had brought down
regulatory barriers but it is technology that has integrated financial
markets around the world in such a way that any reversal of the
process seems impossible. Dealing rooms, traditionally characterised by the noise of traders buying and selling and shouting
information, now feature an arresting range of electronic machinery
used not only for information but also in trading. Dealers who for
years lived on the telephone and cultivated the salesman's skills in
winning clients, are increasingly operating through their desk-top
screens.

Information has assumed a high value. The need for up-to-the-
minute information in dealing rooms bears out the assertion—made
in 1983 by Walter Wriston, then chairman of Citicorp—that information about money would become almost as important as money
itself. Wriston, who followed his prediction by joining the board of
Reuters, the world's biggest distributor of financial information,
said: 'The information standard has replaced the gold standard as
the basis of world finance.'

Australia's financial sector enters the 21st century as highly internationalised, electronically sophisticated markets, with as diverse a
product range as could be found in any major world centre. Given
the size of the population and its gross domestic product, Australia's
financial markets are large and well developed.

Eager to find a new star on the horizon, financial markets in
the late 1990s were pinning hopes on government initiatives that
would further enhance Australia's position as a key financial centre,
such as broadening the offshore banking unit regime and abolishing
withholding tax on corporate bearer securities such as bonds and
debentures. Removing the 10 per cent withholding tax, which
applies to the interest paid to non-residents on loans made (securities bought) in Australia, would lift the appeal of these investments
to non-Australians. Markets welcomed the proposal to broaden the
exemption from interest withholding tax to include debt securities

issued by Australian companies in the domestic market but held by overseas investors. This was seen as a positive step, removing a tax impediment to the integration of domestic and international debt markets by enabling companies to issue bearer securities simultaneously to Australian and international investors.

Financiers in today's capital and financial markets focus on protecting their clients (and themselves) as much as possible against unwelcome movements in rates and currencies, maximising returns on capital and assets and, by using arbitrage techniques, making the most of opportunities offered in different markets. The following chapters describe how they do this, and the market sectors in which they operate.

2

How it all began

Financial markets play an intermediary role in that they facilitate the transfer of funds between suppliers and users—they link savers, borrowers and lenders and redistribute risk to those willing or best equipped to carry it.

The focus of the cash market is mostly short-term—that is, cash is borrowed or lent for periods of less than one year and often as briefly as overnight—although loan facilities can be arranged for longer periods. Market participants also trade in securities such as bills of exchange, promissory notes (commercial paper) and certificates of deposit that for the most part will mature in less than six months. At the longer end of the maturity spectrum is the fixed-income market, dealing in bonds which can have maturities ranging from one to ten years or more. The swaps market, which expanded considerably during the 1990s, trades out to 30 years, far longer than government bond maturities.

The financial intermediaries—banks, investment banks, fund managers, building societies, credit unions and brokers—service companies and institutions (often referred to as 'end-users') which operate at the *wholesale* end of the financial markets where cash and securities are traded in large parcels. The small or 'retail' investor can, however, participate through a pooled fund such as a cash management or public securities trust.

Financial intermediaries have existed for centuries in various forms, largely because the cash demands of the community, from government to the householder, are constantly shifting. Bills to be paid do not necessarily coincide with surplus cash; sometimes surplus cash needs a safe and lucrative short-term resting place. One sector or company might have extra cash when another needs to borrow. Matching these needs is the role of the financial interme-diaries. Their skills lie in bringing together the varying demands of government, companies and private individuals, to find a profitable investment outlet for surpluses and to devise borrowing methods to provide funds. Intermediaries help to dovetail otherwise unmatching cashflows; they help smooth the borrowing-lending process and improve the availability of short, medium and long-term funds by matching up entities of different creditworthiness and absorbing associated risk in return for a commission or a spread.

Background

Australia's short-term money market developed after the Second World War. The markets that evolved over the intervening decades have become increasingly complex, in response to a combination of growth in the domestic economy, financial deregulation and closer integration with, and increasing sophistication of, the world's finan-cial markets.

Until the late 1940s, fixed deposits with a bank were virtually the only avenue for the short-term investment of surplus funds. Before the birth of the official short-term money market in 1959, the banks had little choice but to invest *their* short-term funds in 91-day treasury bills (these antecedents of the present treasury notes were available constantly from the central bank). Forty years ago, Australian investors had a narrow choice of investment outlets; the most familiar intermediary was the bank and prevailing regulations severely restricted what banks could offer in the way of attractive investment opportunities. For example, trading banks could not pay interest on deposits placed for less than three months, a feature that attracted depositors towards hire-purchase companies (forerunners of finance companies). Certainly the community was less interest-rate conscious in those days of low interest rates and, more important, low inflation. There was, nevertheless, a growing aware-ness that it would be profitable to have idle funds earn some return rather than lie in a non-interest-paying cheque account. The diffi-culty was finding an interest-bearing outlet for surplus cash that might be needed at short notice.

The problem of uneven cashflow existed for companies as well as households. Bank overdrafts were not a solution as they were often too small to fund a company's expansion and were hard to find when credit was tight. Companies with offsetting financing needs were encouraged by their banks to help each other out. Such cooperation was the start of the *intercompany* market. Intercompany money-market activity began in the early 1950s, well ahead of the start of the *official* money market. Merchant banks' borrowing and lending activities were an extension of the early intercompany business, with the merchant banks in later years acting as principals rather than solely in a broking role. The official money market, and the secured borrowing and lending handled in the unofficial market, developed from the early 'buy-back' activities of the stockbrokers. The markets in paper, such as bills of exchange, promissory notes and certificates of deposit, were developed to provide additional liquidity and flexibility.

The Australian short-term money market, therefore, has always included several sectors. The markets expanded significantly during the 1980s and 1990s, becoming known as *financial* markets and handling enormous volumes of securities and investments as well as short-term cash, which is generally traded in parcels of millions of dollars. Outsiders find it hard to visualise where all the money comes from, and what the market does. And it is not an easy matter to see operators in action. While share and futures activity, before the advent of electronic trading, was traditionally carried out on a trading floor and observers could watch the activity from a public gallery, money-market business has always been handled by telephone, telex and computer screens. The market is a network of traders spread around Australia—although most are in Sydney and Melbourne—who are in continuous communication, buying and selling parcels of money and securities for themselves or as brokers on behalf of clients. Internationalisation of financial markets has brought global integration, so that financial markets operators, who routinely deal overseas, are constantly watching developments in major world markets and events that have occurred during the northern-hemisphere day and the Australian night. Electronic communication, through services such as Reuters, Bridge Telerate and Bloomberg, has helped bring markets together. Internationalisation of world financial markets has broadened horizons for traders and investors. Domestic traders in Australia follow overseas developments in interest rates and inflation, keep an eye on currency moves and liaise with their counterparts in foreign exchange.

Objectives have changed with new market conditions. Since the Reserve Bank began, in 1990, using a target for the overnight cash rate (see chapter 4) as its main instrument for implementing monetary policy, volatility in short-term interest rates has been substantially reduced and trading for trading's sake has largely evaporated; financial markets operators structure their business around the needs of their clients, providing financing packages for clients and using the different markets to offset their own risks. The financial markets span a range of instruments and activities: short-dated securities, long-term fixed-income markets, derivatives such as financial futures and options (over-the-counter and exchange-traded), swaps, equities, securities underwriting, corporate finance and advice, structured finance, securitisation and foreign exchange.

The official market

For decades, until the 'official' or 'authorised' dealers were disbanded in mid-1996, the domestic market was often described as either the 'official' or 'unofficial' market. Australia's official short-term money market originated in the late 1950s. It corresponded approximately with the UK's discount-house market, the primary dealers in the US and the investment dealers in Canada. Many central banks, in their market activities, have dealt with a limited group of specialist securities dealers. An exception has been New Zealand, where the central bank deals with any institution or individual judged trustworthy and capable of settling a minimum amount of stock. In Germany, the Bundesbank deals directly with the banks. The reasons central banks created and maintained a specialist group with whom to deal were twofold: it gave the central bank scope to buy or sell securities, and provided a channel through which to implement monetary policy. Since the termination of Australia's authorised dealers in 1996, the Reserve Bank has dealt with any entity which is a member of the Reserve Bank Information and Transfer System (RITS, see chapter 4). The authorised dealers—rendered irrelevant by the switch to a real-time gross settlements system which minimises settlement risk in high-value payments (see chapter 4)—had been the conduit through which the Reserve Bank influenced interest rates and so they had an important role in monetary policy. The overnight cash rate remains the benchmark rate, with any change affecting other interest rates, trickling along the spectrum from those paid in the wholesale financial markets to those paid by Mr and Ms Australia for their mortgage.

Authorised dealers' origins

The origins of the official market lie in the 'buy-back' activities in government securities in the 1950s. These were handled by a number of stockbrokers, around the time that hire-purchase companies were starting to borrow from the public and an embryonic intercompany market was developing. Stockbrokers had begun to offer clients facilities for investing temporarily surplus cash. The brokers sold government bonds to the clients and the parties agreed that the brokers would buy the bonds back at a future date and at a set price (a practice now known as repurchase agreements, repos or RPs.) In effect, the brokers were borrowing their clients' funds and securing the borrowings with government bonds. The clients were lending funds (investing) and taking the bonds as security. Such clients would probably have willingly bought government bonds had they been certain about the length of time they could afford to invest; but they were reluctant to buy bonds outright in case they had to sell them within a short time, possibly at a loss. Short-dated government securities at that time were not available in sufficient quantity to guarantee a thriving market. With the brokers' methods, funds were on loan for short periods, from a few days to one month.

The buy-backs were an important catalyst. Despite the risks and disadvantages they carried, they grew sufficiently in volume to prompt concern at government level about the continuing health of the arrangements. A central bank examination of the buy-back activity resulted in the concept of establishing a defined and formal market in government securities, operated by a number of accredited dealers. The original brief for the 'authorised' or 'official' dealers included establishing a short-term money market and stimulating trading in government securities. The broking firms which had already been involved in the buy-back transactions had the dealing expertise, so it was logical that most of the official dealer companies established had strong connections with broking houses.

In February 1959 the central bank (then the Commonwealth Bank and since January 1960 the Reserve Bank) announced the launch of the official short-term money market. Four companies were accredited as official money-market dealers. They were created by the stockbroking firms shifting their buy-back business into new organisations. A further five companies were accredited as authorised dealers in 1960. The authorised dealers were accorded certain privileges but in return they had to comply with a number of Reserve Bank requirements governing the structure of their portfolios and the nature of their activities. However, the rules under which the authorised dealers operated were progressively relaxed to enable the dealers to compete effectively with an expanded and freer banking system. The refinements were intended to strengthen their role as traders of short-term government securities and as a mechanism through which the central bank managed day-to-day fluctuations in liquidity and pursued its longer-term monetary policy objectives.

Dealings between the Reserve Bank and the authorised dealers were based on short-dated commonwealth government securities: government bonds with less than one year to maturity and treasury notes. The Reserve Bank also bought and sold these securities through repurchase agreements which reposition funds and so help to reduce day-to-day fluctuations in the level of cash in the system.

The unofficial market

The term *unofficial market* has become an anachronism, but it is worth explaining for the sake of history. Until the authorised dealers were disbanded, the Australian financial markets were distinguished as 'official' and 'unofficial'. Operators in the unofficial market included banks, merchant and investment banks and brokers. The users of the market ranged from finance companies and large insurance offices and fund managers, building societies and credit unions, to individuals and companies wanting to trade in cash or securities. The unofficial market always had far more involvement with the private sector than its official counterpart, concentrating to a greater extent on matching and servicing the funding requirements of companies and individuals and having no direct interaction with the Reserve Bank. Its role, as is the role of financial markets generally, has been in mobilising funds from one private-sector user to another. The unofficial market had greater freedom than the official to select its areas of activity, and this increased its potential for profit; it was not compelled, as the official market was, to trade in government securities and any decision to do so would be based purely on commercial considerations.

The unofficial market grew enormously, partly because it was unhampered by controls and partly because its growth was boosted by what seemed for years to be an unending expansion of investment (formerly merchant) banks in Australia. Their growth, in turn, was helped by a combination of innate conservatism on the part of the banks and the constraints placed on them by government regulations. Early merchant bank growth also owed much to the eagerness of foreign banks to establish a foothold in Australia, which they did through the only vehicle available at the time—a merchant bank subsidiary. Most have converted to bank status.

An early sector of the so-called unofficial market was the *intercompany market;* it was the first to sidestep conventional borrowing methods, such as bank overdrafts. This market had no counterpart overseas; the US, for example, traded one or two-day promissory notes to accommodate ultra-short-term cashflows. The intercompany market predated the official short-term money market; its beginnings were in the early 1950s, when several large pastoral and finance companies lent surplus cash to companies which were known to be top-class credits. The intercompany market, one of the simplest and least formal areas of the financial system, enabled companies to offset their different financial requirements. The banks also initially encouraged companies to use their spare cash to mutual benefit, but subsequently complained that companies frequently made substantial use of bank overdrafts to boost the amounts they could lend. It became common practice for a company with an unused overdraft to lend the funds to a company looking for money—always provided that the difference between the two interest rates made the deal profitable for the lender.

The informality of the intercompany market was both its strength and its weakness. A significant risk was that a company assessed as a good-name borrower could get into unexpected financial difficulties between assessments. A company could be on the list of several lenders and have borrowed to its limits with each, without any individual lender being aware of the borrower's total commitments in the market. This lack of disclosure was highlighted in well-known crashes, and reinforced the wisdom of lending against security. It was long predicted that the intercompany market would fade into history as the markets diversified in forms of funding.

Investment (merchant) banks

The development and growth of merchant banks, later known as investment banks, in Australia is interwoven with the evolution of the financial markets. The increase in the number of merchant banks largely reflected the high level of overseas interest in Australia; many merchant banks were formed by overseas banks, sometimes in consortium with domestic banks. The merchant banks continually expanded their services and range of clients. Merchant bank strategies have varied. Some operated as quasi-banks, concentrating on borrowing and lending and making profits from the spread in interest rates—an activity that lost its appeal after August 1984, when the banks were allowed to pay interest on overnight deposits. Others turned to specialised areas such as project finance or funds management; many developed expertise in underwriting and corporate finance and advisory work. The energetic and entrepreneurial merchant banks pushed along the development of new financial instruments; they were at the forefront of the drive to develop a market in bills of exchange and they vigorously promoted the promissory note. Many also made a significant contribution, in the late 1970s and early 1980s, to the growth of the currency hedge market. (Investment banks, whose activities have become increasingly indistinguishable from those of banks—many of which have investment banking functions—are discussed further in chapter 5.)

Banks

Until the early 1980s banks were constrained by a range of controls. This facilitated the rapid growth of the merchant banks and other non-bank financial intermediaries, such as building societies, credit unions and finance companies. Many of the 'fringe' banking operations, notably finance companies and merchant banks, were subsidiaries of banks, so the banks were able to engage indirectly in business that was otherwise off-limits. As banks were progressively freed from controls, the rationale for these subsidiaries was largely removed and most were folded into their banking parent. Banks now operate more freely but remain subject to a range of prudential controls. (See chapter 5.)

Fund managers

A growth industry since the mid-1980s, fund managers enjoy an important profile in the financial markets and the wider economy, largely thanks to government initiatives in superannuation which have underscored the increasing importance of the need for the average individual to save for retirement. Fund managers, operating on behalf of investors, have hundreds of billions of dollars of funds under their stewardship, a level that is tipped to increase enormously as individuals add to their pot of savings and superannuation. Investment banks, through their fund management subsidiaries, are important players in the industry, challenging the more established life offices and insurance companies for market share (see chapter 5).

Building societies and credit unions

Building societies and credit unions, long-established cooperative entities operating under state or territory legislation, from 1998 came under the supervision of the Australian Prudential Regulation Authority. Building societies and credit unions borrow from, and provide finance to, their members for general consumer purposes. Building societies are active in the financial markets to help balance cashflows, raise term funds and manage interest-rate and liquidity risk. The number of building societies has fallen as many converted to bank status in the late 1980s and into the 1990s. Credit unions are involved in the financial markets more as 'end-users' than major players.

Evolution of financial instruments

In the early days of the Australian money market, funds were borrowed and lent in uncomplicated transactions—money changed hands, at a rate, between the parties to the deal. The volume of trading in government securities was far lower in the days before the Australian government ran large budget deficits. But during the second half of the 1970s, for most of the 1980s and, again, in the 1990s, the government was a big borrower and hence a regular, and dominant, issuer of securities. The financial markets developed in sophistication and flexibility to cater for the expanding funding needs of companies and governments. A client approaching a bank or investment bank looking for finance would now be offered a selection of financial packages which would include the option to use foreign currencies, fixed or floating-rate securities and one of the many twists available in the growing derivatives markets. The drive to improve financing methods was the impetus behind the development of financial instruments such as bills of exchange, promissory notes, certificates of deposit, swaps and other derivatives, mortgage-backed securities, corporate bonds and euro-$A securities. These financial instruments provide a marketable security or a technique that can be structured to suit an individual client's requirements. And securitisation—parcelling up assets and selling securities against them—has provided additional flexibility.

3

Regulation and self-regulation

Regulation of the Australian financial markets was overhauled in the late 1990s as the federal government introduced several recommendations of the Wallis committee, a committee of inquiry the government had appointed in 1996 under the chairmanship of leading industrialist Stan Wallis to examine the financial system and related regulatory and supervisory issues. Such an examination was felt to be timely, after more than a decade of financial deregulation and rapid change which had followed from the recommendations of an earlier, landmark inquiry headed by the late Sir Keith Campbell, whose six-person taskforce undertook the first thorough examination of the Australian financial system since the 1930s Royal Commission into Money and Banking. The Campbell committee's 1981 report provided a blueprint for reform of the Australian financial system. Since the early 1980s, however, the financial landscape had altered considerably, specifically through progress in electronic communications and developments in the payments system, as well as through the impact of deregulation and greater integration with world markets, so that it was considered appropriate, in some quarters, to undertake another examination to ensure that the financial system was sufficiently flexible to adapt to further change.

Significant outcomes of the Wallis report for regulation of the financial markets were:

- Bank supervisory functions of the Reserve Bank of Australia (RBA) were transferred to a new regulator, the Australian Prudential Regulation Authority (APRA), with the RBA extending its role and powers over the payments system and retaining its responsibility for day-to-day liquidity management and

Regulatory body	Legal basis	Responsibilities
Pre-Wallis regulatory system		
Reserve Bank	Reserve Bank Act 1959, Banking Act 1959 (updated 1989), Banks (Shareholdings) Act 1972, Financial Corporations Act 1974	prudential supervision of banks; oversight of the financial system
Australian Financial Institutions Commission (AFIC)	AFIC legislation 1992	national coordination of state supervisors of building societies, credit unions and friendly societies
Insurance and Superannuation Commission (ISC)	Superannuation Industry (Supervision) Act 1993	prudential supervision of the life insurance and superannuation industries to protect policy-holders and fund members, and ensure compliance with the commonwealth government's retirement income standards
Australian Securities Commission (ASC)	Corporations Act 1989	regulatory oversight of companies, regulation of brokers, dealers, investment advisers, ASX and SFE
Australian Competition and Consumer Commission	Trade Practices Act 1974, Prices Surveillance Act 1983	consumer protection, misleading conduct or advertising, deceptive practices in all industries
Foreign Investment Review Board	Foreign Takeovers Act 1975	review of all foreign investment
Post-Wallis		
Reserve Bank	Reserve Bank Act, Financial Corporations Act	financial system stability, payments system
APRA	Banking Act, APRA Act	deposit-takers, insurance and superannuation companies
ASIC	ASC (now ASIC) Act 1989, amended 1998	combination of those of ASC and some of the ISC and including market integrity, consumer protection in financial services sector
ACCC	Trade Practices Act, Prices Surveillance Act	consumer protection in relation to credit and foreign-exchange contracts covered by Trade Practices Act, input under Section 52 of the act
FIRB	Foreign Takeovers Act 1975	review of all foreign investment

overall stability of the financial system. An element of overlap continued, however; in fact, close coordination between the RBA and APRA was entrenched through the appointment to the APRA board of two RBA *ex-officio* members and establishment of a bilateral coordination committee chaired by the RBA deputy governor. Full exchange of information between the RBA and APRA was assured.

- Non-banks such as building societies and credit unions, which since 1991 had been supervised by state supervisors under the umbrella of the Australian Financial Institutions Commission (AFIC), were to come under APRA, and became members of the payments system. AFIC was to be disbanded as state governments agreed to cede their powers to regulate non-banks.
- The Australian Securities Commission and some functions of the Insurance and Superannuation Commission were joined as the Australian Securities and Investments Commission.

The Payment Systems (Regulation) Bill, passed by parliament in 1998, established new powers and authority for the Reserve Bank to set standards for, and collect information about, the payments system and to set conditions of access to the system; other legislation amended the Banking Act and the Reserve Bank Act. APRA began operating on 1 July 1998.

The Reserve Bank of Australia

A strange profession, little understood by members of the public whose interests it exists to protect, by governments with which it shares responsibilities or by financial institutions whose activities it to some degree controls. Those who practise it often feel themselves to be members of an international freemasonry, a kind of 'mystery' in the medieval sense of a group who possess some exclusive knowledge or skill, and indeed there has always been an element of mystery in the contemporary sense of the word about what central bankers do.

—from *Trial Balance*, the autobiography of Dr H.C. (Nugget) Coombs, governor of the Commonwealth Bank 1949–60 and of the Reserve Bank 1960–68

Central banks face in the 21st century the continuing challenges of ensuring stability and integrity in financial systems that are increasingly seamless following the unprecedented integration and internationalisation of world financial markets in the 1980s and 1990s. This was facilitated by advances in technology and electronic communications as much as by dismantling of earlier regulations which, among other influences, discouraged rather than encouraged global interaction. These changes affected central bankers as much as market operators. Financial deregulation made central banks more prominent and the Reserve Bank of Australia was no exception. Central banks in all deregulated economies became more visible; they were no longer able to hide behind rules and lay down the law without explanation. A deregulated financial system forces central bankers to exercise judgment and discretion. Their critics say central bankers, in the past—when they *thought* they set, say, exchange rates—overestimated their influence. In a deregulated system they can wield considerable power.

Moves in the 1980s to free the Australian financial markets from government controls were not intended to signal an end to discipline. The purpose was to remove regulations which were deemed of doubtful value. Freer markets heightened the importance of the Reserve Bank's monitoring role, from the standpoints of economic management and prudential control. The guidelines on bank capital, discussed in this chapter, are one example of action taken by central banks around the world to try to ensure that free markets do not become synonymous with instability or a lack of confidence in the financial system.

The Reserve Bank's function in respect of the banks—which from 1998 shifted to the Australian Prudential Regulation Authority and encompassed all deposit-taking institutions—altered during the 1980s from one of enforcing regulations to one of detailed and constant supervision, with the objective of ensuring that the safety and stability of the banking system was maintained. The Reserve Bank of Australia had stepped up prudential supervision of the banks but stopped short of offering explicit insurance. Central banks or bodies supervising banks and deposit-takers do not want to appear to be providing a safety net; however, market operators generally believe that no supervisor would stand back and allow a large-scale financial institution to collapse if that were likely to endanger the stability of the financial system (create systemic risk). The difficulty for supervisors is not only the extent to which they should protect banks and other deposit-taking institutions, but how clearly they should signal the steps they would take in a crisis. The objective of prudential supervision is to prevent a crisis occurring in the first place.

History of the Reserve Bank

The history of Australia's central bank dates from an act of parliament in 1911, which created the Commonwealth Bank of Australia. For almost half a century this bank had the dual roles of a commercial bank and a central bank. The first central banking powers were obtained in 1924, when the Commonwealth Bank was given control over the issue of notes. A bill was introduced in parliament to endorse these powers but was defeated in 1930. At that time the private banks vigorously opposed the formation of an institution such as a central bank.

The role of Australia's central bank was first properly examined in the 1936–37 Royal Commission into Money and Banking. The Second World War interrupted application of the royal commission's recommendations, although wartime national security regulations bestowed quasi-central banking powers on the Commonwealth Bank. The 1945 Banking Act confirmed the Commonwealth Bank's status as central bank and drew a clearer distinction between its commercial banking and central banking activities. This laid the groundwork for the subsequent separation of central banking functions. Legislation passed in 1959 split the savings and trading bank operations from the central banking activities. These came under the responsibility of the newly created Reserve Bank of Australia, which began operating in January 1960.

The Reserve Bank's role combines responsibility for financial system stability and for the payments system. The RBA is also banker and adviser to the federal government, but some elements of government banking will go out to tender. The bank carries out its monetary and liquidity management program through open-market operations in the money and securities markets (see chapter 4). Its duties lie in overseeing the activities of Australia's financial markets; the central bank is not a government department, such as treasury, and operates with a considerable degree of autonomy in its day-to-day business and independence in conducting monetary policy. The federal government, however, retains an influence over the RBA through its ability to make appointments to the bank's board, and by requiring the bank to submit its accounts to the commonwealth auditor-general for examination.

The Reserve Bank sits somewhere between the government of the day and the market. In his autobiography *Trial Balance,* the late Dr H.C. Coombs, points out the separate, and at times conflicting, lines of responsibility of a central bank. The bank has a duty to the government, to the banking and financial system, and to the profession of central banking, and these do not necessarily all point in the same direction. Coombs said a central banker feels a member of a different species from commercial bankers, however little this difference is appreciated. He wrote that a friend of his, to whom he tried to explain the difference, commented: 'Come the revolution, you will be hanged as high as the rest, but as they bear you off to the nearest lamp post, you will be crying plaintively, "But I am a CENTRAL banker!"'

The powers of central banks vary from country to country. The Reserve Bank of Australia enjoys a degree of independence bestowed by legislation and in the 1990s increasingly exercised that, although not yet to the extent of achieving the independent profile of, say, West Germany's Bundesbank or the Federal Reserve in the US. The Bundesbank Act of 1957 gives the central bank independence in its pursuit of stability in prices (while also supporting government economic policy). Paul Volcker, chairman of the US Fed from 1979 to 1987, was at one stage voted the second-most powerful figure in the US. Australia has not yet produced a central bank governor of that status; rather, the system has favoured close cooperation between governor and federal government. The governor of the Reserve Bank and the secretary to the treasury are required under the Reserve Bank Act to establish and maintain a close liaison so that each may be fully informed on matters of mutual concern. The practice has developed of briefing the treasurer after each monthly bank board meeting, with the governor and/or deputy governor meeting the treasurer to inform him of the board's views. Contact between the bank and the treasurer, though, is far from limited to such formal occasions.

The possibility that the government and the Reserve Bank might clash over an issue is covered by legislation; section 11 of the Reserve Bank Act sets out the procedures to resolve policy differences between the RBA and the government. These procedures allow the government to determine policy should a material difference arise, however the procedures are politically demanding and their nature reinforces the RBA's independence. If the treasurer and the RBA board cannot agree, the board has to prepare an explanation of the matter in dispute for the treasurer. He may then make a recommendation to the governor-general (effectively the federal government), who might decide on the policy to be adopted by the Reserve Bank. The treasurer would then inform the bank of the decision taken, and would tell the bank that the government accepts full responsibility for the bank's adopting the decided policy. The board is then under a statutory obligation to ensure that the stated policy is carried out. Should matters get to this stage, the government has to notify the parliament of what has occurred, and provide the parliament with statements from the government and the bank setting out their respective views on the issues involved.

This section of the Reserve Bank Act has been criticised as both an intrusion on the independence of the bank and an impingement on the powers of a democratically elected government. Although the federal government has the final word and ultimate responsibility for monetary policy, any serious disagreement between it and its central bank would be publicly aired. There has been considerable support at times for greater independence for the Reserve Bank, and this has borne fruit in the 1990s, particularly in the context of RBA independence over the conduct of monetary policy; meanwhile, no government has yet had to resort to the tactics spelled out in section 11 of the Reserve Bank Act.

Legal framework

The Reserve Bank's activities, powers and responsibilities are set out in the Reserve Bank Act 1959 (revised 1998).

Under the Reserve Bank Act the central bank is responsible for ensuring that its monetary and banking policies contribute to the stability of the Australian economy and to the welfare of its people. The charter of the Reserve Bank (section 10 of the Reserve Bank Act) outlines the bank's duties:

> It is the duty of the Board, within the limits of its powers, to ensure that the monetary and banking policy of the Bank is directed to the greatest advantage of the people of Australia and that the powers of the Bank under this Act . . . and the regulations under that Act are exercised in such a manner as, in the opinion of the Board, will best contribute to the stability of the currency of Australia; the maintenance of full employment; and the economic prosperity and welfare of the people of Australia.

This act spells out the relationship between the Reserve Bank and the federal government and describes the bank's objectives in monetary policy. The Reserve Bank has all the capabilities normally associated with a bank, but it is required to employ them only as a central bank. It has the scope to borrow and lend money, and to buy and sell government and other securities. It is through these activities, and its advisory role to the federal government, that the Reserve Bank can influence the price and availability of money and credit in Australia.

The scope of the Reserve Bank Act has been augmented by the 1996 *Statement on the Conduct of Monetary Policy* (see chapter 4) between the federal treasurer and the RBA governor which both reinforces the independence of the Reserve Bank in setting monetary policy and gives priority to the central bank's achieving price stability, that is, low inflation.

The Reserve Bank's role

The Reserve Bank is active daily in the financial markets through its day-to-day liquidity management role, offsetting (as it chooses for monetary policy objectives) the ups and downs in government accounts as they might affect the overnight cash rate and so other interest rates (see chapter 4). The central bank's charter also includes responsibility for the payments system. The central bank is banker to the banking system and to a few specialist local and overseas financial institutions. It acts as banker and financial agent for the federal government, providing similar services for some state and territory governments. As agent for treasury, it is responsible for managing the federal government's debt, managing issues of treasury notes, short-term government securities used in short-term liquidity management, and of government bonds which play a role in debt management.

The Reserve Bank is responsible for printing and distributing the currency notes in daily use in Australia. This is carried out at the bank's subsidiary at Craigieburn, Victoria, by a separate corporatised entity called Note Printing Australia, which also prints currency for several other countries as a commercial activity. The bank does not mint Australian coins; this is done by the Royal Australian Mint, a part of treasury. However, the bank distributes the coins to the banking system as agent for the mint. The Reserve Bank handles the fixed-income investments in Australia by some foreign governments and foreign banks.

Structure of the Reserve Bank

The Reserve Bank has its own board, governor, deputy governor and staff. The board consists of the governor (chairman of the board), deputy governor (deputy chair), the secretary to the treasury and up to six other members appointed by the governor-general of Australia. The governor, deputy governor and treasury secretary are *ex-officio* members of the board. At least five of the six members must not be officers of the bank or of the Australian public service. The governor and deputy governor are appointed for terms of seven years and are eligible for re-appointment. Other members are appointed for up to five years and are also eligible for re-appointment.

Governors of the Reserve Bank

Dr H.C. Coombs	1949–68 (1949–60 governor of the Commonwealth Bank of Australia)
Sir John G. Phillips	1968–75
Sir Harold Knight	1975–82
R.A. (Bob) Johnston	1982–89
Bernie Fraser	1989–96
Ian Macfarlane	1996–

The payments system

Reform of the payments system has been an area of focus in many countries as regulators and supervisors try to minimise risk in high-value payments and improve efficiencies in low-value (high-volume) payments. There have been a number of important initiatives aimed at reforming and opening up the Australian payments system.

Background

In 1984, the federal treasurer established an advisory body, the Australian Payments System Council (APSC), chaired by the Reserve Bank of Australia, with representatives from payment services providers. During its early years, APSC concentrated on improving access to the payments system for non-bank financial institutions, and helped to negotiate cheque agency arrangements through which building societies and credit unions issued banks' cheques to their customers. More recently, APSC focused on consumer-related matters and codes of conduct for financial institutions. In the late 1980s the Australian Bankers' Association formed a task force to examine the payments system, then the RBA established a Reform of the Clearing System Steering Committee which included representatives from the banks, building societies and credit unions.

These initiatives led to the formation of the Australian Payments Clearing Association (APCA), an unlisted public company with a brief to manage payments clearing arrangements. APCA's shareholders include the Reserve Bank, the banks, building societies and credit unions; its role includes development of the payments system, control of settlement risk and improvement of the system's efficiency.

Responding to the recommendations of the Wallis committee, the federal government in 1998 gave the Reserve Bank increased responsibilities and powers to determine payments system policy and regulate the payments system. A second RBA board, the Payments System Board, was established, chaired by the RBA governor, to carry out these responsibilities. The government also abolished the APSC and transferred its responsibilities for monitoring codes of conduct to ASIC.

The system

The payments system is an area where technology and communications have had a major impact, especially at the retail level but spreading beyond that into the wholesale markets. Sophisticated communications systems and electronic payments have opened the payments system, once the preserve of banks, to a number of others including providers of credit-based payments such as American Express, Visa and Diners Club, building societies and credit unions and, increasingly, supermarkets. In the UK, for example, major supermarket chains such as Sainsburys and Tesco offer banking-type services through joint ventures and alliances with banks. In the US, major credit card companies such as American Express and department stores such as Sears Roebuck have for years offered services that compete with those from banks.

The Australian payments system can be broken down into components: source of value (deposits/credits), payments instruments (cheques/electronic messages), clearing and settlement. Before 1970 almost all non-cash transactions were in the form of cheques and legislation restricted cheque issuance to banks, giving them a virtual monopoly over the payments system. Other financial institutions such as building societies, credit unions and merchant banks offered savings and investment accounts but they could not offer a cheque-writing facility with these accounts. Since the 1970s the payments system has expanded to include a wider range of instruments and participants: in 1974 Bankcard began operating as a credit card, Mastercard was introduced in 1979 and Visa in 1981; enormous progress has been made in the use of automatic teller machines (ATMs) and electronic funds transfer at point of sale (EFTPOS). Technology progressively facilitated more efficient processing of cheques and newer payments instruments. Since 1986 building societies and credit unions have been able to offer cheque facilities through agency arrangements with banks.

A recommendation of the Wallis committee, since adopted by the government, was that access to the payments system be widened. This would occur at two levels: one would enable non-financial organisations, for example, Australia Post, Telstra or a supermarket chain, to provide payments services to the general public, while a second option would be to provide exchange settlement accounts (held by banks with the Reserve Bank, see chapter 4) to a wider range of organisations. Under this extended access, building societies and credit unions, which have effectively been participants in the payments system since the mid-1980s, no longer need a bank name on their cheques but can issue their own (although they may not necessarily clear the cheques themselves but could still have a bank as clearing agent). An essential preliminary to opening the payments system to a broader range of participants was the introduction of a real-time gross settlement (RTGS) system for high-value payments (see chapter 4).

Australian Prudential Regulation Authority

The Australian Prudential Regulation Authority (APRA) is the commonwealth agency which took over prudential supervision functions from the Insurance and Superannuation Commission (ISC) and from the Reserve Bank, but with the addition that non-bank deposit-takers such as building societies, credit unions and friendly societies also come under its net. APRA took over the responsibility for superannuation funds, life and general insurance companies from the ISC and took over prudential supervision of banks from the Reserve Bank. Building societies, credit unions and friendly societies previously came under the supervision of the Australian Financial Institutions Commission, established in 1992, which coordinated prudential supervision of them along similar lines and standards as those that applied to banks. With the establishment of APRA, AFIC was to be disbanded. APRA is a statutory authority, headquartered in Sydney but with interstate capital city offices, with its senior executives drawn from established prudential regulators formerly employed by the ISC and the Reserve Bank and its policies and operations determined by a nine-member board.

The Australian Securities and Investment Commission

The Australian Securities and Investment Commission (ASIC) is a blend of the Australian Securities Commission (ASC) and the ISC. ASIC combines the functions of:

- The ASC, formed in 1991 as the successor to the National Companies and Securities Commission and the sole national authority responsible for administering a national Corporations Law regulating companies and securities and futures markets. The ASC also ensures public disclosure of information needed by investors and creditors and undertakes market surveillance and law enforcement.
- Some responsibilities of the ISC (the bulk of ISC staff went to APRA), responsible for regulating the insurance and superannuation industries. It also has a consumer-protection and market-integrity role, supervising insurance and superannuation industries, protecting the interests of policyholders and fund members and ensuring compliance with federal government legislation.

The government also established a Financial Sector Advisory Council (FSAC) to advise it on developments in the financial sector and to report to the federal treasurer. Council members include the chief executives of several banks and major institutions. FSAC's Regional

Financial Centre Task Force is charged with advising the federal government on developments in international financial markets and measures to boost Australia's profile as a financial centre. Members of the task force include the heads of the Australian Stock Exchange, the Sydney Futures Exchange, the International Banks and Securities Association and the Australian Financial Markets Association.

Prudential supervision

Supervision of all financial institutions has been progressively evolving as regulators and supervisors refine and improve the system to cope with the dynamics of an internationalised financial system. The business of banking, whether that is undertaken by banks or other financial institutions such as building societies or credit unions which take deposits from, and lend funds to, the public, involves taking risk. At the same time, there is an acknowledgement that individual savers (in contrast to sophisticated investors or wholesale financial markets operators) ought to have an outlet to which they can entrust funds. For many years banks were considered too important a component of the financial system to be left to manage their affairs entirely on their own; confidence in the banking system was seen as essential and a prerequisite was a system of sound prudential supervision to maintain depositor confidence. From the mid-1980s, direct controls over banks in Australia were replaced by a specific framework of prudential supervision underpinned by legislative changes which came into effect in December 1989. The amendments expanded the Banking Act to give the Reserve Bank explicit powers in supervision of banks, a framework which did not, however, replace the banks' own responsibility. Prime responsibility for prudent management rested with a bank's individual management.

In its second submission to the Wallis inquiry, the Reserve Bank summed up the differing views on banking:

- Banks are too powerful and too profitable, a position they are able to maintain because they can keep competitors at bay by their own efforts, and with the help of regulations which discriminate against potential competitors.
- Banks are a threatened species. New technology and competition from non-banks such as software firms, communications companies, retailers and specialised finance companies are taking away the most profitable parts of banking and leaving existing banks with the unprofitable residue.

In 1992, with the formation of the Australian Financial Institutions Commission, non-banks such as building societies and credit unions became formally subject to the same prudential controls as banks. In the interest of simplicity, this chapter follows the path of the RBA in its submission to Wallis and uses the term *bank* to refer to an institution which takes deposits from the public and holds loans on its balance sheet.

Bank supervision encompasses:

- reaching agreement on prudential standards, in consultation with banks;
- collecting and analysing statistical information from the banks;
- ensuring the individual institutions have adequate management systems for limiting risk;
- liaising with banks' external auditors regarding certain prudential matters (this enables the supervisor to rely with a high degree of certainty on the statistical information banks provide, as well as to ascertain that banks' management systems are in place and are operating soundly).

The Reserve Bank, in its role of bank supervisor until 1998, published prudential standards in a booklet, *Prudential Supervision of Banks*. The key features of the supervisory framework are: management systems, the role of external auditors, concentration of risk, liquidity management and, most important, capital adequacy and a recognition of impaired assets.

Management systems

The bank supervisor expects banks to have adequate expertise and management resources to support all areas of their operations. Management has to be able to demonstrate that it knows and fully understands the individual and overall risks associated with its operations, including new activities. In this context effective management and control systems are essential for prudent business management. These systems need to be reviewed and tested regularly to ensure that they remain relevant and effective in controlling exposures and limiting risks in respect of on and off-balance-sheet business. Banks must be able to identify and measure the risks inherent in new and complex types of off-balance-sheet business. The bank supervisor is concerned particularly with systems to manage credit risk, liquidity risk, market risk and operational risk.

External auditors

Banks have established links between themselves, the bank supervisor and their external auditors; under these arrangements each bank's auditor gives an opinion on a number of points including:

- whether a bank is observing the prudential standards set down by the supervisor;
- whether information provided by the bank to the supervisor is reliable;
- the adequacy of nominated aspects of a bank's risk-management systems.

There is also provision for the auditor to bring to the attention of the supervisor, through and after discussion with the bank's management, any matters which, in the auditor's opinion, may have the potential to prejudice the interests of depositors of the bank. At least once a year, normally after a statutory audit has been completed, there is an opportunity for a three-way discussion between bank, external auditor and supervisor; any of the parties may propose a tripartite discussion at any time. Within three months of annual balance date of each bank, the supervisor should receive a declaration from the bank's chief executive, endorsed by the board or, in the case of a foreign bank branch, an appropriate senior officer from outside Australia, attesting that 'the board and management have identified the key risks facing the bank, have established systems to monitor and manage those risks including, where appropriate, by setting and requiring adherence to a series of prudent limits, and by adequate and timely reporting processes; that these risk-management systems are operating effectively and are adequate having regard to the risks they are designed to control; and that the descriptions of systems held by the supervisor are accurate and current'.

A major initiative was the move, from 1993, to conduct onsite inspections where each bank is visited annually by the supervisor, with visits alternated between its credit-risk and market-risk supervisory teams.

Concentration of risk

The supervisor expects banks to establish systems to monitor and control their concentration of risk exposures. This includes concentration of exposures by country, sector and individual counterparty. A concern for the supervisor prompted it to require each bank to submit a quarterly report detailing by number and dollar amount any exposure to an individual client, or group of related clients, that equates to more than 10 per cent of the bank's consolidated group capital. Banks are also subject to an upper limit on exposures to non-bank, non-government clients; a bank has to have approval from the supervisor before lending beyond that limit and such approval would be given only in exceptional circumstances. A bank wishing to maintain a high volume of large exposures could be required to maintain a higher capital ratio.

Liquidity management

The Reserve Bank announced new guidelines in April 1998 for liquidity management which replaced the prime assets ratio (PAR), a prudential requirement that all banks at all times hold a minimum level of assets of undoubted quality, in the form of commonwealth government securities, notes and coin and balances with the Reserve Bank. PAR's objective was to ensure that, in times of pressure on liquidity, banks had an emergency line of defence. PAR was initially set at 12 per cent of banks' liabilities (excluding shareholders' funds) but was progressively reduced and by June 1997 was at 3 per cent and the definition widened to include state government securities. Under the framework announced in April 1998, the RBA would agree with each bank a liquidity policy setting out how that bank would manage liquidity under two scenarios: normal day-to-day liquidity management and under a specific crisis. Each bank would be expected to be able to withstand outflows for a minimum of five days, which should give sufficient time to address an underlying problem. The absence of a formal PAR reflected the RBA's view that it was no longer appropriate to impose a common ratio or minimum level of liquid assets on all banks because that did not adequately take account of the different structure of banks' on and off-balance-sheet business. The RBA, however, expects that banks, in the interests of prudent liquidity management, would hold a minimum amount of high-quality liquid assets. Also, the RBA continues to deal only in assets which met the PAR definition in its market operations and when providing intraday liquidity under real-time gross settlement (see chapter 4). Details of the liquidity management statement are contained in prudential statement D1.

Capital adequacy

Capital adequacy is the key element in bank supervision. Supervisors around the world regard capital as a cornerstone of a bank's strength because it:

- demonstrates the owner's commitment to the banking enterprise;
- provides the wherewithal to fund a bank's infrastructure;
- insulates a bank's depositors and other creditors from loss; and
- acts as a shock absorber to help carry a bank through hard times.

By the early 1980s bank supervisors in most countries applied forms of capital adequacy standards to their banks (the US first introduced formal guidelines for capital in 1914). The Bank of England had introduced a form of risk-based capital standard and the Reserve Bank of Australia had implemented an informal capital test for banks relating shareholders' funds to total assets. In 1986 the Bank for International Settlements (BIS) published a report documenting the potential risks associated with new financial instruments such as swaps, options and forward-rate agreements which, being off-balance-sheet activities, were not caught by the prevailing capital ratios. Discussions about how to define and measure capital resulted in the Basle Supervisors Committee introducing, in 1988, international, risk-weighted capital adequacy measures which capture off-balance-sheet as well as on-balance-sheet activities. These produced a uniform definition of capital, applied to the global consolidated on and off-balance-sheet activities of banks and have been incorporated into the capital adequacy requirements set by central banks of most major countries.

The chief features of the risk-weighted capital adequacy arrangements are:

- assets are weighted for risk;
- the system takes account of off-balance-sheet as well as on-balance-sheet activities; and
- capital ratios are applied to both the bank and the consolidated group.

Under the risk-based guidelines for capital, banks have to maintain a minimum level of 4 per cent of 'core' (Tier 1) capital and a ratio of total capital (Tiers 1 and 2) to risk-weighted assets of no less than 8 per cent. Tier 2 capital cannot exceed Tier 1. The supervisor can require a bank to hold additional capital if special circumstances make that appropriate. The characteristics of capital include:

- being fully paid-up and permanently available;
- being freely available and not earmarked to particular assets or activities;
- having the ability to absorb losses in the course of business;
- representing no fixed charge on earnings (applies to Tier 1 only); and
- ranking below the claims of all other creditors in the event of liquidation.

Tier 1 capital consists of paid-up ordinary shares, non-repayable share premium account, general reserves, retained earnings, non-cumulative irredeemable preference shares and minority interests in subsidiaries.

Tier 2 or supplementary capital includes general provisions for doubtful debts (subject to a limit), asset revaluation reserves, cumulative irredeemable preference shares, mandatory convertible notes and similar capital instruments, perpetual subordinated debt and redeemable preference shares and term subordinated debt (up to a limit).

The main features of the risk-based measure of capital adequacy are:

- a 'risk ratio' is calculated by dividing a bank's capital base by the total of its risk-weighted assets;
- the focus is on credit risk and, since 1998, market risk;
- on and off-balance-sheet exposures are weighted for risk in three broad groups—government, bank and others;
- risk-weights are assessed in five general categories—0, 10, 20, 50 and 100 per cent; and
- off-balance-sheet transactions are converted to balance-sheet equivalents before being allocated a risk weight. The process involves two stages: an exposure is first converted to an on-balance-sheet equivalent by multiplying the nominal principal amount by a credit conversion factor. The resulting credit equivalent amount is then weighted according to its counterparty, for example, a two-year $100 million standby funding facility has a conversion factor of 50 per cent which creates a credit equivalent of $50 million; its risk weighting is 100 per cent of the exposure, that is, the bank holds a risk-weighted asset of $50 million.

The credit equivalents for market-related exchange-rate and interest-rate transactions are calculated in a more complex way. The special calculations for these transactions reflect the fact that the credit risks associated with them are generally only a fraction of the gross value of the contracts. Banks have a choice of methods for these calculations. The more 'professional' method is based on a 'current exposure' approach in which financial instruments are marked to market regularly to measure prevailing replacement value (current exposure), plus an allowance for potential future exposure based on residual maturity. A less sophisticated method takes a 'rule-of-thumb' approach based on original maturity, where a simple conversion factor is applied to the notional principal amount of each instrument. Banks which conduct a significant volume of market-rate-related business are expected to adopt the 'mark-to-market' method of calculation.

Irrespective of the method used, the resulting credit equivalents represent a substantial reduction from the notional value of market-related transactions. Foreign-exchange contracts out to fourteen days, and instruments traded on futures and options exchanges that are subject to daily mark-to-market and margin payments, are excluded from risk weightings. Further, when the credit equivalents are assigned to their counterparty risk weighting, a maximum weighting of 50 per cent is applied which represents a 50 per cent reduction on the risk weighting normally applicable to corporate customers.

Items carrying a zero credit risk weight include notes and coins, gold bullion (matched by gold liabilities) in banks' own vaults, balances with the Reserve Bank and commonwealth government securities with less than twelve months to maturity. Commonwealth government securities with more than twelve months to maturity carry a 10 per cent risk weighting, as do state government bonds. Claims on most banks, Australian local governments and public-sector organisations carry a 20 per cent risk weighting. Home loans secured by a mortgage against residential property for owner occupation or rental carry a risk weighting of 50 per cent. Claims on private-sector entities (companies or individuals) carry a 100 per cent risk weighting.

From January 1998 capital adequacy requirements were extended to cover market risk, being defined as the risk of losses in on and off-balance-sheet positions arising from movements in market prices. The guidelines, set out in the Reserve Bank's prudential statement C3, address the risks relating to interest-rate-related instruments and equities and foreign-exchange risk and commodities risk.

Impact of capital adequacy requirements

A risk-weighted approach to capital adequacy brought subtle changes to banks and the financial system generally as the system had an impact on the structure of banks' business and on their pricing. Astute management of capital became extremely important. Banks became more conscious of how they allocate capital, becoming keen to preserve it and maintain good rates of return. Instead of expanding their balance sheets through lending where, because of increased competition, margins tend to be unrewardingly slim, they have turned to fee-based activities. The desire for optimum capital management has fed the drive to securitisation (see chapter 11) because this technique—grouping assets together and selling securities backed by these assets—enables a lender to get assets, which require funding, off the books so that capital is freed to be used in more lucrative pursuits. Bank supervisors have taken steps to ensure that when banks securitise assets such as loans, the assets are removed from the balance sheet in a way that leaves the bank with no residual obligation—a 'clean sale' is effected.

Prudential statement C2 spells out guidelines for banks in the areas of fund management and securitisation. Supervisors worry about any moral responsibility that banks might be perceived to have regarding assets they have originated so they are anxious that banks distance themselves from any obligations associated with securitised assets. The issue of moral responsibility is relevant in fund management, an activity in which banks have become increasingly involved. Supervisors want to ensure that banks are not perceived as responsible for the activities of, say, a managed fund or a trust operated by a bank subsidiary. The assets of such a fund or trust are not assets of the bank but belong to the fund's clients or trust unitholders, on whose behalf they are managed, however a decline in the value of the assets is not a problem to be borne by the bank. Under prudential guidelines, these funds and trusts are structured so that they operate at arm's length from a bank, with a separate management company and an independent trustee.

Recognition of impaired assets

Prudential statement L1 sets guidelines covering the recognition and measurement of impaired assets, security valuation and provisioning, and credit-risk grading systems. The Reserve Bank said that maintenance of sound asset quality is a fundamental aspect of banking. In the RBA's view, it is the prime responsibility of each bank's management to set policies and procedures to ensure that banks maintain sound asset quality, strong portfolio management, prudent risk controls, effective credit review and classification procedures, and appropriate methodology for dealing with problem exposures. The RBA established a set of minimum standards, common language and methodology for identifying impaired assets to improve the quality and consistency of data received from banks.

Self-regulation: the Australian Financial Markets Association

> A primary reason for utilising self-regulation is that self-regulatory organisations know more about the technical aspects of the securities markets and more about the possibilities for market breakdown and market fraud than do government regulators.
>
> —David Ruder, a former chairman of the US Securities and Exchange Commission

The development and growth of the Australian Financial Markets Association (AFMA) in many ways encapsulates the evolution of the markets and their shift to a more serious profile in the economic and financial community. As the 1990s got under way, the financial markets shed the cowboy, screen-jockey image of the 1980s to become a sector with a genuine focus on servicing its constituents, the wholesale investors and borrowers who rely on financial markets' skills to meet their funding and investing requirements and the companies which turn to the financial markets for risk-management advice and help. Even in wilder times, dodgy dealers were given short shrift in the Australian financial markets. The treatment used to be quick and simple: if someone fouled the nest, his or her colleagues would turn their backs and freeze the culprit out. In the 1990s, it was more likely that the Australian Securities Commission would wield its big stick. There might be investigations, court cases, fines and prison terms.

Life is like that in the financial markets: more serious. Once, ways of doing business became common market practice because dealers gave them the nod over a few beers. Then rules and conventions were drafted and given legal status; market practices became mandatory. Once, almost anyone who could operate a telephone could be a dealer. Now, there is dealer accreditation, barring entry to the markets to those without special qualifications, and codes of conduct to be followed once in.

Getting the markets to grow up was largely a matter of pushing, shoving, coaxing and wheedling in an industry that was too busy making deals—and having fun—to be bothered with formality. A major push has come from AFMA, which began in the early 1980s as a rag-bag of bank-bill dealers chatting informally about new-fangled dealing screens and grew into an educational and policy-development machine of some profile. One of the association's most significant accomplishments has been to foster a disciplined structure. Information about how to work and behave in the financial markets, once passed on by tribal elders to aspiring young dealers in favoured city watering holes, is now codified.

Management of AFMA is in the hands of an appointed chief executive and a market-elected executive committee, representing member institutions. AFMA derives its imprimatur from the wholesale over-the-counter financial markets it represents—fixed interest, interest-rate and currency options, cash and repos, FRAs, swaps, commodity derivatives and short-dated securities.

In the 1990s AFMA expanded its purview exponentially, forming committees representing the various market sectors, standardising paperwork, setting down trading conventions, compiling a code of conduct and taking up any issue of concern to the wholesale markets. It pushed the markets to take themselves seriously, organising a program of workshops, seminars and annual conferences featuring speakers from organisations such as the Bank of England and US Federal Reserve. The association has the ear of influential regulators—it liaises with the Reserve Bank of Australia, the ASC and the Australian Tax Office on issues affecting the markets.

The maturing of Australian financial markets mirrors patterns overseas and, given the increased challenges of global trading in complex financial instruments, was inevitable. But it has not been easy. The markets tended to attract highly motivated people who, in many cases, resented interference and begrudged time spent on drafting and learning rules. They set the limits of behaviour themselves. Then came the 1980s and the explosive expansion in the range of products and number of participants. The cosy club was blown apart. And in the fallout the ASC, which in common with all regulators was concerned about transparency and accountability, became interested in the activities of the high-volume but informal and largely invisible wholesale over-the-counter (OTC) markets.

The rationale behind the moves to formalise arrangements in financial markets is not hard to discover. In the mid-1990s the ASC let it be put about that if the markets did not adopt some form of self-regulation the regulator would step in and do it for them. Regulators are rarely sufficiently equipped to do so.

AFMA has drawn praise for its role in raising awareness of the need for high ethical standards, documenting what was already accepted market practice, codifying conventions and standardising documentation. Growth in the swaps market has been a factor driving the need to streamline arrangements. As the swaps market grew the exposure to longer-term commitments also increased; this contrasted with the 1980s when trades were more short-term or involved bonds where the risk was the underlying security rather than the counterparty. Swaps involve a five or ten-year or even longer risk, so documentation became a major issue.

Until the introduction of a dealer accreditation system, dealers operated as authorised representatives of the institutions for which they worked, which in turn were licensed under the Corporations Law. Driving the accreditation proposal was a view that if the markets did not insist on specific qualifications and professional competence, the ASC might. Trading skills are one element, education and training another. The complexities of financial markets placed an increasing onus on traders to understand parts of the law, which in turn demanded continuing professional training. In 1997 AFMA published a revised edition of its *Dealer's Handbook*, the definitive guide for dealers in the Australian over-the-counter markets and which complements the AFMA manual which provides detailed guidelines as to best practice for AFMA members.

AFMA in no sense carries a regulatory function; rather, an emerging preoccupation has been education. The appetite for information about financial markets appears insatiable; tertiary institutions running relevant courses attract torrents of students. AFMA has sharpened its focus on education and training; its education handbook, regularly updated, provides extensive information about courses that can enhance market skills and status.

In shaping itself, AFMA took a line from two overseas organisations, ISMA (formerly the Association of International Bond Dealers) and ISDA (International Swaps and Derivatives Association). ISMA, which produces a range of high-quality publications, is a London-based self-regulatory organisation; it levies fees and runs a trade confirmation system. AFMA, however, is far from the only association to have sprung from the developing financial markets. Longer-standing organisations include the Australian Bankers Association, the Securities Institute of Australia and the International Banks and Securities Association (formerly the Australian Merchant Bankers Association, see chapter 5). Inevitably there is some overlap among the associations and occasionally some clashes over territory. Given the commonality of members, it has been suggested that it would be logical to look for some pooling of resources and skills. AFMA, though, grew up with a very defined focus on ground covered by no other organisation: the treasury dealing areas of the banks, investment banks and other institutions among its more than 100 full members.

4

The Reserve Bank's role in the financial markets

Australia's central bank for many years had a reputation as a gratuitously secretive organisation, given to speaking in obscure bureaucratic language and unwilling to divulge its motives or intentions to the market. This image has progressively changed, first with deregulation which, during the 1980s, thrust the RBA into the spotlight and to which it responded by stepping up its flow of information to the financial markets. The deregulatory moves threw greater emphasis on the bank's open-market operations, requiring a higher degree of communication between the bank and the market. Observers commented on a change of philosophy within the bank, a greater recognition of the need, in a highly deregulated environment, to be more communicative with the institutions with which it deals. The bank's critics, though, remain dissatisfied, believing that the central bank could be more open about its deliberations, possibly publishing details of its monthly board meetings some weeks after the event, in the manner of the US Federal Reserve; such disclosure is now being made by the Bank of England. Experience there, however, suggests that releasing this type of additional information can lead to greater, rather than less, confusion. Other commentators see the Reserve Bank as being adequately transparent, since it explains policy changes publicly, expresses the stance of policy openly in terms of the cash rate and operates within a defined policy framework, that is, an inflation target.

An influential agent in the change of image was R.A. (Bob) Johnston, governor of the Reserve Bank from 1982 to 1989, who took up the post at a crucial time in the reform process that was under way. The will existed within the bank to move with the times and, coincidence of timing or not, Johnston and his senior staff were credited with helping to drag the Reserve Bank out of the closet and on to centre stage.

A pivotal change for the central bank, however, and one which had far greater impact on financial markets operators, was the decision in January 1990, under RBA governor Bernie Fraser (1989–96), to announce changes to the cash rate and to state a cash-rate target. This brought an unprecedented degree of predictability to interest rates. With the central bank virtually setting short-term interest rates for a foreseeable period, opportunities to trade what had been volatile markets significantly diminished and the need for risk-management products declined.

This policy of greater transparency continued with the appointment of Ian Macfarlane as governor in August 1996. On his appointment, he and the federal treasurer agreed on a *Statement on the Conduct of Monetary Policy* which enshrined the Reserve Bank's inflation objective, while also requiring that the bank issue a semi-annual statement on monetary policy containing an inflation forecast, and that the governor appear before a parliamentary committee to discuss the statement. In some respects these requirements are similar to the Humphrey–Hawkins Congressional appearances of the chairman of the US Federal Reserve—six-monthly testimonials which date from 1970s legislation sponsored by Senator Hubert Horatio Humphrey and Congressman Augustus Hawkins requiring the chairman of the Fed to appear before Congress twice a year to report on the central bank's success or failure in achieving its targets. These testimonials have come to be regarded in world financial markets as the definitive statements concerning US monetary policy.

The Reserve Bank Act gives the RBA the power to determine its monetary policy and to take whatever action is necessary to implement policy changes. These powers were recognised in the 1996 statement on the conduct of monetary policy between the RBA governor and the federal treasurer. In the statement, among other things, the government declared its recognition of the independence of the RBA and of the bank's responsibility for monetary policy matters and its intention to respect the central bank's independence as provided by statute. The statement said:

> Monetary policy is a key element of macroeconomic policy and its effective conduct is critical to Australia's economic performance and prospects. For this reason, and given the appointment of a new governor of the Reserve Bank, it is appropriate and timely for the governor and the government to set out clearly their mutual understanding of the operation of monetary policy in Australia.
>
> It is expected that this statement will contribute to a better understanding both in Australia and overseas of the nature of the

relationship between the Reserve Bank and the government, the objectives of monetary policy, the mechanisms for ensuring transparency and accountability in the way policy is conducted, and the independence of the central bank . . . Consistent with its responsibilities for economic policy as a whole the government reserves the right to comment on monetary policy from time to time. However, the government will no longer make parallel announcements of monetary policy adjustments when the Reserve Bank changes the overnight cash rate. This will enhance both the perception, as well as the reality, of the independence of the Reserve Bank decision making . . . In recent years the Reserve Bank has taken steps to make the conduct of policy more transparent. Changes in policy and related reasons are now clearly announced and explained. In addition, the central bank has upgraded its public commentary on the economic outlook and issues bearing on monetary policy settings, through public addresses and its regular quarterly report on the economy . . . the governor has also indicated that he plans to be available to report on the conduct of monetary policy twice a year to the House of Representatives Standing Committee on Financial Institutions and Public Administration.

Macfarlane described the statement as a 'means of clearing up any remaining ambiguity about the relationship between the government and the Reserve Bank'. In an address in September 1996, shortly after becoming governor, he spoke of why the Reserve Bank was 'always on the back foot' having to defend itself against a charge of political interference. The Reserve Bank, he said, was getting recognised as a reasonably independent central bank, but 'this is only a very recent phenomenon'. Macfarlane's predecessor, Bernie Fraser, was constantly defending the central bank against the charge that it was subject to political interference. While the Reserve Bank Act gives the RBA a high degree of legislative independence, there was, said Macfarlane, a widespread assumption that the act gave the Reserve Bank little independence. He said:

This assumption arose because, for virtually 30 years after it was enacted . . . monetary policy was implemented as though the Reserve Bank had no independence. Decisions were taken mainly in Canberra, with the treasurer and the treasury usually having a bigger say in any decision than the Reserve Bank. Generations of economists, politicians and journalists grew up with this and accepted it as the natural order of things . . . How could this situation persist for so long, if the act clearly said that decisions on monetary policy should be made by the Reserve Bank? The answer to this riddle is that the Reserve Bank did not have instruments of monetary policy at its disposal—before deregulation, they were nearly all in Canberra.

Financial deregulation brought a big change for the Reserve Bank because it set aside controls on interest rates and the exchange rate, enabled budget deficits to be financed at market-determined interest rates and left the Reserve Bank's open-market operations as the chief instrument of monetary policy and effective determinant of short-term interest rates. This, said Macfarlane, placed the Reserve Bank operationally in the same position as the US Federal Reserve or the Bundesbank.

The Reserve Bank conducts monetary policy within an inflation-targeting framework. The inflation target is expressed as maintaining underlying inflation in a range of 2–3 per cent on average over the economic cycle. This framework implies that the central bank should reassess monetary policy if the forecast profile of inflation deviates from the target: generally, other things being equal, if inflation is expected to remain above 3 per cent for a sustained period, the cash rate should be increased, while when inflation is projected to remain sustainably below 2 per cent, policy should be eased—that is, interest rates reduced. A number of countries operate within an explicit inflation-targeting framework, including the UK, Canada, New Zealand, Sweden and Finland. The target inflation rate, and the specification of the target, varies among these countries.

The Reserve Bank and monetary policy

Monetary policy covers actions taken by central banks to affect financial conditions (interest rates and exchange rates) in a way that enables the central bank to achieve broader economic policy objectives such as low inflation and sound, sustainable economic growth. Financial markets have an important role to play in this because the Reserve Bank operates in the financial markets to achieve the desired monetary policy position; also, financial markets are the channel through which the effects of RBA action are first transmitted, and the markets provide feedback to policymakers. (Reserve Bank activity in the foreign-exchange markets, where it intervenes from time to time, is discussed in chapter 12.)

The target cash rate

Monetary policy is implemented in two stages. As a first step when changing policy, the RBA announces a new target for the cash rate (the overnight interest rate on funds borrowed and lent in the financial markets); next the central bank operates daily in the market to ensure that the cash rate is held close to the target. Through these operations, often referred to as 'open market operations', the RBA influences the level of liquidity in the banking system by buying or selling securities to add or withdraw funds to or from the banking system. In doing so, however, the RBA's focus is on a *price*, not quantity, of liquidity in the banking system; it operates to influence the cash rate, not a volume of money. If monetary policy is being tightened the central bank operates to raise the cash rate; if monetary policy is being relaxed, the cash rate is lowered.

The RBA's target cash rate reflects the stance of monetary policy (tight or easy). Between 1990 and early 1998 policy was changed 23 times, through fifteen easings between 1990 and 1993 which saw the cash rate fall from 18 per cent to 4.75 per cent, three tightenings in late 1994 which pushed cash rates up by 2.75 percentage points and five easings between mid-1996 and mid-1997 which cut the cash rate by 2.5 percentage points to 5 per cent. The RBA describes the cash rate as 'an intermediate or operating objective of monetary policy: the ultimate goal of policy is inflation and economic growth, not a particular level of interest rates'. The RBA cannot dictate the level of inflation or determine full employment as it wishes; rather, it relies on adjusting the factors that it can influence, to set the economy on course for low inflation and high employment.

Flagging the target cash rate publicly and explaining the reasons for a change in its level is a key part of monetary policy framework. It telegraphs a message to banks and other financial intermediaries about their funding costs and underpins the link between the cash rate—the interest rate that reflects policy—and the lending rates that prevail in the wider market where households and businesses borrow, lend and spend. Announcements about a change in the target cash rate receive widespread media coverage and help reinforce the policy message to the wider community (a sharp contrast to earlier times when the Reserve Bank talked obliquely about 'snugging' interest rates up or down and a disproportionate amount of financial markets resources went into trying to guess what the central bank was about to do or not do). The transparent framework that has been operating since 1990 sends a clear signal about the RBA's intentions with monetary policy and, by explaining why policy has been changed, helps lift understanding about how monetary policy is set so that there is a greater chance of influencing behaviour in directions that support policy aims.

As the RBA states in a paper on the *Implementation of Monetary Policy* delivered at a seminar for teachers in mid-1997, 'the target itself plays a major role in anchoring expectations about the cash rate and adds to the effectiveness of policy'. The RBA's announcement of a target cash rate is the key difference between its operations before 1990 and since. Before 1990, financial markets (and far less the general public) could never be certain about the level of cash rate the RBA was aiming to achieve. As the RBA says: 'This resulted in a high degree of volatility in the cash rate, which often caused confusion because it was unclear whether day-to-day movements in the cash rate were "noise" or actually reflected a change in the policy stance'. For example, in the late 1980s, as it became clear that policy had been too relaxed, the central bank raised interest rates to try to cool economic activity but the message was too muted and even punishingly high interest rates, such as mortgage rates at 17 per cent, failed for a time to drive home the message that borrowers and consumers should rein in their activities. The cash rate became much steadier, and the stance of policy much clearer, after the RBA began in January 1990 making announcements about the target. The ultimate decision about the cash-rate target rests with the Reserve Bank board, whose members draw on staff recommendations about monetary policy which derive from analysis of the economy and of developments in financial markets. This process is forward-looking. Since monetary policy affects inflation and the economy with a lag of perhaps one to two-and-a-half years, policy settings today are made to influence inflation a year so hence. When a decision is made to change the target cash rate, the change is achieved on the day of the announcement by RBA buying or selling operations in the domestic money market. The RBA, however, is active virtually daily in the domestic market, irrespective of policy changes, as it operates to hold the cash rate as close as possible to the target.

Liquidity management

When the Australian financial system was regulated, monetary policy operated through edicts to the banks stipulating the levels of interest rates they could pay and charge and the volume of lending they could undertake. That was normal in countries with regulated financial systems before the realisation spread that regulations were not always effective or efficient. With a deregulated system, central banks use a short-term interest rate as an operating target for monetary policy objectives. The Reserve Bank of Australia achieves a level for the cash rate as close as possible to its target by influencing supply and demand in the money market, being the market for the liquid funds needed by banks to settle obligations among themselves and with the Reserve Bank. Ultimately, these transactions are settled in exchange settlement accounts which each bank holds for this purpose with the Reserve Bank. Accordingly, these funds are known as exchange settlement or ES funds.

Exchange settlement funds: supply and demand

As with any market, the level of ES funds reflects supply and demand. Demand for ES funds is an outcome of banks' settlement obligations, which fall into two categories: obligations among the banks and obligations between the banks and the Reserve Bank.

Each days sees millions of private transactions in the economy and it is these which give rise to settlement obligations between banks as they transfer funds within the banking system. For example, a customer of bank X writes a cheque to pay a customer of bank Y, creating a settlement obligation between the two banks with bank X owing funds to bank Y. A bank making a payment to another bank credits that bank with ES funds from its own ES account; if a bank facing a payment does not have enough in its ES account, it borrows from another bank. Irrespective of how a bank funds such a payment, however, the volume of ES funds in the system remains unchanged by cash transactions within the private sector; interbank transactions have no impact on the overall demand for ES funds. There is, in addition to obligations generated by banks' traditional business, a huge professional money market with both bank and non-bank participants. Some institutions have large short-term funding needs, for example, to finance a bond portfolio. Other institutions tend to be 'cash-rich' and have funds to invest for short periods. The two kinds of institutions come together in the cash market. While the non-bank fund managers exchange short-term funds in the money market, the flow of cash will occur through exchange-settlement accounts in their respective banks. So, as with settlement obligations arising from banks' traditional business, activity in the professional money market cannot add to the available pool of ES funds.

ES funds can only be created when private banks conduct transactions with the Reserve Bank. Payments from the banking system to the Reserve Bank reduce ES funds and payments by the Reserve Bank to the banks increase ES funds. It is through these changes that the Reserve Bank can influence the cash rate.

A number of underlying transactions give rise to transactions between the banking system and the Reserve Bank. A major source of fluctuations in the banking system's level of ES funds, though, is the Reserve Bank's role as banker to the commonwealth government, with the RBA making payments for the government and receiving funds on its behalf. Tax payments flow out of the banking system to the commonwealth government's accounts at the RBA and so drain the banking system: when a company pays tax it writes a cheque on its own bank in favour of the commonwealth government so that when the company's bank pays the cheque the balance

Figure 4.1 Money-market cash position

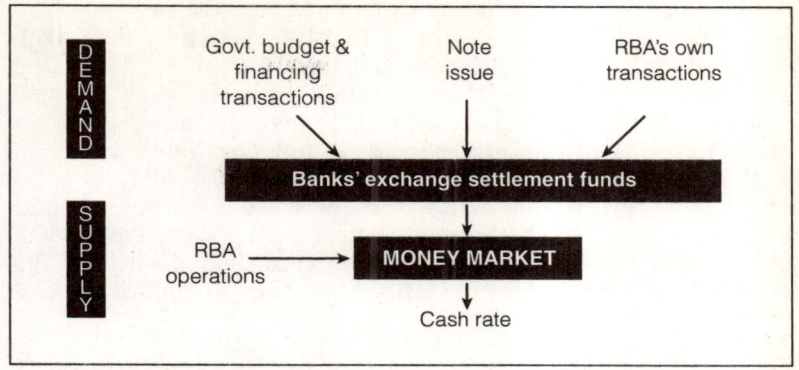

Source: Reserve Bank of Australia

in its ES account falls and the commonwealth government's balance rises. Similarly, a bank paying for a new issue of commonwealth government bonds reduces ES funds. Funds flow in the opposite direction, from the Reserve Bank to the banking system, when commonwealth government spending (pensions, tax refunds and so on) sends funds out of the commonwealth's account at the RBA initially into the banks' ES accounts, so lifting the system's holding of cash.

The Reserve Bank's transactions on its own account also influence system cash.

Reserve Bank operations in foreign exchange, for example, have an impact on ES funds. If, say, the RBA sells $US and buys $A then the ES balance of the bank with which it deals would be reduced as Australian dollars are withdrawn from the banking system. A further, less significant, influence on the level of ES funds is banks' purchases of bank notes from the RBA, as when banks need notes to sell to customers they buy these with ES funds.

If the Reserve Bank did not in some way offset these transactions which affect demand for ES funds there would be big swings in the cash rate as banks short of liquidity bid for it from a diminishing supply. To offset such fluctuations, the RBA operates in the domestic markets to maintain a steady cash rate. When there is a deficit in the banking system (an outflow of ES funds which causes the system to be 'down'), the RBA would tend to buy securities from the market, thus restoring ES funds and, all things being equal, stopping the cash rate from rising. On the other hand, if there is an inflow of ES funds, causing a surplus in system cash

91

(the system is 'up') the RBA would tend to sell securities to withdraw excess funds from the system and stop the cash rate from dropping. The determining factor in the RBA's actions is their likely impact on the cash rate. On most days this means keeping the cash rate steady but, on a day when monetary policy is being changed, it means operating so that the cash rate moves to the newly established target—buying securities to add to liquidity if policy is being eased and selling securities to tighten liquidity if policy is being tightened. A key element here is that the RBA is the sole supplier of ES funds; these can be created for the banking system as a whole only through transactions between the banks and the RBA. This monopoly position enables the RBA, over time, to control the cash rate.

The RBA's market operations

About 90 per cent of the Reserve Bank's market operations is undertaken through repurchase agreements (repos, which averaged $900 million a day during 1998) where a holder of securities sells them for cash but also agrees to repurchase them at a fixed price on a fixed future date. The flexibility of repos (see chapter 9) makes them highly suitable for managing liquidity because their terms can be tailored to different circumstances and securities of all maturities can be used. The RBA uses commonwealth and state government securities in its repo transactions. The RBA also buys and sells outright commonwealth government securities such as treasury notes and bonds with less than one year to maturity. If cash is particularly tight the RBA might undertake a swap in the foreign exchange market to manage liquidity flows (an FX swap is a purchase and sale and, at a pre-agreed rate and date, a subsequent sale and repurchase of currency).

A key change in the RBA's market operations was the termination, in August 1996, of the authorised money-market dealers—an elite group of some ten or so companies (the numbers fluctuated over time) which had direct access to the RBA and which the central bank had used as its conduit for market operations to influence conditions in the wider financial system. The introduction of real-time gross settlement, discussed below, eliminated the need for the authorised dealers and from June 1996 the RBA has dealt in its market operations with all members of the Reserve Bank Information and Transfer System (RITS, discussed later in this chapter).

The RBA follows an established routine in its daily market operations. At 9.30 am each day the central bank announces on the major electronic screen services the cash position of the market. In effect, the RBA tells the market whether it expects a deficit or surplus (whether the system is down or up) and of what size (the system cash position is the movement in exchange-settlement funds on that day if the RBA did not undertake market operations). The RBA also publishes details of commonwealth government settlements due that day because they affect ES balances. The bank at the same time announces its dealing intentions for the day (and any change to monetary policy accompanies this announcement): if there is a shortfall in the system it usually offers to inject funds by buying government securities or repos from the market and it might offer to reduce a surplus by selling. Whether the system is in deficit or surplus is not a crucial consideration for the market because, whichever the position, the market accepts that the RBA undertakes whatever transactions are required to hold the cash rate close to target.

Market participants interested in buying or selling securities have to inform the RBA by 10 am of their intentions, the rates at which they are prepared to deal and the term of repos. The RBA responds by 10.15 am with its acceptance of the most attractive bids and rejection of unsuccessful bidders.

Real-time gross settlement

A real-time gross settlement (RTGS) system enables large-volume payments between financial institutions to be settled immediately (real time), with each payment settled individually (in gross amounts) as it arises and each payment irrevocable, that is, funds cannot be withdrawn or dishonoured. The Bank for International Settlements, in its report prepared by the Committee on Payment and Settlement Systems, defines an RTGS system as:

> . . . a gross settlement system in which both processing and final
> settlement of funds transfer instructions can take place continu-
> ously (that is, in real time). As it is a gross settlement system,
> transfers are settled individually, that is, without netting debits
> against credits. As it is a real-time settlement system, the system
> effects final settlement continuously rather than periodically at pre-
> specified times provided that a sending bank has sufficient
> covering balances or credit. Moreover, this settlement process is
> based on the real-time transfer of central bank money. An RTGS
> system can thus be characterised as a funds transfer system that is
> able to provide continuous intraday finality for individual transfers.

Until the full introduction of RTGS in mid-1998 Australia operated with a deferred net settlement system which allowed banks to make payments during the day with final settlement of the net amount of all debits and credits not taking place until 9 am on the following day. A payment made by a customer with a bank cheque

Figure 4.2 The RTGS day

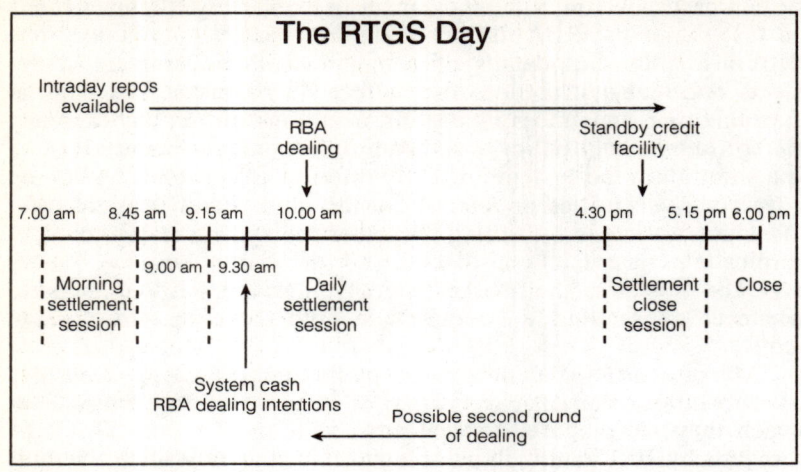

Source: Reserve Bank of Australia

affected the bank's ES account on the following day (deferred settlement) because settlement took place overnight through the clearing house, where banks present all cheques and electronic claims held against other banks. On the following day, the net amounts flowed through the banks' ES accounts. The true level of interbank intraday exposures within the payments system was not clear, and the system was potentially vulnerable to systemic risk should a major bank fail. Potentially, there was a delay of 24 hours before a central bank might learn that a bank was unable to settle obligations incurred. The likelihood of a bank failing was remote but, should a default or near-default occur, there was potential for havoc, or a serious loss of confidence, given that the average day saw payments exchanged between banks—but not settled until the following day—of about $100 billion, or around 20 per cent of Australia's annual gross domestic product. (Of these transactions, 60 per cent have a value of less than $1 million but account for 1 per cent of the total value of transactions; 4 per cent have a value of more than $50 million but these account for 60 per cent of the total value of transactions.)

RTGS is a global initiative as regulators everywhere search for ways to minimise or eliminate the risk of default in an increasingly integrated global financial system. A few countries have had RTGS systems for high-value payments for some time. In the US, the Fedwire has operated since 1918; an RTGS system, SIC (Swiss

Interbank Clearing), has been in place in Switzerland since the mid 1980s; Japan has had real-time funds transfer through BOJ-NET since 1988; and RTGS systems also operate in several European countries, in the UK since 1995 and in Canada since 1997. Many others, including several Asian countries, are developing RTGS systems. In July 1995 the Reserve Bank of Australia announced that it would proceed with a proposal to introduce an RTGS system for high-value interbank payments which would be based on RITS (Reserve Bank Information and Transfer System). This decision followed an extensive period of consultation with individual banks, the Australian Payments Clearing Association and the authorised dealers in the short-term money market. It was taken with a view to eliminating interbank settlement risk in high-value domestic payments and to keep Australia in line with international best practice. Other important objectives include addressing settlement risk in foreign-exchange markets and promoting efficiency and competition in payments arrangements.

The chief advantages of RTGS are that it minimises interbank settlement risk among banks operating in the domestic payments system and payments are irrevocable at the time of receipt. In preparation for the introduction of RTGS, the RBA announced in June 1996 that it would undertake its domestic markets operations with all members of RITS. This electronic settlement system, owned and operated by the Reserve Bank, enables commonwealth government securities to be transferred and settled simultaneously on an assured payments basis—that is, neither a RITS member selling securities nor a member paying cash to buy securities can revoke a transaction once it has been settled and both receive good title at the time of settlement. RITS was enhanced to accommodate RTGS; in July 1996 the RBA began paying a market-related interest rate on overnight balances left in ES accounts (initially at a rate of ten basis points below the cash rate target and, from 1 October 1997, at 25 basis points below the target) and in the following month the authorised dealers' licences were withdrawn. In October 1996 the RBA, with Austraclear Ltd, began working on the RITS system to integrate RTGS and by the end of the year the central bank was testing communications links to the RITS/RTGS system. Further testing and progress continued during 1997.

Under RTGS the RBA continues to announce its money-market cash position at 9.30 am and deal between 10 and 10.30 am. Because high-value payments are settled during the day, the 9 am settlements for overnight clearing obligations are smaller than was the case with deferred net settlement. And liquidity for the 9 am deadline is ample because banks have access before 9 am to the free intraday repo facility offered by the Reserve Bank (discussed below). RITS opens at 7 am each day and shortly after that the RBA makes payments due by it that day, such as large payments by the commonwealth government. The RBA's morning operations remain the chief vehicle for achieving its cash-rate target, however under RTGS a further round of dealing might be needed later in the day because the system cash position announced each morning is an estimate, not a figure derived from overnight clearing operations as was the case under deferred net settlement. So morning operations might need to be supplemented by activity later in the day. In fact, it is possible that under RTGS some pressure could emerge towards the end of the settlement day, between 4.30 pm and 5.15 pm, as banks and others with ES accounts balance their liquidity positions and bid for funds to unwind intraday repos.

To avoid undue disorder, the RBA provides holders of ES accounts with an end-of-day standby facility, in the form of overnight repos priced at 25 basis points over the cash-rate target, under which they can generate liquidity at their own discretion. In offering such a facility the RBA is trying to strike a balance between providing an element of certainty about the cost and availability of end-of-day funding without reducing incentives for market participants to settle among themselves rather than routinely turn to the standby facility. The end-of-day facility, available only to those with ES accounts, operates only after 4.30 pm when RITS is closed to non-ES transactions. A combination of a margin (penalty) of 25 basis points above the target cash rate for an end-of-day repo and 25 points below the cash rate for balances in ES accounts is regarded by the RBA as an incentive to borrowers to find funds in the market rather than use an end-of-day repo, and an encouragement to those with surplus funds to lend them rather than leave them in an ES account. Overall, then, this should stimulate money-market activity. The treasury note rediscount facility remains as a general safety valve for the system.

To prevent gridlock and ensure that payments in the RTGS queue can be made, the RBA has introduced a *bilateral offset facility* designed to make the best possible use of banks' liquidity, and an intraday repo facility under which the RBA provides ES funds in exchange for securities. Under its auto-offset facility, the system automatically searches the system queue for offsetting payments and if payments between two banks can be offset and settled simultaneously without breaching limits, the system does so automatically. These payments are settled in full, simultaneously. The intraday repo facility enables banks to generate additional liquidity to meet payment demands either manually or using an *autorepo* facility. Under autorepo, banks lodge securities in autorepo securities sub-accounts. If a bank needs liquidity, the system automatically provides it by selling sufficient securities from autorepo to the RBA under an intraday repo to settle a particular transaction. Under a manual repo, the banks control the amount of securities used to provide intraday liquidity. The RBA eased concerns among banks about finding adequate liquidity through the day when it confirmed that it would not levy an interest charge for within-day repos; so long as banks have the securities they have access to free liquidity for RTGS transactions.

Given the important role of liquidity in the new system, however, banks have upgraded their systems to provide real-time, centralised control of their liquidity positions. This has had a flow-on effect on customers, particularly the larger corporate clients, as banks moved to intraday customer credit limits and consolidated customer credit limits. RTGS itself does nothing to remove the normal credit risks between bank and corporate customer but it prompted banks to focus more closely on credit exposures; a bank making a high-value payment for a corporate customer through RTGS knows that the Reserve Bank will act on its instruction as soon as funds are available in its ES account, and the payment is irrevocable.

Delivery v. payment (DVP)

The RBA has introduced RTGS in a way that ensures a tight integration of the payments and securities settlement systems. The RTGS system is in fact a component of RITS and closely linked to Austraclear's FINTRACS system for settling transactions in securities other than those issued by the commonwealth government, that is, state government and private-sector securities. This enables the RBA to offer a system of complete delivery v. payment (DVP) so that ownership of securities, customer funds and bank funds all move simultaneously. Interbank settlement risk and the possibility of unwinding a transaction at the end of the day are eliminated. RTGS, however, does not remove the market risk associated with securities transactions in that a counterparty could become insolvent in the intervening time between trade and settlement.

Foreign exchange settlement risk

RTGS eliminates settlement risk in domestic high-value payments but it does not address the issue of settlement risk in foreign exchange. This is often referred to as 'Herstatt risk', after a small German bank that was closed in 1974 by its authorities before—because of time-zone differences—the second leg of a foreign-exchange transaction could be completed. How to eliminate foreign-exchange settlement risk is being addressed through a private-sector initiative, Continuous Linked Settlement Services (CLSS), established by a group of banks from the main OECD countries. Membership of CLSS is restricted to countries with real-time gross settlement systems in place. Work on the project is being supervised by the US authorities, with central banks involved to ensure they are comfortable with what is proposed.

The transmission mechanism

This refers to the process by which the Reserve Bank's actions either to tighten or ease monetary conditions feed through to the ultimate objectives of monetary policy.

In its first stage, the process operates through an interest rate—the overnight cash rate—which has little direct effect on the average individual or on most businesses. The cash rate is determined in the sector of the financial system in which the Reserve Bank deals with the banks to provide ES funds. The ultimate effect on inflation and unemployment of changes in the cash rate depends on how these changes are conveyed through the financial system and the economy, and on how businesses and people react. The cash rate is important, however, because any tightening or easing in the cash rate quickly flows on to other interest rates, especially rates on short-dated securities such as bills of exchange and certificates of deposit.

Changes in monetary policy generally feed through to the 90-day bank-bill rates which occasionally anticipate moves in the cash rate but for the most part hover around it. The bank-bill rate is a useful measure of the cost to banks of raising new funds in the short-term money market. So, when monetary policy changes, banks' costs of funds change accordingly and this feeds through into the rates they charge for lending money. At this stage monetary policy is transmitted to the real economy because banks' lending rates influence decisions of individuals and businesses on borrowing and spending and so the effects show up in the demand for money and credit and in the real economy. For example, the effect on a family's household budget of a rise in mortgage rates might argue against buying a bigger home and the impact of a rise in business lending rates on small business might lead it to postpone expansion plans.

Changes in the cash rate usually cause changes in the lending rates of financial intermediaries (this is the intention). Lending rates of intermediaries are somewhat higher because these intermediaries charge a margin for the risk they take in advancing funds, to cover costs and to earn a profit. The margin between the cash rate and lending rates can fluctuate. Increasing competition has narrowed the gap, with this most evident in housing interest rates. The margin between mortgage rates and the cash rate closed from more than 4 percentage points in 1994 to about 1.7 percentage points in 1998, largely because of competition in lending for housing, spurred in particular by the mortgage managers such as Aussie Home Loans and RAMS which fund themselves in the wholesale markets at rates around the cash rate. This, and their lower-than-bank overheads, enabled them to undercut the banks substantially when offering home loans, and so increase their market share. Banks have been forced to trim their home lending rates to competitive levels. In 1998, the impact of competition was becoming more apparent in margins for small business loans.

The relationship between the cash rate and longer-term interest rates, such as the ten-year bond rate, is less clear-cut because long-term rates are influenced by other factors such as expectations about inflation and international interest rates. A change in monetary policy setting can also have an effect on the exchange rate; a tightening of monetary policy would bring an appreciation, and an easing a depreciation, in the exchange rate.

Reserve Bank information sources

Regular sources of data are the Reserve Bank monthly *Bulletin*, the RBA's annual report, information booklets and occasional papers. These provide information and statistics on Australia's economic and financial health. The RBA website www.rba.gov.au is a valuable source of up-to-date information, including recent announcements and press releases, speeches by senior RBA officials, articles from the *Bulletin*, information about the conduct of monetary policy, and the history and structure of the RBA. The bank regularly supplies a range of details to the financial markets through the wire services such as Reuters, Bridge Telerate, Bloomberg and AFMA*data*.

5

Financial intermediaries: banks, investment banks, fund managers and others

Participants in the Australian financial markets include the banks, investment banks, superannuation and other fund managers, insurance companies, brokers, unit trusts, building societies and credit unions and larger corporations. Participants can be divided into *financial intermediaries* and *end-users* of market services but there are overlaps in activities. For example, typically included among end-users are fund managers, building societies, credit unions, insurance companies and big corporations which borrow and lend, issue paper and invest in securities but these entities are also involved, to varying degrees, in their own treasury and financial risk management and in trading securities, which takes them into financial intermediation. The professional financial intermediaries—banks, investment banks and brokers—play a matching or link role between borrowers, lenders and investors with banks and investment banks earning fee income for risk-management services as well as from their traditional role of intermediating between borrowers and lenders.

Banks

It is often claimed that banks will continue to thrive, but that banking will become smaller and less significant over time. That is, banking—the activity of raising deposits to fund loans which are kept on the balance sheet—will decline . . . banks will respond by moving into other profitable areas of financial activity. There is a lot of truth in this characterisation, but it is often overstated . . . Our forecast is . . . [that] banking [will be left] as a very important part of the economy. Where there is most truth in the claim is that banks have diversified their sources of income.

—Reserve Bank of Australia's Supplementary Submission to the Financial System (Wallis) Inquiry

As we enter the 21st century the banking industry faces no fewer challenges than over the past couple of decades from unrelenting competition in financial services. In the 1970s banks had to cope with increased competition from less-fettered non-banks, in the 1980s they had to come to grips with financial deregulation and an increasingly internationalised world, in the 1990s banks had the task of cleaning up the consequences of the boom-bust cycle of the 1980s, including a daunting level of bad and doubtful debts, and of coping with world pressures and new, internationally accepted guidelines on capital requirements. At the end of the 1990s banks were coming to grips with the challenges presented by relentless innovation in financial markets, competition from growth in the fund management sector (in 1998 the amount of money in US mutual funds exceeded bank deposits for the first time), advances in electronic communications that both enhance and threaten their business and legislative changes that were likely to widen access to areas that were previously bank monopolies, such as the payments system.

Background

Banks are Australia's oldest and largest financial institutions. Australian banking dates from 1817 when the Bank of New South Wales, the forerunner of Westpac Banking Corporation, was founded. The banking explosion of the 1980s reversed a shrinking process that had characterised the Australian banking system since the first half of the twentieth century. During the nineteenth century Australia had more than 30 private banks; that number was reduced through failures and mergers to 21 at the beginning of the First World War and had fallen further to nine by the outbreak of the Second World War.

The Australian banking system, in the form that prevailed after the Second World War, was an oligopoly—a fairly benign rivalry among a small number of giants. The Trade Practices Act 1974 had prohibited collusion on charges and interest rates, but there was a significant similarity among the banks' rates, particularly in the days before ceilings on deposit rates were removed. One reason for this conformity was the strict government control on what the banks could charge for loans and pay for deposits. Regulations also controlled the extent, and at one time the nature, of bank lending. Banks frequently complained about the degree to which they bore

Table 5.1 Growth of banking sector

	1980	1990	1998
Domestic owned	16	16	13
Foreign-owned			
—incorp. locally	0	15	7
—branches	2	3	24
TOTAL	18	34	44

Source: Reserve Bank of Australia, figures as at June 1998

the brunt of government monetary policy, complaining that this hampered their performance (although it did not noticeably affect profits). It did, however, contribute to reducing the banks' share of business.

The emergence of rival non-bank financial institutions, such as finance companies and merchant banks, was a direct result of the restrictions placed on banks. Their existence also enabled the banks to skirt some of the controls by taking shares in those other, freer organisations. The arrival of other savings institutions that chased the public's dollar, such as building societies and credit unions, gave the banks more competition in the struggle to attract deposits. The financial deregulation of the 1980s unshackled the banks, which had been losing market share to less controlled and, in many cases, more dynamic and aggressive non-bank financial institutions. An outcome of the Campbell Inquiry into the Australian financial system, concluded in 1981, was a big win for the banks: they were freed from onerous controls and entry to the banking system was relaxed; from 1985 banks increased substantially in number as foreign banks entered the sector, building societies converted to bank status and, in the 1990s, several large investment banks began operating as licensed (wholesale) banks.

By the 1990s, fund managers were stiff competition for the savers' dollars and that change in the nation's savings pattern, plus developments in electronic communications, significantly altered the nature of banking and hence the role of banks. Gone were the days when banks simply focused on taking deposits and making loans and earning a spread along the way; banks now use balance-sheet and capital management to maximise returns, and offer a wide range of financial services to customers at the retail and wholesale levels. While banks have been operating in a vastly more deregulated and freer environment than that which prevailed before the 1980s, they also operate under a system of progressively increased scrutiny. Regulators and supervisors are keen to ensure that banks comply with a comprehensive framework of prudential standards, including rigorous capital standards which, banks claim, are more onerous for them than for many of their financial-sector competitors.

Banking now

The Australian banking industry, in common with banking sectors in many other countries, has undergone enormous change, a process that continued in the 1990s. A combination of domestic and international pressures pushed banks towards either lifting market share and world presence through mergers, or remaining fairly small, selective and focused and, hopefully, still profitable. While the political climate in Australia remained unaccommodating towards large bank mergers, on the world scene the late 1990s saw a flurry of mergers that created megabanks.

Banking activities span the retail—individuals and households—and wholesale—high-value transactions—levels. Banks deal with private individuals, large corporations, other financial institutions and government bodies. They are major players in the wholesale financial markets, in cash, foreign exchange and fixed-income securities, they provide risk-management services through derivative products such as caps, collars, options and swaps, they offer corporate advice and project and structured finance and they provide investment and fund management products. Most of these activities are also offered by investment banks, some of which are subsidiaries or specialist arms of large banking groups.

Deregulation undoubtedly strengthened banks' foothold in the financial system, enabling them to operate more freely and to increase in numbers. As table 5.2 shows, the banks' market share of all financing, measured by assets, has risen, that of non-banks has declined, while that of superannuation and other funds has also increased. Banks participated in the rapid growth of managed funds as they acquired an increasing share of the industry, about 40 per cent compared with 20–25 per cent at the start of the 1990s. In its *Supplementary Submission to the Financial Inquiry*, the Reserve Bank noted that between 1965 and 1995, bank deposits grew at a rate slightly ahead of Australia's gross domestic product, with the ratio of bank deposits to GDP rising from 49 per cent in 1965 to 63 per cent in 1996. Between 1980 and 1996 the assets of all financial institutions grew at an annual rate of 13.5 per cent but there was a downward trend in the ratio of bank deposits to all financial assets as individuals became wealthier and inclined to hold more of their financial wealth in assets offering higher returns (though with a correspondingly higher risk). Compulsory superannuation has also been an influence.

Despite the opening of the Australian banking sector to new

Table 5.2 Changes in market share (%)

	1985	1990	1995	1997
Banks	44	48	50	49
Non-banks	30	21	15	13
Subtotal	74	69	65	62
Life & super	21	23	29	30
Other funds	4	7	7	8
Subtotal	26	31	35	38

Source: Adapted from Reserve Bank *Bulletin* December 1997

entrants and the consequent increase in the number of banks to 44, Australian banking is still dominated by the Big Four major domestic banks—ANZ Banking Group, Commonwealth Bank of Australia, National Australia Bank and Westpac Banking Corporation. These banks operate extensive, national retail branch networks, although the trend is towards reducing the number of branches in favour of increased electronic services and centralised processing of customer transactions. The Big Four have a high profile in wholesale, as well as retail, banking and in the financial markets and, to varying degrees, operate overseas. ANZ has positioned itself as an international bank, with extensive operations in the Asian region through its earlier acquisition of Grindlays Plc. Westpac, while it has scaled back from its ambitious international strategy of the 1980s, operates a successful global treasury operation and retains a strong regional focus. NAB is positioning itself as a global retailer of financial services and the CBA's focus is predominantly Australasian. State-based banks, which expanded vigorously during the 1980s, and underwent a corresponding contraction in the 1990s, have in many cases come under new owners. Examples are Colonial State Bank in New South Wales, BankWest in Western Australia which is 54 per cent owned by Bank of Scotland and the troubled State Bank Victoria, which in 1991 was bought by the Commonwealth Bank. Regional banks have grown out of former building societies, such as Advance Bank and St George Bank in NSW, Bank of Melbourne (part of the Westpac group), Bendigo Bank in Victoria, Adelaide Bank in South Australia, Metway Bank in Queensland. Macquarie Bank, a leading investment bank focusing on wholesale and corporate finance, was born when the merchant bank Hill Samuel Australia Ltd took up a banking licence in the 1980s. In the 1990s, several leading investment banking names have converted to licensed bank status and operate as branches of overseas parents which gives them access to the parents' balance-sheet strength.

Table 5.3 Banks operating in Australia

	Assets ($ millions)
ABN AMRO	209
Adelaide Bank	4017
ANZ Banking Group	79 847
ANZ Grindlays Bank	1258
Arab Bank Australia	265
Asahi Bank	619
Bank of America	1716
Bank of China	2133
Bank of Queensland	2548
Bank of Tokyo-Mitsubishi (Aust)	2862
Bankers Trust Australia	8234
BankWest	13 797
Banque Nationale de Paris	7205
Bendigo Bank	2805
BZW	1740
Chase Manhattan Bank	5913
Citibank NA	3519
Citibank	7853
Colonial State Bank	17 800
Commonwealth Bank	94 438
Commonwealth Development Bank	5913
Credit Suisse First Boston	441
Dai-Ichi Kangyo Bank	1949
Deutsche Bank AG	6794
Dresdner Bank AG	1296
First National Bank of Chicago	684
HongkongBank of Aust	4881
Midland Bank PLC	2418
IBJ Australia Bank	1814
ING Bank NV	208
ING Mercantile Mutual Bank	891
International Commercial Bank of China	165
Macquarie Bank	6133
Morgan Guaranty Trust Co of NY	2097
National Australia Bank	110 649
NatWest Markets Australia	1240
Oversea-Chinese Banking Corp	1340
Overseas Union Bank	918
Rabobank Nederland	467
Primary Industry Bank	3825
Royal Bank of Canada	853
St George Bank	31 959
Advance Bank	21 934
Standard Chartered Bank Australia	1214
State Street Bank & Trust Co	981

	Assets ($ millions)
Suncorp-Metway	16 622
QIDC	2950
Trust Bank	1970
United Overseas Bank	663
WestLB	795
Westpac Banking Corp	80 099
Bank of Melbourne	11 012
TOTAL	578 931

Source: Reserve Bank *Bulletin* May 1998

Of the foreign banks which entered Australia in 1985, only Citibank has made a sustained successful impact on retail banking; others have focused on specialised areas, such as Bankers Trust's strength in fund management and treasury. Some, through mergers and acquisitions in Australia and overseas, have the might of a global investment house—the various arms of Deutsche Bank create an organisation with a range of skills that covers all banking and financial service functions. During 1998, the banking sector acquired another major player when the AMP Society took up a bank licence. Banking services are expected to expand further as supermarkets in Australia follow the successful UK precedent where major names chains, in partnership with banks, offer deposit and lending products.

Operations of the banks

Banks and the money markets work closely together. The two sectors deal in the same commodity—money—although banks' activities span both the retail (general public) and wholesale (business, corporate and institutional) sectors. The daily flows of funds into, and around, the banking system have an influence on conditions in the money market (see chapter 4 for a discussion of influences on the money market and interest rates). Banks are key players in the foreign-exchange market, accounting for 90 per cent of activity; they account for 80 per cent of the activity in exchange-traded and over-the-counter derivatives and are large holders of securities such as bank bills, treasury notes and government bonds. Their size and capital base enables the banks to be dominant players in the markets, where their role as quoters of two-way prices underpins liquidity. Banks offer a gamut of risk-management products to help customers hedge interest-rate and currency exposures, manage their own interest-rate and foreign-exchange risk and, to varying degrees, undertake proprietary trading.

The Australian banks operate nationally, although some have a regional focus and some have important international operations. Banking relies on an efficient clearing system to ensure that cheques drawn on any branch are readily accepted and cleared in any other part of the country. The Reserve Bank, as banker to the federal government and the banking system, is part of the clearing system and exchanges its debits and credits through the clearing system in the same way as other banks. The different banks' cheques are exchanged at designated premises in each capital city and in some regional centres. Cheque-clearing operations in each state are monitored by committees consisting of representatives of the member banks. Cheques may be exchanged by the banks several times during the day. Suburban branches generally clear through the head offices in each city. In distant suburbs and small towns, clearing is handled by warrants drawn by branches on their capital-city office and later cleared through the larger centres. Balances are settled daily by adjustments to the banks' exchange-settlement accounts with the Reserve Bank.

Banks increasingly operate as large-scale financial services groups, whose different units offer fund management, insurance, cash management and investment, stockbroking and futures trading as well as the traditional banking business of deposits and loans. These specialised divisions tend to function as business enterprises within a banking group. Product innovation has brought customers at all levels an increasing choice of loans and investment outlets. Electronic banking has altered the distribution of many of these products. This trend towards financial conglomerates (groups of companies under common ownership whose main activities include two or more elements of financial services) has contributed substantially to a perception that distinctions between institutions in the financial sector have blurred. A major challenge for regulators and for banks themselves will be the supervision of, and management of, such diverse conglomerates within a banking structure. The move to a single prudential regulator, APRA (see chapter 3), partly springs from a need for a regulatory framework that can handle conglomerates.

Technology

Australian banks have been quick to adapt to electronic banking services. These have been well received by customers who make high use of automatic teller machines (ATMs), electronic funds transfer at point-of-sale (EFTPOS) and telephone and computer banking. In 1997 a total of 7816 ATMs and 169 739 EFTPOS terminals operated in Australia. Thus the ways in which banks deliver products and services to customers have undergone radical change, a trend that will endure with continuing advances in technology and the banks' unremitting drive to cut costs. Customers in search of banking services will increasingly be heading for a supermarket, a banking kiosk in a shopping complex, an ATM or their telephone instead of a one-to-one encounter with a teller or account manager.

Risks

Risks in banking merit an entire book. The Reserve Bank's *Prudential Statements* (August 1997) sets out the framework with which banks have to comply in areas such as capital adequacy, liquidity management, credit exposures, off-balance-sheet exposures, associations with non-banks and asset quality. Central banks and other supervisors have been at pains to encourage banks to improve the level of disclosure and of risk-management techniques. Banks' annual reports today contain far more information about policy towards derivatives and the management of credit, market, liquidity, operational, legal and other risks. The move to real-time gross settlement (see chapter 4) goes a long way towards virtually removing settlement risk from high-value payments.

Banks and fund management

Banks have not been slow to identify opportunities in the burgeoning fund management industry, a trend that is a direct reflection of the increase, at the individual level, of a focus on savings and investment. The rise in the level of funds under management has been at the expense of bank deposits and, recognising this, banks have lifted their presence in fund management and investment and financial services to ensure they retain their role in this growing savings pool.

Investment banks

As the twentieth century draws to a close, the distinction between the activities of banks and those of investment banks has diminishing relevance. Investment banks, however, have enjoyed a rich history in Australia and have made a significant contribution—which has largely stemmed from foreign banks—to the development and growth of the country's capital and financial markets.

Investment banks, known until the early 1990s as merchant banks, tend in Australia to be mostly the local operations of foreign banks or investment banks active in this country's wholesale financial markets, or the wholesale market activities of an Australian bank. As the nature of banking changed, and banks moved increasingly towards operating as financial services organisations offering not just deposits and loans but a range of investment and fund management products, the distinction between a bank and an investment bank became less and less apparent or even relevant. Many members of the investment banks' industry group, the International Banks and Securities Association (IBSA), are also members of the Australian Bankers' Association and some banks, although not the big four majors, are members of IBSA. Investment banks often distinguish themselves by specialising in niche market areas, for example, corporate services or fund management, whereas others offer a fuller range of financial services. Generally, though, the focus of investment banks is at the wholesale end of the financial markets where their client base comprises corporations, financial institutions and governments.

At times, Australian investment banks exhibited spectacular growth, especially during the 1980s—a decade of swinging fortunes, intensified competition and changed economic conditions. As the 1990s got under way, however, it became apparent that not all the growth in assets had been well-founded and several high-profile names in Australian merchant banking came to grief, brought down by overly zealous lending in deals that seemed, at the time, too attractive to reject but which, in many cases, brought problems. By 1990 Australia had about 90 merchant banks, more than double the number operating in the early 1980s but fewer than the peak of more than 100 reached in 1988. By the late 1990s IBSA members totalled 48. Most of Australia's merchant banks are owned by the world's top 100 financial institutions and securities houses. Australian investment banks have left behind the business of building assets (lending) in favour of improving their return on equity by generating fees. The shift towards generating income through advisory work and fees takes Australia's investment banks closer than before to their UK and US counterparts.

Background

Merchant banks emerged in Europe in the sixteenth century as financiers of trade. Their counterparts appeared in Australia in the 1950s. The first Australian merchant bank was formed in 1953, when Australian United Underwriting Company was registered. This grew into the merchant bank AUC Holdings Ltd, becoming a public company in 1957 and attracting the US bank Morgan Guaranty Trust Company of New York as a substantial shareholder in 1961. Morgan Guaranty progressively increased its stake, moving to full ownership in March 1985 of what is now J.P. Morgan Australia Limited. A mere two Australian merchant banks were operating in the 1950s;

by the late 1960s that figure had risen to twelve and from the mid-1960s to the mid-1970s merchant bank business grew at an annually compounded rate of 40 per cent. Since then, merchant (investment) banking has at times been one of the fastest-growing sectors of the Australian financial system. Merchant bank numbers increased during the 1980s, virtually doubling between 1984 and 1987 and then stabilising, although with some rationalisation in numbers and activities. Even though the industry was quickly becoming over-crowded, new merchant banks continued to arrive in Australia throughout the 1980s. Australia held considerable appeal as a young country with a stable economy, a growing population and an expand-ing and increasingly deregulated financial sector which filled an attractive slot in the international clock, well placed in the promising growth area of the Pacific Basin. All these factors helped bring overseas investors into Australia. And the country's comparative lack of exposure to third-world debt was another point in its favour.

The merchant banks, as they were then known, that were established in Australia from the 1950s bore little resemblance to either the US investment banks—which are closely identified with underwriting and distributing securities on behalf of companies—or the UK merchant banks, which earn fees by structuring deals that generally are funded by other people. In neither country was mer-chant banking characterised by strength in lending—a quality traditionally associated with banks. But the effect of government regulations was that many of Australia's merchant banks developed as lenders: many were established as quasi-banks by overseas bank-ing parents which, at the time, could not operate as banks in Australia. Merchant bank subsidiaries gave them a foothold in the Australian financial markets. Some merchant banks were launched by domestic banks to secure access to the type of business from which prevailing regulations excluded them. But as the domestic banks were unshackled in terms of how much and to whom they could lend, and the banking sector was opened up to new domestic and foreign entrants, Australia's merchant banks found themselves squeezed on all fronts.

Australian merchant banks are grouped together for statistical purposes as 'money market corporations' but this label masks vari-ations and distinctions in size, contribution and activities. Merchant banks played a significant role in the innovation and enterprise that has marked the development of Australia's money market. The merchant banks were established for a variety of reasons but an early incentive was the government controls that, until the 1980s, restricted banks' operations in short-term borrowing and lending. Merchant banks benefited for years from being able to operate unhindered by the kind of government controls that constrained the banks. The merchant banks were free to respond to the growing demand for financial services. It is true that some of the financial innovation introduced by the merchant banks could have been handled by the banks, but for a number of years the banks were hobbled not merely by external controls; they were remarkably conservative, and complacent and reluctant to push into new areas. Another strong motive behind the rapid growth of the merchant banking community was the legislation which, until 1985, barred foreign banks from operating as banks in Australia—although they could establish merchant bank subsidiaries.

The resources booms of 1968–70 and 1978–81 had boosted overseas banks' enthusiasm for a foothold in Australia. The boom years, combined with a local need for overseas connections and funds, brought waves of merchant banks and representative offices to Australia. The first wave had consisted mostly of US and UK organisations; the second wave in the late 1970s brought a number of European and Asian financial institutions. A third wave arrived after September 1984, when the federal government allowed foreign parents of Australian merchant banks full ownership of their subsidiaries. This saw the dismantling of a number of consortium merchant banks, with the owners setting up new subsidiaries, each carrying its parent's name. The 1984 announcement enabled Australia's merchant banks to restructure on a stronger footing. Lines of ownership became more clear-cut, removing doubts about who might stand behind a merchant bank should a crisis arise. This was particularly important for the merchant banks operating in the foreign-exchange market, where those which could point to one committed parent, rather than a diverse group of shareholders, fared better when securing credit limits.

Local banks moved to full ownership of merchant bank subsidiaries and overseas banks which ranked low in the queue for bank licences seized the chance to establish wholly-owned merchant or investment banks. Some representative offices upgraded to merchant/investment bank status, enabling them to trade in the domestic markets. The removal of the restrictions on foreign ownership of merchant banks prompted a significant increase in the number of Japanese-owned investment banks.

By the end of the 1980s, merchant banks were under pressure to write business in an over-serviced market, facing competition from a significantly more energetic and imaginative banking sector and shrinking margins in virtually all areas of activity. The decline in activity in commonwealth bonds had reduced business for fixed-interest operators, and continued high interest rates cooled the private sector's enthusiasm for borrowing. It was hardly surprising that merchant banks were contracting and refocusing. The need to reassess business directions was underscored by disappointing results for the late 1980s. Whereas merchant banks had performed well during 1986 and 1987, before the sharemarket crashed, profits subsequently dropped significantly. Merchant banks which had made loans to highly-geared companies whose fortunes plummeted after the sharemarket collapse were faced with bad and doubtful debts and, in some cases, large losses. As the combined effects of the sharemarket crash and high interest rates filtered through the business sector, some merchant banks fell victim to the boom-bust cycle. Merchant and investment banks had been redefining their objectives for years but the sharemarket crash of October 1987 forced another rethink, not only in Australia but in world financial capitals such as London, New York and Tokyo.

Many Australian merchant banks had by then turned their backs on lending, scaled down their operations, focused on fee-based activities or particular 'niches', closed state branches and centralised treasury and foreign-exchange operations in one city, most of them in Sydney. By 1989, 43 members of the 49-member Australian Merchant Bankers' Association had head offices in Sydney and in recognition of this AMBA moved its headquarters to the NSW capital in January 1989. Then, in 1993, in view of the increased internationalisation of financial markets, AMBA changed its name to International Banks and Securities Association (IBSA), reflecting its role as the national organisation representing the interests of investment banks and securities houses in Australia. Members of IBSA include the Australian operations of foreign-owned banks operating in wholesale financial markets either as a branch, subsidiary or representative office of the parent; the Australian operations of foreign-owned investment and merchant banks; wholesale banking activities of Australian banks; and Australian investment and merchant banks. Several foreign-owned investment banks took the opportunity, following the federal government's further relaxation of constraints on the banking sector in February 1992, to convert from a subsidiary to branch status of their parent bank, reflecting a mounting view that those conducting the business of banking should be licensed banks.

Activities of the merchant/investment banks

At their broadest, merchant/investment banking operations have covered trading in money, securities and financial futures, arranging longer-term finance for company expansion, providing working capital, arranging project finance, advising clients on foreign-exchange cover, and advising on mergers and takeovers. Several merchant banks also offer portfolio investment management services and underwrite corporate and state-government issues of securities. Some operate unit trusts, such as cash management trusts, property trusts and equity trusts, and many are active in fund management.

Australia's merchant banks have to meet financial and other requirements to deal in or advise on securities and futures markets. The administration and enforcement of companies and securities legislation was changed with the passing of the Australian Securities Commission (ASC) Act through the federal parliament in June 1989. Legislative changes introduced in 1998 brought investment banks under the stewardship of the Australian Securities and Investment Commission (ASIC, discussed in chapter 3).

Investment banks which are members of IBSA must meet the association's requirements regarding capital, liquidity and ownership. IBSA has taken account of the Reserve Bank's risk-weighted capital adequacy regulations, which apply to banks, by varying its membership requirements. Many investment banks owned by banks have responded to the new risk-weighting guidelines by securing guarantees from their banking parents, which substantially cover their on and off-balance-sheet liabilities. An investment bank which is not a subsidiary of either an overseas or Australian bank will find it harder to obtain bank loans because it attracts the 100 per cent risk weighting which applies to non-bank borrowers, rather than the 20 per cent risk weighting which applies to investment banks guaranteed by an Australian or foreign bank.

Various areas of activity have generated bursts of enthusiasm and energy at different times over the past 40 years. The means of survival for the investment banks has been their ability to diversify, and to adapt to changing circumstances as other operators make inroads into financial services. In the late 1990s typical investment banking services included corporate finance (encompassing advice on mergers and acquisitions, project and infrastructure finance, debt and equity funding and underwriting), money market (cash and securities trading, arranging and placing issues of securities and derivatives and risk-management facilities), foreign exchange and equity market activities, securitisation, fund management, commodities trading and offshore banking services. Investment banks have developed specialist skills in corporate finance which is often the heart of an investment bank's operations and covers advisory and funding services to a broad range of corporate and government clients. Many of the earlier merchant banks which came to Australia in the 1960s and 1970s brought expertise in project finance; more recently, private infrastructure has become an important element in investment banking business and in their role in helping finance private-sector infrastructure the investment banks make a significant contribution to the economy. Moreover, Australian expertise in financial services, particularly infrastructure financing and treasury technology, has been recognised overseas so that a new dimension has been created in the export of financial expertise. Key domestic private-sector infrastructure projects include the Sydney Harbour Tunnel and a number of tollways and power stations, as well as social infrastructure projects such as hospitals and prisons.

Many investment banks seized the opportunity to acquire the status of *offshore banking unit* when this regime was introduced in 1992. OBUs benefit from a concessionary tax rate of 10 per cent on profits generated by offshore banking. This sector is still developing, with a mere dozen or so of the 73 OBUs active. The federal government's *Investing for Growth* statement, launched in December 1997 to foster innovation and investment and boost Australia's position as a financial centre, was seen as an important step towards enhancing the effectiveness of the country's OBU regime.

Equities

The equity, or share, markets play a key role in raising capital for listed companies and also provide an important investment outlet for individuals and institutions. Turnover on the Australian Stock Exchange (ASX) reflects the high liquidity of shares. A combination of increased attention on savings and investment, largely driven by the compulsory nature of superannuation, and a succession of privatisations which have turned previously government-owned entities into private hands, has vastly increased the level of Australian share ownership to the point where, according to the ASX's 1998 *Shareownership Survey*, 40 per cent of the Australian adult population directly or indirectly own shares. For the first time, the level of direct ownership of shares exceeded that of indirect, a shift that resulted from the number of individuals buying shares for the first time in the 1997 Telstra float. Equity derivatives (see chapters 13 and 14) provide an avenue for managing risk.

Investment banks play an important role in equity raisings and are active in equity markets generally through stockbroking subsidiaries and through their corporate finance and fund management divisions. Investment bank participation in privatisation is evident in the following three examples (sourced from IBSA's presentation to the Wallis Inquiry, September 1996) which do not include legal advisers and accounting firms, registrars or trustees. Investment banking roles covered issues associated with listing, financial and strategic advice to the federal government and the listing entities, underwriting and domestic and international distribution of the securities.

- *GIO Australia* (June 1992) where the financial adviser to the government was BT Australia Ltd and the underwriters were

County NatWest Securities Ltd, Bain Capital Markets Ltd and Potter Warburg Capital Markets Ltd. Retail brokers included BOS Stockbroking, Hambros Equities Ltd, Macquarie Equities Ltd and James Capel Australia Ltd; the international selling group comprised ABN AMRO Bank NV, Credit Suisse First Boston and James Capel Australia Ltd.

- *Qantas* (June 1995): financial adviser to the government was Bain Capital Markets Ltd and financial adviser to Qantas was Baring Brothers Burrows & Co Ltd. Joint lead managers were McIntosh Corporation Ltd and Potter Warburg Capital Markets; domestic co-lead managers were BZW Australia Ltd, Ord Minnett Corp Services Ltd, J.B. Were Corp Services Ltd, ANZ McCaughan Corporate & Financial Services Ltd; international co-lead managers were McIntosh Securities Ltd, Salomon Brothers Inc and SG Warburg Securities.
- *Commonwealth Bank* (May 1996 share offer): business adviser to the government was Bain & Co Corp Finance Ltd and global coordinator was J.B. Were & Son. Joint lead managers were County NatWest Securities, CS First Boston, Salomon Brothers Inc, J.B. Were & Son; domestic co-lead managers were Macquarie Underwriting Ltd, McIntosh Corporation Ltd and Ord Minnett Corp Finance Ltd; international co-lead managers were ABN AMRO Hoare Govett Ltd, Cazenove & Co and Daiwa Securities Australia Ltd.

Fund managers

The fund management industry has grown enormously since the mid-1980s and the federal government's introduction of compulsory superannuation, which has spread superannuation to the point where more than 90 per cent of the full-time workforce have accounts with retirement funds. The figures show the rise of fund managers' share of financial intermediation: in 1995 the assets of all financial institutions totalled $882 billion and assets of super funds under management were $253 billion; in 1998 these figures were $335 billion in super funds under management out of a total financial institutions assets of $1.122 billion.

Fund managers by the late 1990s enjoyed a far higher presence not just in wholesale financial markets but in the wider community. Whereas the average household used to channel whatever it had in the way of savings into a term deposit at a bank, building society or credit union, the emphasis on superannuation and saving for retirement shifted household savings more towards investments which provide a market-linked return. With managed funds, investors turn over their savings to professional managers who pool the funds, invest them in a mix of assets and manage them to produce, ideally, optimum returns for investors. Fund managers use investment outlets such as unit trusts, superannuation funds and insurance bonds, as well as equity and fixed-income markets.

For their part, the fund managers have successfully marketed their services to a public eager to maximise investment opportunities across the traditional range of asset classes—cash, fixed income, shares and property. Unit trusts have sprung up to cater for these needs. Investment banks, through their fund management subsidiaries, have claimed a considerable slice of the fund management market, with global names such as Bankers Trust and Rothschild as well as Macquarie Bank challenging traditional life-office players. Investment banks account for a large part of the fund management industry and, according to IBSA's submission to the Wallis Inquiry, six of the top fund managers are investment bank subsidiaries.

Unit trusts

Unit trusts are professionally managed investment vehicles which enable small (retail) investors to pool their funds so that they earn a higher return than could be achieved individually with smaller amounts of money. Unit trusts can be independent entities but often come under the management umbrella of a bank, investment bank or fund manager which uses the financial markets (domestic and international) to manage the portfolios of investments in the different asset classes. Common types of unit trust are:

Cash management trusts

The advent of the cash management trust in Australia marked a watershed in financial markets' history in this country. Cash management trusts are a variety of the unit trust, an investment that has been part of the Australian scene for several decades. However, it was not until December 1980 and the launch of a cash management trust by the investment bank Hill Samuel Australia Ltd (now Macquarie Bank Ltd), that trusts became linked to the money market, an initiative that opened the door to the professional money market for individual investors, enabling them for the first time to achieve wholesale market rates on deposits of only a few thousand dollars. For the first time since its inception in the 1950s the money market became accessible to a wider group of investors who could participate, along with the large companies and professional traders, in the attractive interest rates available in the wholesale market.

Cash management trusts had emerged in the 1970s in the US—where they are known as money-market mutual funds. The big growth of the US money funds began in 1978 in response to high interest rates. Money that poured into the trusts took funds away from traditional borrowers such as savings and loan institutions (the US equivalent of building societies) which could not match the high rates available from the money funds. In Australia, the traditional recipients of household savings, the building societies and credit unions, were hurt in the early 1980s by the rise of the cash trusts.

Cash management trusts, offered by banks, investment banks, fund managers, stockbrokers and professional trustees, invest in a range of money-market securities such as bills of exchange, promissory notes, treasury notes and government bonds. They have the conventional trust structure: the management company, which looks after the day-to-day investment strategy; unitholders who supply the funds and a trustee who safeguards the trust's assets and ensures investments are in line with the trust deed's specifications. Cash management trusts operate by pooling relatively small individual amounts of cash (by wholesale money-market standards) and investing the aggregated amounts in securities previously accessible only to those with big sums to invest—wholesale financial markets discourage 'piggy-bank' (retail) deposits because of the turnover and paperwork involved in servicing small deposits.

Equity trusts

Equity trusts can be in the form of a trust that invests in domestic or international equities (shares). By using a trust, an individual has immediate access to a far more diversified investment than would be possible had he or she entered the sharemarket directly. Investors pay fees (upfront and management) to a manager whose job is to draw on experience and skills to achieve the optimum return. International equity trusts invest in overseas sharemarkets, providing an element of diversification that would otherwise be beyond the means of the average individual investor, as well as an element of additional risk because of exposure to currency fluctuations (most trusts offer to manage this risk).

Property trusts

These can be listed and unlisted but, in either case, the trusts invest in commercial, residential and industrial property to produce income and capital growth. In the case of listed property trusts, their units trade on the stock exchange and their price is determined in the market and published daily, so that investors have immediate liquidity, should they wish to sell, and a day-to-day valuation of their investment. With an unlisted trust, an investor wishing to sell has to agree on a price with the trust manager and has to wait between seven and thirty days for funds.

Public securities (fixed-income) trusts

These trusts invest in commonwealth and state-government bonds and offer a secure, medium-to-long-term investment with generally a low level of volatility over the longer term but with the occasional short-term gyration. International fixed-income trusts invest in foreign government and bank securities, generally on major world markets and, as is the case with international equity trusts, can be advantageously or adversely affected by movements in currencies. This presents an additional risk, although, in most cases, the trusts offer to manage any foreign-currency exposure associated with the investments.

Mortgage trusts

With these trusts, investors' funds are placed in residential, commercial and industrial property mortgages, usually for terms of three-to-five years and offering a variable rate of return.

Central financing authorities

State-based authorities such as New South Wales's Treasury Corporation (NSW TCorp), Queensland Treasury Corporation (QTC) and Treasury Corporation of Victoria (TCV) are active in the financial markets in the context of interest-rate and other financial risk management for themselves and their client authorities (see chapter 7).

Building societies

Building societies grew out of the financial cooperatives established to lend funds for housing and the main focus of their business continues to be providing mortgage finance to home buyers. Australian building societies date from the 1840s and over the past 50 years have become an increasingly important element in the Australian financial system. They raise funds from individuals and the wider markets and use these funds to lend to home-buyers. The number of building societies peaked in the 1970s. Between the mid-1980s and mid-1990s, as banks deregulated and expanded, a number of building societies converted to bank status and by 1998 the number of building societies had dropped to 23 from 71 in 1985. Building societies came under state supervision and, from 1992, under the aegis of the Australian Financial Institutions Commission.

AFIC's powers were transferred in 1998 to the Australian Prudential Regulation Authority (APRA, see chapter 3). In the financial markets, building societies mostly rank as end-users, especially for treasury management.

Credit unions

Like building societies, credit unions are a product of the financial cooperative movement. They primarily take deposits from, and lend funds to, their members (retail customers) and are essentially end-users of the financial markets. Credit unions, totalling 271 in June 1997, also came under state supervision and the AFIC umbrella and, from 1998, moved under the wing of APRA.

Finance companies

Finance companies borrow funds from the public and from the professional and institutional markets. These non-bank financial institutions lend in areas such as commercial property, motor-vehicle finance and through leasing; specialising in commercial and consumer finance, they are end-users in financial markets. Historically, controls on banks fed strong growth among finance companies in the 1950s and 1960s and, as deregulation took hold, it was widely forecast that finance companies, many of which were subsidiaries of banks, would disappear. Several finance companies were folded into the parent bank but, as a species, finance companies have survived as specialists in consumer and commercial finance, often concentrating on motor-vehicle finance, leasing and lending for commercial property.

Finance companies that are affiliated with a banking conglomerate have benefited from the status of a banking parent. This has enabled them to borrow and lend at slightly lower interest rates compared with competitors with no equivalent banking link. The parent bank does not provide any explicit guarantee to a finance company subsidiary but circumstances where a bank parent has provided a rescue package for a finance-company affiliate, such as Westpac's bail-out of Australian Guarantee Corporation in the early 1990s, have highlighted the distinction between a bank-owned finance company and one that is not affiliated with a bank.

The late 1990s witnessed a resurgence in finance-company activities with the addition to the sector of strong names such as AT&T Capital, GE Capital, BMW Australia Finance and Mercedes-Benz Finance. And the industry's profile was further boosted by the 80-strong Australian Equipment Lessors Association, whose members account for 90 per cent of leasing activity in Australia.

Brokers

Stockbrokers trade shares and securities on behalf of clients in return for a commission (brokerage) and most also provide research and investment advice. *Foreign exchange/fixed-income brokers* arrange deals between two over-the-counter players in the financial markets, earning brokerage on the deal. These brokers are not a source of investment advice.

Corporations

Publicly listed and private companies use the financial markets as borrowers to raise funds as needed and as lenders to invest temporary surpluses. They also draw on financial markets' expertise to help manage interest-rate and foreign-exchange risks incurred in running their businesses. They are considered end-users of financial markets' services, particularly in areas such as treasury risk management and corporate finance and advisory services. Some major corporations undertake their own treasury risk management but, increasingly, companies focus on their core business and outsource treasury management.

6

Short-dated securities

Financial instruments such as bills of exchange, promissory notes (also known as commercial, or one-name, paper), negotiable certificates of deposit and longer-term bonds are traded to varying degrees in the financial markets. These securities also serve as investments for superannuation fund managers, cash-management trusts, banks and others including individual investors. Traders can use the securities as collateral against deposits and loans, as investments in a portfolio or as instruments to be traded, ideally, for profits.

Financial instruments can be either short or long-term: examples of short-term paper are bank bills of exchange, promissory notes/commercial paper, negotiable certificates of deposit and treasury notes. Longer-term securities include government, state and territory government bonds, corporate bonds, inflation-indexed bonds, debentures and mortgage-backed securities. The widespread use of swaps has considerably diminished the distinction between short and long-term securities because borrowers can raise funds through, say, short-term notes and then exchange the terms of the funding with a longer-term fixed-interest borrower (see chapter 13 for details on swaps).

Financial instruments can be further distinguished as either *discount* or *coupon* securities: bills of exchange, commercial paper, certificates of deposit and treasury notes are discount securities that sell at a discount from face value; bonds and debentures are fixed-interest securities carrying a coupon that identifies an annual return.

This chapter details the features of the short-dated securities. Turnover in these instruments has gone against the general market trend of recent years in that it has declined, although in 1997 activity picked up from the big dip of 1994 and 1995. The drop in trading volumes in bank bills, a major element of the short-term debt market, reflects changes in the Australian market. In fact, in earlier years the huge turnover in bank bills was an idiosyncrasy of the Australian market, resulting from banks' channelling most of their lending through bank bills to avoid the penalty associated with the Statutory Reserve Deposit (SRD) requirement. This stipulated that banks hold a proportion of their deposits (liabilities) in low-interest accounts with the Reserve Bank. There was an incentive for banks to avoid this cost by funding their business with off-balance-sheet activities such as discounting—selling—bills into the market. With the shift from SRDs to non-callable deposits (NCDs), bank bills lost a great deal of their relative appeal for banks because *all* liabilities became subject to the NCDs. With the artificial prop of SRDs removed, bank-bill outstandings fell from a peak of $70 billion in 1990 to $65.6 billion in early 1998 and turnover in the bill market correspondingly also declined. The trend was reinforced by the Reserve Bank's decision in January 1990 to announce changes in monetary policy in terms of a target for the cash rate, and to flag such changes in public announcements. This greatly reduced volatility in short-term interest rates and so tended to curtail trading opportunities. Trading for trading's sake, which had been a key feature of the Australian short-term money market, largely evaporated; those keen to punt on short-term interest rates instead turned to the more 'transparent' (and leveraged) financial futures and options markets whose turnover often exceeds activity in the physical, or underlying, markets. And trading futures contracts removes the need to fund a stock of bills or commercial paper. While the professional money-market dealers' activity in short-term securities has dropped, companies, superannuation fund managers and cash-management trusts have become significant investors (end-users) in short-term instruments such as bank bills and commercial paper.

Bills of exchange: background in Australia

The bill of exchange, in its present form, came to prominence in Australia in the mid-1960s. It is not, however, a modern invention: the Greeks in the fourth century BC used bills of exchange. Its original purpose is thought to have been associated with eliminating the problems of transporting large amounts of money (or, in very early days, gold) between distant places. Using a bill of exchange, a debt owed by one party to a second can be used to pay the second party's debt to a third. The real growth in the instrument's use occurred in the eighteenth and nineteenth centuries, with the expansion of international trade and the importance of London as a financial centre. The bill drawn on London played a significant part in financing trade flows within the British empire. The increase in trade was promoted by the development of merchant banks—those traders who became active in financing other traders rather than in merchandising. The early merchant banks discounted bills of exchange, drawn by the seller and accepted, as evidence of debt, by the buyer.

Bills of exchange have long been used to finance Australia's international trade, both imports and exports. As an instrument for domestic financial transactions, however, it did not feature until fairly recently. It was not until 1963 that attention seriously focused on the bill, and its flexibility and versatility were recognised. This popularity was no mere coincidence. By the early 1960s Australian companies were spreading their financial wings. Borrowers were looking for alternatives to traditional bank or finance-company credit, and investors were seeking profitable outlets for surplus cash. In earlier days, particularly before the Second World War, the banks were able to accommodate the financial needs of the business community. The growing system needed more.

Accommodation bills—descendants of the earlier trade bills but not necessarily related to a trade transaction—were increasingly seen as an instrument that could fill a gap in the Australian financial system. Official interest was aroused and in 1964–65 the commonwealth government established an inquiry which decided that a bill market was a viable proposition for trading banks and authorised money-market dealers. The authorities were persuaded that the instrument would be a useful addition to Australia's financial markets. The bill market started in March 1965 and developed gradually into two tiers consisting of bank and non-bank bills. Its growth coincided with the expansion of the country's merchant-banking industry, as had been the case in Europe, where the merchant banks contributed substantially to the bill's wider use. In Australia, the bill market blossomed between 1970 and 1975, when the merchant banks developed a secondary market in the paper. In tight credit years, the trading banks would increasingly turn to bills of exchange as a method of lending that enabled them to refinance by selling the bills in the market.

Subsequent changes, particularly the removal in 1988 of the banks' SRD requirement, and the introduction of new rules applying to bank capital, had a big impact on the Australian bills of exchange market. The impact of the new rules applying to bank capital varied, depending on whether a bank held or sold the bills. If a bank sells its own bills there is no impact on capital; a bank holding bills of another bank is exposed to a low risk only. Bank-endorsed bills fell victim to capital adequacy requirements because these raised the cost of a bank's endorsement stamp as a bank had to set aside capital against the contingent liability created; bank-endorsed bills became increasingly scarce and, according to the March 1998 Reserve Bank *Bulletin* accounted for a mere $459 million out of total bank bills of $65.6 billion, or less than 0.1 per cent. As bank bills in general lost much of their popularity, banks increasingly turned to negotiable certificates of deposit as preferred funding instruments.

Definition of a bill of exchange

For money-market purposes a bill of exchange is a negotiable instrument, maturing (usually) within six months, sold at a discount from face value and believed to be the obligation (debt) of a first-class credit. It has loosely been likened to a post-dated cheque.

The rights and obligations of the parties to a bill of exchange are set out in the Bills of Exchange Act 1909–73. (The federal government has indicated that it is considering reviewing the act to enable a move to paperless trading in bills, so that the issue, as well as recording and transfer of negotiable instruments, could be computerised in ways that do not alter their essential characteristics.) The Bills of Exchange Act was adapted, with few changes, from the UK Bills of Exchange Act 1882. The act defines a bill of exchange as:

> An unconditional order in writing, addressed by one person to another, signed by the person giving it, requiring the person to whom it is addressed to pay on demand, or at a fixed or determinable future time, a sum certain in money to or to the order of a specified person, or to bearer.

A booklet, *Bills of Exchange and Promissory Notes*, published by the Australian Merchant Bankers' Association, now the International Banks and Securities Association (IBSA), gave this definition:

> The bill is an order, and not just a request, and that order must be unconditional, must be in writing and must involve three parties, these being the party issuing the order (drawer), the party to whom the bill of exchange is addressed (the drawee who becomes the acceptor) and the party to whom the bill of exchange is to be paid (payee). The bill must be signed by the drawer, the time of payment must be fixed and the bill must be for a specified sum of money, and the order must instruct the drawee to pay the named payee or his order/bearer.

(See figures 6.1a and 6.1b for an illustration of these terms.)

Normally, the amount due under a bill of exchange is paid to the holder, by the acceptor, on the date the bill matures. The holder

Figure 6.1a An example of a bank-accepted bill of exchange (face side)

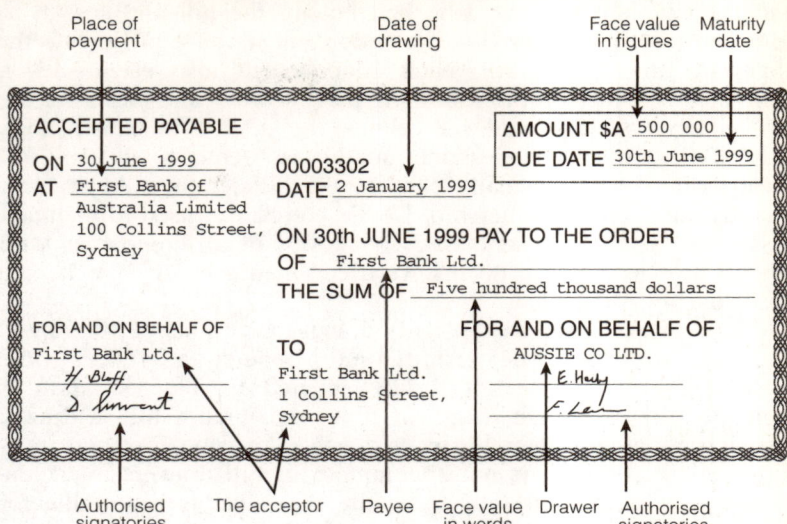

Figure 6.1b An example of a bank-accepted bill of exchange (reverse side)

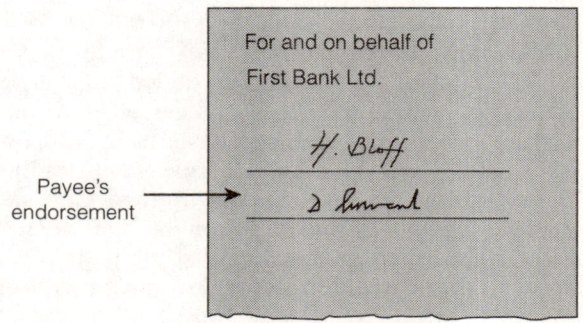

brings the bill to the address specified as the place where the bill is payable. In rare cases a bill has been dishonoured by the acceptor. The Bills of Exchange Act provides a formal chain of protection to the parties to the bill, which covers such instances. The order of liability for payment runs from the acceptor, to the drawer then on to the endorsers in ascending order from the last endorser, so that the first endorser can claim only on the acceptor or drawer. Endorsements are traditionally stamped and signed on the reverse side of a bill of exchange, starting with the payee's endorsement. Subsequent endorsers would be those who had bought the bill and sold it to someone else in the market. The endorsements on a bill create the chain of title to the bill; each endorsement also establishes a contingent liability on the endorsing party which continues until the bill matures and is paid out. Since the advent of Austraclear, Australia's computerised money-market settlements system, bill traders no longer physically endorse the bills; rather, Austraclear records the chain of ownership. Dealer companies used to maintain up-to-date lists of the approved signatories of all companies with which they dealt; these details, verified when a bill is bought, are now held by Austraclear.

Bills of exchange are normally drawn for periods of 30, 90 and 180 days, with the 30-day term the most popular and 180 days the least. These terms are not rigidly adhered to, but 180 days is generally the maximum length of time for which a bill is drawn; transactions of less than 184 days are exempt from financial institutions duty (FID). It is not uncommon for bill drawers to fix the maturity dates of their bills to ensure the paper is acceptable for delivery under the terms of the 90-day bank-bill futures contract on the Sydney Futures Exchange, because this increases the marketability of the paper—and the more liquid a security, the lower its yield and the higher its market value. Only bills issued by the four major banks are eligible for delivery on the SFE.

Bills normally have a face value of $100 000 or $500 000 and in the professional market they usually trade in parcels of $10 million. The rates at which bills are traded vary, depending on a variety of factors such as the quality of the acceptor on the bills, their maturity and, especially with shorter-term bills, the amount of cash available on a given day. A basic rule when trading bills of exchange is that when a bill is 'acquired in good faith and without notice of fraud', that is, legitimately bought, the buyer has good title to the bill. The rights and obligations of parties to a bill of exchange are well documented in statute law and an enormous body of legal precedent.

Bills of exchange can be either trade bills or the accommodation bills which evolved in Australia in the early 1970s. Accommodation bills are a means of providing working capital. The bills helped investment banks (then known as merchant banks) finance business demand in the days when Reserve Bank controls on bank lending meant bank credit was in short supply. The bills also suited the seasonal fluctuations in liquidity which were a feature of Australian financial markets before changes to the pattern of corporate tax payments and other flows between the government and the private sector virtually eradicated the ups and downs in government cashflows.

Bills can be grouped into various types within the categories of trade and accommodation. Bills can be non-bank (also referred to as commercial bills or commercial paper and rarely seen), generated by investment banks; they can be bank-accepted or bank-endorsed, the latter also being far less common than in the past. With bank-accepted bills the bank's name appears as the acceptor of the paper. Bank-accepted bills now include accommodation bills, financing non-specific commercial requirements.

Users of bills

Public and private companies, and often individuals, use bills of exchange to borrow funds or as investments. The lenders are generally the major banks or investment banks whose clients like bill lines (a line of credit—flexible loan—from a bank, funded by discounting bills of exchange) because they offer a cheaper source of funds than, say, an overdraft or fixed-term loan. The list of those who use the bill market as traders or investors would be long—regular users, though, include the banks, investment banks, superannuation fund managers, cash management trusts, industrial companies, finance companies, building societies, insurance companies, sharebroking firms, and semi-government and local-government authorities.

Dealing in bills of exchange takes place daily by telephone or on broker screens. The most active bill trading takes place among the four major banks because they are the institutions with the large bill drawdowns for clients so they initiate most of the buying and selling. During a telephone conversation involving a bill transaction, dealers (buyers and sellers) discuss the details of the bills, such as the name of the issuer, maturity date and the amount of money involved. Settlement details are agreed after a 'firm deal' has been struck. Financial markets operators' conversations are commonly tape-recorded to provide proof of dealing details, should a dispute arise. Professional market transactions are settled through the Austraclear system.

Establishing a bill line as a form of bank finance involves the normal credit assessment procedures undertaken by a lender. The borrower's starting point is to approach a bank and outline what finance is needed. The lender will want to know details about the borrower, such as cashflow and industry status. Lenders use their own internal credit analysis and/or rely on information supplied by a ratings agency such as Standard & Poor's or Moody's Investors Service. The lender would discuss with the borrower whether the loan is to be secured or unsecured and, if secured, what type and level of security is available and acceptable. The nature of the security provided by the borrower can influence the acceptance fee or credit margin charged by the lender. A bank offering a line of credit would probably quote an all-up price which would include a margin above the prevailing bank-accepted bill rate. The margin would be based on the credit assessment of the borrower, and the extent to which the paper carrying the borrower's name would sell easily in the market.

Advantages for users

A bill line, now regarded as a 'mature', straightforward financial markets product, offers a lender an instrument which can be traded to generate cash (assuming a ready market), and thus reliquefy a loan. This kind of financing illustrates the bridging/matching process which is an integral part of the business of financial inter-mediaries, and which continues to be refined with the use of more sophisticated packages based on arbitrage and swaps. The objective is to increase efficiency in the use of funds, and thus to lower the costs.

Bank lending has become increasingly versatile, with banks offering products that are attractive alternatives to bill lines. Loans can be in the form of cash advances at fixed or floating rates, cash advances with bill options, or drawn bills. They can also include an option to use different currencies. Innovations in bank lending can be driven by a number of factors, not least the banks' and borrowers' preferences for the best deal. A trend seen since the early 1990s has been a drop in the use of bill finance by small business; according to Reserve Bank statistics, in 1997 bill finance accounted for about 11 per cent of small business finance (defined as loans of less than $500 000) compared with nearly one-third in 1993. 'This trend away from bills appears to be driven to an important degree by lenders,' the RBA commented in its April 1997 *Bulletin*. 'The fact that the shift has been into fixed-rate loans suggests that there may also be demand influences at work, as borrowers lock in what are historically low interest rates.'

Bank finance to small business is also available in variable-rate loans such as an overdraft, or an overdraft or term loan secured by residential property and, as banks came to recognise the quality of the security supporting these loans, they correspondingly shaved the interest rates applied. The Reserve Bank's March 1998 *Bulletin* recorded that the weighted-average interest rate on variable-rate loans to small business fell by 3.2 percentage points to 9.4 per cent between June 1996 and December 1997, while the indicator overdraft rate and the cash target rate fell by 2.5 percentage points. The competitive forces which hit the housing loan market (see chapter 11) caught up with the market for small business loans early in 1998; several major Australian banks introduced a number of new, lower interest-rate products and cut their indicator lending rates on standard products independently of a reduction in official cash rates.

At times, uncertainty about interest rates and currencies has left both borrowers and lenders unwilling to lock themselves in for long periods, leading to the popularity of instruments and techniques that allow a renegotiation of terms. Bills offer flexibility to borrowers, enabling them to tailor borrowings under a term bill line to suit their needs. Funds are made available under a bill facility for, say, up to five years, but can be drawn down as the borrower needs. The opportunities offered by the swaps and options markets mean that borrowers and lenders can escape from an unwanted interest-rate structure: fixed rates can be swapped for floating, and short-term funding for longer-term.

Bill facilities

Bill facilities are available in two categories: *acceptance* or *discount*. An acceptance facility is so called because the lender charges an 'acceptance commission' (fee) to bear the risk of the borrower, that is, the acceptor's credit risk is substituted for that of the borrower. When a bank accepts a client's bill it undertakes to accept that client's risk up to a specified amount and for a fixed period. The bills are then sold in the market so that funds are provided by the market and not directly by the acceptor of the bill. An acceptance facility is usually used when the names of the parties to the bill are not widely recognised, and the name of the acceptor, whether a bank or well-known investment bank, adds weight to the bill. Lending using bills saves extensive documentation as the bill itself is evidence of debt and once the bill is sold it is off the bank's balance sheet and is recognised only as a contingent liability until it matures. There are currently no balance-sheet reserve requirements for banks other than capital-adequacy provisions for endorsed bills which have been sold.

With a discount facility (now rarely used) the funds are provided directly by the bank or investment bank, up to an agreed amount for a predetermined period. The decision as to acceptance or discount facility is a matter for negotiation between borrower and lender.

Once agreement has been reached to establish a bill line, the details are set out in document form, separate from the bills. The essential component in the documentation is the letter of offer which has to be formally accepted by the borrower; it includes details of security provided, or negative pledges or covenants entered into, and defines rollover dates during the period for which the facility has been organised. The initial interest rates on the borrowed funds are established and these are subject to regular review at rollover times.

Cost of bill finance

Costs can include a range of fees, which differ from one company to another but broadly include items such as establishment, commitment and acceptance fees and legal costs (most states have abolished stamp duty on bills of exchange). All costs are for the borrower's account. The acceptance fee would reflect the lender's credit assessment of the borrower. The price of funds (the interest rate) is quoted at a discount from the face value of the bill line, and is expressed as a yield per annum. This varies with the term of the bills and the level of interest rates in the market.

Market rates on bills

Bank-accepted bills of exchange trade at the finest bill rates—that is, the lowest yields (interest rates)—in the secondary market. This reflects the perceived security associated with the banks, which flows from their own creditworthiness. Bank bills, particularly bank-accepted bills, traditionally were described as homogeneous, in that all banks have the same status. With the expansion of the Australian banking system, however, this point has come into dispute. Banks rank equally under the law but their paper can trade at different rates in the market, reflecting the fact that pricing is a combination of credit and liquidity; their credit is not in question but the liquidity of a smaller bank's paper is less than that of a major operator and that affects its pricing. Over time, the market has become tiered according to credit-rating, with the four major banks' credits alike and the remaining banks coming under them.

For example, liquidity was a factor influencing the pricing of now-rarely-seen bank-endorsed paper. Because the claim of a holder on an endorser is less direct than a claim on an acceptor, bank-endorsed paper has tended to trade at a marginally higher yield than bank-accepted paper. This implies slightly lower status, but a bank-endorsed bill is secure, because the bank will pay out; it could take more than one day, or even longer, though, for a lender to recoup funds. There is a legal process to go through which would involve costs as well as time. The market in bank-endorsed bills was never as deep as that for bank-accepted bills and this also affected the rates at which bank-endorsed paper trades. Overall, bank-accepted bills traditionally enjoyed greater marketability.

Commercial (non-bank) bills, virtually unknown in the late 1990s although the concept still exists, are those which do not carry the name of a bank as either acceptor, drawer or endorser, and trade at a higher yield than bank-accepted or bank-endorsed bills. This reflects their lower credit rating in the market. A top-name corporate borrower would have paper trading at fairly fine yields compared to a lesser-known borrower.

Several factors affect bill rates on any day in the market:

- the prevailing target for the cash rate (this being the anchor for all short-term interest rates) and expectations that it is likely to be changed before a bill matures;
- the demand for bills in the market;
- the supply of bills;
- the maturity of the bills offered; and
- the names of the parties to the bill and their credit status.

The average bank-bill rate, used as a reference or benchmark rate for other market prices, is published daily on Reuters BBSW (bank-bill reference rate) page at 10.10 am.

Security aspects of bill trading

The arrival in September 1984 of Austraclear Ltd—the money markets' electronic settlements system—removed most of the worries regarding the security aspects of trading instruments such as bills of exchange. Before Austraclear, bill traders had to consider a number of features beyond picking the right rate at which to trade. Traders had to check items such as title to the bill, signatures of the last endorser and maturity date, as well as seeing to the physical settlement of the transaction and safe-keeping of the paper. Austraclear removes such concerns by recording the trades and changes in ownership so that there is no need for the bills (or other securities handled by the Austraclear system) physically to change hands.

Bills of exchange and promissory notes have the legal protection of the Bills of Exchange Act. Bills of exchange are also covered by a number of legal precedents, established in market practice, which contribute to clarifying the rights and obligations of those who trade and hold these securities.

A basic principle in bill trading is to ensure that the holder has good title to the bill. The buyer's title flows from the seller—hence a cardinal rule has been never to buy a bill of exchange from an unknown party in the market. With Austraclear checking the paper lodged in its system, such confirmation is in place when bills are traded. Before the arrival of Austraclear, traders would photocopy all bills bought, front and back, and these would be filed in order of maturity date so that the list could be cross-checked with the bills listed in the trader's portfolio. It is a tribute to the market that, given the rapid and high turnover in securities, there have been few instances of bills or promissory notes being lost or stolen. If a bill is stolen or mislaid, all parties to the bill must be notified, details of the missing bills must be made public as soon as possible to protect the rights of the parties to the bills and the rights of other traders.

Normally, advertisements are placed in the national financial press, listing the details of the missing bills. Unless very rigorous and detailed collusion had taken place among a number of parties in advance, it would be almost impossible for anyone who did not have good title to the bills to cash them. Market practice and the wide circulation of the bills' description would militate against fraud.

Bills of exchange must be presented for payment on the due date. Australian law provides for 'days of grace'; section 19[i] of the Bills of Exchange Act states that three days of grace are allowed after due date, but in practice the days-of-grace clause is eliminated by adding the word 'fixed' to the date on accommodation and trade bills. This minimises uncertainty about payment.

Negotiable certificates of deposit

Negotiable certificates of deposit (NCDs) are bearer instruments; a simple description is that they are basically a promissory note issued by a bank, with only the name of the issuing (borrowing) bank appearing on the paper. Certificates of deposit received a boost with the removal of SRDs and the introduction, in their place, of non-callable deposits. The certificates trade in the market at the same rates as—and rank *pari passu* with—bank-accepted bills of exchange, and are commonly used by banks as a funding method. Borrowing in foreign-currency-denominated certificates of deposit, or in euro-commercial paper (CP) has been possible since December 1983, when exchange controls were virtually abolished.

Negotiable and transferable CDs are issued by banks for periods ranging from a few days to several years. NCDs are a shorter-term instrument and are generally issued for 30 to 180 days with most issues in the 30–90-day period; transferable certificates of deposit (TCDs) are similar to a medium-term-note (MTN) and are issued for periods up to five years.

Promissory notes (also commercial, or one-name, paper)

One-name paper emerged in the Australian markets in the early 1970s and by the end of the decade had achieved widespread acceptance. Australian financial markets operators use the terms 'one-name paper', 'commercial paper' and 'promissory notes' interchangeably while the more common term overseas is 'commercial paper'. These labels cover bearer notes and bearer certificates as well as promissory notes; they all qualify for the tag 'one-name paper' because only one name appears on the security and so repayment is solely dependent on the performance of the issuer. Commercial paper is regularly issued by companies, state central borrowing authorities, other government authorities and finance companies. Issues have also been made in Australia by some off-shore banks which raises their profile in this country.

Promissory notes have been used widely overseas for decades, especially in the US and Canada, where there was no equivalent of the Australian intercompany market. The US's one-name paper market was the closest approximation. The paper in the US market ranges from as short as three or five days to a legal maximum of 270 days, although paper drawn for longer than 45 days is rare. The Australian promissory note market has largely been modelled on the US market.

Credit for pioneering promissory notes (P-notes) in Australia has generally been attributed to General Motors Acceptance Corporation (GMAC) Australia. (GMAC Australia's US parent had contributed to the development of the commercial paper market in the US.) The financier FNCB-Waltons made a brief entry into the P-note market in the early 1970s but GMAC's issue of bearer notes in 1973 is regarded as the start of regular issues in volume. GMAC Australia's notes differed slightly from the conventional promissory notes, being issued at a rate which fluctuated in line with intercompany market rates and escaping stamp duty even when that applied to promissory notes. GMAC Australia's notes subsequently became registered instead of bearer securities which enabled them to be registered electronically and traded through the Austraclear system. GMAC, which had first traded its paper in this way in New Zealand in March 1996, in December of that year became the first corporate to introduce such trading in Australia, with other issuers following.

Promissory notes are among the simplest, most flexible and most convenient methods of raising funds. Initially it was expected that, because of the importance of credit-ratings, only twenty or thirty top companies would use promissory notes but the range broadened considerably with more than 100 private-sector companies and many public-sector authorities issuing P-notes. The notes were originally envisaged as a way of adding term funding to the intercompany market and were even expected to eclipse that market. P-note financing has developed along similar lines to bill finance, with facilities being granted for up to three years. The notes, however, are issued in the same way as bills of exchange, generally in maturities of 30, 90 and 180 days. In the case of a term facility of, say, three years, the notes are rolled over periodically, probably every 180 days or less, to allow for changes in interest rates and to accommodate the borrower's requirements. They are generally priced at a margin over the bank-bill rate of a corresponding maturity.

The promissory note is defined under section 89 of the Bills of Exchange Act 1909–73, as 'an unconditional promise in writing made by one person to another, signed by the maker, engaging to pay, on demand or at a fixed or determined future time, a sum certain in money, to or to the order of a specified person or to bearer'. This definition gives the promissory note the same legal status as a bill of exchange. The promise contained in a promissory note is unconditional, and it must involve two parties—the party making the promise and a receiving party. The party to whom the sum of money is to be paid may be the bearer of the instrument, a specified person or a person nominated by the order of a specified person. A promissory note must be signed by the party making the promise, must be for a specific sum of money, and must specify the time for repayment. Promissory notes are instruments in bearer form, transferable by delivery, without endorsement for value received. The notes are issued at a discount from face value, redeemable at par on maturity. (See figure 6.2.)

The chief advantages of promissory notes are their flexibility and the absence of contingent liability for note-traders. Because the promissory note, unlike a bill of exchange, does not require endorsement when sold in the market, the seller has no further liability. The multiplier effect of the contingent liability aspect of bills of exchange leads to many lenders quickly filling up their lending limits, leaving them little flexibility.

Promissory notes are generally sold by tender, with a bank or investment bank acting as arranger or lead manager to the note program, handling the documentation and organising issues, and a dealer panel appointed comprising three-to-five financial intermediaries which bid for the notes and place them with end-users. The bidding process helps hold down yields for the borrower and panel participants are generally selected because they have a good distribution network and can also warehouse unsold stock. The major issuers can dispense with the auction process and approach the market directly. Some issuers are 'on tap' in that they can be

Figure 6.2 An example of a promissory note (face side)

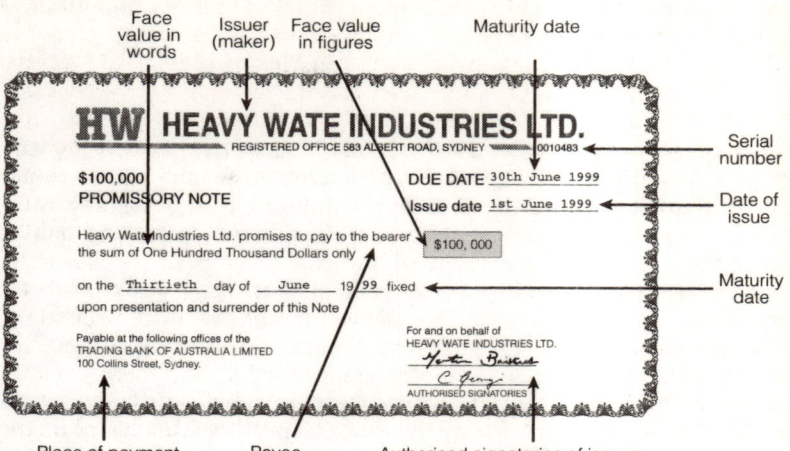

approached on any day by a manager or panel member to issue if the prevailing rates and maturity suit the issuer. At one stage the process of having a P-note issue underwritten brought far more companies than was originally thought possible into the promissory note market; however, underwritten issues by the late 1990s were less common and issues of promissory notes rely on the credit-standing of the issuer. The market was promoted as the preserve of top-name borrowers of unquestionable creditworthiness, because lending through P-notes ranks as unsecured lending. The lower appeal of less-than-prime names shows in the rates at which their paper trades, reflecting lenders' opinion of their credit status. A solution has been to structure a P-note issue with the backing of a letter of credit issued under a trust deed and confirmed by an Australian bank. The lender is thus ultimately relying on the bank, should the borrower default, and the note yields reflect the backing of the bank. The cost of adding this credit enhancement is borne by the issuer, adding to its costs but enabling the P-notes to trade at a lower yield and with wider marketability. Credit-standing is important as some investors, for example cash management trusts, cannot buy paper that is ranked less than A1+ or are restricted in the terms for which they can invest in paper graded A2.

Commercial paper programs can also be backed by a specific asset, in the same way that longer-term bonds can be issued against, say, a pool of mortgages. And many banks, corporates and state-government borrowers have launched euro-CP programs out of

Hong Kong, the US or Europe, using under six-month, multi-currency issues handled by dealer panels and sold to Asian investors and other offshore investors.

Treasury notes

Treasury notes are short-term discount securities issued by the federal government. They are aimed chiefly at the professional money market and are of virtually no interest to the average individual investor. The main holders of treasury notes are the banks, which hold about 70 per cent of the notes on issue because the paper is useful for liquidity management. For many years the notes were used to iron out seasonal fluctuations in liquidity. More generally, they are used chiefly to meet the federal government's need for within-year finance. Treasury notes are sold at times when revenues are less than receipts, that is, when the commonwealth budget is in deficit, and mature when receipts exceed spending. In the past, the amount of notes on issue tended to rise during the first three quarters of the financial year then fall in the June quarter as large tax collections flowed to the government's accounts. This pattern has become less pronounced as the commonwealth government has made efforts to smooth the pattern of tax receipts through the year.

The concept of seasonal notes being issued by the federal government dates from the 1950s, when notes were initially issued fortnightly, by the treasury, for nine months of the year. Treasury notes were first made available on a daily basis in 1962, initially only in 13-week maturities; the 26-week maturity was introduced in 1967 and a five-week maturity added in 1991.

Treasury notes have been sold through regular, usually weekly, tenders since December 1979. This system replaced the earlier method which made the notes available daily, 'on tap' from the Reserve Bank, at a rate that was set by the central bank. Under the tender system, note-buyers bid competitively for the securities, so that the rates are determined in the market. The notes sell at a discount from face value in the same way as bills and promissory notes. A feature of the notes of less than 91 days (13 weeks) to maturity is that they can be converted into cash at any time by rediscounting (selling them back) to the Reserve Bank. Anyone holding treasury notes of the appropriate maturity therefore has a method for generating instant cash. In these circumstances the notes are sold at the *rediscount* rate, which is set by the Reserve Bank. The central bank quotes the yield at which it is prepared to buy the notes, with the yield reflecting its assessment of the market yield plus a fixed margin (0.75 percentage point in March 1998). In addition, there is a ceiling on the penalty so that, regardless of the maturity of the notes rediscounted, the penalty will not exceed that which would apply if seven-day notes had been rediscounted.

The relationship between yield and discount

Bills of exchange and promissory notes are normally traded according to their *yield* which is a different measure from a *discount*. Australia uses a yield formula, whereas the US and UK use a discount; the US bases calculations on a 360-day financial year, whereas Australia uses a 365-day year with no adjustment for a leap year.

The yield on a security refers to the rate of interest expressed as a percentage per annum on the amount outlaid when the instrument is bought. For example, a trader buying a note with a face value of \$100 000 and a term of 90 days at a yield of 5.00 per cent would outlay \$98 782.14. When the note matures the holder (who may or may not be the original buyer) would receive its face value, \$100 000, so that the interest earned would be the \$100 000 less the outlay of \$98 782.14 = \$1217.86.

The yield formula is:

$$\text{price} = \frac{\text{face value} \times (\text{days in year} \times 100)}{(\text{days in year} \times 100) + (\text{yield} \times \text{days to maturity})}$$

$$= \frac{100\,000 \times 365 \times 100}{(365 \times 100) + 5.00 \times 90}$$

$$= \frac{3\,650\,000\,000}{36\,500 + (5.00 \times 90)}$$

$$= \$98\,782.14$$

The discount, however, is calculated not on the amount outlaid but on the face value of the security (\$100 000), taking into account the discount rate and the number of days to maturity. For example, a \$100 000 90-day bank bill bought at a discount of 5.00 per cent would cost a buyer \$98 767.12. The discount, being calculated on the face value of the security rather than on the amount outlaid, is similar to interest paid in advance. The 5.00 per cent earned on the face value of \$100 000 is a greater amount (\$1232.88) than the 5.00 per cent earned by using the yield formula (\$1217.86).

The discount formula is:

$$\frac{\text{face value} \times \text{discount rate} \times \text{days to maturity}}{100 \times \text{days in the year}}$$

$$= \frac{100\,000 \times 5.00 \times 90}{36\,500}$$

$$= \$1232.88$$

The outlay is the face value of $100 000 less the interest for 90 days on $100 000 at 5.00 per cent ($1232.88) = $98 767.12.

The Reserve Bank rediscount rate for treasury notes is quoted as discount rate and not a yield; when converted to a yield it reflects a more expensive 'give-up' rate.

7

Long-term fixed-income government securities

A combination of reduced public-sector spending and further progress with privatisation suggests no let-up in the decline of commonwealth and state-government securities. The full or partial privatisation of government entities such as Telstra which, as its predecessor Telecom, was a major public borrower and so source of paper, shifts ownership of these organisations from government to private-sector investors. Privatised borrowers such as Telstra, however, provide a good benchmark for corporate-sector stock. Early in 1998, $90 billion of commonwealth government bonds were on issue, a figure that was expected to reduce as Australia continued its transition to a low-debt country through privatisation programs and budget surpluses.

Long-term fixed-income securities issued in the Australian financial markets include commonwealth government bonds, state and territory government bonds—in early 1998 still the two most active securities markets—corporate bonds (including medium-term notes), debentures, inflation-indexed bonds issued by the federal government and state government authorities, mortgage-backed securities (discussed in chapter 11), global $A bonds, treasury adjustable-rate bonds (TABs), eurobonds and infrastructure bonds (no longer issued since in February 1997 the federal government withdrew the tax exemptions on coupon payments of new infrastructure bonds; earlier issues exist which continue to be exempt from tax and the concept of infrastructure bonds prevails). This chapter focuses on government fixed-income securities and the following chapter discusses private-sector fixed-income paper.

Long-term fixed-income securities are also traded with the depth of trading largely reflecting the amount of the securities on issue.

Table 7.1 $A bonds outstanding ($ billion)

	1980	1990	1995	1997
Domestic				
C'wth govt	25	34	90	89
State govts	–	39	43	35
Other				
—Corporate	–	13	8	11
—Asset-backed	–	6	8	17
Foreign				
—Issued in Australia	–	–	2	3
—Euro-$A	–	34	44	54
—Dual currency	–	7	24	52

Source: Reserve Bank of Australia

During the late 1980s, when the commonwealth government was reducing its debt, turnover in commonwealth government bonds fell in line with the drop in outstanding bonds, which levelled around $35 billion in 1990 and 1991. In subsequent years commonwealth bond turnover soared as outstandings reached $70 billion in 1994 and $95 billion in June 1997. In contrast, the state governments were reducing debt levels, so turnover in their securities fell, and by 1996 was less than half of that in commonwealth bonds. The 1997 AFMA Financial Markets Report recorded daily turnover of $4 billion in commonwealth bonds and $1.5 billion in state government paper. In March 1998 there were 34 series of commonwealth bonds, five series of capital-indexed bonds and one series of TABs. In mid-1997 about 42 per cent of commonwealth bonds were held by non-residents; the Reserve Bank estimated that around half of those non-resident holders were Japanese and US investors.

Fiscal responsibility, a worldwide trend in the mid-to-late 1990s, together with privatisation, translates into diminishing public-sector debt and highlights a reversal in markets which had thrived on big-spending politicians and massive deficits which had to be funded. It is no surprise, then, that the number of players in the Australian fixed-interest markets contracted sharply in the second half of the 1990s and attention had once again turned to fostering markets in securities other than those issued by the commonwealth and state governments. However, early in 1998 the commonwealth was still by far the largest single issuer of debt securities and because of this, and the undoubted creditworthiness of the commonwealth government, its securities were the benchmark for other paper in the market.

Table 7.2 Securities outstanding ($ billion)

	1997	Average growth (%) over past decade
Bank-related securities		
Bank bills	65	2
Certificates of deposit	47	25
Other securities		
Cwth govt bonds	89	7
State govt	35	7
Corporate bonds	28	–
$A eurobonds	54	9

Source: Reserve Bank of Australia

Fixed income: state your interest

Fixed-income investments provide exactly that: a fixed rate of interest income for a specific period. A broad definition of a fixed-income security is an instrument with a fixed maturity date and yield (interest rate): fixed-income products range from a straightforward term deposit with a bank, building society or credit union, to a simple or compound-interest finance-company debenture and commonwealth or state government bond and more complex inflation-indexed bonds. For the purposes of this chapter, fixed-income securities are defined fairly narrowly as those with a coupon stream (regular, usually twice-yearly, fixed-interest payments) as well as a fixed term to maturity and an unchanging face value.

All interest-bearing securities have four basic features:

- coupon (periodic payment of interest on face value)
- principal amount or face value
- maturity date
- yield to maturity

On stock issued at par, such as a finance-company debenture, the coupon *is* the yield to maturity. For example, you may buy $10 000 of ABC finance company debentures maturing in ten years, carrying an 8 per cent coupon so that you earn 8 per cent each year on the face value invested, that is, 8 per cent on $10 000 paid twice yearly in two instalments of $400 which brings an annual income of $800. On maturity after ten years you get back the $10 000 (assuming the coupon interest is not reinvested, as would be the case with compound-interest debentures).

Two cardinal rules apply to fixed-income securities such as government bonds. First, the capital value of the security fluctuates constantly, rising when interest rates fall and falling when interest rates rise. This contrary correlation is not a worry for the investor planning to hold to maturity and ride out the fluctuations, earning income from the set coupon. But it is of paramount importance to a bond trader or fund manager trying to maximise returns, and its occasionally unsettling consequences show up in quarterly reports from managed funds. Second, the interest rates (yields) quoted in the financial press apply to the $5–$10 million standard parcels traded in the wholesale, professional market. If the yield on $10 million ten-year bonds is 8 per cent, retail investors interested in, say, $10 000 or $50 000 can expect to buy at around 7.85 per cent, inclusive of some 0.15 per cent brokerage. Retail investors can buy fixed-income securities directly from the issuer in the case of a company debenture or state government bond, through a specialist broker or, in the case of commonwealth government bonds, from the Reserve Bank (or they can invest indirectly through a managed fund).

A commonwealth government or state government bond carries a coupon (interest rate), face value and maturity but also involves a yield or price, which makes these securities more complex for the average investor. Bonds are bought at a yield (determined by the purchase price) which varies in line with supply and demand in the market. So a parcel of $500 000 commonwealth bonds, bought on 15 June 1999 at a yield of 9 per cent, with a coupon of 8.5 per cent and a maturity date of 15 June 2009, would entail an outlay of $483 740.00. Fluctuations in yield are reflected in a change in the bond's capital value. Hence, those trading bonds are exposed to potential losses and gains on the face value of their investments (they still earn interest through the coupon on a bond for the period they hold it). On the other hand, long-term investors who hold bonds until maturity are not exposed to fluctuations in income from their bond investments because their income stream is limited to earning interest on the bond through the coupon which remains constant for the life of the bond (the fixed part of fixed-income investments). For the holder-to-maturity, fluctuations in the capital value of the bond remain unrealised losses or gains and, at the maturity of the bond, the holder receives face value.

Fixed-income markets

Fixed-income markets play a key role in the financial system: they provide a fund-raising medium for governments (commonwealth and state) and for companies; and they provide investment outlets for banks, fund managers, investment banks and other financial intermediaries. The Reserve Bank of Australia holds a portfolio of commonwealth bonds and trades in these as part of its monetary and liquidity management; the yields on commonwealth bonds serve as a benchmark for other interest rates in the financial community.

In the late 1980s federal treasury, through the Reserve Bank, began consolidating lines of commonwealth government bonds into sizeable 'benchmark' maturities—*hot stocks* which, by definition, are large liquid lines of actively traded securities, often linked to futures baskets. The concept of 'hot stocks' evolved with the increase in the volume of debt issued by the commonwealth and state government borrowers. The task of selling big volumes of stock is made easier if the stock is divided into large, liquid lines rather than many small, less marketable lines; and the common-wealth treasury, faced with managing a burgeoning debt issue task, was keen to keep costs down. Consolidation into benchmark lines brought the number of series of bonds on issue down from 153 in 1985 to 34 in March 1997, in sixteen benchmark lines of $3–$5 billion. Benchmark series accounted for some 97 per cent of the total value of bonds on issue compared with 30 per cent in the late 1980s. The state government authorities which, since the late 1980s, have operated through *central borrowing authorities*, were in fact ahead of the commonwealth government in streamlining borrowings into large, consolidated lines.

Australian fixed-income markets in the late 1990s extend far beyond domestic horizons. Significant international investor interest, predominantly from Japan, Europe and the US, has been a feature since the mid-1980s in $A securities. The fixed-interest market is not driven solely by domestic factors; the long end of the bond market in particular is vulnerable to overseas influences because Australian bonds compete with all others for a place in the portfolios of overseas investors. Australian commonwealth government secu-rities account for between 1 and 2 per cent of the benchmark indices of major overseas investment banks. Market practices in Australia have developed along the lines of major overseas bond markets where, for example, dealer panels, market-making and two-way pricing are long-established conventions.

The market in fixed-income securities almost exclusively involves institutional and wholesale investors, with small but grow-ing participation from retail investors. Professional market operators are generally unwilling to quote for parcels of less than $1 million; standard parcels traded are $5–$10 million, with many institutions dealing in $20 million or $30 million, even $50 million lots. However, growing retail investor interest, especially from self-managed superannuation funds, has encouraged a few stockbroking houses to cultivate retail interest in commonwealth and state government bonds. They are mindful, though, that these instru-ments carry pitfalls for the unwary. The Reserve Bank provides an over-the-counter purchase-and-sales facility for retail parcels of commonwealth government bonds at its branches in all states.

Retail investors have at times been enthusiastic supporters of other public-sector paper such as bonds issued by NSW TCorp, Queensland Treasury Corporation (QTC) and Treasury Corporation Victoria (TCV) which are often advertised in the print and electronic media. The issuer (borrower) might well offer a buy-back facility should an investor wish to dispose of stock before it matures (with limits on quantity and at a price reflecting the prevailing market for the stock in question). Individual investors have also sometimes been buyers of finance-company debentures—uncomplicated securities which are sold through a prospectus at face value, and which pay interest through a coupon which is fixed for the life of the debenture.

How fixed-income markets evolved

The methods of issuing fixed-income securities, specifically commonwealth and semi—semi-government (state government)—paper, have undergone several changes over the past few decades as the markets developed and the amount of funds to be raised increased substantially (although some quite large amounts were raised in earlier times, relative to Australia's prevailing gross domestic product).

Commonwealth government bonds have been issued under three successive systems. Until 1979, the commonwealth raised funds through periodic issues of bonds, with the government setting the interest rates and selling as many bonds as the market would buy at these rates. The system worked well for most of the post-war period when interest rates were regulated and budget deficits and inflation were low. But by the mid-to-late 1970s two major influences had undermined these arrangements: first, the rise in inflation saw interest rates climb to historically high levels which, given the post-war experience of very low interest rates, government found unpalatable; and, in addition, the process of financial deregulation had begun and instruments were available carrying market-determined interest rates. Yields on bonds became uncompetitive. As a result, the commonwealth government had difficulty selling adequate amounts of bonds at a time when, with large deficits, its borrowing requirement had increased considerably.

The Campbell Committee, in its landmark review of the Australian financial system in 1981, made the point that the earlier methods of selling bonds suited the 1950s and 1960s when inflation was low and interest rates were regulated. There was little competition then from private-sector borrowers and good support from captive investors; also, government borrowings were quite modest.

Between April 1980 and July 1982 a 'tap' system operated, with bonds constantly available from the Reserve Bank. The federal government set the coupons and initial prices (yields); the objective was to adjust the price as necessary to tailor sales to the amounts the government wanted to raise. However, tap stock yields were not always kept in line with market rates, and having bonds constantly available led to a degree of inertia in the markets.

Support had for some time been growing for a move to sell bonds by tender (auction), a system successfully used in the US. The Campbell Committee favoured a tender system where the government, through the Reserve Bank, would offer a known quantity of bonds and the market would set the price. Treasury notes, the short-term government security, had been successfully sold in tenders since 1979. It was decided in June 1982 to introduce a tender system for selling commonwealth government bonds and the first tender was announced on 29 July, offering $350 million in three maturities. As expected, tenders encouraged additional secondary-market trading in bonds. The bond tender system was effective in enabling governments to sell large quantities of stock with minimal disruption to interest rates. The system got off to a healthy start, with the first tender offered in a climate of falling interest rates, reflecting the recessionary conditions of 1982–83. And with demand for funds generally low, the government had a clear run as chief borrower. A further bonus was overseas investors' interest in Australian fixed-income securities, an interest that encompassed semi-government, as well as commonwealth government, securities. Secondary-market activity in bonds increased, encouraged by the tender system and by the larger volume of stock on issue. However, a number of prevailing ratio requirements, compelling various institutions to hold large proportions of government securities, dampened secondary-market trading. These ratio requirements were progressively reduced and then phased out during the 1980s and 1990s, further stimulating market trading.

Australian fixed-income markets have tended to be dominated by commonwealth government securities. However, from 1989 until the mid-1990s the balance shifted in favour of state government paper. The decline in the amount of available commonwealth government paper reflected the government's move from budget deficit to surplus and hence a drop in its need to borrow through selling bonds. This had a significant but not enduring impact on the Australian fixed-income markets which, for more than a decade, had relied on commonwealth government securities as a benchmark stock from which to price other securities such as state paper and corporate debentures. The scarcity of commonwealth paper increased when the commonwealth government began reducing its debt by buying back existing stock. How best to operate in the absence of a large supply of commonwealth paper was a topic of considerable discussion but before the debate could progress very far the problem was reversed as the federal government moved back into operating with a deficit and its bonds were no longer in short supply. By the late 1990s, however, the federal budget was again in surplus, with considerable revenue flowing from large privatisations, and the stock of bonds was again forecast to decline. Attention was increasingly focused on developing corporate bonds, which include bank paper, and the growing market in mortgage-backed securities. In addition, the federal government was acknowledging the need to preserve some form of liquid bond market in the face of budget surpluses and commonwealth treasury was considering options for doing so.

The role of fixed-income markets

Fixed-income markets in Australia are used as a means of raising funds by the federal government and state government authorities and, more recently, by the corporate sector. They are an important outlet for investments by individuals and companies. They represent:

- a method of borrowing for companies, government and state government authorities, and institutions;
- an investment medium for corporate, business, state government, banking and, in many cases, institutional and private investors;
- a means of implementing monetary policy;
- a means by which liquidity (that is, flows of funds) can be transferred between key areas of the financial market.

Fixed-income securities are a key element in the portfolios of insurance companies and superannuation funds because these investments are held to match long-term liabilities. By holding long-dated assets which mature as their liabilities become due, these financial institutions achieve a degree of protection for their portfolios. Banks have traditionally been required to hold a proportion of government fixed-interest securities (prime assets) for liquidity ratio purposes; in 1997 state and territory government paper also became eligible for the banks' ratio requirements (which in 1998 were replaced with new liquidity management guidelines). Borrowers such as state government authorities have at times used long-term securities to fund large-scale capital works projects that generate income over long periods. This income flow matches the coupon and other liabilities created by borrowing using fixed-income securities.

Characteristics of fixed-income securities

Cashflow

A convenient way of examining the returns available from any investment is to identify the source of income. The rate of return from all investments can be defined as the yield, which is the coupon yield plus capital yield (gain). Fixed-income investments provide a coupon yield; some also provide a capital yield. For example, because banks guarantee to repay the amount deposited, an interest-bearing bank deposit relies for its total return on a fixed rate of interest, whereas investors in discount securities such as treasury notes or bank bills rely entirely on a capital gain for their income. A government bond can be a combination of both interest (coupon) and capital gain.

Financial markets operators tend to distinguish between coupon securities, such as government bonds and debentures, and non-coupon instruments such as treasury notes, commercial bills and promissory notes. The frequency of the coupons can vary, but is usually half-yearly or annually. The coupons attached to bonds, semi-government paper, debentures and mortgage-backed securities represent a fixed annual return to the investor.

Market value

Government bonds are bought at a yield, which is determined by the purchase price; the rate of return during the life of the bond is determined by the rate at which the half-yearly bond coupons are reinvested. The bond formula assumes that the bond-holder reinvests each coupon's proceeds. If the bond is held to maturity, the investor receives the principal (face value) of the bond, plus interest through the coupons during the time the bond is held.

Fixed-income securities provide a full redemption value when they mature but their market value can change at any time in line with supply and demand. Say an investor buys a $100 000 five-year 8 per cent coupon bond at par, that is, market yields are also at 8 per cent so the outlay is $100 000. Subsequently, yields rise to 9 per cent so, because of the inverse relationship between price and yield, the market value falls from par to $96 044. A bond-holder receives a constant rate of interest through the coupon on the bond, so that in the case of a $100 000 bond with a coupon of 8 per cent,

Figure 7.1 Coupon flow

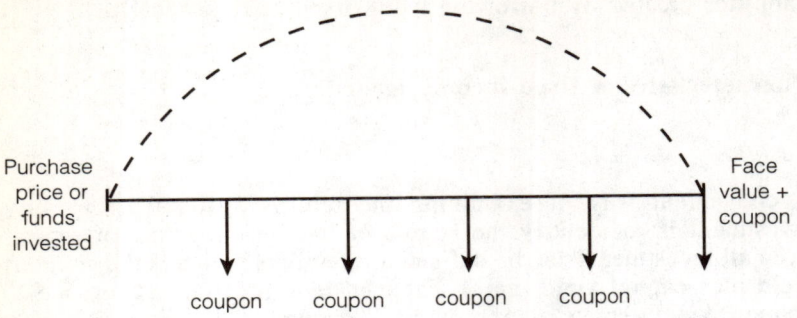

Purchase price or funds invested

Face value + coupon

coupon   coupon   coupon   coupon

a holder would receive $8000 each year, paid in two six-monthly instalments.

Coupon securities are sometimes bought at par but often at a discount or premium. With a discount, the purchase price is lower than face value, enabling greater earnings to accrue for the investor who holds to maturity. Securities which trade at a premium offer a market yield which is lower than the fixed-income payment represented by the coupon, and sell for an amount greater than face value.

Table 7.3 illustrates the gain or loss from a one-basis point movement in yield if $1 million were invested in bonds of different maturities. It shows that the cost of wrongly picking the direction of interest rates is higher the longer the maturity of the bond (as illustrated by looking down the columns) because longer bonds have a greater modified duration, that is, the value of the bonds is more sensitive to changes in yield. Also, the loss is larger if yields are lower, as the modified duration of a bond declines as yields increase (illustrated in the rows of the table).

Variations of the basic types of bonds have been introduced, such as the *deep-discount* and *zero-coupon* bonds. Deep discounts are rarely used now; zero-coupon bonds are mostly issued in private placements and are useful in structuring deals. A deep-discount bond is sold at a large discount from face value and therefore offers a low return through the coupon but substantial capital gain when the bond matures and the holder receives face value. A zero-coupon bond—an extreme version of the deep-discount bond—was designed to provide no income during the life of the bond but a gain when the bond matures. Changes in December 1984 to the tax treatment of securities such as zeros were intended to reduce the after-tax benefits of these bonds and other deferred-interest securities. Broadly, the effect has been to tax the income accruing to the investor from these securities each year, instead of allowing the

Table 7.3 Gain or loss from a one-basis point movement in yields

Aust. c'wth govt security (maturity)	yield @ May 98 (%)	$A per point per $ million @ May 98	Yields 3 percentage points higher than in May 98	Yields 6 percentage points higher than in May 98
July 1999	4.82	120	115	109
July 2000	5.04	225	209	194
Nov 2001	5.20	358	321	288
Aug 2003	5.41	503	431	370
Feb 2006	5.65	723	584	474
Aug 2008	5.80	877	669	514

income to accumulate for tax purposes until maturity or until the security is sold.

Another type of bond is the *inflation-indexed* bond. The commonwealth government first issued such bonds in July 1985 and the market remains dominated by federal government issues. Treasury indexed bonds (TIBs) were initially available in two types: the more common capital-indexed, where the capital value is indexed to the inflation rate, and interest-indexed, where the interest payments are indexed to inflation and the capital or face value is constant. The commonwealth government suspended the issue of these securities in February 1988 and recommenced issuing only capital-indexed bonds in February 1993. The capital value of indexed bonds is adjusted quarterly by a factor based on the consumer price index published by the Australian Bureau of Statistics. The bonds carry a 4 per cent coupon with quarterly interest payments of 1 per cent of the current capital value. The securities trade in terms of real yield and guarantee that real return notwithstanding changes in the level of inflation.

Treasury adjustable-rate bonds (TABs), first issued in November 1994, are like a long-term government floating-rate note as they carry an adjustable or floating-rate coupon which is reset every 90 days at a margin below BBSW (bank-bill reference rate) with the margin determined when the bond is first issued.

Influences on securities

Key influences on yields on securities are credit risk, liquidity and maturity. Securities are generally ranked according to the creditworthiness of the issuer, market or price risk associated with the investment and its maturity.

Credit risk: The commonwealth is the biggest and least risky borrower and for these reasons it is a benchmark from which other issues are priced. Under normal conditions, an investor putting money into, say, corporate bonds could expect a higher return than would be achieved by investing in government securities because the corporate issuer has a higher risk of default than the commonwealth. The margin above commonwealth reflects the creditworthiness of the borrower, although well-timed issues might be able to take advantage of favourable market conditions to shave the margin.

Liquidity: The more liquid a security, the lower the yield tends to be because yields are less likely to move against an investor selling the security. Higher yields are required for investors to hold illiquid stock, to compensate for the prospect of adverse yield movements on the sale of the security. This factor is also evident in adjacent stocks along the yield curve when lines of stock with large issues can track at ten or so basis points below a security of similar maturity with a small issue.

Maturity/time value of money: significant differences can develop in the market between different maturities of the same security. This relates to the time value of money which means that investors normally require a higher return on funds placed for longer terms. The broad categories of maturities are short-term (up to two years); medium-term (two to five years); and longer-term (beyond five years). The increased use of swaps, though, has reduced much of the significance for borrowers and lenders when deciding whether to go long or short-term because funds can be borrowed or lent for a short period and then interest flows swapped for long and *vice versa*.

More generally, supply and demand can alter the margin between commonwealth and private-sector securities. For example, for much of the 1980s the federal government was a big borrower, so that government borrowings were said to be 'crowding out' private-sector borrowers, and the large supply of government bonds reduced the traditional margin between these securities and state government paper. In the ensuing rundown phase of government bonds the margin between commonwealth and semi-government securities waxed and waned, with semis becoming increasingly traded and corporate bonds bought and held for a higher running yield.

Monetary policy has an effect on the yield curve. Normally lending overnight (shortest maturity) should be at a lower interest rate than that applying to a ten-year bond because of the time value of money and market risk that bond yields might change. The Reserve Bank determines the cash rate, the instrument of monetary policy, through its market operations (see chapter 4). When policy is tightened, it is possible that the cash rate will move above bond yields (as occurred in the mid-and-late 1980s). In that case the yield curve is inverse, negative or downward sloping. This configuration reflects expectations that the high level of short-term interest rates will prove temporary and will, on average, be below the bond yields on the yield curve over the relevant period (see illustration of yield curves in chapter 10, figure 10.1).

Major sectors of the Australian fixed-income market

Commonwealth government bonds

Governments issue bonds, sometimes in the past referred to as *loan stock*, in return for cash which is used for current or capital expenditures. Governments all over the world, for centuries, have sold bonds to the public as a means of borrowing, to finance wars or just balance their budgets.

Investors who buy the bonds are in effect lending their money to the government, for a fixed period and at a fixed rate of interest. The government bond rate is regarded as a barometer of the level of Australia's interest rates—although if bonds decline significantly in supply this role can be assumed by other issuers such as, say, state-government or prime corporate and bank borrowers. The government is regarded as the prime borrower in any industrialised country, and therefore it is able to borrow at the cheapest rates. The ability of the government to repay its obligations is secured against its unquestioned capacity to raise funds through taxation revenue. Because of this, government bonds are said to be 'risk-free', in the sense of being free of credit risk—although traders in bonds still face market risk in that they can lose money if interest rates rise and a trader has a 'long' (bought) position and is forced to sell. But the repayment of the face value of the bond is never in doubt.

The most active secondary market trading in bonds was traditionally in the shorter stocks, although over the years increasing Japanese interest boosted activity in ten-year bonds. The secondary-market activity led to a decision in 1984 to introduce bond futures contracts on the Sydney Futures Exchange, to provide a method of hedging the interest-rate risk associated with trading government bonds. Bond futures trading adds depth to the physical bond market and much of the price discovery in the bond market takes place in the futures market where prices are more transparent and transaction costs lower. Further, the exchange-for-physical facility provides a bridge between physical and futures markets by enabling bonds to be exchanged for futures contracts at a margin or spread so that a futures position can be exchanged for a physical (or *vice versa*) without incurring interest-rate risk. EFP also helps visibility of prices, as the brokers' screens show the margin at which physical bonds trade to bond futures. To further encourage secondary-market trading in bonds a group of specialist market-makers in government securities, the reporting bond dealers, was created in December 1984. The list was periodically reviewed according to activity in the bond market. Further developments in the bond market, however, specifically the launch of the Reserve Bank Information and Transfer System (RITS), resulted in the concept of reporting bond dealers being abandoned and the RBA dealing in bonds with any member of RITS.

Bond-market trading, like money-market activity, takes place mostly over the telephone and through a handful of fixed-income brokers. The Reserve Bank has had an important role in the bond market, through its daily liquidity operations and its role as agent for federal treasury in issuing securities. Bonds are traded in the market in a similar way to discount securities such as bills of exchange and promissory notes. Until the early 1980s the bond market in Australia consisted mostly of a captive market—banks and authorised money-market dealers (disbanded in 1996), which had to buy bonds for ratio purposes, and life offices and pension funds which were granted tax concessions in return for holding 30 per cent of their assets in public securities, a requirement that was removed in September 1984. The bond market drew much of its support from these captive buyers. The secondary market in bonds increased in depth and liquidity during the 1980s, partly because of the tender (auction) system and partly because institutions which hold bonds developed a more active approach to managing a bond portfolio. Secondary-market bond rates became an important indicator for the primary (new issue) market rates.

Turnover has increased in the Australian bond market largely because of the increase in the amount of stock on issue, the growth in repo activity (see chapter 9) and futures trading. The increase in overseas interest, the tender system and abolition of captive markets for stock also provided a major boost to secondary market activity. Further, the disbanding of the authorised dealers, with whom the Reserve Bank had carried out its open market operations exclusively, broadened the range of counterparties with which the central bank deals. And the introduction of RITS has enabled a low-cost, efficient and electronic transfer of ownership of bonds. Bond-market turnover is concentrated among banks, investment banks and nominee companies. Investment banks are not big holders of government bonds, rather they are inclined to buy in tenders to redistribute stock.

Bonds in bearer form have not been issued since 1984; this blocked the opportunity to avoid paying tax on interest received by not registering as a bond-holder. The holder of a bearer bond (or any other bearer security) owns it and receives its face value when the security matures. There is no record of ownership, and consequently losing a bearer security is like losing a bundle of banknotes. With inscribed stock, ownership of securities issued is recorded in a registry and the owner receives a certificate detailing the securities held on his or her behalf. This certificate is not transferable; transfer is effected using a transfer and acceptance form (T&A) or, more commonly, through Austraclear (see chapter 16) or RITS.

Selling commonwealth bonds

The amount of commonwealth bonds to be sold each financial year (through the Reserve Bank, as agent for the federal government), is announced by the treasurer in the annual budget and reflects the commonwealth government's financing requirements. The debt issued in 1997/98 was around $6.5-$7.5 billion of which $5-$6 billion was in conventional fixed-coupon commonwealth bonds, inflation-indexed bonds of between $500 million and $1 billion and TABs of $1 billion.

The tenders through which new issues of commonwealth bonds are sold (primary issues) are generally spaced at intervals through the year to allow smooth take-up of the stock. Tenders are held every four to six weeks, with inflation-indexed bonds offered every six to eight weeks. The amount on offer is announced on Monday at 12 noon, with bids to be lodged by 12.45 pm on the following day and results announced by 2 pm that day. This contrasts with the first bond tender held in August 1982, when results were announced 29 hours later. Bonds are settled on the Thursday after the tender. Electronic bidding was introduced in October 1993 and since August 1995 all tender bids must be submitted electronically through RITS, with any member of RITS eligible to bid. RITS members number about 150 and an average of perhaps fifteen bid in each tender. Those bidding in the tenders are seeking stock either for their own purposes or for clients. In the latter context, there may be an element of speculation as to how much will be demanded. New issues of bonds are chiefly bought by investment banks, often on behalf of super funds, insurance companies and overseas clients, which gives them a key pivotal role in the distribution of bonds. This contrasts with earlier times when banks dominated in bond tenders; their declining role reflects changes in regulations which curtailed their demand for bonds. Investment banks' increased take-up of bonds also partly reflects their absorption of authorised dealers which were active bidders in the bond tenders until they ceased operating in mid-1996.

Table 7.4 shows that holdings of commonwealth bonds by banks

Table 7.4 Holders of commonwealth government bonds (% of total)

	1986	1997
Reserve Bank	19	20
Banks	28	17
Authorised dealers	3	0
Life offices	6	7
Other financial institutions	17	16
Other public authorities	1	1
Other	26	39

Source: Reserve Bank of Australia *Bulletin* table E3

have fallen considerably since the banks' prime assets ratio, requiring them to hold a proportion of their assets in commonwealth (and, from June 1997, state) government paper, was reduced from 12 to 3 per cent. The Reserve Bank announced in April 1998 that PAR would be phased out for banks with acceptable internal systems for managing liquidity risk. A big increase in bond-holders is in the category of 'other' which chiefly reflects holdings by nominee companies on behalf of foreign investors and superannuation funds. Overall, the proportion of bonds held by foreigners increased significantly over the decade to 1997 to account for about 40 per cent of commonwealth bonds on issue, excluding official holdings.

The approach of the Reserve Bank and treasury is to keep the market well informed and avoid surprises. To this end, shortly after the annual budget is brought down, treasury announces how it intends to finance the budget deficit and informs the market of its borrowing plans in conventional, indexed and adjustable-rate bonds, its plans for the repurchase of stock and its strategy for holding debt on issue close to the benchmark.

The role of the Reserve Bank

The Reserve Bank participates in the longer end of the bond market to adjust its portfolio or undertake transactions to achieve the commonwealth government's objectives in debt management. On rare occasions, the RBA has operated in the market to restore orderly conditions. In the past, the central bank undertook transactions in the bond market as the counterpart to (or to sterilise) its foreign-exchange intervention (see chapter 12). But, in the late 1990s, these transactions are usually sterilised by offsetting foreign-exchange swaps or repos. The RBA's daily liquidity management operations, which are concentrated in repurchase agreements, provide considerable liquidity to the bond market. The RBA also provides a stock-lending facility.

State government securities

With the borrowing powers of the states liberalised, their borrowing programs became larger, reflecting less fragmentation in fundraisings and a consolidation of borrowings handled by each state's central authority. A combination of progress in privatising previously government-funded projects and increasing attention to fiscal rectitude has shifted activity from simply raising funds to managing state finances as efficiently as possible.

State governments led the way in consolidating debt when, in the early-to-mid-1980s, they began to establish centralised borrowing authorities which successfully increased liquidity in state government securities and reduced borrowing costs. These entities are increasingly referred to as centralised financing authorities (CFAs), to reflect their wider role, and colloquially in the markets they are still often known as semi-government authorities or 'semis'. By the early 1990s turnover in state government bonds exceeded that of commonwealth government securities. Since then, however, turnover in commonwealth paper has risen while that of state securities has fallen, reflecting a decline in the level of state government borrowings and in part associated with the progressive corporatisation of state electricity, transport and port authorities and privatisation programs. Average daily turnover in state government securities in the late 1990s was about half that of commonwealth paper.

A further dampening influence on turnover has been the convergence of credit spreads among state government authorities which has curtailed fund managers' activity in switching from one state's paper to another to achieve a higher yield. State paper in general received a fillip in June 1997 when the Reserve Bank announced that state government paper would be included in the banks' prime assets requirement (replaced in April 1998 with new guidelines on bank liquidity management), that the central bank would undertake intraday repurchase agreements (see chapter 9) using state as well as commonwealth paper and that the credit-risk weighting of short-term state paper was reduced to zero in line with commonwealth government bonds. As with the commonwealth government, fiscal responsibility and increasing privatisation equates to a reduced volume of debt and a reduction in turnover of securities, with a corresponding increase in the appetite for mortgage-backed securities and corporate bonds.

The trend in government thinking is that debt is bad and that government businesses should be sold into private hands to pay down debt. A succession of privatisations of previously government-owned entities has resulted. In particular, the sale of energy utilities has become a high-profile, worldwide trend. As an editorial in *The Economist* commented in March 1998: 'Electricity used to be so important that governments had to control its production and distribution; today it is so important that governments should be kept as far away as possible.'

Centralised financing authorities (CFAs)

Until the 1970s state government enterprises (such as water and electricity boards) raised most of the funds they needed directly from captive institutions such as savings banks and life offices. Greater demand by these borrowers during the 1970s led to their tapping the household market as well as institutions. The size of the borrowings, and the offer of securities to a wider market, entailed greater structuring and marketing and, from 1976 to the early 1980s, the common pattern was to have loans underwritten and marketed by syndicates of brokers, merchant banks and banks. The state borrowers faced increasing competition from some commonwealth enterprises—for example, Telecom, forerunner of Telstra—which from the mid-1970s began to lose their funding from the commonwealth budget.

Until the early 1980s public-authority borrowing programs were very much under the wing of the Loan Council, a body established under the Financial Agreement of 1927 to coordinate commonwealth and state government borrowings, especially their overseas fundraisings. The Loan Council, comprising the prime minister (the federal treasurer usually attends in his place) and the six state premiers, meets formally once a year, in May/June. However, its powers have been progressively and significantly watered down, enabling the states to set their own borrowing terms and conditions and to overhaul the marketing of their stock, a process that culminated in the establishment of the centralised borrowing authorities which took over the borrowing programs of the various state entities.

Semi-government and local-government authorities traditionally borrow funds to finance capital works such as railways, electricity, gas and water supplies and to provide community services such as schools. The states' methods for raising money were refined several times during the 1970s and 1980s, reflecting a combination of changing demands for funds, increasingly larger sums borrowed and a more efficient, professional approach to borrowing reflecting a growing emphasis on public-sector financial accountability.

In the 1990s, in line with generally falling PSBR (public-sector borrowing requirements), the centralised financing authorities—New South Wales Treasury Corporation (NSW TCorp), Queensland Treasury Corporation (QTC), Treasury Corporation Victoria (TCV),

South Australian Government Financing Authority (SAFA), Western Australian Treasury Corporation and Tasmania's TasCorp—have expanded their roles to embrace debt management and financial management for client (state) authorities. Debt management entails moving debt around, restructuring the liabilities according to demand and consolidating them into homogeneous lines of borrowings that can be repurchased at any time. All major semis have significantly streamlined their debt into homogeneous parcels, which has correspondingly increased its marketability. Debt management added a new dimension to the behaviour of the issuers and singled them out from other fund-raisers. To manage debt effectively, the manager must have ready access to an active secondary market so as to be able to change the maturity mix of the portfolio of the debt. The state-government issuers, therefore, actively participate in a secondary market to issue, manage and remove inefficiencies in ways that improve the yields (interest rates) on their stock.

The first centralised authority to begin operating, New South Wales Treasury Corporation (NSW TCorp), was formed in 1983. As the trend spread throughout the states, the process of having loans underwritten was abandoned, and the CFAs placed less emphasis on public issues, turning back to the wholesale market for their funds. Marshalling the semis and smaller authorities under one borrowing entity enabled the one borrower to approach the market on their behalf. If CFAs had not been introduced it is likely that Australian fixed-income markets would be far less sophisticated; the CFA structure enables more efficient operation and concentration of expertise. This has greatly helped the development of skills in debt management. CFAs also provide centralised cash-management facilities to authorities.

The most significant effect of the introduction of the CFAs was the consolidation of debt into a few large lines with a common maturity and coupon, which introduced an unprecedented element of liquidity to the market. Another change with almost equal impact was the move, in 1986, to allow the semis the flexibility to refinance debt before it matured. This was a prerequisite for active debt management because it allowed the authorities to change the average maturity of debt.

The CFAs are run as commercial enterprises, undertaking interest-rate risk management and investment as well as lending to state authorities. Profits may be generated by dealing and risk management and other activities such as stock-lending, where a holder or issuer of securities lends them on a short-term basis, enabling traders to short (sell stock they do not yet have) and still be sure of delivering.

While the model varies from state to state, the CFAs perform functions similar to those of a corporate treasurer; essentially, their mandate is to meet a target level of profitability from fundraising, risk management, debt and asset management and offering financial services to clients including advice and structural finance. For example, NSW TCorp works with electricity utilities on debt management and with other state-owned enterprises on specific risk-management projects, such as the Eastern Distributor road system (with the Roads and Traffic Authority) and the Olympic Stadium (with the Olympic Coordination Authority). TCorp's treasury division in 1996/97 managed ten clients' liabilities portfolios and provided advice to a further five. TCorp works with clients which do not have treasury expertise, in effect taking the role of investment banker to the state government and its activities such as electricity generation and rail transport. TCV, operating since January 1993, functions on the lines of a financial institution, providing all borrowing required by Victoria and its public authorities, centrally managing financial risk for the state, providing loans, risk-management products and cash-management facilities for its clients and working with the Department of Treasury and Finance on government financial policies. An overriding influence on TCV's operations is the Victorian government's privatisation program, on which TCV advises, and the ensuing retirement of state debt. Between July 1995 and July 1997 Victoria completed the privatisation of five electricity distribution companies and three electricity generating businesses, netting $17.9 billion which went towards reducing debt. In 1997 PowerNet Victoria, operator of the state's grid, and Southern Hydro, were sold, and the gas section corporatised ahead of privatisation in 1998. Queensland's program of corporatising its public-sector trading enterprises such as electricity, port and rail authorities, has been under way since 1994 and QTC's responsibilities include evaluating and implementing financing arrangements for corporatisation and commercialisation as well as providing funding and financial risk management to client authorities.

CFAs can raise funds in four ways:

- in the institutional market using tenders;
- by private placement in the institutional market;
- tapping overseas markets; or
- in the domestic retail market (a very small proportion).

Sources of funds

State borrowers have diversified their funding base so that they carry a mix of domestic and offshore funding. For example, NSW TCorp's 1996/97 annual report showed that its liabilities were sourced 45 per cent from domestic bonds and 37 per cent from offshore and, within that, 15 per cent in global exchangeable bonds, 14 per cent in euro-MTNs and 8 per cent in other offshore borrowings. All CFAs have achieved a lower cost of funds by diversifying funding sources, especially through tapping the Japanese retail market and the $A eurobond market. TCV's annual report showed that 40 per cent of its liabilities were international and 34 per cent in domestic hot stocks (major lines); reflecting TCV's strategy of retiring debt, it did not undertake international issues in 1996/97; rather, its overseas activities focused on repurchasing its securities in the secondary market. QTC's liabilities in 1996/97 were mostly in domestic $A bonds, global $A bonds and euro-MTNs (of which the bulk were Japanese issues). State government authorities have made increasing use of indexed bonds and floating-rate notes, and have increased their flexibility through the swaps market. They also regularly tap overseas markets, borrowing through euro-$A bond programs, euro-commercial paper, US commercial paper and multi-currency paper. The Japanese retail market was for many years a major source of funds, principally through the issue of dual-currency bonds. The bulk of state government fund-raisings are borrowings from institutions for periods of one to fifteen years. Retail loans are usually raised for one to three years, euro-$A borrowings for three to five years, offshore foreign currency borrowings for between one and twenty years and euronote facilities from one month to one year. Domestic promissory notes also offer short-term fund-raisings with maturities between a few days and six months. Most CFAs have access to the interbank market for 11 am funds and so have the flexibility to cover the whole spectrum of debt-management options.

Funds raised from institutions are mostly in benchmark stocks (big lines) that are easily managed and restructured. Euro-$A funds can be fairly cheap but are not always readily available. Offshore foreign-currency borrowings require hedging and management to be handled properly and, if fully hedged, may not provide cheaper funding than would be available in $A; however, a lower-than-domestic cost can often be created through a swap. Indexed bonds have not proved to be a significant source of funds. For the investor, the income earned on a semi-government security flows from the coupon, which is fixed. Profits can be made by buying at a high yield and selling when interest rates fall—an option for institutions and professional traders, rather than retail investors, because of the volume and narrow buy/sell spreads in the interdealer market.

Supply and demand

Generally there has been a significant margin (or spread) between commonwealth bonds and semis but in the mid-1990s spreads began to converge, both the semi spread to commonwealth bonds and the spread among semis, reflecting a combination of supply-and-demand factors and an easing of the credit concerns that had dominated the early 1990s. In its 1996/97 annual report, NSW TCorp reported its lowest margin over commonwealth bonds since its inception fourteen years earlier.

Two anomalies occurred in the 1980s which resulted in a flood of demand for issues of state government authorities. The first occurred when the Japanese investors discovered the market. Their enthusiasm for stock exceeded supply despite the willingness of issuers to increase their debt. The second period was when the euro-$A era provided cheap (tax-effective) and plentiful funds for prime credits such as semis. At both times the commonwealth was a very large domestic borrower, so the spread narrowed. Both episodes were short-lived and the spreads returned to normal, first when the Japanese investors decided that the securities were not sufficiently liquid and, in the second case, when the tax loophole closed.

The NSW TCorp set about establishing liquidity. It brought in an outside consultant to advise and implement strategy. Within a year turnover had risen from a mere $1 billion to exceed $20 billion a month. The underlying strategy was similar to that which had made commonwealth bonds liquid in the early 1980s. TCorp set about creating an active interdealer market by issuing an open invitation to join its panel. A condition of acceptance was a commitment to make interdealer prices. The move brought a significant number of new players into the market. TCorp also set up a series of arbitrages against other yield curves. These arbitrages could be against the TCorp curve, other semis' curves, swaps, corporate bonds or commonwealth bonds. This process helped dealers become used to dealing in increasingly larger amounts and so considerably boosted turnover. TCorp established itself as the 'benchmark' semi stock, meaning that other stocks were priced at a margin against TCorp. TCorp's status as benchmark does not mean it always raises funds most cheaply; depending on maturities, others such as QTC and TCV have borrowed at margins below TCorp but TCorp retains the status of benchmark as it represents 50 per cent of the turnover in state government paper.

The role of dealer panels

Dealer panels, established in Australia in the 1980s to handle periodic issues of promissory notes, are the conventional method used to distribute and trade issues of euro-commercial paper. The bill market in London also relies on dealer panels for distribution and sales. From the point of view of an issuer, establishing a dealer panel has the advantage of cutting down the number of operators an issuer has to talk to, so there is better use of resources; it is also likely to improve marketability of the paper on offer and ensures the issuer has a group of traders who have an incentive to promote its securities.

The state authorities were keen to promote liquidity and therefore to encourage turnover in their stocks. This is facilitated by having a group which has access to the issuer's stock, to facilities for borrowing stock and to information. In return, the traders make markets in the paper by quoting two-way prices (buy and sell quotes) among themselves and with their clients. The issuer thus has a commitment from a group of dealers that they will market the securities; and the market recognises that certain organisations have been given the status of 'dealer' in particular stocks, and are the first port of call for those wishing to buy the stocks. The issuers are thus comforted by the efficiency of having a panel of dealers or group of market-makers who will bid for an issue of securities, often on short notice. Some issuers pay fees, some do not. Some regard being on their panel as a privilege in return for which the dealers are willing to tender for their stock, make prices and provide continuing liquidity and advice regarding strategy. Issuers continuously monitor the performance of members of their dealer panels.

Closed panel issues can be *closed auctions*, where members of the panel bid competitively against one another for stock, or *bought deals* where each member of the panel agrees to buy a certain quantity of stock at a certain price before the issue is formally announced. Panel members have greater input into the decisions regarding which securities to issue and when. This method is particularly useful when issuing a new stock for which there might be initially low liquidity which could discourage bids. The closed auction system is the more common, although many issuers use a mix of both systems. Panels for bought deals are usually smaller, often including six to eight members compared with twelve to fifteen in a full panel.

State government securities are traded using a mix of telephone dealing and brokers' screens.

8

Private-sector
(non-government)
fixed-income securities

The shrinking government debt market

For many years Australian fixed-income markets were dominated by federal government and state government securities but by the late 1990s a number of influences—market, structural and legislative—were coming together to change that. These factors included fiscal consolidation at federal and state levels and large privatisation programs which led to a contraction in the volume of government paper. For example, Telstra in its former life as Telecom was a major source of government-guaranteed securities. Now, as a partially privatised entity, it issues bonds which considerably boost the pool of non-government paper. In early 1998 Telstra was the largest issuer of fixed-coupon bonds in the Australian corporate bond market and its lines on issue with maturities of 2000 and beyond accounted for 32 per cent of Bankers Trust Investment Bank's corporate bond index.

Also, legislative moves in the superannuation field, specifically the compulsory nature of superannuation contributions (super covers some 92 per cent of the workforce, compared with 40 per cent in 1983), fed the growth of funds under management and left institutional fund managers facing the prospect of a greater volume of funds to manage at a time when their traditional investment outlets were shrinking. A further influence has been the development of the Australian market to the point where it became sophisticated enough to attract global issues when conditions suited the big international issuers of such paper. In addition, capital adequacy changes for banks have been encouraging a transition from syndicated loans to debt securities.

In its May 1998 *Semi-annual Statement on Monetary Policy,* the Reserve Bank of Australia commented that since 1996 non-intermediated debt, being debt raised by companies issuing securities directly to the market, had risen sharply, with annual growth rates rising from less than 2 per cent in 1995 to around 30 per cent in the year to March 1998. The RBA said:

> Since late 1995 the level of non-intermediated debt on issue has almost doubled, having remained broadly unchanged during the first half of the 1990s. The rate of increase of non-intermediated debt over the past two years has outpaced that of lending by inter-mediaries. Non-intermediated debt, however, remains a relatively minor source of funds; currently it amounts to about $38 billion, compared to intermediated credit of about $530 billion.

The components of non-intermediated debt which have shown the largest growth are promissory notes (discussed in chapter 6) and asset-backed bonds (see chapter 11). The market in private-sector, non-government debt discussed in this chapter includes corporate debt—fixed-rate bonds and floating-rate notes (FRNs) and medium-term notes (MTNs)—euro-$A bonds and global bonds.

Non-government debt

Corporate debt market: bonds and notes

Debt issued directly by companies has been rising. The RBA esti-mates that the corporate bond market—FRNs, fixed-rate paper and medium-term notes and not including asset-backed securities—at $12 billion in 1998, compared with $7 billion in 1996. Financial intermediaries, mostly banks, accounted for about 60 per cent of the issues in both years. Corporate debt in the form of bonds and promissory notes began to increase significantly in volume in early 1996. A growing number of companies have turned to raising medium and long-term funds, at fixed and floating rates of interest, through bonds and notes. Their issues added to the existing stock of paper in a market that has, for some years, been dominated by bank and finance-company securities. The increased use of swaps, and facilities such as medium-term and floating-rate note programs, which provide for term funding but with the ability to reset the interest rate periodically, enable borrowers to achieve the preferred funding profile without committing to fixed-rate, term debt.

Before these developments, the appeal of fixed-rate funding rose and fell in line with expectations about movements in interest rates: borrowers were unwilling to commit to term funding when rates were high but expected to fall and, on the other hand, lenders were equally reluctant to lock in a term loan at a low rate if there was some expectation that rates could rise. Funding has become much more flexible, from the standpoints of borrowers and lenders. At various times borrowers were deterred from turning to medium and long-term fixed-rate debt instruments because of competition from commonwealth and state government borrowers, that is, the private sector was 'crowded out'; growth in the euro-$A bond market and swap opportunities muted enthusiasm for domestic corporate fixed-rate term debt instruments. In the late 1980s, however, there was a discernible shift in trends, leading to sizeable growth in issues of non-government securities. The corporate bond market in Australia first developed in the second half of 1988 and was soon dominated by finance company and bank issuers rather than companies. Several banks found the corporate bond and medium-term note market a useful funding medium but it lacked liquidity and consequently investor confidence. The market proved short-lived: growth stalled and then shrank with the credit crisis of the early 1990s, a legacy of the borrowing binge of the previous decade. As a consequence of the borrowing indulgences of the 1980s, the early 1990s saw companies concentrating on reducing, rather than increasing, debt.

Influences at work in the mid-to-late 1990s, though, suggested that the time had come for Australia to develop a fully-fledged, private-sector debt market. While the sector was developing well, it was still shallow compared with corporate bond markets overseas, for example, in the US where private-sector debt, excluding mortgage-backed and asset-backed securities, totalled around $US1400 billion or, depending on the $US/$A exchange rate, around $A2000 billion compared with Australia's $10 billion. Some explanation can be found in history: Australian companies tended to tap the short end of the financial markets rather than commit to long-term borrowings, or they went offshore where interest rates were often lower. With greater interest-rate stability, and a lower level of interest rates generally, more companies have been enticed to issue bonds domestically and the market developed on the back of a necessary combination of investor and issuer appetite.

Growth in the medium-term corporate bond and note market relies on a continued flow of top-name issuers who can provide investors with paper of sufficient credit status, liquidity and marketability. By the late 1990s the negatives of earlier years had been replaced by more positive influences and in 1997 and early 1998 a number of good-name corporates had tapped this market, generally for terms of two to three years, with investors chiefly representing fund managers and duration managers, specialist funds and European banks operating in Australia. Further reinforcing the rising profile of the corporate bond market, the Australian Financial

Markets Association in November 1997 launched a monthly debt issue revaluation service aimed at improving information on pricing in corporate bonds by providing revaluation rates for 29 domestic bond issues on its AFMA*data* pages on Bloomberg screens. This should improve secondary-market liquidity; inadequate transparency had been identified as a factor inhibiting activity in the corporate bond market where many issues tended to be privately placed. SBC Warburg Dillon Read's corporate bond index, available since 1989, was joined in November 1997 by Bankers Trust Investment Bank's intermediate corporate bond index; in January 1998 Bankers Trust launched the broader BT corporate bond index, the non-government bond index and the BT inflation-linked bond index. The announcement later in the year of proposals to widen exemptions from interest withholding tax was greeted as a positive for the sector's development. It was seen as broadening the market for corporate bonds by facilitating greater integration between domestic and offshore issues. A further plus came from the Australian Stock Exchange's moves to extend its CUFS (CHESS Units of Foreign Securities) facility—a form of depository receipt providing a structure that enables investors to buy or trade foreign securities in Australian dollars—to cover debt instruments as well as equities. These initiatives reflect the increasingly important role, against a background of diminishing government debt, for private-sector financial products in Australian financial markets.

Growth in the corporate bond market is also fuelled by changes in the nature of banking and in banks' relationships with their corporate clients, trends which have led to a reduced role for banks in the intermediation process. Both banks and corporate clients have become less interested in the traditional loan. From a corporate standpoint, a substantial long-term loan from a bank was often hard to achieve, while, from the banks' perspective, the thin margins on lending to corporates left the banks struggling to cover the cost of capital and funding required to support the loan at a time when banks could no longer subsidise lower-margin wholesale business through fat margins in retail products—an outcome of the process of deregulation which was initiated in the early 1980s but which took time to filter through the system. Banks have increasingly preferred to 'take' the corporate client to the market, supporting the issue by being ready to provide liquidity and trade the paper in the secondary market—moving more to an investment bank approach, as facilitator rather than provider of funds, and earning a fee along the way. With this method, the bank earns fee income without having to support a loan with expensive capital and the corporate client probably benefits in terms of attractive borrowing costs.

Except for top-name corporates which can tap markets directly in their own name for funds by issuing bonds or medium-term notes, companies need a specialist intermediary, such as an investment bank, as adviser and manager of a bond or note issue, with the investment bank also absorbing much of the risk and ensuring the paper is distributed to investors. Active secondary-market trading is an essential in a healthy market and, with this in mind, a number of corporate bond market players have expressed their commitment as placers of paper with a vested interest in ensuring the corporate bond market develops the liquidity which is essential if it is to continue to flourish.

A first step in a corporate bond issue is to determine the type of issue and its terms and price; this would normally be done by the borrower in conjunction with its adviser/manager who would also ensure that the issue meets all regulatory requirements. Bond issues can be either by way of a public issue or a private placement. Public issues, mostly made by finance companies when they issue debentures, require a prospectus setting out all details of the issue, whereas with a private placement the lead manager undertakes to place the paper, usually through a panel of other intermediaries, with investors. Most issues are fixed, and bought by fixed-income fund managers, some are floating and a few are a mix of fixed and floating. Less well-rated companies issue short-term floating-rate paper which tends to be bought by cash-management trusts and banks.

A typical corporate (or euro-$A bond) issue would start with a borrower appointing a lead manager with whom it discusses details of a proposed issue, such as timing, terms, size, price and fees. The lead manager, after discussion with the borrower, appoints a panel of intermediaries, selected for their distribution strengths, which bid for the paper and then distribute it to investors. The lead manager and borrower prepare documentation for the issue, including an information memorandum for investors and agreements detailing the obligations of panel members. Panel members meanwhile establish which institutional investors might be interested in the paper, and in what volume and at what price. The lead manager also provides information about the borrower and the issue to major credit-rating agencies to secure a credit-rating. A company that is unrated would have to provide a greater volume of information than one which carries a credit-rating from an acknowledged credit-rating agency. Corporate bonds issued in Australia are generally registered securities settled through the Austraclear system.

Investors in corporate and other forms of private-sector debt face a challenge that does not exist with commonwealth government paper—assessing the credit risk. Because a company can fail, or default on its debt, or an event can alter either the industry in which it operates or the market for its paper, the returns from corporate paper are less assured than those from investments in government securities. An obvious illustration of this is the higher rate which investors demand for placing funds in corporate paper as against investing in government bonds. Credit-rating agencies have a significant role in helping investors determine the credit-ranking of corporate investments; from the company's perspective, being rated adds a discipline on management which is keenly aware that a wrong step or a disappointing performance can result in a downgrading which might deter investors and inevitably leads to an increase in borrowing costs. Even though a borrower is rated, investors are not absolved from undertaking their own research, or a borrowing company from providing information about its activities to potential investors. However, a credit-rating is a useful guide for investors.

Floating-rate and medium-term notes

Floating-rate notes (FRNs) and medium-term notes (MTNs) are usually considered part of the corporate bond market, that is, long-term non-government debt. Floating-rate notes are like a corporate bond but with an interest rate that floats at a margin over BBSW (bank-bill reference rate) rather than a fixed coupon and, while the notes are usually issued under a term facility, the interest rate is reset every three or six months. An MTN can be fixed or floating; under MTN programs, notes can be issued over a specified time, up to a stipulated maximum amount and with the choice of maturity made as funds are drawn down and notes issued. FRNs increased in popularity in the early 1990s and by late in the decade Australia had a growing domestic FRN market (especially so on the back of growth in issues of mortgage-backed paper, see chapter 11). Most regional banks and building societies have made use of the FRN and MTN market as well as a number of high-profile corporates such as Australia Post, Coles Myer, Ford Credit, GMAC, Southcorp and Woolworths. Investor enthusiasm for the paper, initially chiefly from banks but gradually from a wider group, helped bring more issuers to the market. Floating-rate notes have been used extensively overseas as a popular source of medium-term funding. In Australia state-government authorities have made extensive use of floating-rate notes since the mid-1980s, issuing the notes to borrow for periods of around one year and longer. Banks have also used FRNs, sometimes called floating-rate certificates of deposit (FRCDs), which have been issued mostly by regional banks.

Euro-$A bonds

Euro in its earlier usage indicated a security that was issued outside of its country of origin so that, say, euro-$A bonds could be issued in London, Hong Kong, New York, Tokyo or any other centres; the prefix *euro* did not indicate Europe, although that is where the euromarkets began and where the bulk of the issues were sold. The term *euro* has an interesting history. The markets for eurocredits, eurocurrencies and eurobonds began in the 1950s—partly, so the story goes, as a reaction to the cold war between the US and the then Soviet Union. This left the Soviet Union anxious about holding dollars in the US and so it placed them with European banks, which lent them to customers. At the same time, US banks were operating under restrictions which led to their holding $US balances in Europe, particularly London, which developed as the first euromarket centre. Euromarket activity received a further boost in the 1970s as oil-rich Arabs recycled petro-dollars. In the late 1990s, with the development of the 'euro' as a common European currency, *euro* has come to indicate Europe.

A euro-$A bond is denominated in Australian dollars, issued outside Australia and marketed internationally to non-Australian investors. The bond has been particularly attractive to private individual investors and, reflecting this, most issues have been for around $A100–200 million and sold in small parcels. Issues of euro-$A bonds have been made by a range of entities including government, major and second-tier banks, highly-rated corporates and supranational borrowers. However, as the bulk of the investors are retail, they tend to be more comfortable with top names such as commonwealth or state-government borrowers or other easily recognisable identities.

Euro-$A bonds were first issued in sizeable volume in the early 1980s. The market grew rapidly in the mid-1980s when high Australian interest rates and the spread of swaps gave it a significant boost. With Australian interest rates high at a time when rates overseas were falling, investors in the US and Europe were prepared to wear a currency risk to invest in securities that offered coupons as much as 8 per cent higher than was available in their own markets. Australian companies had for years been discouraged by high interest rates from borrowing domestically, so that the domestic term-debt market had shrunk. With foreign investment rules substantially relaxed and exchange controls removed in 1983, borrowing overseas was a very attractive alternative.

The bulk of euro-$A bonds were 'swap-driven', that is, issued solely to be swapped to give the borrower a different interest-rate and/or currency structure, but by the late 1990s real demand for an $A security had developed worldwide. Euro-$A bonds have been bought largely by 'retail' investors in Europe—the ubiquitous 'Belgian dentist'—but also by those from Japan and South-East Asia, and so were sold in fairly small parcels that were bought and held, rather than traded. Several European countries have developed efficient retail distribution systems for euro-$As through their local branch networks. The bonds' status as bearer securities has added to their appeal, enabling anonymity on the part of investors. Institutional interest has been apparent from time to time, particularly from fund managers and hedge funds, which generally prefer the larger, more liquid lines from sovereign and supranational issuers. Since around the middle of 1994, however, issues of euro-$A bonds increased, including at one stage a subset known as *dual-currency bonds* which had cashflows in more than one currency, most commonly the $A and yen. With one form of dual-currency bond the borrower received yen when issuing the bond but $A when the bond was redeemed. During the life of the bond its coupon stream could be denominated in either $A or yen. With a second type of dual-currency bond, also known as a 'reverse dual-currency bond', the principal payment was denominated in yen and coupons in $A.

A substantial proportion of euro-$A bonds have been issued by non-Australian borrowers and, among Australian borrowers, many issues have been made by state-government authorities and banks. Eurobonds do not offer the liquidity available in the larger lines of commonwealth and state-government securities but this is not an issue for retail investors seeking an attractive yield.

The bonds are popular with borrowers because they enable them to tap a wide range of investors. But the market is open only to high-quality, well-known names and the minimum volume of an issue is usually around $30 million. Generally, borrowers have a program running, such as a medium-term note program, where they can issue paper when it suits, with a panel of investment banks appointed which sell the notes when market conditions are favourable and/or when it suits the borrowers. A primary issue is usually open for between three and six weeks, at the end of which the borrower is paid and the securities start to trade in the secondary market with lead managers expected to make two-way markets. After an initial six months of trading, most eurobonds are bedded down with investors. Euro-$A bonds are usually listed on a European stock exchange, often London or Luxembourg, although they are not actively traded on those exchanges which essentially maintain accounting records. The bonds are cleared by CEDEL and Euroclear which also have systems enabling eurobonds to be 'borrowed', that is, lent to investors who are 'short' of certain securities, a feature that adds to market liquidity.

Australian borrowers also issue foreign-currency bonds in the country of the chosen currency, subject to that country's regulations, for example, Yankee bonds (denominated in $US and issued in the

US) and Samurais (yen-denominated bonds issued in Japan by a foreign borrower).

$A global bonds

These are widely distributed bonds which can be sold either in Australia or an overseas market, free of withholding tax, which have attracted foreign sovereign and supranational issuers and have been popular with institutional investors. The first $A global bond was issued in October 1991 by the European Investment Bank (EIB) which raised $A400 million in ten-year bonds, securities that at the time were tagged 'Matildas'.

A handful of other foreign borrowers have made subsequent issues but outstandings in these securities are still quite small. During 1997 the $A global bond market was enlivened by three issues by the Federal National Mortgage Association (Fannie Mae), the giant US mortgage arranger. Writing in *The Australian Financial Review* in September 1997, Bankers Trust head of debt markets research Paul Bide commented that the transaction was 'swap-driven':

> Global issuers are motivated to borrow in any market by the level of swap spreads (the spread between the risk-free government curve and the swap). The wider the swap spread, the greater the chance that the issuer can achieve better funding in that market compared with others, and the better the overall funding the swap-debt package delivers when swapped back to the issuer's domestic currency. In this case, the combination of the Australian bond/swap level and the demand for the underlying securities in the Australian-dollar denominated bond market delivered the cheapest funding opportunity to Fannie Mae . . . [which] found a swap market that worked, and a bond market that wanted its bonds.

Another type of $A bond which appeared briefly was the *Kangaroo* bond, which saw minimal local trading and was largely issued by private placement. Three issues were made, by Korea Development Bank, Korea Long Term Credit Bank and Korea Exchange Bank, in 1996 and 1997. In the wake of the Asian financial markets debacle during 1997, KDB and KEB were downgraded below investment grade and the concept was buried by the malaise pervading the Asian region.

Inflation-indexed bonds

These tend to be dominated by commonwealth and state issues but the Australian market is seeing a small but growing pool of corporate and asset-backed indexed bonds. Inflation-indexed bonds are complex but are gaining a higher profile as a number of intermediaries identified growing retail demand. Typically investors in inflation-indexed bonds have been the major superannuation funds and insurance companies, which use the bonds as a hedge against the inflation-linked products they sell. However, there is also appetite among the do-it-yourself (DIY) super funds. Overall, the low-inflation environment of the 1990s has not fostered roaring interest in inflation-linked products.

According to BZW's *Guide to Index Linked Securities* (second edition), securities that compensate the holder for changes in inflation were first issued some 250 years ago. Australia's first issue of a bond with a capital value indexed to the consumer price index (CPI) was in 1983, by the State Electricity Commission of Victoria. Similar securities had already been issued in several European countries. Until 1987 the Australian market in inflation-linked securities was mostly the preserve of the commonwealth government but since then a number of state-government authorities have entered this market and inflation-linked bonds have been issued in connection with some major privatisations involving tollways and hospitals.

The bonds can be either *capital-indexed* or *interest-indexed*. With capital-indexed bonds, the original capital amount (face value) is adjusted in line with the CPI, usually quarterly. If inflation were 5 per cent in the year following an issue of a \$10 000 bond, then the capital in year two would be \$10 500. In year three, if inflation were 4 per cent, the capital value would increase to \$10 920. The security also carries a fixed-rate coupon, usually of 4 per cent, which is paid on the current face value so that the coupon interest rises with inflation, that is, both income and principal are indexed, thus maintaining real value. Coupon interest is the only cashflow during the life of the bond. As with a conventional bond, the investor receives full face value of the investment when it matures. These securities suit investors who want to receive capital later, in the meantime receiving regular cashflow through the quarterly payments of interest. An investor, however, should take tax implications into account. With interest-indexed bonds, the interest (coupon) component is indexed for inflation but the capital or face value remains unchanged. These appeal to retail investors. The commonwealth government stopped issuing interest-indexed bonds in February 1988.

Whether or not inflation-linked securities appeal to an investor depends largely on his or her expectations about inflation. Promoters of inflation-linked bonds emphasise that they carry a government guarantee and offer protection of capital against inflation. Retail investors can buy capital-indexed bonds through a stockbroker or from the Reserve Bank.

Infrastructure bonds

These bonds, a tax-driven rather than capital-markets product, were conceived in February 1992 as a method of boosting investment in Australian infrastructure (major projects such as tollways, railways, hospitals and proposed privatisation of electricity and gas industries and of airports). The first issue of infrastructure bonds was made in February 1993, with the complex structure aimed at attracting top taxpayers. The volume of issues made, as well as those in the pipeline, raised federal government concerns and in February 1997 it removed the tax concessions on coupon payments of new infrastructure bonds. However, existing bonds remained exempt from tax and are lightly traded. Given the major infrastructure program confronting Australia, infrastructure finance remains a significant area and heavy user of financial instruments, in turn offering investment opportunities for the major asset managers. In recognition of this, Macquarie Bank established the Infrastructure Trust of Australia Group as a listed investment vehicle with a mandate to invest in a range of infrastructure projects. The ITA group already held involvements in four tollway projects when it was listed in December 1996 as Australia's first infrastructure investment fund.

Debentures

Debentures are an early form of the corporate bond, issued at face value for a fixed term, usually one to five years, and carrying a coupon. They are issued mostly by financiers and industrial companies. Offers can be made to the general public through a prospectus, or in the form of a private 'family' issue to existing share and debenture-holders. Debenture-holders' funds are lent to the borrowing company under the terms of a trust deed which sets out the fixed or floating charge over the assets of the company. Debenture-holders rank ahead of preference and ordinary shareholders in their claims on the borrowing company's assets and repayment of principal and interest should the company be wound up.

Finance companies are continuous borrowers. An exception to the finance companies' constant presence in the market as borrowers was in the 1982–83 recession, when demand for funds collapsed. The finance companies had no need to raise new funds for several months until economic activity revived.

The prospectus issued by a finance company details the interest rates available, the amount to be borrowed and the amount of oversubscriptions that can be accepted. Finance companies generally borrow for periods ranging between one month and five years. The interest paid on the borrowed funds is fixed and is usually paid to investors at six-monthly or quarterly intervals. The interest earned on a debenture is expressed as a fixed rate per annum, similar to the coupon attached to a commonwealth bond or a semi-government security. An investment of $50 000 in three-year debentures at 6 per cent would earn 6 per cent per annum on the full face-value amount of $50 000 for the three-year life of the debenture. When the debenture matures, the holder receives the face value, $50 000, plus the final interest payment. Various types of debentures are available, offering compound interest and cumulative interest payments. Finance company prospectuses are available through stockbrokers, from the companies direct, or, in the case of bank-affiliated finance companies, through the branches of their banking parents.

The range of investments on offer to the public, and the increased ability of finance and industrial companies to borrow using more flexible instruments, domestically and overseas, have cut into the popularity of debentures. Finance and industrial companies also issue unsecured notes, which offer a higher rate than debentures (and trade as corporate bonds).

High-yield bonds

A market in high-yield bonds has not yet developed in Australia but is enormous in the US where issues totalled around $US60 billion, or more than $A100 billion, in early 1998. Such bonds earn attractive interest rates for the holder in return for a greater-than-average credit-risk on the investment. The bonds could prove worthless if the issuing (borrowing) company cannot pay out when the bonds mature. The so-called junk bonds were pioneered in the US by the Wall Street investment bank Drexel Burnham Lambert, and were the brainchild of its chief bond salesman, Michael Milken. By the end of the 1980s both Drexel and Milken had fallen from grace. The bonds were issued to raise funds for companies which were rated less than BBB and so were known as sub-investment-grade securities (bonds issued by companies rated higher than BBB are 'investment grade'). Yields on junk bonds were around 5 per cent higher than those on investment-grade securities. Australian investors and fund managers have not been as keen as their US counterparts to chase the extra earnings achievable from junk bonds. A mere handful of Australian companies have issued junk bonds but these have relied on foreign, rather than domestic, investors.

9

Repurchase agreements

Repurchase agreements (repos) are a subset of the fixed-income market, although in themselves are a short-end instrument. They are used both as an instrument for managing liquidity and as a fixed-income trading tool. Repos involve the sale of a security, usually a commonwealth government or state-government bond, with a simultaneous agreement to reverse the transaction at an agreed price on an agreed date. Most banks and investment banks using repos run them in conjunction with their fixed-income desk, although in many cases also with a dotted line to the short-dated securities end of the trading desk because repos are generally written for fairly short periods. The introduction of real-time gross settlement in 1998 (see chapter 4) sparked growth in the volume of intraday repos to balance liquidity. Repos are used:

- as a means of funding bond portfolios (cash repo) where a dealer who has bought bonds then uses them to raise cash by selling the bonds under repurchase agreements. Funding this way is regarded by lenders as more secure than an outright loan, because the lender has a claim on the bonds in the event of default, so the interest rate is usually less than it would be on an outright loan. In this way, repurchase agreements provide a cost-effective form of funding for bond-dealers. The Reserve Bank is a big operator in cash repos, providing liquidity to holders of bonds;

- by bond-dealers to borrow and lend bonds as a way of bridging gaps in their bond portfolios; these transactions can be structured either as a cash repo or as a bond-for-bond switch;

- to cover a short-term liquidity requirement and avoid the need to sell bonds outright, which might involve a capital loss; and
- by someone with a temporary cash surplus which can be invested in a repo.

A repo—also known as a buy-back, sell-back and reciprocal purchase agreement—is similar to a short-term loan secured against commonwealth government bonds or other types of securities (in theory a repo can be based on whatever security is agreed by the parties). A repo gives the holder title to the security; it is not a secured loan. Repos can be 'open-ended', that is, on demand, or overnight or for a fixed term. Generally, repos are arranged for periods ranging between one day and three months, with most having maturities of two months or less and some 80 per cent transacted 'daily but open-ended', that is, 24 hours' notice has to be given to close or unwind the repo. The underlying security to a repo is traded at its market price; the repo is traded at an agreed cash-related rate. Repos have carved themselves an important position, however, to the point where a professional bond-trader shorting a large parcel of bonds would first look at the borrowing cost of a particular maturity. A bond is referred to as being 'on special' when there is strong demand for that particular maturity. In this case, the repo cash-lending rate can become quite low, that is, the borrower of the 'special' stock receives a substantially below-market rate for cash held by the lender. In extreme cases this rate of interest can be close to zero.

A repo is created by two parties agreeing to enter two transactions simultaneously. Bank X agrees to sell bonds to Company Y, at a price for settlement now, or the next day, and Y agrees to sell the bonds back to X at a price agreed now but for settlement at a future date, say, three months hence. The difference in price is the overnight cash rate for the number of days involved. At its simplest, a repo comprises a spot sale and a forward purchase by one party, and a short-term loan, secured by bonds, for a stated amount, by the other. At the specified future date when the repo is unwound, X buys back the bonds and Y gets repaid.

The explosion in options trading and derivatives in general in the mid-to-late 1990s helped fuel an upsurge in activity in repos because these activities increase the need for hedging positions in physical bonds. Repos play a role in providing major derivatives traders with an avenue for funding when they are long physical stock (that is, they are holding bonds) and with a way of gaining access to physical stock when they need to cover a short (sold) position. For example, a trader has bought a put option and sold securities against it as a hedge; he or she would buy stock under a repo to cover that short position. The 1996/97 AFMA annual survey of Australian financial markets showed a 63 per cent increase in repos turnover to $2.4 billion ($1.4 billion in 1995/96). Reflecting the contraction in the number of participants in the fixed-income market, however—itself a function of the decline in issues of government paper—turnover in repos became more concentrated, with the top five players accounting for 80 per cent of turnover. Growth in repos during 1997 and into 1998 was such, though, that the market attracted additional broker interest.

Repos and the Reserve Bank

Repurchase agreements make up the bulk of the Reserve Bank's liquidity-management operations in the market, with most activity in transactions for less than 30 days and of that, most within seven days. When the central bank offers to 'buy repos' it is normally a day when there is a deficit in the cash system, so the central bank puts cash into the banking system, and agrees to sell that stock back (taking cash out of the system) at a future date. On a day with a cash system surplus, the RBA might offer to sell repos, with its transactions taking cash out of the system.

Repos are useful in repositioning funds and help reduce day-to-day fluctuations in the level of cash in the system. When the Reserve Bank is offering to buy repos, that is, putting funds into the system, it takes into account the liquidity effects of unwinding the repo (which takes funds out of the system) when selecting repos of different terms. When buying repos, the Reserve Bank sorts the bids into descending order of yield (the bank is looking to provide funds at the highest), and into maturities. When selling repos, the Reserve Bank, being effectively a borrower, sorts the bids into ascending order of yield. However, maturity can often be a more important consideration than price.

As discussed in chapter 4, the RBA also offers, to those with exchange settlement accounts, an end-of-day funding facility in the form of an overnight repo. Reflecting the view that this should be used only rarely, the RBA charges a margin of 25 basis points over the target cash rate for this facility. Banks can generate liquidity during the trading day through an *autorepo* function by lodging securities in an autorepo securities sub-account with the RBA. When a bank needs funds to settle a transaction, the system automatically provides it by selling securities from the autorepo account to the RBA under an intraday repo. Banks can activate or deactivate their autorepo accounts at any time. A within-day repo can also be activated manually at the discretion of a bank, through the manual repo facility, using securities available in a bank's securities sub-account. Whether a repo is effected using the autorepo function or manually, when the first leg is completed the RBA credits the exchange settlement cash account of the bank selling securities with the amount of the purchase price and debits the relevant repo account (autorepo or designated sub-account for a manual repo) of the bank with the securities sold. RBA intraday repo liquidity is provided free of charge, apart from a RITS transaction fee of $3 per line of stock in each leg of each transaction.

The Reserve Bank also makes outright purchases and sales of commonwealth government securities but, when undertaken for liquidity-management purposes, these are restricted to short-term securities. Securities used in repos can be of longer maturities, and their term is not related to the maturity of the repo agreement. This enables the Reserve Bank to use a far wider range of securities, for example, a repo in long-term bonds can be used to achieve the same impact on liquidity in the cash market as an outright transaction in short-term treasury notes.

Repurchase agreements have enjoyed a surge in popularity in recent years but are not a recent phenomenon. A form of repos dates from the 1950s and the beginnings of the 'official' short-term money market, when a number of stockbrokers began 'buy-back' activities in government securities. By 1954 the stockbrokers had begun to offer clients facilities for investing temporary surpluses of cash. The brokers sold government bonds to the clients and the parties agreed that the brokers would buy the bonds back at a future date and at a set price. In effect, the brokers were borrowing their clients' funds and securing the borrowings with government bonds. The clients were lending funds (investing) and taking the bonds as security. Such clients would probably have willingly bought government bonds had they been certain about the length of time for which they could afford to invest but they were reluctant to buy bonds outright in case they had to sell them within a short time, possibly at a loss. Short-dated government securities at that time were not available in sufficient quantity to guarantee a thriving market, nor was there much secondary-market trading. With the brokers' methods, funds were on loan for short periods, from a few days to one month.

In *In Reserve—Central Banking in Australia 1945–75*, Professor Boris Schedvin records that, by the late 1950s, 'there were . . . distinct signs that the market in government securities was increasing in sophistication'.

Early in 1957 the [central] Bank was approached by the ES&A [bank] to enquire whether a buy-back arrangement in relation to government securities would be considered. Such an arrangement was advantageous to an institution with excess short-term liquidity because it obtained 3 per cent on money that otherwise would have been idle. The offer was accepted, the Board approved the arrangement in February 1957, and during the year the Bank entered into a small number of repurchase agreements amounting to about $27 million.

Repos and the market

The repo market has hugely expanded, with most repo business carried out by the major market-makers in fixed-interest securities. The stocklending facilities provided by state-government financing authorities such as NSW TCorp and Queensland Treasury Corporation, in furnishing an additional port-of-call for those in need of stock, deepened market liquidity by fostering market-making, and so contribute to increased activity in repos. Repos offer a way to obtain otherwise scarce stock and they foster market-making in the underlying securities, by providing an extra dimension of flexibility in turning over stock. Banks and investment banks running large bond books are major repo players, undertaking repos among themselves and with clients.

Sellers

At its most straightforward, a seller of repos gains short-term liquidity at an attractive rate.

Typically a seller of repos could be a party which is a natural holder of stock—an institutional investor whose business includes holding bonds or a dealer holding securities as part of his or her stock-in-trade—and is looking to gross up his or her portfolio by selling the stock under repo at a cash rate below that at which the proceeds can be reinvested. For example, assume that a fund manager (natural holder of several hundred million dollars' worth of bonds) has stock that is keenly sought by traders who are short of the stock; the fund manager sells the stock under repo at a cash rate of, say, 5.25 per cent, then reinvests the proceeds in the cash market at 5.50 per cent, realising a 25-basis point profit.

A seller might also be a trading house or investment bank which has taken a position in bonds that has to be funded—but does not operate with a deposit base so it borrows the cash it needs by putting stock out on repo. Or a bank might sell a repo as an alternative to raising deposits in the wholesale market; it can fund its bond position through the repo market.

Buyers

On the other side are the buyers—investors keen to place cash through repos because that offers top-class security. Most, though not all, repos are based on commonwealth or semi-government bonds and so carry minimum credit risk. (A small proportion of repo activity is based on corporate bonds.) Someone with a short position in bonds would buy securities under a repo to cover that position. In the past, a bank buyer of securities under a repo could obtain stock to satisfy the prime assets ratio which prevailed until 1998, for example by buying commonwealth government securities on a short-term basis through the repo market in preference to buying long-dated securities, resulting in considerably less exposure to movements in interest rates. Under real-time gross settlement, banks continue to require holdings of commonwealth government securities to be able to generate intraday liquidity, often using repos.

Repos and securities lending

Activity in securities lending (stock lending) increased enormously around the world in the mid-to-late 1990s, often associated with equities but also with fixed-interest securities. Securities lending in Australia dates from 1984 and the creation of the reporting bond-dealers which were a considerable catalyst to market-making. A pioneer in the area was The Bond Lending Company, established in 1984 by Australian Gilt Securities as a special-purpose company focusing on fostering trading in bonds. The volume of activity in securities lending—transacted between professional trader and institutional client or between institutions—is considerably lower than that of repos but securities lending business generates stock for the repo market (the preserve of the professional traders).

Some institutions prefer to *lend* their securities rather than execute a repo. Securities lending, carried out for a fee, is a borrowing-lending exercise that does not require any movement of cash; the lender of the stock is paid a fee by the borrower who also provides the lender with 'substock' (substitution stock). A repo, on the other hand, is a buy-sell transaction where cash changes hands, giving operators potentially large cashflows to reinvest. There is a degree of uncertainty associated with the reinvestment rate and an element of credit risk on the reinvestment. Many non-professional operators prefer securities lending because it does not generate cash that has to be reinvested in the market and is a simpler process to administer because it eliminates tax and accrual complications. Also, the mark-to-market risk associated with securities lending is minimal because bond-holders have 'swapped' stock whose yields and

Figure 9.1 Example of a repurchase agreement

9 December
$20m 10.5% 15/9/05

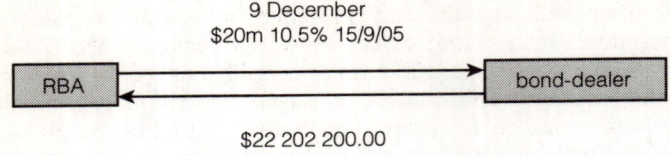

$22 202 200.00

Figure 9.2 Reversal of the repurchase agreement

12 December
$20m 10.5% 15/9/05

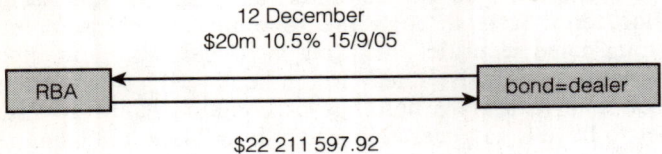

$22 211 597.92

duration are similar so that even with a major market move, their yields will shift in tandem.

From a practical point of view, notional ownership of stock changes hands with securities lending, because the two main settlement systems, RITS and Austraclear, can only handle buy-and-sell (not lending) transactions. So for the purposes of settlement a transaction is processed as a buy-sell, irrespective of its being a securities loan or a repo.

The mechanics of a repo

The mechanics of a transaction in which the Reserve Bank sells a repo and a bond-dealer purchases it (the deal could be between any two parties as buyer and seller, for example, bond-dealer and client) are:

The Reserve Bank sells a repo of $20 million of commonwealth government securities with, say, a 10.5 per cent coupon, maturing September 2005, and a market yield of 7.57 per cent. The RBA repos the stock for three days, say, 9 to 12 December, at a rate of 5.15 per cent. The price of the securities is $111.011 per $100 face value, $22 202 200 for $20 million.

The transaction is reversed on 12 December. Through RITS, the securities are transferred back to the original seller (in this case the Reserve Bank), which in return credits the bond-dealer's account with $22 202 200.00 plus interest at 5.15 per cent per annum for three days. The bond-dealer has earned $9397.92 in interest.

Price of a repo

The price of a repo, in terms of the premium/discount to the cash rate, varies depending on the demand for, or supply of, the underlying stock. If the stock is in plentiful supply and regularly issued, the premium is low, for example, a repo would be transacted at about 4.85 per cent against a cash rate of 5 per cent. If the stock were very actively traded and in short supply the premium would be higher; stocks have been known to trade 300 points or more under the cash rate for brief periods.

Market risk

A repo with a maturity of more than one day involves a potential risk of a change in the market value of the relevant securities (which are owned for the time being by the purchaser of the repo). Exposure can be limited by marking the security to market at regular intervals. The market value of the repo is sometimes altered, by mutual agreement, to reflect a change in the yield of the securities—for example, a repo has been transacted at a yield of 7 per cent and a cash rate of 5.50 per cent but the market moves to 8 per cent so the stock's market value has been reduced. While the market value of the repo is sometimes changed, the face value and the repo rate remain unaltered. When the yield rises (price falls, because of a general movement in interest rates), a margin call is made which increases the face value of the stock underlying the repo, thus maintaining market value.

Settlement

Repos may be settled through RITS or Austraclear. Commonwealth government securities are settled through RITS, while semi-government and most other money-market securities are settled through Austraclear. With transactions involving institutions or corporate clients which are not members of RITS or Austraclear, settlement involves the physical exchange of securities and bank cheques.

Repo settlement or securities lending transactions look like outright purchases or sales, except that in RITS the transaction can be flagged as a repo for statistical purposes (although many participants do not do so).

Documentation

Each repo transaction is agreed individually. The repo interest rate is determined when the repo is initiated, as is the agreed repurchase price. Where a repo is not 'open-ended', that is, on demand, the sellback/buyback date is agreed at the outset of the transaction. When this date arrives the counterparties decide whether the transactions are to be rolled over or terminated.

There are two documents endorsed by AFMA. The *PSA/ISMA Agreement*, devised in 1994 by the US's Public Securities Association and Europe's International Securities Markets Association, is a globally recognised document and has become the standard documentation used in the Australian market. The investment house Deutsche Morgan Grenfell introduced the agreement to the Reserve Bank of Australia in 1995 and the central bank adopted it in mid-1996 as the exclusive basis for its repo transactions. Major repos players use the PSA/ISMA Agreement which clearly defines features such as the maintenance of margins and repricing, thus removing considerable uncertainty from the impact of price movements on repos. The *ISDA Master Agreement*, prepared by the legal firm Mallesons Stephen Jaques for AFMA and ISDA (International Swaps and Derivatives Association), can also be used for repos if Addendum Number 9—Reciprocal Purchase Agreement—is included.

Advantages in using the ISDA Master Agreement include providing participants with the choice of using one master agreement for all transactions, including swaps, options, FRAs and repos; using one master agreement simplifies documentation; and it gives the option of specifying net payments for corresponding payment dates for all transactions, reducing settlement costs and risks. With all transactions regulated by the same agreement, the amount payable on early termination will be payable by reference to aggregate net exposures under all transactions and therefore would not exclude amounts payable in connection with repos. By incorporating Addendum Number 9 in the ISDA Master Agreement, the parties agree that every repo between them is governed by the agreement, whether or not its confirmation refers to the Master Agreement or Addendum Number 9 and whether or not the parties state in their confirmation that the repo is governed by the terms of any other master agreement.

There is no standard documentation for securities lending, although the Overseas Securities Lenders' Agreement (OSLA) is gaining acceptance while the Australian Securities Lenders' Agreement (ASLA), used chiefly in equities, is seen as adaptable for fixed-income markets. In the absence of standard documentation, agreements are arranged between individual parties.

10

Trading and investing in long-term fixed-income securities

Trading the instruments

Financial markets traders buy and sell the securities described in chapters 6, 7, and 8. The difference between the rates at which these are bought and sold represents trading profits (or losses); true profits are the difference between the purchase and sale prices adjusted for the cost of funding the asset over the period held. Bonds are priced at a margin to the three-year or ten-year futures contract, depending on the maturity of the bond. If the maturity is close to the three-year part of the yield curve then it is priced against three-year bond futures; if closer to the ten-year part of the curve then it is priced against ten-year bond futures. The turning point for this price convention is somewhere around the five-to-seven-year maturity. Price discovery is carried out in the futures market because of the transparency of futures markets. The liquidity of bond futures adds to the appeal.

Traders aim to make a profit by buying assets at low prices and selling when they appreciate; they do not expect to hold assets for the term of an investment.

Buying a security is similar to *lending* money—both require an outlay of funds. The purchase of a security at a higher rate of interest means the buyer/lender is earning a better return on the cash. *Selling* a security is like *borrowing* funds, so that a lower yield on the security sold is as welcome as a cheaper rate of interest on borrowings. Issuers and investors both act to secure the best rate they can. An issuer seeks to sell its paper (borrow) at a low yield (low interest rate) while an investor wants to invest (lend) funds at a high yield (high interest rate). A trader is interested solely in trading profitably, so he or she must buy and sell bonds so that purchases and sales result in a profit, that is, from buying at high yields and selling at lower yields.

Traders are not like investors and issuers because they are not 'end-users' of a bond—they are neither borrowing nor investing. They function as financial intermediaries—providing liquidity for both sides of the market. The particular positions they take and subsequently clear on behalf of their issuing and investing customers depend on their judgment as to the future course of interest rates. Volatility in price provides trading opportunities. Such volatility, though, is also a function of risk: asset prices both fall and rise. An understanding of the role of the *yield curve* is a prerequisite to grasping why securities are traded and what advantages can be gained from this.

The yield curve

The Language of Money (Carew, Allen & Unwin 1996) defines yield curve as: 'A graph showing the relationship between the yield to maturity and the term to maturity of a group of similar securities.' According to the County NatWest *Dictionary of Investment Terms*, the yield curve is 'a visual representation of the term structure of interest rates at a point in time. It shows the relationship between bond yields and maturity length. A normal or positive yield curve signifies higher interest rates for long-term investments while a negative or downward curve indicates higher short-term interest rates.'

The yield curve moves around in response to unfolding economic developments and events. The short end of the curve is tied down by the setting of monetary policy—the cash rate (see chapter 4). The long end of the yield curve reflects expectations about interest rates over the period to maturity. If expectations of a tightening of monetary policy emerge, this would be reflected in short-term interest rates, such as those on 90-day bills, which would lift the short end of the yield curve. If, on the other hand, inflation expectations improved, but the market saw this as unlikely to produce an easing of monetary policy, short-term rates would probably remain steady, while bond yields might fall, leading to a flattening in the shape of the yield curve (and illustrating that the long end of the yield curve can move independently of the short end). Experienced traders position their portfolios to take advantage of such movements.

There are a number of basic types of yield curve (see figure 10.1). A curve is plotted on a graph showing the yield to maturity on the vertical axis and the maturity of the investment on the

Figure 10.1 Types of yield curve

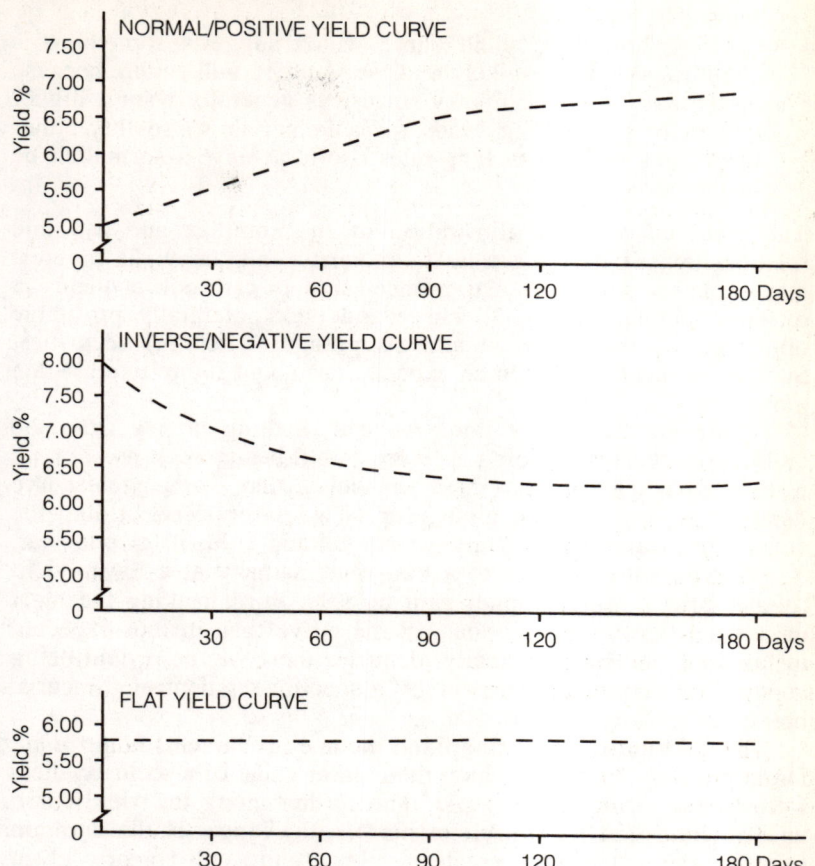

horizontal. The shape of the yield curve reflects prevailing economic conditions as well as market expectations of the future level of interest rates. The yield curve encapsulates the stance of monetary policy, confidence, economic activity, expectations about inflation and about influences in international markets. The most common types of yield curve are:

- the normal, positive, upward-sloping yield curve, reflecting investors' conventional expectation of a higher interest rate if funds are committed for a longer period;
- the downward, negative, inverse yield curve, illustrating high

short-term rates to slow economic activity and the view that rates will fall later;
- the flat, horizontal yield curve which suggests something is about to give; it is unlikely that the situation will endure because of the time value of money (investors generally want a higher return for committing funds for a longer term) so that either short rates will fall or long rates rise to achieve a normal shape in the curve.

The yield curve is an illustration of the complex and dynamic relationship between the time to maturity and the yield (interest rate) value of a security. Experienced traders can look at yields at different parts of the yield curve and pick potentially profitable opportunities for arbitrage and swapping (switching) securities. Such activity will be based on expectations about future interest-rate movements.

There are essentially three ways of making money from the yield curve (besides holding a security until it matures): positioning to take advantage of movements in yields, that is, the yield curve itself moves up or down giving capital gains or losses; riding the curve—if a trader buys a three-year bond and holds it for one year, it will have moved down to a two-year maturity at a lower yield (higher price) with a capital gain on sale; third, making the most of anomalies, or imperfections, in the curve that are not expected to last long. A trader normally identifies these by their yield being above the interpolated curve or by a specific segment of the curve being particularly steep or flat.

A vital tool for managing fixed-income investments is *duration*. Duration is the extent to which the market value of a security alters following a movement in yield. The further along the yield curve an investor positions himself or herself, the longer is the duration of an investment and the greater the loss (gain) will be for a given rise (fall) in yield.

Traders and portfolio managers talk of yield-curve positioning, that is, going long or short (duration). When interest rates are expected to rise, traders will take a short position, to avoid capital losses. When interest rates are expected to fall they will take a long-duration position to reap capital gains. They also focus on trading the shape of the yield curve, which involves picking the maturity that, they believe, will perform best to increase profit opportunities and reduce chances of loss. What traders do with an investment—whether they buy, sell, hold or swap—will be determined by what they see as its prevailing market rate compared with where they believe the yield curve will be in the near future. Riding the yield curve down, an important part of active portfolio management, means locking in a high interest rate that looks increasingly attractive as it matures.

Credit curve

The credit curve adds a fresh dimension to trading and investing in Australian fixed-interest markets. Whereas commonwealth government securities represent a homogeneous market of absolute creditworthiness, this is not the case with corporate paper. And there is an increasing trend towards investing in lesser credits to achieve a higher return—to ride the credit curve.

An understanding of credit, in the sense of the creditworthiness of a borrower and the credit-rating that can attach to its paper, assumed increasing significance in the late 1990s as Australian fixed-interest markets diversified from a reliance on virtually homogeneous government paper to include a range of corporate and other issuers, and fund managers broadened their investment base to encompass a bigger range of private-sector products. Whereas the far larger and more diversified US markets have been trading credits for years, developing a clear understanding of credit in this sense is a fairly new challenge for Australian financial markets. As a consequence, demand for credit analysts has risen, investment banks and fund managers place increasing emphasis on credit research, and institutions recruit analysts familiar with the dynamics of a corporate balance sheet, with specific industries, with changing market conditions, who can examine debt and estimate the likelihood of its being repaid. While the major credit-rating agencies provide invaluable information, credit analysts can identify variations even within a single credit-rating band. This puts pressure on everyone in fund management to sharpen their grasp of the dynamics of private-sector debt and how to incorporate it in a fixed-income portfolio.

Also driving the focus on credit is a need for fund managers and investors to maximise performance, and taking on a judicious element of credit risk is seen by many as essential to this end. With its focus on mostly investment-grade securities, Australia is years away from developing a high-yield (sub-investment grade) bond market on the scale of that seen in the US but its fixed-income markets are slowly expanding to include higher-yielding products that appeal to many specialist and self-managed funds.

Portfolio management

Financial markets activities in fixed-income securities vary between those who issue paper to raise term funding, those who trade and those who invest on behalf of superannuation funds, insurance companies and other asset managers. Even for investors, though, flexible management of a portfolio has been important. Portfolio management in Australia has undergone considerable change over the past several decades. Portfolio management no longer means buying parcels of securities from time to time and sitting on them until they mature. No-one can afford such a completely passive approach: the objective, rather, is to buy to maximise return, taking a view on the direction of interest rates, that is, the shape and position of the yield curve and exploiting opportunities in different markets. Choices exist between domestic and overseas assets, between different securities and between different maturities.

A portfolio manager is constantly looking for a balance between the accounting effects, the taxation effects and the investment effects of any trading or investment decision. The objective is to maximise income, subject to risk; this calls for management of both risk and return. The shape of a portfolio will depend on the investor's or portfolio manager's appetite for risk. Most, however, would regard some stability of income (or cashflow) as desirable, which means that a diversified portfolio is optimal because it spreads risk over a range of instruments and asset classes. The ultimate position on risk depends on the investor's appetite for reward.

The differing accounting treatments of investors and traders give rise to different activities. Trades are reported that can appear to make no sense as investments but could be accounting or taxation manoeuvres. Banks, dealers and institutions have varying objectives. A good bond-dealer would be aware of a client's position and aims regarding taxation, accounting and investment objectives. (Such strategies would be detailed in a textbook for an advanced course in portfolio management.)

A typical portfolio of fixed-income securities would include commonwealth bonds and state government securities, corporate bonds and mortgage-backed securities and would also include foreign government bonds, foreign corporate paper and global bonds. A dealer would run a portfolio of such securities, combined with swaps and options. It is impossible, even dangerous, to generalise about objectives, given the different requirements mentioned above, but portfolio managers and fixed-income strategists would often be influenced in their thinking—which dictates whether the trader buys, sells or holds particular securities—by factors such as:

- *liquidity*, whether they need funds soon, and how much they can invest in long-term stock;
- maintaining a level of *income* which can accommodate potential loss or risk, or maximise cashflow;

- *strategy*, taking into account market outlook on interest rates;
- *inflation*, the *exchange rate,* opportunities that can be maximised, risks to be avoided;
- *flexibility*, leaving sufficient breadth so that strategy can be altered if conditions change;
- relative *performance* of asset classes (for example, equity, property, foreign v. domestic instruments).

Strategists have to take into account different forms of risk when structuring a portfolio—risk being the possibility that returns will not meet expectations. Such risks relate to movements in interest rates, to the liquidity and marketability of the securities, inflation, creditworthiness and changes in economic conditions that can affect business and industry. An essential buffer in avoiding or at least minimising credit risk is to invest in securities issued by entities of the highest credit-standing such as domestic or foreign governments, highly-rated banks and institutions. But portfolio managers and strategists also have to achieve good returns on the investments under their stewardship and the twin pressures of security and performance lead them to diversify, spreading exposures over a variety of assets, currencies, maturities, sectors and credits, monitoring the relative performance of each and adjusting as appropriate, perhaps overweighting in an asset that they believe is undervalued and poised to rise and underweighting in an asset they believe is likely to fall in value. Portfolio managers establish 'benchmarks' against which returns on their portfolios are regularly measured. The level of technology in the average dealing room has expanded enormously, with sophisticated programs written to cope with swaps and complicated transactions involving forward decisions about securities with different coupons and maturities and, increasingly, in different currencies.

Despite the innovative techniques and more complex transactions, trading securities still hinges on a basic objective: making the most out of interest-rate (and currency) movements. Changes in interest rates and differing outlooks for the relative asset classes are key factors affecting portfolio management. Changes in interest rates are important because a rise in interest rates means a fall in the capital value of a security, that is, a capital loss because, for a given movement in yield, the capital loss rises with the term of the investment. The traditional reaction to rising or uncertain interest rates among portfolio managers and bond-holders is to reduce interest-rate exposure either by selling bonds outright or moving to shorter-term investments.

Inflation

A big influence on portfolio managers and the value of the investments under their control is expectations about inflation. This arises from the effect of inflation on the purchasing power of the dollar and hence on interest rates, being the domestic price of money. If inflation is running at an annual rate of 3 per cent and an investor is earning 8 per cent per annum (pre-tax) from a security, the pre-tax real rate of return is 5 per cent; but take off the effects of, say, a 50 per cent tax bracket on the nominal return of 8 per cent, and the real after-tax rate of return is a mere 1 per cent. If expectations are for rising inflation, and an investor wants to protect his or her real rate of return, the nominal interest rate has to rise to compensate. Thus an increase in expectations of inflation implies higher interest rates and capital losses. Because rising interest rates reduce the capital value of a security and because this intensifies with the term of the security, inflation expectations are likely to be especially important for long-dated rather than short-dated securities.

The exchange rate

Expectations about the exchange rate also play a part in a portfolio manager's thinking, although portfolio managers tend to handle currency risk as a separate asset class—a contrast to, say, the early 1990s when currency risk was not as actively managed in this way. Overseas investors have been enthusiastic buyers of Australian fixed-income securities, and these foreign investors take into account expected currency movements (as well as interest rates) when deciding where to place their funds. For example, predictions of a strengthening $A may encourage foreign investment. But predictions that the $A might weaken or indications that it was near a peak might discourage overseas buyers. An efficient foreign-exchange market enables local managers of offshore bonds and overseas managers of local bonds to hedge currency exposure. These hedging costs also influence the decision about whether or not to invest in foreign assets. Hedging costs may be favourable or unfavourable for an investor in bonds. (A portfolio that is not hedged would be managed.)

Funding

The portfolio manager also has to consider cashflow and the funding cost involved when investing in securities. The funding cost has to be included when calculating the overall return from securities that have been bought. The professional money market pays interest monthly on call deposits and cash management funds generally pay interest quarterly. Cashflow calculations must take account of differences between securities such as state government paper, which provides six-monthly income, and deposits which have a monthly or quarterly flow. This usually requires an adjustment either to the cost of funds or to the yield earned on the security to bring the comparison into line. Individual investors should also be aware of factors that determine the effective interest rate earned on an investment, such as whether interest is paid monthly or quarterly, whether it is calculated daily or on the minimum monthly balance and whether or not interest is reinvested. A rate of 10 per cent per annum, for example, on an investment paying interest quarterly provides the same annual return (assuming quarterly reinvestment of the interest payments at 10 per cent) as an investment offering 10.13 per cent and paying interest semi-annually. This relates to the time value of money: the more frequently interest is paid, the greater the compound effect and running yield on the original investment.

Active or passive portfolio management

Holders of fixed-income securities have the ability to hedge and reduce risk by using futures and options and other risk-management products, or a form of portfolio insurance. Portfolio managers have to consider whether to follow a strategy of *active* management, riding the yield or credit curve to lift returns or undertaking active duration management through yield curve plays (duration management being managing maturity *and* value), or to take a more *passive* or *structured* approach, aiming to match and hedge. (The relative merits of active and passive portfolio management are the subject of considerable debate in the industry, with lengthy and complex arguments that deserve a textbook of their own.) Briefly, an active approach in portfolio management entails continuous monitoring and analysis of factors that can affect investment returns, such as interest rates and inflation, and adjusting the distribution of assets to favour those that are expected to increase most in value. With the passive approach, a manager sets out an investment strategy and more or less sticks with that, shifting only if there is a major development that would have significant long-term impact on the investments. The passive manager's objective generally is to match the performance of the portfolio under management with an appropriate market index. Active managers, on the other hand, aim to outperform a relevant index and take bigger bets against it.

Trading techniques have been described here mostly in the context of dealing in fixed-income securities. The same principles apply when trading in the short-term instruments described in chapter 6. Traders in bills of exchange and commercial paper have to make investment decisions when buying and selling, but their horizon tends to be limited to six months or one year, rather than longer-term projections.

These shorter-term securities are more vulnerable to day-to-day influences whereas the longer-term securities react to broader trends in the economy, such as the inflation rate and the general direction of interest rates. The most obvious risk in trading securities is that a trader might incorrectly pick the trend in rates. This can result in a bond having to be sold at a higher yield (lower price) than it was bought for, or it could mean a loss on funding while the paper is held. Traders have to be constantly aware of reinvestment opportunities for their funds (computer technology plays a big role here in speedily identifying opportunities that might provide a better return). For example, a trader might improve the return by cutting losses on a particular security because fresh opportunities have arisen that offer a greater chance for profits or a higher running yield.

Market-making and the convention of two-way pricing

Professional market-makers quote two-way prices because that provides a visible spread for traders and evidence of fair value to clients. Making two-way prices is virtually a definition of a market-maker, showing that a trader can get in and out of a stock. Two-way prices also help to keep margins fairly narrow. Margins of around two basis points in commonwealth bonds and up to three basis points for state paper are regarded as quite fine. Clients often demand two-way prices. Some houses discourage this but, although the professional market is not obliged to quote two-way prices to clients, such is the competition for client business—the muscle of the bigger clients—that customers tend to get what they want. Often a spread can be narrower between professional and client than between two professionals. A client can get a quote without being compelled to deal; equally, he or she can ring around and get a range of quotes. A quote would be made as '50/47' and the other party is expected to know the 'big figure'. Correct telephone dealing etiquette requires that, before hanging up, the trade details are repeated in full, including the big figure.

Short-selling

A major benefit of market-making is that it provides a high degree of liquidity. A consequence of active market-making has been a growth in the volume of short-selling. The ability to short-sell is fundamental to the liquidity of the market; by definition, as turnover increases (as it has), so the volume of short-selling also rises. It is not uncommon for a big trading house to have a junior on the desk whose job is to borrow stock to cover short-selling in the repo market (see chapters 4 and 9).

Short-selling can result for one of two reasons. A dealer may consciously decide to short on the basis of an expectation of market movement, or short-selling can result from active market-making, with the trader aiming to cover the position quickly. Very little short-selling took place before the establishment of dealer panels and market-making. And bond tenders have also been conducive to short-selling, with a considerable amount taking place ahead of a tender. Short-selling has been facilitated by the states' establishing stock-lending facilities which enable traders to sell stock and borrow from the issuer to cover the position for a specific period. The growth of repos (reciprocal purchase agreements) in bonds and semis has also been a boost to short-selling. The Reserve Bank is active in repurchase agreements as part of its daily liquidity management; repos are also used by market-makers as a way of gaining additional flexibility and making profitable use of surplus stock in portfolio.

Insufficient volume of issues and the absence of an active repo market in corporate bonds has inhibited that sector from establishing a liquid trading market.

Settlement procedures: RITS and Austraclear

Commonwealth bonds are cleared through RITS; state government and corporate securities are cleared through Austraclear.

Austraclear, introduced in 1984 and owned by a wide range of financial institutions, handles all debt securities except commonwealth government stock. Trade settlements are not final and irrevocable until the members' cash positions are agreed by their banks through Austraclear. Special arrangements can be made to settle immediately; otherwise, trades are generally settled at the end of the day. Only a small proportion of fixed-income transactions in ineligible securities is settled outside the Austraclear system; these involve smaller companies and individual clients who are not members of the system.

RITS, operated by the Reserve Bank, is a derivative of the Austraclear system. When a trade is arranged, usually by phone, a trader fills out a deal chit which is sent to the back office where it is keyed into a computer and transfer of cash and securities is effected once the counterparty enters its side of the deal (a participating bank is needed to guarantee payment). The trade, once settled, is irrevocable. Irrespective of which system is used, deal checks are carried out within an hour of a deal being done, to ensure deal details are correct regarding stocks, amounts and maturities, for settlement T+3.

Some trades in commonwealth securities are settled outside RITS; some overseas authorities require securities to be held with a custodian. If a deal is executed with a client not on RITS, the professional trader is expected to travel to carry out the settlement by delivering cheques and transfer-and-acceptance forms. The choice of bank cheque or company cheque is up to the individual trading organisations.

11

Mortgage and asset-backed securities

Fancy investing in a security whose payoff depends on how much beer is sold in British pubs? How about a bond to be paid by collections of overdue parking fines in New York city? . . . If you'd prefer . . . the royalties earned by pop stars such as David Bowie and Rod Stewart. There is barely a cash flow anywhere, it seems, that cannot be reassembled into a bond-like security that the most conservative of investors might buy. Putting such strange instruments together has become one of the hottest businesses on Wall Street.

—The Economist *9 May 1998*

Attempts to define securitisation invoke argument but broadly it can be said that securitisation enables funds to be recycled—it presents lenders with an opportunity to repackage comparatively illiquid assets such as mortgages and, more recently, other types of commercial and consumer loans, into highly-rated marketable securities (bonds or notes), thus generating cash for other, ideally more lucrative, activities. Instead of having to fund a conventional loan that would appear on the balance sheet, tying up capital and probably earning a low return on it, a seller of a securitised product sells the asset in a way that transfers certain risks, such as credit or maturity risk, to investors. Where the asset sold is prepayable, as in the case of a mortgage or loan, an important benefit for the seller of the asset is that the asset is funded for its life, with investors accepting the risk of prepayment. For the seller, this eliminates the liquidity risk associated with funding long-term loans such as mortgages with short-term liabilities because the term of the mortgage-backed securities is matched against that of the underlying assets.

Securitisation involves collecting assets representing cashflows, such as mortgages or loans, and issuing bonds backed by them. This is done by establishing a special-purpose vehicle (SPV), either a trust or a corporate structure, which buys the assets.

The process can offer benefits to investors, governments and financiers, in that it enables assets to be broken down into component risk parts, with these being sold to appropriate parties: the risks can be 'unbundled' and rebundled so that they are managed by the parties best able to do so.

According to reviews by leading ratings agencies such as Standard & Poor's and Moody's Investors Service, securitisation in Australia grew by 90–95 per cent in 1997, a significant increase over growth in the previous two years. Activity has been such that Australia is ranked as the second-most active market in mortgage-backed securities after the well-established and large US market. Moody's estimated that mortgage-backed securities on issue totalled $10 billion in 1997; S&P reported it had assigned ratings to $18.53 billion of mortgage and asset-backed securities and commercial paper programs backed by Australian and New Zealand assets, compared with $6.2 billion in 1995 and $10.6 billion in 1996. Other estimates put the Australian mortgage-backed securities market around $20 billion. Of the securities issued, 42 per cent were in the form of floating-rate bonds, 37.8 per cent as commercial paper, 8 per cent as fixed reverting to floating-rate bonds and the balance as a mix of floating-rate notes, medium-term notes and indexed bonds. Issues of mortgage-backed securities during 1997 were fuelled by a rush of banks entering the securitised loans business for the first time; however, some have had a growing involvement in securitisation since 1995. Such was the new-found enthusiasm from banks that in 1997 they accounted for 35 per cent of the issues of mortgage-backed securities, up from 14 per cent in 1996. Established operator PUMA—a non-bank securitiser originally launched by the investment bank Schroders Australia and acquired by Macquarie Bank in 1991—retained its dominance with a 20 per cent market share. Two other non-banks were in the top five issuers— RAMS Mortgage Management Pty Ltd, a member of the Allco Group, which specialises in asset-based finance, and Super Members' Home Loans, a program launched in 1994 by National Mutual Funds Management and the Australian Council of Trade Unions. Bank competition came principally from securitisation programs of established issuers Westpac and Citibank, but also from banks entering securitisation for the first time, such as St George Bank, Colonial State Bank and Commonwealth Bank of Australia.

In mid-1993 Citibank had created a breakthrough when it launched Mortgage Power, lead-managed by Bain Capital Markets (now Deutsche Bank), a landmark deal which securitised revolving home equity lines of credit secured by a first mortgage over property. In a subsequent initiative, Citibank in 1995 launched SAMT (Securitised Australian Mortgage Trust), its first issue of long-dated, amortising principal-and-interest mortgage-backed securities.

In 1996 Westpac established its mortgage-processing centre in an Adelaide suburb to centralise and streamline processing of mortgages from around Australia to reduce costs and facilitate securitisation. Reflecting the influence of several US executives at the bank who would be familiar with the spread of securitisation in the United States—where some two-thirds of mortgages are securitised—Westpac was an early mover among Australian banks in recognising that banks could not continue to rely on margins from traditional lending practices but needed to reduce costs and earn fee income. In September 1996 it became the first major Australian bank to securitise its own home-loan assets. Westpac maintained its lead in securitisation among Australia's four major banks and has gone on to securitise billions of dollars worth of its home loans, removing assets from its balance sheet to free capital for more productive purposes and originating assets directly into off-balance-sheet structures. Westpac was one of three issuers which launched mortgage-backed securities in the euromarkets in 1997; PUMA made two transactions and St George Bank one. According to Moody's, during 1997 about 31 per cent of Australian mortgage-backed securities were issued offshore. In 1997 National Australia Bank bought the leading US mortgage servicer and producer HomeSide Inc. NAB followed in April 1998 with the announcement that HomeSide Lending had entered into a 'strategic' alliance in the US with Banc One Mortgage Corporation, a further step in NAB's strategy of building global mortgage-based activities. And in June 1998 Westpac broke new ground with a $US1.4 billion global mortgage-backed securities issue which was sold to investors in the US, Europe and Asia. It was the first global Australian mortgage-backed securities issue, the largest debt issue by an Australian borrower and the first asset-backed program by a foreign issuer in the US markets to be registered with the US's Securities and Exchange Commission (SEC). That issue took Westpac's home-loan securitisation programs to a total of $5.5 billion.

In the late 1990s securitisation was spreading from a focus on mortgage-backed instruments. It was no longer regarded as an arcane technique with highly specialised application; rather, its use had extended to encompass financing areas as diverse as credit-card receivables, government-guaranteed lease streams for buildings and car fleets and, in the US, show business, particularly future earnings in the film industry.

Background

Securitisation has its origins in the US in the years of the great depression. In 1933 the federal government started buying mortgages that were in default, grouping them together and issuing mortgage-backed securities to fund the purchases. The objective was to enable impoverished families to stay in their homes. From this beginning grew the Federal Housing Association, an agency established in 1934 to ensure there was an adequate supply of long-term, fixed-rate finance for home-buyers. The Federal National Mortgage Association (FNMA, known colloquially as 'Fannie Mae') was created in 1938 as a vehicle through which mortgagees (lenders) could sell mortgages. FNMA pioneered a secondary mortgage market, buying mortgages from lenders and so providing them with funds for new lending. The US secondary mortgage market developed steadily over the ensuing decades. In the mid-1950s it produced a new industry—private mortgage insurers. The first, established in 1956, was Mortgage Guaranty Insurance Corporation (MGIC).

The secondary mortgage market's growth continued at a sedate, rather than explosive, pace, and it was not until the late 1960s and early 1970s that a secondary mortgage market became an important source of funds for the US housing industry. A significant spur to developing the secondary mortgage market in the US was the practice of providing fixed-rate home loans, which locked lenders into assets whose low yields at times compared unfavourably with higher deposit costs. A milestone was reached in 1968 with the creation of the Government National Mortgage Association (GNMA, known as 'Ginnie Mae'). At the same time, FNMA changed its structure to that of a federally chartered, privately owned corporation. GNMA was the catalyst in getting the secondary mortgage market off the ground with the release, in 1970, of its pass-through securities—certificates issued against a pool of mortgages guaranteed by the Federal Housing Administration and Veterans Administration. Investors in GNMA certificates have the protection of a GNMA guarantee which is backed by the US government. The establishment of the Federal Home Loan Mortgage Corporation ('Freddie Mac') in 1971 was the birth of the third in a group of organisations that helped fuel the huge US secondary mortgage market. This federal government support was a crucial ingredient in the development of the US market. Also, the creation of these three bodies enormously boosted securitisation, largely because they encouraged loans to be standardised. The result was a perceptible trend in the US away from the traditional view that a mortgage is a loan that a lender has on its books until it matures or is paid out. An increasing proportion of residential mortgages in the US were funded through securitisation, with individual investors enthusiastic buyers of mortgage-backed certificates. Mortgage originators in the US include traditional lenders such as commercial banks, mortgage bankers and credit unions; institutional investors come from life offices, pension funds, banks and money managers.

Securitisation thus began in the US with mortgage-backed securities—financial instruments (bonds, notes or certificates) whose cashflows are secured by a pool of homogeneous mortgages owned by a special-purpose vehicle that issues the financial instruments. The special-purpose vehicle can be a trust or a corporation limited by the terms of its charter solely to hold assets for the benefit of investors in the mortgage-backed securities. A significant break-through came with the advent of the collateralised mortgage obligation (CMO) which, by selling in tranches, enables a variety of average maturities to be offered to investors to suit different preferences. With a CMO, securities are issued mostly as floating-rate notes with the coupon reset quarterly. It soon became clear that almost any loan that produces a predictable cashflow could be securitised. And so, in the mid-1980s, some 50 years after the early initiatives in securitisation, its principles were applied to other assets. The receivables—of whatever kind—form the underlying collateral for the securities issued, and the cashflow from the pool of assets matches and services the interest payments on the securities issued. These asset-backed securities are similar to mortgage-backed securities, in that they too are financial instruments (bonds, notes or certificates) whose cashflows are secured by a pool of homogeneous asset receivables, owned by the special-purpose vehicle issuing the financial instruments.

Receivables-backed bonds first appeared in the US in 1985 when Sperry Lease Finance Corp became the first computer company to undertake a public issue of securities backed by computer lease receivables. At the end of that year First Boston lead-managed a significant issue by General Motors Acceptance Corporation (GMAC) of securities backed by loans for motor vehicles. The first issue backed by credit cards was made early in 1987. By this time banks had come to recognise that when credit from traditional sources is tight and expensive, alternative sources tend to emerge which enable participants to obtain funds at reasonable rates; also, they identified the advantages of securitisation from a capital-adequacy standpoint, and were displacing the US auto finance companies as the major originators of asset-backed securities. Banks in the US were helped into securitisation by a Supreme Court ruling, early in 1990, permitting them to package and place their own mortgage loans and other assets as securities. The decision cut considerable ground from beneath the Glass Steagall Act of 1933, which separates the banking and securities industries.

Recent developments

The US securitises a range of assets beyond mortgages and commercial loans, including future revenue streams from the film industry with deals involving leaders such as Disney films, Twentieth Century Fox and Steven Spielberg's Dreamworks. In Tokyo, Disneyworld's gate-takings were first securitised in 1988 in a deal that combined securitisation and currency hedging techniques. It gave Disney a part of the profits of the ensuing twenty years and protected the company from vagaries in the $US/yen exchange rate. The deal was refinanced in 1997. Securitisation has spread to Europe, especially in the UK, and, generally, has evolved into a world-wide trend driven by a desire to improve returns on equity and returns on assets. Rock music stars David Bowie and Rod Stewart have securitised their future royalties, although in Stewart's case it would be more accurate to say that he raised a $US15 million loan against the security of future royalties.

Securitisation, a global guide, an *Asia Law* supplement published by *Euromoney*, cites Hong Kong as probably the most developed securitisation market in Asia, with a number of residential mortgage and credit-card backed deals executed in 1994, followed by securitisation of car loans and commercial real estate in 1995. Securitisation in Japan dates from the late 1980s but the market was fairly quiet until the early 1990s; Japanese credit-card and leasing companies have securitised receivables since 1993, transactions have taken place involving other types of assets and Japanese banks have been raising capital by repackaging their loans into marketable financial products which have been bought by Japanese institutional investors.

Australian background

In Australia, the development of securitisation began at state, rather than federal, level. Efforts to establish a secondary mortgage market in Australia date from the late 1970s but mortgage-backed securities were not issued in large volume until the late 1980s. However, a breakthrough was achieved in 1984 when the New South Wales and Victorian governments removed *ad valorem* stamp duty from the transfer of mortgages. (Most states have since removed stamp duty on the transfer of mortgage-backed securities and corporate debt instruments.) In 1986, Victoria launched its National Mortgage Market Corporation (NMMC) and the NSW government established FANMAC (First Australian National Mortgage Acceptance Corporation) Limited to foster a market in mortgage-backed securities.

The market in mortgage-backed securities added a new dimension to Australia's capital markets. By mid-1990 FANMAC had issued about $4.7 billion in securities, half of the total volume outstanding in the Australian mortgage-backed securities market. FANMAC—25 per cent owned by the NSW state government, the rest by shareholders associated with the mortgage market—issued fixed-rate prepayable mortgage-backed bonds against housing loans made under the NSW Department of Housing HomeFund Program. The FANMAC structure hit difficulties in the early 1990s, when a period of sustained low interest rates encouraged high prepayments of the fixed-rate mortgages. If interest rates are falling, mortgage-holders are inclined to refinance at lower interest rates and pay out their existing higher-rate mortgages. When they prepay, they do so at par, while investors—now holding high-coupon bonds in an environment of falling interest rates—value the bonds at a premium, thus causing immediate underperformance. Conventional fixed-income securities pay interest on the (constant) principal or face value semi-annually through a coupon and repay principal at maturity. And whereas falling interest rates increase the capital value of a conventional fixed-interest bond (discussed in chapter 7) and rising interest rates reduce its capital value, bonds that can be prepaid underperform in both cases. With FANMAC, investors discovered what is termed *negative convexity:* just when the interest-rate climate suggested returns should rise, they did not—and that jaundiced the investors' view of fixed-rate mortgage-backed securities.

The FANMAC scheme undertook no new loans after 1993 and its book was run down. HomeFund was discontinued and by the late 1990s was a modest operation. FANMAC's Victorian equivalent, the Melbourne-based National Mortgage Market Corporation (NMMC)—launched by the state government of Victoria, the South Australian Financing Authority (SAFA) and the State Housing Commission of Western Australia and a range of other shareholders —financed different types of mortgages in different ways. In 1995 NMMC was taken over by Bendigo Building Society—a shareholder and major user of NMMC—which subsequently converted to Bendigo Bank.

By the late 1990s the climate for securitisation had changed for the better as understanding and acceptance of the concept spread. The drive to liberate cashflows, unbundle risks and maximise returns, particularly on the part of banks and other corporations judged increasingly by the returns they can produce on their assets and equity, fuelled growth in the application of securitisation techniques across an increasing range of assets and businesses. According to S&P's review, the top Australasian operators of securitisation programs were Macquarie's PUMA, RAMS Mortgage Corp Ltd and Westpac, with Société Générale's ACE ranked as the major repackager of mortgage and asset-backed securities. Three issuers had gone overseas, with Macquarie, Westpac and St George Bank, taking issues of Australian mortgage-backed securities to the euromarkets. Major distributors of the securities included Deutsche Bank, Bankers Trust Australia, Macquarie Bank, SBC Warburg, Westpac Banking Corporation and Credit Suisse First Boston.

Incentives to securitise

Securitisation of mortgages marks a major breakthrough in Australia by severing the nexus between lending and capital—no longer does a lender require a large balance sheet to be a major force in lending. Securitisation, because it enables funds to be recycled, has allowed mortgages to be written by non-bank lenders, bringing unprecedented competition into the mortgage market. The market was initially driven by non-bank issuers but banks have increasingly engaged in securitisation as they strive for balance-sheet improvement and making the most out of a given level of capital.

Securitisation provides banks with an opportunity to sell assets that in themselves are not very liquid but can be converted into marketable parcels, then re-applying the proceeds to higher-yielding activities. And if banks securitise assets in a way that takes them completely off their balance sheets, so that there is no recourse to the bank, then central banks take the view that any capital requirement has been removed. Central banks, though, conscious of the appeal of securitisation to banks keen to free up capital (and increase fee income), have issued guidelines regarding securitisation in the light of their concern that banks should be under no risk—either credit, interest-rate or even moral risk—when they securitise assets. The Reserve Bank of Australia, for example, insists on a clear separation between a banking group and any special-purpose vehicle it has established to securitise assets. The RBA's prudential statement C2 comments that as a consequence of securitisation activities, banking groups can incur financial, operational, legal and other forms of risk. C2 quantifies and provides adequately for the potential liability of a banking group's involvement in a securitised scheme, with the objective of neutralising moral risk, that is, the possibility that a banking group might feel a 'moral obligation or commercial need' to support a securitisation scheme beyond any legal obligation to do so. C2 emphasises disclosure, the separation and limitation of liability, outlines what constitutes a 'clean sale' of assets by a banking group and defines the arm's-length nature of any facility provided by a bank to an SPV.

Any market needs investors as well as issuers. Investors were initially concerned about a new asset class and possible lack of liquidity in mortgage-backed securities. Many investors had been seared by early experiences in securitisation in Australia, either through the FANMAC program or buying three-to-five-year bullet securities backed by commercial property loans. In the early 1990s securitisation in Australia was struggling for credibility. Then a number of factors combined to breathe new life into the mortgage securitisation market. The arrival in 1992 of Aussie Home Loans, which quickly became Australia's most successful mortgage manager, busted the cosy cartel of the banks which had enjoyed fat margins from home-mortgage lending business. Aussie Home Loans, followed by the financier RAMS Mortgage Corporation and others, issued mortgage-backed bonds which enabled them to provide cheaper-than-bank home finance. These new non-bank lenders appeared at a time when banks were preoccupied with recapitalising after corporate and property losses in the early 1990s. Moreover, residential mortgages with a loan-to-valuation of less than 80 per cent attract a 50 per cent risk-weighting for capital adequacy purposes of banks, as against a 100 per cent risk-weighting for a commercial loan, so there was less incentive for banks to securitise housing loans. At that time, the banks tended to view securitisation as something of a gimmick that could fade off the scene.

Events, however, unfolded differently. Citibank had helped turn the tide with Mortgage Power. And banks found they had no choice other than to enter this growing mortgage market if they wanted to remain competitive with non-banks on pricing. A crucial factor in helping turn the tide was the development in 1994 of prepayment analysis undertaken by Deutsche Bank director Dr Richard Mason, whose work helped remove a significant element of uncertainty for managers of, and investors in, mortgage-backed securities. Over time, the increased volume of issues and the willingness of investment banks to quote in the secondary market improved turnover and contributed to alleviating the concerns. By the late 1990s the mortgage-backed securities market was increasingly viewed, along with the smaller corporate bonds market, as the sector most likely to fill a gap left by a decline in public-sector securities. In Australia, as in the US, investors in mortgage-backed securities have chiefly been the life offices and superannuation and other fund managers. The asset-backed commercial-paper programs (conduits) such as Société Générale's ACE, ABN AMRO's Tasman and Deutsche

Bank's SABRE, are also buyers of the securities. These conduits fall into two categories: those which purchase high-quality assets and issue commercial paper against them, and those which buy rated securities and sell commercial paper against them, taking advantage of the arbitrage—spread—between the rates on the securities and those on commercial paper. Securitisation and related techniques in structured finance are being energetically applied in areas associated with state and federal government initiatives to privatise so that private-sector funds and skills are used to support public infrastructure that was previously government-funded.

Supply and demand

A combination of circumstances has led to an upsurge in activity in asset-backed securities which, early in 1998, were still chiefly in the form of mortgage-backed securities. These instruments marked a shake-up in the home-financing market as mortgage managers have been able to deliver home loans at cheaper-than-bank rates to borrowers. By the late 1990s the edge that banks and building societies had long enjoyed in home lending—a position largely underpinned by their extensive branch networks—had been significantly chipped away by the new breed of mortgage managers. Home loans provided by mortgage managers are funded by securities issued to the wholesale financial markets and taken up by investors such as life offices and fund managers, so that the mortgage managers perform something of a broking role between home loan borrower and professional market investor. Consumers have benefited from this: not only are the mortgage managers a source of lower-cost mortgages but their emergence forced banks to compete more vigorously on rates and terms.

A significant factor in the growth of the mortgage-backed securities market has been a more competitive environment for fund managers whose performance is regularly judged in performance surveys and who, as a consequence, are constantly searching for investments that offer the favoured combination of low risk and good performance. This contrasts with a less demanding environment in the 1980s and even early 1990s, when fund managers were long-term, comparatively passive investors. While the supply of mortgage-backed securities built up somewhat in the early 1990s investors, overall, remained rather shy of the product; subsequently, though, the scarcity of government paper forced investors to examine alternative sources of AAA-rated securities. At the same time, the growing level of funds pouring into superannuation was seeking remunerative investments. As the imbalance between supply and demand grew, it was increasingly widely predicted that the gap would be filled by mortgage-backed securities and corporate bonds. A substitute investment for government and state government paper had to be of high credit quality, and in sufficient volume to meet demand.

Mortgage-backed securities met both criteria. And as market liquidity grew, the credit-ratings agencies became increasingly satisfied with the performance of the mortgage-backed securities sector. Some comfort could be drawn from the fact that these securities are backed by loans that, in Australia, carry a historically very low level of default; lenders have experienced minimal credit losses through mortgage finance. The presence of primary mortgage insurers, especially Housing Loans Insurance Corporation (HLIC, which until January 1998 was commonwealth-government owned), gave mortgages very strong credit backing which, coupled with the sound asset-backing of real estate, makes them very attractive investments. The tricky element in mortgages is not related to credit but to the payment pattern associated with them: borrowers might take out a long-term mortgage but they frequently prepay, move house or refinance. Considerable research has gone into refining mortgage-backed bonds into readily marketable, well-rated, liquid securities. Prepayment analysis (see below) has grown into a science, with the research effort bearing fruit in the form of vastly increased volume of data on the behaviour of mortgagors and mortgages in Australia; on a more general level, there is also a far wider range of publications providing Australian-based and global information on trends in securitisation.

Financing an increasing proportion of mortgages by selling assets backed by pools of mortgages enables the wholesale capital markets to channel funds into housing. Most of the funds provided by Aussie Home Loans by way of mortgages are supplied by institutions and then securitised. The borrowers' relationship is with Aussie Home Loans, with the financing of the loans in the background. Likewise, borrowers deal directly with RAMS, which also draws on funds raised by institutions.

Securitised products

Securitisation, or securitising products, is a further stage in a process that began in Australia with bills of exchange and promissory notes. These securities represented an early form of securitisation in the sense that they enabled an item that is not readily marketable—a loan—to be sold. They also enabled a corporate borrower to bypass conventional lenders, such as banks, and go direct to the market for buyers or investors in its paper. In early 1998 the volume of mortgage-backed securities issued in Australia ranked that market second-largest after public-sector (commonwealth and state) government bonds. Mortgages offer volume, and so economies of scale; growth in securitising credit and charge-card receivables is expected to continue to develop as credit cards are prised out of the banks' grip in the same way that mortgages have been levered out of their domain.

Developments in non-mortgage-backed securities include:

- Citibank, a leading world player in securitisation, broke new ground in Australia in December 1997 when it launched a $A586 million program securitising cashflows from its corporate loans, ICONs (Initial Corporate Obligation Notes), the first collateralised loan obligation (CLO) in Australia; and
- asset-backed commercial paper programs (conduits) such as ABN AMRO's Tasman, Deutsche Bank's SABRE, Société Générale's ACE, Westpac's WARATAH and Macquarie Securitisation's POLAR. Moody's estimated that outstanding asset-backed commercial paper conduits increased their issues by 90 per cent from $2.3 billion in 1996 to $4.4 billion in 1997, with the number of conduits rising to 22.

The list of assets which can be securitised has increased exponentially. However, products conventionally regarded as suitable for securitisation are characterised by:

- standardised loan documentation;
- historical portfolio characteristics;
- homogeneous assets; and
- well-defined process for originating the assets.

Once packaged, the products to be securitised are transferred to a specifically created, special-purpose vehicle which buys the assets from the originator. Generally, the originator is retained to deal with customers, but the assets bought by the SPV are kept separate from the originator's funds and assets. The SPV issues securities, raising funds which in turn pay for the assets bought. The principal and interest owed to investors in the securities is funded out of the cashflow received from the financial assets. Often enhancements such as a letter of credit or some form of credit support are used to ensure that the securities receive as high a credit-rating as possible to underpin their appeal to investors.

Each securitised structure is unique, so each series of securities has its own characteristics. However, a typical structure would involve a trust, a trust manager and a trustee. The trust is created to own the assets which are accumulated in a warehouse before being securitised. Once created, the asset-backed securities are issued through a dealer panel, who are also the market-makers and bring the issue to investors. The trust manager administers the assets, invests the liquid funds and liaises with investors, underwriters and the trustee. The trustee is the watchdog over the trust manager and a security trustee keeps an eye on security through having a charge over the assets for the benefit of investors.

Prepayment risk

A feature that differentiates mortgage-backed securities from conventional long-term fixed-income paper, and which makes them a more complex investment, is the prepayment element of mortgages. Borrowers might take a 25-year mortgage but, for a variety of reasons—personal, financial or economic—they prepay, or pay out or pay down the mortgage well ahead of that term, perhaps because they refinance to a cheaper loan. The decision or frequency of prepayment of fixed-rate mortgages carrying no prepayment penalty is a function of the direction of interest rates; this was borne out in the US and in the FANMAC model used in New South Wales.

However, the majority (around 85 per cent) of Australian mortgage-holders borrow at floating or variable rates which are reset regularly to reflect prevailing market conditions. As interest rates rise and fall, their mortgage payments generally increase and decrease with a lag, but prepayments are largely unchanged as there is little incentive for borrowers to refinance when most lenders' floating-rate products are similarly priced. However, there is still substantial incentive for borrowers to partially repay owner-occupied home loans because the interest cost of these loans is not tax-deductible. Most securitisations in Australia are structured with floating-rate medium-term notes (MTNs), based on pools of floating-rate mortgages, because it reduces investors' prepayment risk and the bonds generally trade close to par. An exception is Macquarie's PUMA program, lead-managed by Deutsche Bank, which issues fixed and floating-rate bonds, but with its fixed-rate issues in the form of bullet securities which cannot be repaid before maturity. With MTNs, the coupon changes monthly or quarterly as it is reset in line with BBSW, a trend that satisfies investors because their coupon is following market cycles in interest rates. However, investors still face term risk, as there is no certainty as to the eventual term of the securities. Using mortgage substitution, also known as *substitution period* and usually limited to two years, a mortgage manager can overcome this by 'topping up' after prepayments with new mortgages which come from a warehouse or have been freshly originated. This enables the mortgage manager to keep the pool open, and also extends the average life of the mortgage-backed securities by reducing the impact on their average life of any increase in prepayments.

Securitisation's role in financing projects

The skills developed in securitisation and related techniques have been applied in project finance, leading to the birth of innovative structured finance deals using securitisation (in its widest sense) to finance hospitals, airports and tollways. Banks and investment banks have applied securitisation techniques to projects especially where governments are keen to transfer risk. (Some banks and investment banks have securitisation as part of a structured finance or asset finance division, others operate the two separately.) An early example of a structured finance deal was the 1986 $500 million funding of the Sydney Harbour Tunnel, which was a first in terms of selling long-term inflation-linked bonds issued by private enterprise to finance construction of a major public development. Westpac subsidiary Partnership Pacific Ltd devised inflation-linked bonds as a way of offsetting construction costs against toll income in future years.

Structured finance techniques have been applied in:

- Victoria's new Latrobe Regional Hospital project, which is an example of private-sector participation in providing hospital services and forms part of the state's broader strategy of privatisation where private-sector skills are applied to provide public infrastructure. Latrobe Regional Hospital Pty Ltd, a special-purpose vehicle established to build, own and finance the hospital and lease it to the operator, Australian Health Care, issued CPI-linked annuity bonds. Under a twenty-year 'build-own-operate' agreement, the Victorian Department of Human Services buys health services on behalf of public patients in the Latrobe Valley and in return LRH Pty Ltd has exclusive rights to provide public hospital and healthcare services in its area for the life of the contract. Payments to bond-holders come from revenues received from the state for health services delivered to public patients at the hospital.
- Western Australia's Peel Health Campus, a $55 million redevelopment of an existing public hospital with new private facilities, which was funded by issuing fixed-interest bonds for seventeen years. And a structured bond issue was used in the sale-and-leaseback of the WA Government Vehicle Fleet, with the $150 million financing including securitisation of lease payments made by the WA government for some 10 000 vehicles.

- The M2 tollroad in Sydney, where CPI-linked bonds were issued to finance construction and long-term funding, with the debt a securitisation of the projected tolls over the first 25 years.
- Privatisation of Perth airport, where twenty-year bonds were issued, backed by the aggregated revenue streams from sources such as government landing charges, car-parking charges and lease payments of the domestic terminals.
- Securitisation techniques have also been used in the acquisition and privatisation of state power utilities.

12

Foreign exchange and the foreign-exchange markets

Foreign-exchange markets developed to cater for the supply of, and demand for, different currencies by governments, companies and individuals. They exist to serve international trade and the international movement of money. Individuals, companies, banks and governments can use foreign-exchange markets to settle their debts by exchanging one currency for another.

A rate of exchange is the price of one currency in terms of another, such as the price of Australian dollars in terms of US dollars. This price or rate of exchange is expressed in a 'spread'—for example, the value of the $US in terms of the yen may be 127.70/80 and the value of the $A against the $US may be 65.50/53 US cents. The spread is the difference between the bank's buy and sell (bid and offer) rates, and represents the profit or margin the bank makes when it handles both sides of a transaction. A simple rule to remember when converting into a foreign currency is that the customer always gets the smaller amount, the bank the larger. Thus, in the above example, the customer received 127.70 yen and 65.50 US cents for every $US or $A sold to the bank, while it would cost the customer 127.80 yen and 65.53 US cents to get back one $US or $A.

The Australian dollar is usually measured against the $US or in terms of the trade-weighted index (TWI) which is not a price but a measure of the general value of the $A. The $A/$US rate is important because the bulk of the foreign-exchange trading in the $A is in terms of its US counterpart, as is the case for most world currencies, and the greater part (51.4 per cent) of Australia's imports are paid for not in $A but in $US. The TWI, a basket of two-way exchange rates against the $A for around 25 countries, each weighted in line with its trade with Australia, shows whether the

$A has been rising or falling on average against the currencies of our major trading partners. The TWI is reviewed annually and reweightings published in the Reserve Bank's monthly *Bulletin* (usually in the October issue).

Currencies are usually quoted either *spot* (settlement in two working days' time) or *forward* (settlement on an agreed future date). Spot transactions are uncomplicated, standardised trades taking place in a highly liquid market. A survey in 1995 by the Bank for International Settlements noted that while the spot market used to be the most important segment in foreign-exchange trading, accounting for more than half of the volume, by 1995 that had changed so that forward transactions accounted for more than half of the total, although the spot market still recorded healthy growth of 30 per cent between 1992 and 1995. In foreign exchange, a quote is assumed to be spot unless otherwise specified. Currencies can also be dealt through a *swap* which is the simultaneous purchase and sale of spot and forward foreign-exchange transactions at rates agreed between two counterparties.

Australia's foreign-exchange markets have grown substantially, as activity resumed after a lull in the early 1990s. By 1997 average daily turnover, according to Reserve Bank figures, had risen to $A70 billion, which represents an average annual increase of about 7 per cent since 1990. Expansion in Australia's foreign-exchange markets since the mid-to-late 1980s has mirrored the increase in global foreign-exchange trading and the willingness of global investors and money managers to look beyond their own markets; during those years Australia secured for itself a niche in global foreign-exchange business by filling the time-slot between the close of the active New York markets and the opening of major centres such as Tokyo, Hong Kong and Singapore. However, as foreign-exchange activity becomes increasingly concentrated on key world centres such as Tokyo, London and New York, it is possible that the significance and advantages of Australia's niche position could diminish. An unknown for foreign-exchange operators in the late 1990s was the impact of the shift, starting in January 1999, to a common European currency, with monetary policy coming under the wing of the European Central Bank. Under this European Monetary Union (EMU), the eleven currencies of France, Germany, Spain, Italy, Luxembourg, Belgium, Ireland, the Netherlands, Austria, Finland and Portugal joined to form the European currency unit (ECU) or 'euro', eliminating the volume of business transacted by key currencies such as the deutschmark. Trading of the euro against the $US could grow or, so it was thought until the Asian financial debacle of late 1997, major Asian currencies could take up the slack.

Most trading desks start early; in Sydney, 5 am Monday morning

(7 am New Zealand time) is the official start of foreign-exchange trading so that Sydney can squeeze maximum advantage out of its time zone position. Interbank traders aim to capitalise on the few hours' start before the active Singapore market opens and takes over. Heavy-volume trading in $A formally opens around 8.30 am but effectively never stops. Local foreign-exchange traders, whose days have been lengthened by the international integration of markets, deal until at least 7 pm Sydney time which is only 8 am that day in London (although the time-difference varies between seasons). Several major players run 24-hour desks. The segmentation of foreign-exchange activity into shifts in the 24-hour clock has cut into the former, cosier sociability in foreign-exchange markets.

Reflecting the increasing sophistication of financial markets around the world, spot foreign-exchange trading ranks as a 'vanilla' or 'mature' product compared with more exotic risk-management facilities and margins from basic foreign-exchange trading have been declining. An important trend has been a massive increase in electronic foreign-exchange trading as technology plays a bigger role in the markets; the Australian foreign-exchange market uses two electronic broking systems, EBS (Electronic Broking Service) and Reuters Dealer 2002 and automated trading systems are increasingly being developed. There has also been an increased concentration of foreign-exchange business among the top handful of players. Banks have become the dominant participants in foreign exchange and the major fund managers and hedge funds have also become players of significance in world foreign-exchange markets. In Australia, most corporates have retreated from having active in-house treasuries which trade foreign currencies and take a more defensive approach to foreign-currency management; the gap has been filled by fund managers. With credit-rating and balance-sheet size important factors in an institution's capacity to deal effectively in foreign-exchange markets, the less-than-behemoth players have opted for foreign-exchange advisory roles or niche positioning rather than trading activities. Whereas in the past foreign-exchange traders undertook a great deal of trading for trading's sake, and the more aggressive made (and lost) money from taking big positions, the trend has shifted from aggressive risk-and-position-taking to undertaking packaged, structured deals for clients using derivative products such as options and swaps rather than basic (vanilla) foreign-exchange transactions. This is part of the financial markets' restless search for new markets where profits are fatter than in the older, established 'mature' markets.

The 1995 BIS survey showed daily turnover in foreign exchange to be $US1.1 trillion, representing growth of 45 per cent since the

Table 12.1   Currency composition of gross (that is, not adjusted for double counting) foreign-exchange turnover in Australia: % of total turnover

	April 1995	January 1998
$A/$US	42.0	57.4
$US/deutschmark	21.7	11.3
$US/yen	13.3	11.5
Pound sterling/$US	7.0	3.9
$NZ/$US	3.2	6.5
$US/Swiss franc	2.6	0.8

Source: Reserve Bank of Australia

previous BIS survey in April 1992. Australia was ranked the ninth-largest foreign-exchange market, accounting for 2.5 per cent of world turnover; the three largest foreign-exchange markets, the UK, US and Japan, accounted for 55 per cent. The next five most important centres were Singapore, Hong Kong, Switzerland, Germany and France. The UK, the largest single centre for foreign-exchange trading, alone accounted for almost one-third of all foreign-exchange turnover globally in 1995. This dominance is attributed to London's favourable position between the Asian and North American time zones and the depth of capital and derivatives markets in the UK capital. The BIS survey showed that the $US continued to dominate world foreign-exchange trading, with the US currency involved in 83 per cent of all transactions worldwide.

With average daily turnover of $A70 billion, the Australian market has grown by 36 per cent since the 1992 BIS survey. A significant proportion of $A trading takes place outside Australia, with an estimated 40 per cent taking place in Australia and the rest in Asian, European and US markets—a trend that reflects increasing interest by international fund managers in Australian-dollar investments. The Australian dollar is not alone in being widely traded outside its own country; for example, only about 16 per cent of $US trading takes place in the US, while 10 per cent of deutschmark activity takes place in Germany and 35 per cent of yen trading occurs in Japan.

Australia's foreign-exchange market has grown significantly since December 1983 when the $A was floated and most exchange controls removed. Before the float, physical trading in foreign exchange was handled by fourteen banks, whereas by the late 1990s about 70 institutions were authorised to trade foreign exchange.

Most foreign-exchange market activity is prompted by speculation, arbitrage and professional dealing, with currencies being bought and sold as if they were a commodity such as apples or

Table 12.2 Australian foreign-exchange market activity: average daily turnover ($US billion)[1]

	April 1989	April 1992	April 1995	Jan 1998
By type of transaction				
Outright spot	18.0	12.6	17.6	19.4
—of which against $A	9.1	3.5	5.6	8.9
Outright forward	1.5	1.2	1.3	2.5
—of which against $A	1.1	0.7	0.8	1.6
Swaps	9.4	15.1	20.6	23.4
—of which against $A	5.7	7.4	10.0	15.0
By type of counterparty				
With customers	6.1	5.8	9.0	11.3
With other resident dealers	7.5	5.6	8.0	8.7
With overseas banks	15.2	17.6	22.5	25.4
Total	**28.9**	**29.0**	**39.5**	**45.3**
—of which transactions through brokers	9.7	9.4	9.8	10.8

[1] Adjusted for double counting. Items may not sum to totals due to rounding.
Source: Reserve Bank of Australia

potatoes. Unlike such commodities, though, currencies and their prices have important implications for government policy.

Foreign-exchange markets are understood most easily by those who already have a working knowledge of the money markets. Like traders in the money market, foreign-exchange traders deal in money, but whereas money-market dealers for the most part handle cash and securities denominated in their domestic currency, foreign-exchange traders handle cash and paper denominated in different currencies, although the distinction between foreign and domestic financial markets activities has become increasingly blurred in contemporary globalised markets. Traders share the dealing-room environment, and the accompanying pressures of making split-second decisions about handling large volumes of money.

The Reserve Bank commented on Table 12.2:

> Spot transactions, which involve outright trading of currencies for settlement in two business days, are becoming a less prominent part of market turnover. Spot transactions in Australian dollars, for example, are now little more than half the peak level of the late 1980s. This reflects a maturing of the market and a decline in speculative activity. The main growth in the market has been in swaps activity, which has reflected the general trend by market participants to make greater use of derivatives in all markets or to use forward currency markets to establish speculative interest-rate positions. Swaps—transactions in which parties agree to exchange

two currencies and to reverse the exchange at a later date—account for virtually all the derivatives trading in the foreign exchange market. There is no Australian futures market in Australian dollars, and only trading in outright forwards—the exchange of two currencies for settlement more than two business days after the conclusion of the deal—and options. This is not dissimilar to patterns of trading elsewhere in the world.

As in all over-the-counter markets, customer-based business in the foreign-exchange market is only a small part of total turnover; it has typically averaged around 20 per cent of the total. Most turnover is what is often referred to as 'inter-dealer', which involves dealers transacting currencies among themselves to lay off positions resulting from customer deals and to determine the exchange rate at each point in time. In Australia, an increased proportion of this inter-dealer trading is with dealers in other countries, reflecting the growing importance of trading in currencies other than the Australian dollar.

Foreign exchange has been a market where, traditionally, a large proportion of deals have been executed through brokers. In recent years, however, reflecting advances in electronic technology, there appears to have been some move away from use of voice brokers; transactions through voice brokers have declined to about 22 per cent of total turnover, compared with about one-third in the late 1980s. Greater use of electronic deal-matching services is one reason for this.

Around 70 foreign-exchange dealers operate in the Australian market but turnover has always been fairly concentrated and has become even more so over the past few years. The top ten dealers account for around 75 per cent of turnover, compared with around 60 per cent at the end of the 1980s. Most of these top ten dealers are banks. While non-banks comprise 40 per cent of the total number of foreign-exchange dealers, their share of turnover is only 7.5 per cent of the market.

Trading foreign exchange

Because the $US is the dominant currency in foreign-exchange markets it is common practice that major currencies are quoted against the $US or 'greenback'. 'Dollar' in foreign exchange is taken to indicate the $US; any other currency expressed as a dollar has to be identified, for example $A, $NZ, $HK. A quote that is expressed as so many units of currency to one US dollar can be termed a *direct quote*; for example, one $US = 127 yen or 1.8 deutschmarks. An exception to this is the former 'sterling bloc'—the UK's pound sterling and the Australian and New Zealand dollars. These currencies are quoted *indirectly*, that is, in terms of so many US dollars per unit of currency, and read:

one $A = $US0.6500 or 65 US cents
one $NZ = $US0.5500 or 55 US cents
one pound sterling = $US1.6650

If the Australian dollar were quoted directly its price would be given in Australian dollar units per one $US, for example, $A1.5385.

Foreign currencies are traded for a variety of reasons, but transactions broadly fall into three categories:

Covering trade or investments

- to pay for imports;
- to convert proceeds from exports;
- to repay an overseas borrowing or pay dividends or interest to overseas investors;
- to convert funds that have been borrowed or invested from overseas.

Arbitrage

A trader arbitraging different markets or currencies has no inherent foreign-exchange risk that requires covering. The arbitrager is taking advantage of opportunities for profit arising out of short-term discrepancies in the prices of currencies or in interest rates. Arbitrage is a highly professional business. Windows of opportunity generally open and close very quickly. To arbitrage markets successfully, a trader needs extensive credit lines and the ability to move rapidly.

Speculative transactions

A speculator in foreign exchange is someone who accepts the possibility of adverse exchange-rate movements in the hope of making a profit from favourable movements in currencies.

Covering foreign-exchange risk

Transactions in foreign exchange do not always relate to the immediate future. Often traders need to cover a known future commitment, such as a foreign-currency bill that will fall due in six months or a foreign-currency loan that is due to mature three months hence. An importer pays for goods not when they are ordered, but when they are supplied; an exporter does not receive the proceeds of a sale until the goods have been delivered to the buyer. In the intervening weeks or months, exchange-rate movements could significantly alter what an importer or exporter expects to pay or receive.

The risk of exchange-rate variations can be covered by buying or selling foreign currencies forward, that is, by agreeing that the future settlement of the transaction, when it falls due, will take place at a predetermined exchange rate. Forward markets have developed to cope with such needs, to allow buyers and sellers, exporters and importers, to take cover (or insurance) against fluctuations in exchange rates. Forward contracts provide for delivery of a foreign currency for periods ranging from a few days hence to one year or longer.

Forward prices take into account the different delivery dates, based on the spot rate of a currency plus or minus a margin which varies with the period for which the forward contract is written. The forward rate therefore has two components: the spot rate and the forward points, or margin. An 'outright forward' is the total of the spot rate and the forward points. The forward margin between two currencies largely reflects the differential in *interest rates* between the two countries concerned. For example, if Australian interest rates are higher than those in the US, the forward points are deducted from the spot $A/$US rate; if Australian interest rates are lower, the forward points are added to the spot rate.

Calculation of forward points

A simple way to think of the interest-rate differential is in terms of what you might earn in Australia as against what a borrowing might cost in the US. For example, assume that Australian interest rates are lower than those in the US and that the three-month interest rate is 6 per cent in the US and 5 per cent in Australia and that the spot $A/$US exchange rate is $A1.00 = $US0.65 or 65 US cents.

In Australia, in three months' time, $A1 will be worth $(1 + (1 \times 0.05 \times 92/365 =))$ 1.01260. In the US, 65 cents in three months' time will be worth $(0.65 + (0.65 \times 0.06 \times 92/360 =))$ 0.659968 (US uses a 360-day year).

The implied spot $A/$US exchange rate in three months is thus $(0.659968/1.01260) = 0.65175$, a difference from today's spot rate of 17.5 points. Australian interest rates are lower so the points are added and so are ascending around a mid of 17.5 to give forward points of 15/20 and forward rates of 0.6515/20.

If Australian interest rates were higher than those in the US, the forward points would be deducted. Assume the three-month interest rate is 5 per cent in the US and 6 per cent in Australia and the spot $A/$US exchange rate is 0.6500.

In Australia in three months' time $A1 is worth $(1 + (1 \times 0.06 \times 92/365)) = 1.01512$. In the US in three months' time 65 cents will be worth $(0.65 + (0.65 \times 0.05 \times 92/360)) = 0.65831$ so the implied spot $A/$US exchange rate in three months is $(0.65831/1.01512) = 0.6485$ or 15 points less than today's spot exchange rate. Using 15 points as a midrate, forward points of 17/13 would be deducted from the spot rate to give forward rates of 0.6483/87.

During 1997, the gradual easing in Australian interest rates saw the interest differentials between Australia and the US cross as Australian interest rates became lower than those prevailing in the US. This occurred initially in the shorter maturities but then spread across the spectrum. For the first time since the $A floated, sellers of the currency (importers) received a benefit for holding forward positions, whereas exporters were penalised in terms of forward points in that they received fewer Australian dollars in the forward maturities for every $US sold than they would have received at the spot dates. The forward margin is called a premium when the forward price of the foreign currency against the domestic currency is higher than the spot price. This means it costs more units of the domestic currency to generate one unit of the foreign currency:

If Australian interest rates are higher than those in the US and the spot $A/$US rate is (that is, $A1.00 = 65.50/53 US cents)	65.50/53
The forward margin (2 weeks) is deducted to get the	23/20
outright forward of	65.27/33

This numerically 'lower' rate means that the $US is worth more Australian dollars, or buys more Australian dollars in the forward market than in the spot market. The premium is deducted from the spot rate, therefore the $A is lowered in value and the foreign currency buys more $A. A $US premium in Australia favours the exporters, who sell their foreign-currency proceeds in exchange for Australian dollars.

If Australian interest rates are lower than those in the US and the spot $A/$US rate is	65.50/53
The forward margin (3 weeks) is added to get an	30/33
outright forward of	65.80/86

The numerically 'higher' rate indicates that one Australian dollar buys more $US in the forward market than in the spot market.

Table 12.3 Cross rates

	$US	deutschmark	£stg	yen
$US	1	1.7773	0.6127	140.52
deutschmark	0.5627	1	0.3447	79.06
yen '000	7.1164	12.6481	4.3600	1
£sterling	1.6321	2.9010	1	229.36

Rates as at June 1998

Importers prefer a $US at a discount because they need fewer $A at the future (forward) date to buy $US.

A general guide to the calculation of outright forwards is that when the forward points are ascending (for example, 20–23), they are added to the spot rate. When the forward points are descending (for example, 23–20) they are subtracted from the spot rate.

The future value of a currency is determined by a number of factors, but predominantly by interest-rate differentials between the domestic and overseas market.

Reciprocal rates

The reciprocal rate is the inverse of a conventional quote. For example, sterling is normally quoted in terms of US dollars and cents; the reciprocal would show US dollars in terms of sterling. If one pound sterling is worth $US1.6127, the reciprocal quote would be calculated by dividing one by 1.6127 to give 0.6200, that is, $US1 is worth 0.6200 pounds.

Cross rates

Currencies regarded as 'exotics' are usually traded in terms of the $US; also, for historical reasons, currencies such as sterling, the $A and $NZ are expressed in terms of the US currency. To trade, say, the $A against a currency other than the $US, one must first relate that currency to the $US and then the $US to the $A. For example, an exporter who has to convert 10 million deutschmark export receipts into Australian dollars would first gather the market rates for the $A/$US and the $US/DEM, and use these rates to arrive at a rate for the $A/DEM. If one $US were equal to $A1.651 and one $US were equal to 1.7773 deutschmarks one deutschmark would be equal to $A0.9289. A typical cross-rates table can be seen in table 12.3

As in the money markets, there is no physical trading floor for foreign exchange. Foreign-exchange traders deal by telephone and also use telex and facsimile machines to confirm details. The

219

interbank market increasingly uses the Reuters Dealing System to trade because it provides an instantaneous printed confirmation of deals executed, which avoids disagreements.

The volume of foreign-exchange trading has increased to such an extent that business in a treasury operation is divided among specialists. One trader might focus on 'spot yen', that is, yen transactions to be settled in two business days. Another concentrates on forward trades and another runs a swaps desk. Currency swaps and options are discussed in chapter 13. (Foreign-exchange trading is discussed in greater detail in *FOREX: the Techniques of Foreign Exchange* by Edna Carew and Will Slatyer, published by Allen & Unwin.)

Background to floating currencies

Floating currencies are not a phenomenon of the late twentieth century: they existed in the late nineteenth century and were tried again in the 1930s. Support for floating exchange rates re-emerged in the 1950s and 1960s, when the philosophy of free markets—most noticeably espoused by the American economist Milton Friedman—argued that floating exchange rates would bring greater stability in currency markets. There was considerable enthusiasm for floating exchange rates among academic economists who placed more faith in markets than in the ability of governments to determine exchange rates.

The search for the most satisfactory method of managing exchange rates is decades old. From the late nineteenth century until the early 1930s the world operated with a gold standard which set the levels of currencies in relation to gold. The First World War and the disruptions that followed in world economies destroyed the system. By 1933 only five countries remained on the gold standard and it was becoming increasingly difficult to maintain exchange-rate parities in the face of rising inflation. The Second World War brought further problems and interruptions, but in 1944 the representatives of 44 nations met in Bretton Woods, New Hampshire, US, to work out a new international monetary system. The conference also established the International Monetary Fund (IMF) and International Bank for Reconstruction and Development, popularly known as the World Bank. The Bretton Woods proposals were accepted in the hope that they would bring about some stability in exchange rates and avoid competitive devaluations. The new system bore some resemblance to the gold standard; exchange rates would continue to move but in an orderly way and in specific circumstances. And no change in the value of a currency could take place without the approval of the IMF. The $US held a key role in the new system, because each member country of the IMF set a level for its currency relative to gold or the $US; most currencies were tied to the $US which remained convertible into gold. The system maintained fairly stable exchange rates until the late 1960s.

By the late 1960s the US was issuing an excessive amount of paper money, largely to finance the war in Vietnam, and this prompted other countries, notably France, to cash their paper dollars for gold. But the US had issued more paper money than could be backed by gold, so the link between gold and the currencies had to be broken. On 15 August 1971, the US government suspended redeeming paper certificates for gold. This signalled the final stages of the Bretton Woods system. In December that year central bankers and treasury officials put together a new policy, known as the Smithsonian Agreement, under which the official price of gold rose from $US35 to $US38 an ounce—effectively a 7.9 per cent devaluation of the $US. The agreement also recognised that the $US was no longer convertible into gold. The Smithsonian Agreement was short-lived, largely because the world had lost confidence in the $US. The US currency was heavily sold, to an extent that forced an official closing of foreign-exchange markets on 1 March 1973. When the markets opened several weeks later there was no further attempt to hold exchange rates within official limits. Rates between the $US and other currencies were free to float, subject only to the forces of supply and demand. Various degrees of managed floats were tried during the 1970s but from 1973 the main currencies of the world were subject to little discipline. The change, by many major economies, to floating exchange rates in the early 1970s was a vote in favour of market forces. The optimism surrounding the move proved ill-conceived, mostly because it was based on the premise that exchange rates are mainly influenced by shifts in countries' current accounts. In reality exchange rates are manipulated by short-term capital flows which represent a large pool of mobile funds chasing the best interest rates.

By the late 1980s imbalances in trade and in world economies had brought an unwelcome degree of volatility to currency markets, forcing a reassessment of the advantages of floating currencies. Central banks began to intervene more frequently in currency markets and a particular feature of the late 1980s was a new form of concerted intervention by the main central banks. This recognised that one central bank acting alone could do little to change the course of a currency; but by acting in concert, and with judicious timing, the central banks could have an influence over the direction of a currency.

By the late 1990s it was not evident that flexible exchange rates were universally favourably viewed. A number of countries, including Argentina, Estonia, Lithuania and Bulgaria, had followed the example of Hong Kong and adopted a system where their currency is pegged to a major, hard currency. In Hong Kong's case this is the $US but the deutschmark or sterling could be used. In January 1998 the IMF commented in a study, *Currency boards: the ultimate fix*, that currency boards (a new name for a 'peg') were back in fashion (at their peak in the 1950s about 50 countries operated with a currency board). Australia used a currency board or peg to the $US in the years before the $A floated. A variant of a currency board is to have the currency fixed to a basket of currencies of the countries of major trading partners, or have a 'loose peg' where a currency is fixed to a band around a major currency, perhaps 5 per cent above or below it. However a currency board operates, it removes control of domestic monetary policy from the local authorities as interest rates are left hostage to biases in the foreign-exchange market, for example, pre-float a big sell-off in Australian dollars used to mean the supply of $A dried up and interest rates soared, whereas with a float the currency itself takes the brunt.

What affects floating exchange rates?

Exchange rates are affected by a number of factors, especially the main economic indicators such as inflation and interest rates, a country's balance of payments, fiscal and monetary policies, international political and economic developments, government attitudes to intervention and—as the events in Asia in late 1997 and early 1998 demonstrated when a number of regional currencies were pushed to levels regarded as quite out of line with fundamentals in their economies—investor confidence. Investors and speculators can influence the direction a currency takes. Also important is market sentiment. Foreign-exchange markets tend to over-react to news, so that currencies are often pushed too far in one direction and they 'overshoot'. Foreign-exchange traders are prone to focus on the very short term and to mark a currency up or down accordingly, usually ignoring longer-term fundamentals. This adds to the volatility and can cause sudden, inexplicable movements in exchange rates which can drive these rates to levels that are difficult, if not impossible, to explain in the context of economic conditions.

Another factor that influences floating exchange rates is central bank intervention. Foreign-exchange dealers can regard central bank intervention as a guide, or they can take it on as a challenge. If dealers interpret intervention as a guide then they have an indication of where the government and central bank would like to have the currency. Central bank intervention is discussed more fully below.

Foreign-exchange market players

Australia's foreign-exchange markets operate with around 70 authorised or licensed foreign-exchange traders which include the four major domestic banks and large global investment banks. Other significant participants in foreign-exchange markets are fund managers, corporations, central banks and foreign-exchange brokers. Wealthy individuals also participate. The dominant sector of the foreign-exchange market is the interbank market, where the banks trade with each other, either directly or through a broker. Capital movements, rather than trade flows, are the main focus of business.

International investors

Portfolio managers investing overseas first consider the currency and interest-rate risks but also take into account the liquidity of an overseas market, its regulations and settlement procedures and ability to hedge against the relevant currency. Portfolio managers use international fixed-interest markets in their push to maximise returns (through income, currency and capital appreciation), diversify currency risk and find different, possibly longer-term, maturities compared with what is available domestically. International investors have a variety of markets from which to choose; popular examples include the Swiss franc market, US treasury bonds and UK gilts, as well as currency derivatives such as options and swaps and eurodollar and eurobond markets which offer securities denominated in, say, euro-$US, euro-sterling, euro-yen, euro-$A and so on. Australian fund managers have access to all these markets.

Foreign borrowers are often blocked from using the domestic bond markets of other countries and so specific securities have been designed for use by non-resident borrowers. These include *Yankee* bonds, being bonds issued in the US, denominated in $US, the UK's *Bulldog* bonds, denominated in sterling, and Japan's *Samurai* bonds. Australian companies have at times capitalised on the appeal of high (relative to other countries) Australian interest rates to offer $A-denominated securities in the euromarkets—euro-$A bonds—which were energetically sold in the 1980s to the mythical 'Belgian dentist', the stereotype of the affluent retail buyer looking to earn a high return through the coupon on the bond.

Euromarkets is a generic term for currencies and securities held outside their country of origin. Active euromarkets began in 1957 when non-US banks holding $US deposits began to re-invest them in Europe instead of in the US. The UK banks played a major role in lending $US to European banks, companies and individuals. Euromarkets are also said to have been encouraged by the cold war between the US and the Soviet Union, with the Soviet Union placing

$US with UK banks rather than holding them in the US. At the time, US banks were operating under restrictions which held their deposit rates substantially lower than those of their European counterparts, so that European banks attracted $US deposits. Euromarkets subsequently got a big boost in the 1970s from Arab oil money following the oil price rises. These large surpluses of petro-dollars were looking for an outlet and the Arabs were unwilling to place all of the funds in the US. The *euro* in the late 1990s signifies Europe's common currency.

Banks

As well as the highly publicised and highly leveraged hedge fund operators, the big players in foreign exchange are the large, internationally operating banks and global investment banks which are active in financial markets and fund management. It is these institutions which can influence currencies and which share the multinationals' capacity to 'move the market' (significantly influence exchange rates up or down). The banks are active in foreign-exchange markets on behalf of their customers (exporters and importers, borrowers, lenders and investors) and on their own accounts; they are both intermediaries and principals. A bank's objective in foreign exchange is to profit by earning a margin from the client for facilitating the business and to use its knowledge of market demand to outperform interbank competitors. A corporate client, on the other hand, will be trying to hedge or protect its cashflow from movements in exchange rates (although it is not unknown for companies to speculate, too). Banks tend to take a short-term view in foreign-exchange trading; corporates often have a medium to longer-term focus.

Banks carry out foreign-exchange transactions at the retail level, exchanging one currency for another either in cash (currency notes) or travellers cheques for tourists. The rates applying to these transactions are related to those that prevail in the foreign-exchange dealing room (the professional or wholesale market) but are less attractive because of the administrative and processing costs of such 'small' business.

The larger banks are professional foreign-exchange dealers; they are market-makers who quote two-way prices—prices at which they will buy and at which they will sell. The spread (difference) between the bank's buying and selling prices represents its profit on the deal. Banks operate in foreign exchange under internally imposed limits set by the board; for the most part these fall within the capital adequacy supervision undertaken by external regulators which takes into account foreign-exchange and other market risks. The limits relate to overall exposure in all currencies, in each individual currency, and in individual and total spot and forward positions. Banks' overnight limits are more restricted than those that prevail during the day's trading, and overnight positions smaller, for prudential reasons. Central banks and banks prefer to reduce exposures during hours when senior executives are not at the trading desk. Even banks which run a full overnight shift operate with smaller limits overnight than during the day when senior people are present to take decisions.

Investment banks

Investment banks, formerly known in Australia as merchant banks, were active in the Australian currency hedge market, the 'grey' or *de facto* market which, before the foreign-exchange market was freed in 1983, provided facilities to protect against exchange-rate movements for those ineligible, at the time, for the banks' forward market. Most merchant banks with involvement in foreign exchange sought the status of authorised foreign-exchange trader when this became available in 1984. Although the currency hedge market ceased to exist, the hedge settlement rate, published in the *Australian Financial Review*, is still used as a benchmark, with long-dated forwards priced off that rate.

Financial institutions

Big financial institutions, such as fund managers and insurance companies, have developed significant offshore investments and are an increasing force in foreign-exchange markets as they manage their international assets and liabilities. These financial institutions might not be continuously active in foreign exchange, but when they do enter the market, they come in with big volumes that can have an effect on exchange rates. The major Japanese life offices have at times been big investors in Australian fixed-interest securities because of the attractive differential between the interest rates on Australian and Japanese government debt. Australian fund managers have become increasingly global in their outlook and activities. Growing use of foreign-currency investments on the part of fund managers has led to a rise in *currency overlay managers* who, for a fee, manage currency risk for fund managers. Usage varies, with some fund managers choosing to manage their currency exposures themselves, some appointing currency overlay managers to handle the deals and some using currency overlay managers as advisers and handling the dealing in-house.

Corporations

Companies use the foreign-exchange market to protect themselves against exposure to unfavourable movements in the exchange rate. A large company might run an in-house treasury division; a smaller organisation would employ one or two traders. Trading companies have as much need to monitor and participate in the foreign-exchange markets as the banks. Shifts in exchange rates can throw their financial planning off course, so it is important that they take out some form of insurance or protection against such movements— that is, they *hedge* or *cover* their position. Companies and individuals in countries with high interest rates use overseas markets as a source of cheaper funding, but they must take into account the currency risks on principal and interest payments. Those who assume that low interest-rate currencies are an automatic source of cheap funds run the risk of coming to grief. This was demonstrated by the rush, during the 1980s, by Australian and New Zealand borrowers to raise funds in Swiss francs, only to find the repayments crushing when the domestic currencies dropped in value against the strong Swiss currency. Company boards therefore set limits and dealing policies for their traders. Organisations which borrow off-shore to fund overseas projects add to Australia's foreign debt problem, but if a debt is matched, in the same currency, by assets, then the borrower has a natural hedge.

Foreign-exchange brokers

Brokers became a significant feature of the London interbank market because until 1979 London banks were not allowed to deal directly with each other in foreign exchange but had to transact business through a third party. By the time this was no longer the case the brokers had carved out for themselves a role and reputation as useful, instantaneous conduits of market and price information. The key broking houses in foreign exchange operate as a worldwide network, acting as middlemen in a role that is broadly similar to that of money and sharebrokers who stand between buyer and seller and execute deals in return for a commission.

Brokers tap their wide network to find the best available rate for a client. Their activities, though, involve more than just quoting a price. They are constantly in touch with as wide a range of market players as possible. They thrive on information, on gaining it and dispersing it, and are often a rich source of market rumour. They use the latest in electronic communications, a combination of phones, fax, screens and, less commonly, 'squawk boxes' (speakers that relay market information to the dealing rooms) as well as absorbing information from newspapers, television, radio and news services. Brokers tend to service mainly the interbank market. All bank and professional foreign-exchange dealing rooms maintain a direct telephone link to a broker, if only for information purposes.

Broker activity probably peaked in the late 1980s and early 1990s and has since been declining. Staff numbers in the four main foreign-exchange broking firms in Australia were substantially cut in 1997 as the brokers felt the combined pinch of a smaller client base and the impact of electronic broking.

Electronic trading

Electronic trading in foreign-exchange markets has increased significantly with both Reuters and EBS providing electronic broking services where banks deal on screens which show their best bid-and-offer prices in a range of currency pairs. Either price can be hit (taken or accepted) by pressing a button and a deal ticket is printed automatically. This method of trading has brought greater transparency to foreign-exchange dealing than was available when trading took place solely by telephone. Corporate end-users of the market can see prices on the screens. A combination of electronic and direct (not brokered) conversation-dealing is available on Reuters systems where traders communicate electronically, carry out a typed conversation, agree a price and confirm through automatically printed deal tickets.

Central bank intervention

Central banks are key players from time to time in foreign-exchange markets, even in a climate of floating exchange rates. This is part of their role as guardians of their countries' monetary and banking systems, and holders of foreign currency reserves.

Central banks intervene in foreign-exchange markets to counter disorderly market conditions, to provide stability in special circumstances such as a major political event, or to support or depress the local currency if the market pushes it to a level that the bank (or government) feels is inconsistent with monetary policy objectives, or to offset speculative moves that the central bank believes to be potentially destabilising.

The purpose of intervention is to provide greater stability. Such intervention allows time for domestic policies to take effect on other aspects of the economy. Internationally, the fraternity of central banks aims to encourage market confidence by exhibiting coordinated policies. To be effective, a central bank must choose the time and the reason to intervene, and intervention must be supported by appropriate economic policies—if not, the bank can pour good money after bad.

Floating exchange rates have diminished the central banks' role in the sense that they—theoretically—no longer directly intervene in foreign-exchange markets (though most reserve the right to do so), but retain a key role as the institutions responsible, usually under a charter, for maintaining economic prosperity, low inflation and stable conditions. Central banks tend to talk as much of 'reweighting their reserves' as of 'intervention', reflecting a world-wide trend of paying greater attention to managing reserves. That central banks have become more active in managing their foreign-currency reserves is itself a reflection of the greater level of financial accountability among central banks and a tendency to manage their balance sheets more efficiently.

The question confronting central banks is how to choose the best (least costly) system of exchange-rate management, based on their experience of the flaws in both fixed and floating exchange-rate systems. Few countries can claim to operate 'clean' floats. Most countries have had their floats muddied at times by central bank activity.

Central banks have differed over the years in their attitudes to intervention in foreign-exchange markets. Renewed support for intervention during the 1980s stemmed from disappointment with the shortcomings of floating rates, and a wish to offset longer-term swings in exchange rates, particularly when these swings take an exchange rate to a level that is incompatible with fundamentals. Equally, central banks know they do not have the power singlehandedly to prevent a realignment of the exchange rate that, however unpalatable, is justified by fundamentals. Governments and their central banks had hoped that floating exchange rates would see currencies in line with economic fundamentals in a way that would ensure a degree of monetary independence. This did not happen. The role of central banks in trying to overcome the problems associated with floating exchange rates has been the subject of considerable debate.

International agreements, such as the 1985 Plaza Agreement and the 1987 Louvre Accord, endorse coordinated intervention. In 1985 there was a widespread view that the $US was overbought and clearly overvalued; the central banks put their heads together and said 'enough is enough, exchange rates should reflect fundamentals', and took action which contributed to pushing markets in the right direction and driving the $US lower. The Plaza Agreement was critical of markets:

> The ministers and governors [of the G5 countries] agreed that
> exchange rates should play a role in adjusting external imbalances.

In order to do this, exchange rates should better reflect fundamental economic conditions than has been the case. They believe that agreed policy actions must be implemented and reinforced to improve the fundamentals further, and that in view of the present and prospective changes in fundamentals, some further orderly appreciation of the main non-dollar currencies against the dollar is desirable. They stand ready to cooperate more closely to encourage this when to do so would be helpful.

Early in 1987 the Louvre Accord applauded the changes that had taken place since 1985 and endorsed prevailing levels:

Further substantial exchange-rate shifts among [these] currencies could damage growth and adjustment prospects in [these] countries. In current circumstances, therefore, [ministers and governors] agreed to cooperate closely to foster stability of exchange rates around current levels.

The two agreements underscored an acknowledgment that central banks and their governments could achieve more together than when acting individually, and moreover expressed a willingness to act in concert when necessary.

In June 1998 the US and Japanese monetary authorities entered the foreign-exchange markets in support of the beleaguered yen, stemming its tumble, with the US treasury secretary Robert Rubin stating that the US was prepared 'to continue to cooperate in exchange markets, as appropriate'. The effectiveness of the joint intervention contrasted with an earlier, less successful attempt by the Bank of Japan to defend its currency alone.

Sterilised and non-sterilised intervention

Sterilised or 'pure' intervention occurs when a central bank offsets its actions in the foreign-exchange market so that they have no effect on the domestic money supply. The authorities can thus affect the price level of the domestic currency without upsetting interest rates or other areas of the economy. The intervention can affect the exchange rate *and* market expectations by signalling official intentions about the currency. Sterilised vs non-sterilised intervention had become less of an issue for Australia by the late 1990s but remains an important theoretical question. When the Reserve Bank has intervened it has sterilised the effects; that is, if it bought $A, it replaced cash in the banking system so that there was no effect on interest rates. It replaced liquidity either by buying commonwealth government securities or, more commonly in the late 1990s, it would execute an FX swap: if buying foreign exchange, the first leg of the swap would be to sell foreign exchange with an agreement to buy it back again at a future date. In this way the cash impact of the initial intervention would be deferred until the foreign currency was delivered under the second leg of the swap. Then the transaction might be reversed in the market, delivered if that suits domestic liquidity or rolled over with another swap to buy time until market conditions suit.

Sterilised intervention might take place, for example, when the domestic currency is rising and the authorities (government and central bank) believe this to be inappropriate. The central bank will sell the domestic currency and buy foreign currency. But the central bank's sales of domestic currency will have added to the domestic money supply, so the bank counters this by selling government securities into the market, thereby draining off funds and offsetting the liquidity effects of selling the domestic currency.

Non-sterilised intervention involves doing nothing to offset the liquidity effects of action in the foreign-exchange market. Such inaction would follow a deliberate decision on the part of the central bank. Non-sterilised intervention can have a big impact on the exchange rate because, in reality, it is equivalent to monetary policy action. It is normal practice for central banks to offset any large injections of cash into, or withdrawals of cash from, domestic money markets. If the injection or withdrawal were caused by central bank purchases or sales of foreign currency, the central bank would offset this by an equal sale or purchase of government securities. Choosing not to do so would signal that the central bank wanted to change monetary conditions, that is, it wanted its foreign exchange activities to have an effect on, say, interest rates.

Central banks' justification of their intervention in foreign exchange, under a system of floating exchange rates, shows how far the debate about the efficiency of a float has progressed beyond the idealism of the early 1970s, when freely floating exchange rates were regarded as the proper substitute for an imperfect system of fixed rates. Critics of the floating system point to the degree of intervention as evidence that a float is unworkable and claim that in reality it is little different from a managed rate. Central banks retort that there is a world of difference between maintaining stability through a lightly managed or controlled float and imposing a system of fixed or heavily managed currencies supported by exchange controls.

The Australian experience

The Australian experience with intervention since the $A floated mirrors the general trend and provides an example of its effective use. The Reserve Bank, as is the case with most central banks,

Table 12.4 Foreign-exchange market transactions: summary statistics

	Total post-float period	1 Dec 83– June 86	2 July 86– Sep 91	3 Oct 91– Nov 93	4 Dec 93– June 95	5 July 95– mid-97
No. of days of transactions	1430	331	967	132	nil	273
% of days of transactions	49	52	72	24		59
Average of absolute value of transactions ($Am)[a]	50	13	58	147		38
Max daily transaction ($Am)	−1300	−90	−1000	−1300		286

− implies sales of foreign exchange
[a] Calculated on basis of days when transactions took place

intervenes to calm markets which are threatening to become volatile and disorderly, to try to reverse an overshoot in the currency level (up or down) and sometimes to help monetary policy aims. Sometimes the amount of intervention is less important than the mere news that the RBA had indeed intervened; that alone sends a signal to markets.

When the Reserve Bank intervenes by buying or selling $A, nearly always in exchange for $US, it can deal with banks anywhere in the world, at any time during the 24-hour trading day. The RBA's main foreign-exchange dealing room in Sydney opens at 6 am until 6.30 pm (local time) but the bank also deals from its offices in London and New York. If the $A is rising, the RBA sells it and buys foreign currency; if the $A is falling, the RBA buys the local currency and sells foreign exchange. Like its overseas counterparts, the Australian central bank is not intervening specifically to target a particular level in its currency but to promote stability in its foreign-exchange markets. Central banks abhor volatility in their currencies; they do not always discourage their currencies from shifting to a new level but like to see them do so in an orderly way.

In a seminar paper delivered in May 1997, the Reserve Bank's international department summarised the central bank's approach to intervention as evolving through five fairly distinct phases.

During the immediate post-float period from December 1983 to June 1986 the RBA's approach was to leave the exchange rate to market forces and, when necessary to intervene, to do so only in small amounts. The central bank's favoured description of its approach at that time was one of 'smoothing and testing'. From the middle of 1986 the $A began to experience some large falls; the big swings in the currency's value led the RBA to intervene more frequently and in large amounts as it tried to keep conditions stable while still allowing large moves in the exchange rate. During this period there were several episodes when, in the RBA's view, the $A exchange rate had overshot and it intervened to signal this to the market, for example, in July 1986 when the $A was falling, again in February 1989 when the exchange rate rose to nearly 90 US cents and for a third time in October 1990 when the $A rose sharply following the invasion of Kuwait.

The Reserve Bank succeeded in putting a floor under a falling $A in 1986, through a combination of intervention and adjustments to monetary policy which included a 2 per cent hike in cash rates in one day. As the then deputy governor, John Phillips, later commented when addressing the Australian Forex Association: 'Market conditions were disorderly and we stepped in to calm things down. That was a high-profile and substantial exercise which we judged to be appropriate to the circumstances.' Phillips talked of a later incident, in January 1987, after an announcement of the European currency realignment:

> Nothing much had occurred to alter Australia's economic circumstances, but so-called 'selling on the cross-rates' produced a panic situation in the market for a couple of days. Again we decided that we should be willing to enlarge the scale of our operations to encourage a return to good order. In neither episode did we seek to defend a particular exchange rate or to stay within some preselected exchange rate band. We set out to achieve greater stability in the market. We were delighted, of course, when the market decided enough was enough and that some kind of floor existed for the time being. We don't even mind being given credit for laying of the floor . . . We certainly don't want to fall into the trap of seeking to manage the exchange rate—we have been there before.

The Reserve Bank again intervened in foreign exchange markets, effectively and over a short period, early in 1989. By early February that year the $A was close to 90 US cents, propped up by high interest rates but substantially overvalued when set against economic fundamentals. There was a clear risk that a savage correction would take place. This view was endorsed when, on 31 January, statistics showed that Australia's inflation rate was romping well ahead of budget projections, at close to 8 per cent instead of the hoped-for 5 per cent. The news prompted heavy selling of the $A. The $A, though, swiftly regained strength, hitting a four-year high of 89.60 US cents in February. The Reserve Bank demonstrated that the $A had risen too far by selling the currency. Then the release of a disappointing current account figure pulled the $A down. Reserve Bank selling of the currency, in a climate of bad economic data, brought the $A down by 7 per cent over the course of a week. The central bank had set out to achieve two goals: it wanted to break the nexus between high interest rates and the $A, so that one did not constantly chase the other. It also set out to take advantage of a growing view that at close to 90 US cents the $A was overvalued, and was happy to foster a fall, although not a 'free' fall, and so intervened by buying to check the decline. The Reserve Bank also capped a rally of the $A when it hit 84 US cents, showing its intention was to steady the currency at an acceptable level. Between October 1991 and November 1993 the Reserve Bank intervened infrequently but when it did, it was there in large quantities to maximise the impact.

Between October 1991 and November 1993 the RBA's approach to monetary policy was one of keeping conditions easy to foster economic recovery, a policy that often led to downward pressure on the $A. The RBA did not want to sacrifice an easing in monetary policy to support the exchange rate so any intervention had to be carefully managed as to size and timing. Between December 1993 and June 1995 the RBA did not feel a need to intervene in foreign-exchange markets. From 1995 to mid-1997 the $A was generally rising in value; the RBA's activities chiefly involved buying foreign exchange to retire swaps built up between 1991 and 1993.

The Reserve Bank's first major intervention in foreign-exchange markets since late 1993 occurred in late 1997 and early 1998. The $A had come under a cloud, falling from 74 US cents at the end of October 1997 as Asian currencies tumbled; during that time, however, the TWI rose slightly. In the year to January 1998 the $A fell against the $US by around 20 per cent but the overall depreciation of the $A was not of this dimension because the move against the $US also reflected the strength of the US currency, which ranked the strongest of world currencies. In TWI terms the $A had been more stable, with its fall against the $US offset by large appreciations against currencies of several of Australia's key East Asian trading partners. So there were contrasting influences on the $A from a strong $US and weak Asian currencies. The world view of the $A, however, was to link it with the problems in Asia, trading the currency down to a twelve-year low of less than 60 US cents in June 1998, despite considerable Reserve Bank intervention estimated to total $3 billion in 24 hours. Concerted intervention by the world's two economic giants, the US and Japan, in support of the yen pulled the $A back over 60 US cents later in the month.

Table 12.5 Trade weights and currency movements (%)

	Export weight	Import weight	Movement in $A since beginning of 1997[a]
United States	7.9	24.3	–19.9
Japan	22.0	14.1	–8.4
ASEAN–4 & South Korea	22.4	10.7	88.1
Other East Asia	19.6	14.1	–10.3
European Union	10.4	23.6	–8.6
New Zealand	8.8	5.1	–0.2
Other	9.0	8.1	–12.3

[a] Increase indicates appreciation against the currency/currencies concerned
Source: Reserve Bank of Australia *Bulletin* January 1998

Australian background

Australia has moved through a range of exchange-rate regimes. Until December 1971, for historical reasons, the Australian currency was pegged to sterling. The value of the Australian currency against all other currencies was a reflection of sterling's movements. Under this fixed-exchange-rate system, the Reserve Bank set the rate for all sterling transactions and banks were not allowed to offer concessional, or very high, sterling rates without the Reserve Bank's approval (although they were free to set rates in other currencies).

Between December 1971 and September 1974, the Australian currency was fixed to the $US—a fixed peg. With this system the $A held constant in relation to the $US but varied in its relationship with other currencies. From September 1974 until November 1976, the $A was fixed to the average value of a basket of currencies weighted in proportion to each country's trading importance to Australia. After November 1976, when the $A was substantially devalued, the fixed peg to the basket of currencies was replaced with a variable link to the basket—a flexible or crawling peg. This system, with the $A being valued daily against the trade-weighted basket of currencies and expressed as a midrate in terms of the $US, lasted with some modifications until December 1983 when the $A was floated. The system was intended to work using small, frequent adjustments rather than periodic large movements in the currency. Time was to show, though, that speculation could build up with small, frequent adjustments just as much as in the days of big once-off devaluations or revaluations. As long as someone's hand was on the currency helm the market would try to guess the currency's movements.

During those years, at 9.30 am each day, the Reserve Bank

announced to the banks the public rates for the $US; that $A/$US midrate was the rate for the day. The Reserve Bank set outer limits at or within which the banks had to set rates for their spot transactions in $US. The banks set their own buying and selling rates for currencies other than the $US. The banks operated under strict guidelines: they were not allowed to hold 'open positions' in a foreign currency—at the end of each trading day they had to settle an overbought or oversold position (any surplus or shortfall) with the Reserve Bank. Banks had an important privilege, though—at that time they were the only intermediaries allowed to trade physical foreign exchange. This dominance led to the establishment in the early 1970s of a *de facto* market, operating beyond formal guidelines in foreign exchange and known as the currency hedge (grey) market. This market enabled those not eligible for the banks' forward market to take out cover against exposure in foreign exchange. The hedge market, operated by currency brokers and merchant banks, was based on offsetting, rather than physically deliverable, contracts, and for some three years it was Australia's chief market in foreign exchange. Variations and trends in the hedge market, combined with some weaknesses in exchange controls, ultimately put heavy pressure on the prevailing exchange-rate system.

Australia's move to floating exchange rates

The system of exchange-rate management in Australia came under severe pressure in 1983. Domestic markets had by then been substantially deregulated, so that interest rates were market-determined; the exchange rate, though, was controlled by the monetary authorities, leaving an uncomfortable imbalance in monetary management. Exchange controls prevailed, but by the early 1980s Australian banks and merchant banks had such well-established overseas links (which facilitated large corporate flows) that movement of funds into and out of the country was fairly easy. This was possible because of a flaw in exchange controls which enabled merchant banks to bring in or repay 'working capital' in huge amounts, several times a day, to speculate against the fixed exchange rate. Pressures during 1983 led to some technical adjustments to the existing system which took effect on 31 October 1983—but Australia had reached a turning point in the country's financial history. Money had been flowing into Australia throughout the second half of 1983 but the weeks that followed the introduction of the modified system were marked by excessive speculation on the $A. The authorities had loosened the controls on the forward market but left the shackles on the spot rate. The $A began to be traded around the clock, the Australian operators watching its movements overseas and tuning in early in the Australian day to trends that had developed overnight in the major world markets. The new system had been introduced to quell speculation during the Australian trading day but overnight speculation continued. And expectations had begun to build that the $A was heading for a revaluation. This translated into substantial capital inflow, a trend that makes forecasts of a currency revaluation self-fulfilling.

The authorities' attempts during November 1983 to tinker with the trade-weighted index and fox the markets were unsuccessful. By the end of trading on Thursday 8 December, it was clear to the monetary authorities that extreme measures would have to be taken to halt the flow. Later that evening the Reserve Bank got word from its New York office that a substantial amount of money would be arriving in Australia the following day. That information set off a round of telephone calls between the Reserve Bank and the government, discussing the options available. Their choices were to sit out the situation, shift the exchange rate, introduce capital controls—or take the big step and let the market find its own level. By the end of the night arrangements had been made for senior Reserve Bank officials to fly to Canberra the next day to thrash out a decision with the government and treasury. Meanwhile the foreign-exchange markets were to be closed, to give the decision-makers time to review the situation. It was an unusual step. On arrival at their desks on Friday 9 December, foreign-exchange traders were greeted with a message from the Reserve Bank:

> The Reserve Bank has announced that dealing in foreign currencies by Australian banks has been suspended for the time being. Banks' authorities to deal in foreign currencies have been withdrawn except that they may at their discretion meet the needs of *bona fide* travellers for essential travel needs.

Foreign-exchange traders had not seen such a move since the chaotic days of the early 1970s. For most in the Australian foreign-exchange market it was a new experience. Friday 9 December became a day to remember. Senior ministers and treasury and Reserve Bank officials consulted in Canberra; markets buzzed with rumours and counter-rumours. Late that afternoon, when it seemed unlikely there would be an immediate decision, a press conference was called. It was announced that the historic decision had been taken to float the $A and to lift most exchange controls.

The new system began operating on Monday 12 December 1983. The exchange controls left in place related to transactions with tax havens, to foreign investment policy and to foreign official institutions and foreign banks holding investments in Australia. This ended a system that had begun in Australia in August 1939, six days before the outbreak of the Second World War, partly for defence purposes. (The regulations had stated that no person could undertake foreign-exchange dealing except the Commonwealth Bank, at that time the central bank, or a trading bank as appointed agent. Exchange control was administered by the central bank under the Banking (Foreign Exchange) Regulations of the Banking Act.)

The removal of most exchange controls meant that restrictions were withdrawn from the timing of payments for trade transactions; importers could 'lead and lag' payments, depending on their expectations of currency movements. Restrictions on Australian residents' investing overseas and non-resident participation in Australian markets were also withdrawn. Australian financial institutions, such as banks and merchant banks, could offer their customers accounts denominated in foreign currencies. These moves opened up overseas equity and futures markets to Australians and enabled foreigners to trade on Australian markets. Trading banks could deal in 'third' currencies, that is, undertake transactions that did not involve a $A/$US leg.

The switch to a floating currency brought a greater element of stability to domestic interest rates as inflows and outflows of funds show up, in theory, in the price of the currency. The exchange rate, instead of interest rates, absorbs shocks. A shift to a floating exchange rate therefore gives the government, through the Reserve Bank, greater control over domestic monetary policy.

13

Over-the-counter derivatives: swaps, options, forward-rate agreements and credit derivatives

A derivatives transaction is a contract whose value depends on (or derives from) the value of an underlying asset, reference rate or index.

—Group of Thirty, Global Derivatives Study, 1993

Growth in over-the-counter derivatives has continued, although at a slightly more moderate pace than in the heady days of the mid-1990s: in 1996 this fairly new market ballooned by 86 per cent over the previous year, according to a study by the Bank for International Settlements. Over-the-counter derivatives activity increased by a further 11 per cent in 1997 to $US357 trillion ($A597 trillion). Volatility in world prices for commodities such as oil, gold, wheat, cotton and aluminium has made hedging, or price protection, a greater priority for commodity producers and consumers, feeding demand for commodity derivatives.

Derivatives might seem less daunting if they were referred to by the more familiar names of futures, forwards, options and swaps. But daunting they can be: over the past ten years, derivatives have been associated with some chilling losses, such as the high-profile collapse of the UK's pedigree, 233-year-old Barings Plc in early 1995 following a billion-dollar futures-related trading loss in its Singapore office. Such episodes brought the burgeoning derivatives markets unwelcome publicity. Futures and options, however, have been used for centuries. Swaps, which developed in the 1980s, had earlier counterparts in the 1960s and 1970s in the less sophisticated form of parallel loans. Computer technology has enabled these established instruments to be traded at greater speed and to be restructured in seemingly infinite variations. The more 'exotic' derivatives—swaptions, spreadtions, lookback options, knock-in options and so on—are variations on earlier, simpler concepts.

The 1997 AFMA financial markets survey, prepared by The Financial Products Research Group, showed $1.3 trillion in over-the-counter derivatives traded in Australia, with significant increases in swaps, interest-rate and currency options and a decline in forward-rate agreements. Rapid growth of derivatives would not be possible without technology, deregulation of global financial markets and the facilitation by advances in communications technology of the integration of those markets. Derivatives have capitalised on the seemingly never-ending demand for risk-management products; alternatively, they can in themselves create an exposure. Used intelligently and with care, they are extremely useful; they are flexible and involve less credit risk than lending or borrowing principal amounts. And because the credit risk is lower, the capital charge for banks is lower—that is, banks need less capital to support a derivative product than, say, a loan. An attraction of derivatives is the capacity they provide for *leverage*, for example, by outlaying $10 an investor can leverage or gear up to receive returns commensurate with an outlay of, say, $50 or $100. Leverage need not be reckless; used wisely, it enables low-cost risk management. Used over-zealously it can be disastrous if the markets take an unexpected turn.

Derivatives are mainly used to manage market risk, the risk arising from possible fluctuations in price. Using derivatives, traders can change exposure to a range of price risks relating to interest rates, currencies, equities or commodities, without altering the underlying principal element of a transaction, in ways that may bring reduced risk, a reduction in borrowing costs or an improvement in returns. Derivatives can be used in portfolio management and in risk management through hedging, speculation and arbitrage. In practice, the distinction between these activities is not always clear-cut. Hedging is defined as taking a form of insurance to offset investment risk, speculation implies a high-risk strategy taken knowingly in anticipation of a gain (and recognising the possibility of a loss), and arbitrage involves 'riskless' trading so as to profit from changes in the differential between related commodities or securities.

In terms of the structure of trading, settlement systems and characteristics of contracts, derivatives have tended to fall into two groups: over-the-counter (OTC) and exchange-traded although, by the late 1990s the distinction was becoming less relevant and many players were active in both. OTC contracts are privately negotiated by banks and investment banks and their clients and specifically tailored to customer needs. Exchange-traded derivatives, discussed in chapters 14 and 15, are traded on a recognised exchange such as the Sydney Futures Exchange or the Australian Stock Exchange's derivatives market (ASXD), typically using a standard contract specification. Counterparty risk is much less of a concern for exchange-traded instruments because of the role of the clearing house (each trader's exposure is to the clearing house, not to another market participant) whereas with OTC derivatives counterparty risk is an important feature.

How derivatives provide benefits*

Properly used, derivatives offer very real benefits and play a genuine role in risk management, as the following examples show.

An airline

An airline is in the unusual position of operating with a highly mixed receivables side in its balance sheet, with ticket income flowing in a variety of currencies, the mix constantly changing and the volume unpredictable. Its shareholders' funds would be denominated in its domestic currency, as would most expenses and wages. An airline, however, also has to cope with significant fuel costs so it watches the oil price carefully. It also watches its competitors closely, because the behaviour of competitors is an important element in any company's approach to hedging. Hedging at a time when your competitors are not and then finding the hedge unnecessary, because prices have moved in your favour, is a costly exercise. The management and board of an airline have no control over the unknowns, such as how many passengers they might carry in a year, but they can take steps to manage risks such as the company's exposure to currency fluctuations and to changes in the price of oil. Derivatives can play a role in this risk management.

Bank

Banks' activities can produce a structural mismatch in their balance sheets. They offer products such as fixed-rate home loans (a bank's assets) while they take deposits (its liabilities) at variable rates and usually for shorter terms. When interest rates are rising, borrowers want to fix rates to lock in a known cost but on the other side, depositors are reluctant to place funds in a fixed deposit because a higher return might be on the horizon. Conversely, when interest rates are falling borrowers want floating rates that shift in line with the market but depositors want to fix the rate rather than see their returns decline. Banks use interest-rate swaps (and futures) to hedge exposures incurred as a result of the mismatch in rates.

Mining house

Mining houses live with volatility in the prices of the resources they dig out of the ground, often unpredictable costs of production and equally unknown but frequently high exploration costs. Moreover, their timetable of production can be uncertain. A gold-mining house could be anticipating a production flow in six months' time but that could be delayed and meanwhile the spot price of gold could drop. Mining houses offset some of the uncertainty by selling a proportion of their production forward but they cannot commit 100 per cent of production in case forecasts prove wrong. Mining companies make prudent use of the forward market for their production, generally adhering to fairly straightforward hedging techniques.

Other sectors of the Australian economy also use derivatives to hedge. Many state government infrastructure projects have been facilitated by the borrower's ability, through the swaps market, to raise foreign-currency funds and swap back into $A finance. Companies use derivatives to protect against interest-rate, foreign-exchange and commodity risk. Fund managers, being buyers of securities, are exposed to interest-rate, foreign-exchange and equity-price movements and use derivatives such as swaps to improve their returns.

* This section is drawn from an address by Ian Moore, executive vice-president, Bankers Trust Australia Ltd.

Swaps

The liquidity of the Australian swaps markets has improved substantially over the past few years. As a result, the swaps market is now at least as liquid as the bond market by three key measures: transaction size, maturity profile and bid/offer spreads. In addition, turnover has increased substantially, almost doubling since 1993.

—J.P. Morgan Australia Ltd, Australian fixed-income research, March 1998

A swap is an over-the-counter (OTC) contract between two parties, with each agreeing to exchange his or her respective obligations. Swaps can be used to arbitrage capital markets to reduce the cost of funds, to increase returns by changing the interest stream of an underlying asset or to eliminate the risks involved in funding fixed-rate or long-term assets with floating-rate or short-term funds.

Development and growth

Before the advent of swaps, a lender providing fixed-rate, term funds was locked into the conditions of the loan for the specified term. Many suffered when market rates rose (if market risk had not been covered in some other way) because they were unable to vary their charges. Credit-tiering resulted in rigidities. For example, governments would have access to fixed-interest markets where, as long-term borrowers, they prefer predictable interest costs. At the other end of the spectrum would be companies which, with the exception of top-class credits, could not raise fixed-rate funds because those lending to them prefer to provide floating-rate finance. In between were the banks, which largely lent at floating rates because this matched the generally floating-rate nature of their borrowings, and the institutions, which borrowed long-term fixed-rate funds as a counterpart to their long-term investments.

Swaps brought a way to manage these cashflows more flexibly. Swaps enable a state government borrower, for example, to raise floating-rate debt at a cheaper rate than through traditional sources; at the same time they provide companies with access to fixed-rate finance—if that is what better suits each party's cashflow. The determining factor is that traders and company treasurers—anyone managing cashflows—cannot afford to ignore the risks associated with funding fixed assets with floating-rate liabilities, or $A liabilities with yen assets. Such practices could involve opportunity costs, or worse.

Swap techniques have been used increasingly in Australia since the mid-1980s. The two main categories are interest-rate swaps and cross-currency swaps, with interest-rate swaps by far the larger. The development of the swaps market was a response to restrictions on international capital flows (and was also fuelled by arguments about comparative advantage, domestically and internationally). The search for a mechanism to bypass these restrictions led to the emergence of currency swaps, which evolved from the parallel and back-to-back loans popular in the late 1960s and 1970s. In the case of parallel loans, these were structured through, say, a UK company lending sterling, for a fixed term and at a fixed rate, to the UK subsidiary of, say, a US company. Across the Atlantic, the US company would lend an equivalent amount of $US for the same maturity to the US subsidiary of the UK company. This transaction avoided any cross-border movement of funds and so avoided exchange controls. According to Satyajit Das in *Swap Financing Techniques* (published by The Law Book Company), this led to the first currency swap in 1976, arranged by Continental Illinois and Goldman Sachs for a Dutch and a British company and involving guilder and sterling. The World Bank gave a boost to the use of swaps when it entered into a swap agreement in 1981 with IBM which enabled IBM to pay the World Bank's $US obligations while the World Bank serviced IBM's obligations in Swiss francs and deutschmarks. In *Swap Financing Techniques*, Das writes that the first interest-rate swaps were also arranged in 1981, initially between Citibank and Continental Illinois. The first swap in Australia was transacted in 1983 between the Commonwealth Bank and AIDC. Just over a decade later, in the year to June 1994, the total volume of swaps dealt was $A274 billion, an increase of 41 per cent over the previous year's $A195 billion, according to a survey carried out for AFMA by Financial Products Research Group.

Although the currency swap came first, the dominant type of swap used in the markets is the interest-rate swap, which grew out of the earlier currency transactions. This reflects two factors: most borrowers raise funds in their own currency, and interest-rate swaps involve less credit risk than currency swaps because, with interest-rate swaps, there is no exchange of principal amounts. The basic concept of a swap remains fairly simple but details can become complex. In its most straightforward form, a plain vanilla/generic swap involves two parties exchanging interest payments for a certain period; one pays floating rate, the other fixed rate and the settlement is for the net difference between the two interest costs.

A further stage in the development of swaps came with eurobond credit arbitrage. While the euromarkets helped drive swaps, they did not necessarily underpin the swaps market which went on to develop a maturity of its own. However, the $A eurobond market flourished during the mid-1980s because of the wide interest-rate differentials between the Australian and European currencies which attracted substantial interest from retail investors in Germany, Belgium and the Netherlands.

Australian state-government borrowers, such as NSW TCorp and Queensland Treasury Corporation, provided a major boost to the swaps market when they grouped their debt into big, liquid lines of 'hot stocks' which were actively traded. The state authorities became major users of the swaps market as part of their liability and asset management. The consolidation of debt into hot stocks, and active fee-based stock-lending programs (which improve the market-makers' ability to provide liquidity) have led to state-government bonds being increasingly used as benchmarks for pricing.

The swaps market was also fuelled by the reverse dual-currency bonds. These bonds were very popular with borrowers, mostly European banks, which issued bonds with an $A coupon and a yen principal. Dual-currency bonds generated a large volume of swap deals before narrowing interest-rate differentials and changed currency levels removed much of the appeal.

Types of swaps

Interest-rate swaps

Interest-rate swaps help in the management of interest-rate exposures. Fixed-floating interest-rate swaps form the largest category, accounting for $305 billion out of a total of $409 billion $A interest-rate and cross-currency swaps executed in the year to June 1997 (an increase of 19 per cent over the previous year).

An interest-rate swap is a contract between two parties under which they agree to make periodic payments to each other based on a known interest rate and a notional principal amount. Generally, this involves the exchange of fixed-interest payments for floating-interest payments, or *vice versa*, with the exchange of interest payments usually quarterly, half-yearly or annually. Payment of fixed and floating-rate obligations are generally made on the same day and are settled by calculating and paying the cash difference, which reduces the credit exposure between counterparties and simplifies administration.

The driving feature that makes a swap worthwhile is one party's relative credit advantage in a particular market, that is, it can borrow in a number of markets but at especially favourable rates in one. The swap technique enables each party to the transaction to borrow in the market where it achieves the best terms and then exchange the conditions of its borrowings to achieve a lower cost and the desired interest-rate profile.

For example: Aussie Co has taken on a $30 million three-year floating-rate bill facility which includes three-monthly rollovers and wants to protect against rising borrowing costs through a swap. It approaches First Bank Ltd to organise a three-year swap, with the swap rate agreed at 8 per cent. When Aussie Co's first rollover arrives, the 90-day bank-bill rate is 8.25 per cent; the borrowing is rolled over with a settlement amount exchanged between Aussie Co and First Bank based on the difference between the bank-bill rate in the market (8.25 per cent) and the agreed swap rate of 8 per cent. The settlement amount is calculated as the difference between:

$$\frac{\$30 \text{ million (principal amount)} \times 8\% \text{ (agreed rate)} \times 91 \text{ (days of contract period)}}{36\,500}$$

and

$$\frac{\$30 \text{ million (principal amount)} \times 8.25\% \text{ (market rate on rollover)} \times 91}{36\,500}$$

$$= \$18\,698.63$$

First Bank pays Aussie Co $18 698.63 which has the effect of lowering Aussie Co's borrowing cost from 8.25 per cent to 8 per cent. If, on the other hand, the market rate for a 90-day bank bill at rollover time were 7.75 per cent, Aussie Co would owe First Bank the difference between the agreed swap rate of 8 per cent and the 90-day bank-bill rate of 7.75 per cent. The settlement amount would be calculated as the difference between:

$$\frac{30\,000\,000 \times 8\% \times 91}{36\,500}$$

and

$$\frac{30\,000\,000 \times 7.75\% \times 91}{36\,500}$$

$$= \$18\,698.63$$

Under the swap, Aussie Co would pay First Bank $18 698.63, which effectively lifts Aussie Co's borrowing cost from 7.75 per cent to the agreed rate of 8 per cent. The same calculation is repeated at each of the remaining rollovers under Aussie Co's borrowing facility so that irrespective of movements in prevailing interest rates, Aussie Co's borrowing cost is fixed at the swap rate of 8 per cent.

Swaps are generally organised and traded in market parcels of between $10 and $30 million, regardless of their maturity. A professional swaps player's preference is for a parcel of $20 million, with $10 million regarded as a minimum (otherwise a premium might be charged for illiquidity). Companies usually approach the swaps market to pay fixed and receive floating, to generate synthetic fixed-rate funding, while state borrowers, which mostly issue fixed-interest debt, use swaps to receive fixed and pay floating, to raise synthetic floating-rate funding more cheaply than would be available from traditional sources.

Swaps involving an exchange of fixed for floating rates, with interest calculated in arrears, usually pay interest quarterly or semi-annually. When the interest payment on a swap is calculated using the formula for a discounted bill of exchange, that is, the discount or 'up-front' method, the swap is known as a *discounted swap*. The formula used when settling a discounted swap is the same as that used for a forward-rate agreement.

Swaps transacted on an exchange-for-physical (EFP) basis now account for more than half of interbank trading. An EFP is the simultaneous purchase and sale of a physical instrument (including swaps) with a corresponding opposite futures contract taken out.

This leaves both parties with a hedged position which can be managed at the discretion of each.

Pricing

Interest-rate swaps are generally priced relative to an underlying physical instrument, usually a commonwealth or state bond or a eurobond, or, in the case of shorter swaps—say, up to two years in maturity, off a bond/bill futures strip (a continuous string of sequential contracts created by buying or selling bank-bill futures). As with other interest rates and prices, swap prices are influenced by supply and demand in the market, with the demand for, and supply of, fixed-rate money determining the swap rate. Indicative rates for swaps are displayed on screens and are also published in the daily press.

Variants of the interest-rate swap

Complex versions of the interest-rate swap can be achieved by adding 'exotics' to a standard or 'vanilla' product.

Forward swaps start from a future date. For example, an intending borrower with a debt due to start in three months' time can lock in a fixed rate now instead of waiting until the borrowing is drawn down. Forward swaps could go out as far as a bank's credit risk and policy will allow, for example planning a six-year swap to start four years hence.

Zero-coupon swaps are those in which the fixed-interest payment due is paid out as a lump sum, in the form of a 'bullet' payment, when the swap matures.

Amortised and *escalating swaps* involve a swap where a single swap rate applies to a principal which increases (with an escalating swap, also known as *accreting* swap) or decreases (with an amortised swap) over time.

Basis swaps differ from regular swaps in that they involve different time periods and/or an exchange of two different floating interest rates, for example, US three-month treasury bills for three-month eurodollar deposit rates, or a 90-day bank-accepted bill rate for a 180-day bank-accepted bill rate.

Non-par swaps are swaps where the fixed and floating rates are based on a non-market interest rate with appropriate cash adjustments.

Rollercoaster swaps involve a variation of the principal or the coupon during the life of the swap.

Currency swaps

Cross-currency-and-interest-rate swaps, known as currency swaps or currency-and-interest-rate swaps, where each side is denominated in a different currency, may involve an exchange of the principal amounts, at an agreed exchange rate, as well as an exchange of interest payments in the two different currencies. (This differs from the foreign-exchange or 'FX' swap which is purely a purchase and sale, and, at a pre-agreed rate, a subsequent sale and repurchase of currency on maturity. The interest differential in this case is reflected in the contract price on maturity.) With currency swaps the interest differential is handled through mutual exchange of interest flows. Many currency swaps are structured using euro-$A bonds and other euromarket issues. These swaps may be on a fixed-to-fixed, fixed-to-floating, or floating-to-floating interest-rate basis.

Commodity swaps

Australia, as a major commodities exporter, has developed considerable expertise in derivatives applied to the commodities markets, although this activity is dwarfed by volumes in the overall derivatives markets. An RBA survey of derivatives markets in Australia in 1995 showed commodity derivatives accounted for 2 per cent of activity and within that commodity forwards and swaps were the more important, with more than two-thirds of the notional principal amounts being in gold contracts.

Commodity swaps have emerged as risk-management tools for the 1990s, propelled by the same factors that drove the popularity of currency and interest-rate swaps: volatility and uncertainty—this time, volatility and uncertainty in the price of, say, oil, gold, wool, wheat or cotton and, most recently, electricity. So far, there has been growing Australian activity in oil swaps; gold, aluminium and copper tend to be traded forward rather than swapped. Airlines have been major users of oil swaps. A commodity swap enables a producer to fix future revenues at a specified level and, on the other side, enables a consumer to set future costs. Each gives up any increased income or reduced costs should prices move in his or her favour. Commodity swaps are similar in structure to the earlier financial swap but are still in a growth phase compared with the volume transacted in interest-rate and currency markets where swaps are ranked a 'mature' product. To commodity producers, a swap is a long-range forward sale: a commodity price is fixed against a benchmark price or index for the commodity. Others liken a commodity swap to a single interest-rate swap—the two parties to a commodity swap, producer and consumer, through an intermediary, exchange a stream of payments (fixed for floating cashflow), with no exchange of principal. A commodity swap does not involve a physical swap of commodities; only payment streams are exchanged. A bank or investment bank acts as intermediary, bringing the two parties together and taking a spread between payments for bearing the credit risk of each. (Derivatives used in commodities are discussed in detail in *Derivatives Decoded* by Edna Carew, published by Allen & Unwin).

Electricity: The introduction of a competitive Australian national electricity market, and corporatisation and privatisation of the industry, have prompted growth in electricity-based derivatives to assist generators, retailers and end-users of electricity to manage price risk. An electricity swaps market began operating in May 1996, pioneered by Macquarie Bank Ltd, and the Sydney Futures Exchange introduced electricity futures contracts in September 1997 (discussed in chapter 14). Financial intermediaries in the swaps market deal over-the-counter with generators and retailers in New South Wales and Victoria and, as other states deregulate, with operators there. Swaps are priced off the spot price for electricity, the reference point determined by supply and demand in each state. Swaps can be short-term or for as long as a couple of years. Increased activity in electricity derivatives is expected to develop as demand grows from buyers and sellers of electricity to hedge price risk in a competitive market in which, since the commodity cannot be stored, prices tend to be volatile.

Oil: The oil market centres mostly on the New York time-zone but some Australian intermediaries quote oil prices for clients and several banks run large energy books out of Singapore which would be coordinated with their bank's global book. The oil market quotes several indexes. West Texas Intermediate (WTI) crude oil, listed on NYMEX (New York Mercantile Exchange) and the world's most actively traded energy futures contract, is regarded as the benchmark indicator of world oil prices. Tapis, a light Malaysian crude oil, is very relevant for Asian and Australian markets but is less freely traded than WTI and so less of an indicator of world supply-and-demand factors. The Sydney Futures Exchange has forged a link with NYMEX, placing its WTI oil futures and option contracts in the Asia–Pacific time-zone (see chapter 12).

An over-the-counter oil swap is a common commodity swap. This enables a producer to receive a fixed price for a barrel of a specified type of oil and in return pay a floating price set according to a market index. Tapis swaps are quoted out to two years and longer if necessary. Swaps prices in $US per barrel give the fixed price that an intermediary would pay a producer in return for a floating payment over the same period. The floating index generally used is the APPI (Asian Petroleum Price Index) Tapis price published every Thursday, averaged over a month or quarter. At the end of the swap period the producer either makes or receives a payment, depending on the movement in the floating price. The swap market has reasonable depth, with quotes available out to five or even ten years.

Equity swaps

Equity swaps are used in Australia although not to the extent of interest-rate and currency swaps and are more common in the US and Europe. They share the characteristics of a conventional swap such as notional principal, specified term, predetermined payments made at intervals, a fixed rate (swap coupon) and an exchange of income streams by the parties to the swap. A basic equity swap would involve an end-user and an equity swaps dealer, with the end-user perhaps running a diversified share portfolio whose return is much in line with, say, the All-Ordinaries index but who wants to receive a fixed rate of return. The end-user would enter into a swap with a dealer/investment bank, agreeing to pay the All-Ordinaries-related return and receive a fixed rate of return for the term of the swap. Payments would be made periodically on the notional principal which remains constant for the life of the swap. The notional principal is not exchanged and is used merely as a base to calculate the regular payments.

Various parties use equity swaps but key examples would be foreign fund managers keen to gain exposure to Australian equities but wanting to avoid going through a local manager, and corporations seeking to change their exposure to equities or protect the price risk of an equity portfolio. An organisation with a diversified share portfolio could use an equity swap to convert an unpredictable return on shares into a fixed income or return based on a floating interest-rate indicator. Using an equity swap, the end-user has converted its unpredictable return from a share portfolio into a stable fixed return. For their part, equity swaps dealers hedge their risk by dealing in the underlying shares or baskets of shares or by using share-price index (SPI) futures, with the choice of hedge used depending on the kind of shares involved in the swap.

Swaps market participants

Derivatives such as swaps, options and FRAs involve two main categories of participants—sellers of, or dealers in, the products (intermediaries such as banks and investment banks) and end-users, which covers a wide range including overseas investors, companies, fund managers and state government borrowers.

Banks and investment banks market swaps to corporate clients who want to improve their risk-management techniques. These intermediaries play an active role in organising swaps, identifying organisations with offsetting needs, arranging the different forms of financing, negotiating terms, organising documentation and watching market movements to find the right moment at which to execute a deal. Good timing is important in swaps transactions because even a small movement in a currency or interest rate can make a difference to the fixed swap rate, which is the important number in the transaction.

The intermediaries, usually banks, also have a 'client' in their own internal asset and liability management needs. Much business, though, centres on structuring swaps to suit clients. Banks use swaps and other derivatives to manage the interest-rate risks in their own products, for example the offer of a capped or fixed housing loan to a retail borrower. Until recently, retail customers had virtually no access to derivatives but they can benefit from them because derivatives enable the bank to package products and to manage its liabilities more efficiently and to provide a wider choice to customers.

By using swaps, an end-user transfers performance (market) risk (but not the underlying position) to the provider (intermediary) who, in return, earns a spread or margin. End-users enter the swaps market for a number of reasons: to achieve a lower cost of funds or higher returns, to hedge an interest-rate or currency exposure or to improve asset or liability management.

In addition, there is an active broker market in swaps, with brokers acting as agent and earning brokerage for finding the best price. Brokers handle a sizeable volume of interbank business; however, a bank would not place a corporate deal through a broker because that would involve a weakening of the bank-client relationship on which the bank wants to build.

Risks associated with swaps

Given the flow of supply and demand, it is unlikely that swaps held by the principals exactly offset each other, so the principals are exposed to various types of market risk; they would take steps to hedge such risk. All market prices move according to supply and demand and the swaps market is no exception. A principal taking on a swap could hedge against the underlying instrument, although such a decision would depend on the structure of his or her swaps book. A principal can also 'warehouse' a swap until an opposite deal is found.

As with other derivatives, swaps do not present new forms of risk; they involve risks with which traders are well familiar, such as those associated with credit, market, liquidity and documentation. Interest-rate swaps involve a credit risk which reflects the ability or otherwise of each counterparty to make payments owed under the swaps agreement. (This credit risk is less than would be the case with an outright loan because, should a default occur, the counterparty is not exposed to loss of the principal amount.) The payments involve the outlay or receipt of the net differences between the fixed and floating rate. Because swaps carry a credit risk, a swap obligation cannot be assigned to another party without the consent of the first counterparty.

Outright risk occurs when a swaps trader is not completely square (balanced) but has some exposure to a particular level of interest rates or change in the slope of the yield curve.

Basis risk involves the risk of a movement between the swap and the product used to hedge it.

In managing the market risks on swaps, dealers focus on the net cashflows of the entire swap book, rather than the flows on individual swaps. Mismatches are usually hedged with bond futures contracts.

Options

Development and growth

Options have developed in two broad categories: over-the-counter (OTC) and exchange-traded options. OTC options are tailored by banks and investment banks to suit the needs of their clients. Exchange-traded options are available on the Sydney Futures Exchange (options over futures contracts) and the Australian Options Market, a division of the Australian Stock Exchange (ASX), which offers options over shares (see chapter 15). Options have become increasingly popular in recent years as a risk-management tool. While a product of the 1980s and 1990s, options are by no means a purely recent innovation; evidence of option contracts dates from at least the Middle Ages and, in the seventeenth century, options were traded on exchanges in Holland (over tulips) and in the UK.

The meteoric growth in OTC options—bond options, caps and floors, and swaptions—in the late 1980s stabilised in the early 1990s. The 1997 AFMA survey showed currency options up on the previous year by 57 per cent, interest-rate (bond) options up by 50 per cent, caps and floors down by 34 per cent and swaption growth 'erratic'.

The volume of options written is similar to that of swaps but options have long been regarded as the sector with the most potential for further growth because of the limited risk for option buyers. When purchasing an option, the option buyer pays a premium at the outset for the right to hold the option and this represents the maximum loss the buyer can incur, irrespective of the subsequent trend in market prices. On the other side, the option writer (grantor or seller) carries potentially unlimited risk while profit is limited to the premium received.

Options are chiefly used either to hedge or to produce income. Buying an option is commonly compared to buying insurance: the buyer pays a premium to protect against unwelcome movements in interest rates or currency or commodity prices. The initial spurt in growth in over-the-counter (OTC) options came in bond options, caps and floors. Bond options have been popular despite having an entry price never viewed as cheap. Banks were the first to sell over-the-counter bond options, then fund managers realised they too could sell the options and reap an improved return. This gave the options market a further boost. The appeal of OTC options, tailored to specific stocks, lies in their ability to provide a more precise match-out for risk.

Option terminology

Options can be either *puts* or *calls*. A put option grants to the buyer, in return for paying a premium, the right, but not the obligation, to sell at a specific rate or price; a call option gives the buyer, in return for paying a premium, the right but not the obligation, to buy at a specific rate or price. The *strike* or *exercise* price of an option is the price at which an option buyer may exercise his or her right to buy or sell the underlying asset over which the option was written.

Options are further defined as *in-the-money, at-the-money* and *out-of-the-money*. A strike price is in-the-money if the option can be exercised at a profit at that time. For example, a call option (an option to buy) is in-the-money when the strike price is below the prevailing price of the relevant obligation. The opposite of in-the-money is out-of-the-money. A put option (an option to sell) is out-of-the-money if the strike price is below the prevailing price. An option is at-the-money if the current strike price is the same as the prevailing market price.

The cost of an option is known as the *premium*. From the point of view of an option buyer, a premium is similar to a one-off insurance premium. For the option writer or seller, the premium is the reward for taking the risk in granting/selling the right conveyed by the option. A high premium is in the grantor's interest but a grantor is constrained from overcharging by competition from other grantors and the level of demand from takers. Another influence on the level of an option premium is the *intrinsic value* of an option. This is the amount by which an option is in-the-money. By definition, an out-of-the-money option has no intrinsic value, but it is still bought because, from a hedger's point of view, it provides some protection (it has a time value). The premium asked for an out-of-the-money option varies depending on how far the strike price is from the market price. The further an option is out-of-the-money, the cheaper becomes its premium, because it is less likely to expire in-the-money, that is, to be exercised.

A deep in-the-money option costs more than an at-the-money option because it has an intrinsic value and is more likely to expire in-the-money and be exercised. Put premiums move in the opposite direction to call premiums. If a call option is in-the-money, then a put option (over the same underlying instrument and at the same strike price) is out-of-the-money.

The longer the life of an option, the longer the period for which the grantor has to carry a risk, so the grantor demands a higher premium. Further, the more volatile the price of the underlying asset, the more risk the grantor is being asked to assume, so the grantor will want a higher reward in the form of a higher premium. Volatile prices also tend to increase the likelihood of an option being exercised, which further influences a grantor to demand a higher premium. Options that are not exercised become worthless and simply expire. Option traders talk of an option having an *expiry*, rather than maturity, date.

Pricing an option

Pricing is critical with options. The option price (premium) takes into account two features, the intrinsic value and the time value of the option. The intrinsic value is the profit available to the option holder if the option were immediately exercised, that is, the difference between the market value of the underlying asset or instrument and the exercise price of the option. The time value of an option represents the chance that the price of the underlying asset (for example, bond, currency, share or commodity) will move in a favourable direction, causing the option to become in-the-money; time value declines as the option approaches its expiry date.

There are six key influences on the option premium:

- the strike price;
- the price of the underlying asset or instrument;
- the time to expiry of the option;
- market volatility in the underlying asset;
- interest rates; and
- market expectations.

A number of formulas are used for pricing options. Most European options pricings, however, are derived from the Black-Scholes pricing model. (A European option is one that can be exercised only on its expiry date. An American option can be exercised at any time up to expiry date.) Developed in the early 1970s by two US economists, Fischer Black and Myron Scholes, the model highlighted the potential of options for limiting risk. Computers have played a vital role in the proliferation of option-pricing models, with systems available as 'off-the-shelf' purchases for those who do not want to develop their own.

The valuation of option premiums is of interest both to the grantor (seller) and to the buyer. Those choosing to ignore the calculations and make judgments about market forces do so at considerable risk. On the other side, the hedger who takes or buys options generally merely takes a view about the cost of the premium and whether it is affordable as part of an overall hedging strategy. The more sophisticated hedger trades the market regularly, using options and futures, and structures trading strategies and monitors the actual, not just implied, value of premiums.

Over-the-counter options

Interest-rate options, caps and floors

Over-the-counter (OTC) options are customised, that is, privately negotiated and tailored to suit each client. Within the OTC category of options come variations such as caps, floors, collars and swaptions. These are basic option products offered by a bank or investment bank for a client but banks and investment banks also write options for their own interest-rate risk management.

A *cap* (put option) is the maximum rate a borrower will be required to pay for funds and so offers protection to a borrower. By placing a ceiling on interest rates, it provides the borrower with a form of protection or insurance against rate movements. A *floor* (call option), on the other hand, guarantees a minimum rate of return by providing protection against falls in interest rates and so offers protection to investors. In both cases, investors are free to benefit from favourable movements in interest rates by simply abandoning the option and forsaking the premium paid. *Collars,* also known as tunnels or cylinders, set both minimum and maximum rates beyond which the borrower's interest costs will not move. Because collars have the effect of locking a borrower into an interest-rate band, they involve smaller premiums; they can also be designed as zero-cost collars, with the premium paid equal to the premium received. Demand for caps and collars is likely to increase when traders believe that the interest-rate cycle has bottomed. Caps and floors are quoted out to five years and are generally fairly liquid out to three years.

Swaptions are options to enter into an $A swap at a future date, giving this right to the buyer but without imposing an obligation to do so. Growth in swaptions has been slower than that of, say, swaps and options. The small size of the swaptions market has been attributed to the discouragingly complicated pricing models used, and to the preference of many investors for 'plain vanilla' products with deep, liquid secondary markets. Caps and floors offer similar protection and are easier to price and to market. An example: Aussie Co is tendering on a project and, if successful, will require fixed-rate debt for five years. Aussie Co will not know for two months whether its bid is successful; however, the five-year swap rates are attractive now. To ensure that it does not miss the desired swap level, Aussie Co buys an option to pay fixed-rate debt at today's strike price, with the option exercisable at the end of the tender period. Swaptions include the credit risk of an option and that of, say, a five-year swap; a large number of swaptions are transacted on a cash basis to avoid the credit risk, that is, when the option expires and is in-the-money, the parties to the agreement decide to cash-settle rather than enter the swap.

Options are available over a number of financial instruments but most commonly, in the case of interest-rate options, over commonwealth and state bonds and bank bills. An interest-rate option gives the buyer, in return for paying a premium, the right, without the obligation, to borrow or lend at a predetermined rate. For example, a borrower wishing to limit interest costs buys a put option (cap) at a strike price of, say, 6.5 per cent. That borrower can borrow at 6.5 per cent and has paid a premium for that right to the grantor (writer) of the option. The borrower has effectively bought insurance. The day arrives when the borrower has to decide whether to draw down bank bills under the borrowing facility: if interest rates are above 6.5 per cent the borrower would exercise the option to borrow at the specified strike price of 6.5 per cent; if rates were below 6.5 per cent the borrower does not need the option and so does not exercise it. A floor provides the opposite to a cap—a level below which a lender or investor's rate cannot fall.

Currency options

Standard currency options give the option-holder, in return for paying a premium, the right, but not the obligation, to buy or sell a specified amount of a foreign currency at a specified exchange rate at some future date. There are a number of variations to standard options, including so-called *knock-in* and *knock-out* options which are conditional on whether the exchange rate remains within a certain band. Currency options are available over a wide range of currencies but generally in Australia are mostly used over $A, $US, deutschmark, yen, sterling and $NZ. Currency options are sold by banks to a mix of end-users in which the big exporting companies and mining companies are predominant. Exporters and fund managers use currency options, as do importers, although to a lesser extent. While normally considered buyers, end-users do have the choice of buying or granting currency options. As grantors they are exposed to greater risk but, provided they fully grasp how options work, have the chance to gross up their returns (as is the case with, say, fund managers using interest-rate options). Currency options showed significant growth between 1993 and 1997, according to the Financial Products Research Group's survey for AFMA, rising from $257 billion to $349 billion.

Options over commodities

Commodity options, such as those over gold, wool and cotton, are used by producers and consumers. Derivatives activity in gold in Australia is largely over-the-counter, privately negotiated between bullion bank and client. Whereas New York gold banks have grown up around trading and dealing at the more speculative end of the market, Australian gold banks have grown around the mining industry. Gold producers have long used forward selling as a way of fixing future prices. (Australian mining companies hedging metals other than gold have used the London Metals Exchange, which trades base metals, for some twenty-five years.) The gold-mining community is often cited as one that is highly sophisticated and makes good use of hedging opportunities. Australian gold producers, faced with relatively high costs of production compared with other major world producers, rank among the world's most skilled gold hedgers, using basic put and call options, options combined with forwards and other, more complex, facilities. As with other options, the premium (cost) of a gold option is based on a combination of factors: the spot price of gold, the strike price, prevailing interest rates, time to expiry of the option and the expected volatility of the gold price (the unknown factor). Since gold, in common with other metals, is denominated in $US, companies have to consider whether their shareholders want to be exposed to the $A or $US price of gold. Companies can hedge their foreign-exchange exposure, leaving shareholders exposed only to fluctuations in the $US gold price. Exposure to currency fluctuations demands active foreign-exchange risk management; this has encouraged Australia's evolution as a resourceful provider of innovative foreign-exchange risk-management techniques which have been adapted for the gold market.

The end of the Reserve Price Scheme for wool in 1991 signalled increased exposure to price risk for the Australian wool industry. As discussed in chapter 14, the Sydney Futures Exchange responded by reactivating a wool futures contract. The search for the optimum price protection method led Macquarie Bank to develop an over-the-counter contract which offers price protection: Macquarie Wool Futures. This cash-settled hedge market enables participants—growers, wool brokers, processors and spinners—to transfer price risk to another party without committing to make or take physical delivery. Wools can be bought or sold, in microns ranging from 19 to 25, for specific forward maturities and volume. Prices are based on the micron price guides published by the Australian Wool Exchange. Macquarie Wool Futures contracts are flexible and may be tailored to suit individual hedging needs, for example, maturity can be customised so that the hedge closely matches physical purchase and sale of wool.

Who uses options?

Financial institutions use both OTC and exchange-traded options; corporates and a broad range of users tap the OTC market and the small player uses exchange-traded options. Specifically, borrowers tend to buy caps for protection. However, the use of options as protective devices rises and falls with uncertainty over interest rate and prices; the more certain the outlook for interest rates, and the lower the level of debt, the less demand there is for risk-management products such as options.

Most OTC option business falls into two groups—that generated by institutional holders of bonds and transactions by state borrowers with big portfolios of fixed-interest, fixed-term debt. The market is highly client-driven, particularly by the demands of the state authorities and fund managers. Clients shop for the most competitive premiums, and most have a good idea of where the price level should be. Brokers add to activity levels, ringing around the market on behalf of potential participants. Brokers are also an additional source of information about prices. Fund managers tend to approach the market directly themselves, rather than have a broker chase a price for them.

The OTC bond options market is dominated by professional, wholesale-market players; it does not cater for the small retail trader. Nor are corporates major players in bond options; corporates prefer caps and swaps, which better suit their funding needs (generally short-term, three years and less). Banks and investment banks are active in a small interbank market in options, making prices to each other and running portfolios of options over various instruments. Most transactions in options represent hedging or portfolio management; the remainder, possibly 10 or 20 per cent of activity, represents speculation, and most of that takes place in the exchange-traded options.

Running an options portfolio: option sensitivities

Banks and investment banks running an options portfolio operate with overall trading limits and limits applying to each counterparty with whom they deal. These limits are set by management. Option books are closely monitored and reports made of trading and positions at the end of each day. Option traders have to be alert to the fact that their hedge positions change with a change in any of the factors (expressed as Greek alphabetical symbols) affecting the market value of the option. One of these is *delta* (δ), that is, the expected change in the option price for a given change in the price of the underlying asset or instrument, expressed as a decimal fraction of that change. The option trader has to run through the positions held and identify the exposures to determine what would happen if the market were to rally or dip. Many option books are revalued and rehedged daily to take account of volatility (a significant risk). Option traders must also be aware of funding rates; a trader might execute an options deal and buy stock to hedge it, and must take into account the cost of funding the stock. Another important factor is *theta* (θ), which measures the effect of time on the value of an option (a bought option decreases in value as it gets closer to expiration date). Theta can be shown by the expected change in the option price in cents per day or, more relevantly, in the value of the option contract in dollars per day.

Gamma (γ) measures the change in delta given a change in the price of the underlying asset; it shows the sensitivity of the hedged position and thus what hedging adjustment might be required if the price of the underlying asset moves. *Ega*, also known as *kappa* (κ), measures the change in the option price given a change in volatility of the underlying asset or instrument and *rho* (ρ) is the sensitivity of an option price to a change in funding costs (interest rates). Like theta, this can be shown by a change in the option price in cents for each 1 per cent change in rates, or a change in the value of the option contract for a 1 per cent change in interest rates.

Banks, investment banks and others running a portfolio of options use computers to monitor the associated risks. Computer reports would show the position of each option held over a specific underlying instrument, giving its position in the prevailing market and how that would be affected by a rise or fall in interest rates, a change in volatility, a change in the number of days until the option's expiry and, of course, a change in the price of the underlying instruments. Computer reports break the portfolio down into the different expiry dates. The portfolio manager would try to avoid having large options positions expire on the same day; however, an option trader would know from its price whether or not an option is likely to be exercised.

Traders of option portfolios are, among other things, trading volatility—their exposure is a function of how much interest rates, exchange rates or share prices are likely to move. In assessing volatility levels traders can base their judgments on previous volatility levels over a defined period (historical volatility) or on the volatility levels derived from the option premiums traded in the market (implied volatility).

Risks

For an option seller, there is no credit risk outstanding once the buyer has paid the premium, although there is a very large market risk arising from the possibility that the buyer might exercise the option. Buyers bear the risk that sellers might not be able to fulfil their obligations under the contract when the option is exercised. However, the seller has no control over whether the option is exercised.

Forward-rate agreements

Derivatives in the form of forward contracts have been used for centuries. As well as being one of the earliest forms of derivatives, forward contracts are also one of the simplest. Under a forward contract, one party commits to buy and another to sell a specific item at a specific price, for a specific amount, at a date in the future. The contract operates like an over-the-counter futures contract. Unlike futures markets, however, where contracts are standardised and traded on an exchange, forward contracts are negotiated between two parties—they are 'customised' as to terms and conditions to suit each individual counterparty's business and risk-management needs.

Forward contracts exist for a variety of underlying assets and instruments, ranging from the traditional agricultural commodities to gold, currencies and interest rates. For example, in a forward-rate agreement, two counterparties would agree to exchange interest-rate differentials on a notional principal amount at a given future date.

A forward contract in gold would involve, say, a gold producer and a bank agreeing to a purchase and sale of gold at some future date, possibly one, three, six or twelve months hence—whatever time-frame is acceptable to the market. Or a bank could write a forward foreign-exchange contract with a client, agreeing to sell to, or buy from, the client a specific quantity of foreign exchange at a set future date at a price agreed now. Contracts are settled either by calculating net differences or by the exchange of gross amounts. The currency hedge market that developed in Australia in the 1970s, in the days when the 'official' foreign-exchange market was closed to all but trade-related transactions, operated with non-deliverable contracts and the hedge contract was in many respects a forerunner of later forwards and swaps that now fall under the umbrella of 'derivatives'.

Both parties to a forward contract are vulnerable to the risk of default for the life of the contract, so the credit risk created by a forward contract remains until the contract matures. Credit risk dictates that counterparties to forward contracts are generally well-rated companies, banks, financial institutions, institutional investors or government bodies.

Development and growth

Growth in interest-rate FRAs turned negative in 1997, according to the annual AFMA report, with volumes down by 27 per cent to less than half of the peak levels seen in 1995. This trend reflected not just the prevailing stability in interest rates but the increased visibility and certainty in their direction. The Reserve Bank's efforts to reduce volatility and remove uncertainties from the interest-rate outlook have caused a corresponding decline in products devised to protect against such vagaries.

The FRA market began in London in 1983 and quickly spread to Australia where it became a sizeable sector of the OTC derivatives markets, for several years (1993–96) far outdoing swaps and currency options which, by 1997, had caught up with FRA volume. FRAs enable interest-rate exposure to be altered. They are short-term agreements between two parties wishing to protect themselves against the risk that interest rates might move against them. For example, a lender providing fixed-rate funds could be locked into the conditions of the loan for the specified term. Being unable to vary charges, the lender suffers if market rates rise and market risk has not been covered in some other way. Likewise, a borrower would be disadvantaged if rates fell during the term of a fixed borrowing, or if rates rose before a future known borrowing could be put in place. An FRA operates like an over-the-counter futures contract but with greater flexibility in that any starting date and term can be struck. It is similar to a synthetic forward bank-bill purchase or sale and has also been described as a single-period interest-rate swap (and a swap likened to a string of FRAs). The contract is made at an agreed interest rate, for a specified period, based on an agreed notional principal amount, between any two parties looking to protect themselves against a future movement in interest rates. Each party's exposure is to the difference between the rate agreed under the FRA and the settlement rate.

Use of FRAs

FRAs help manage interest-rate exposures related to bank-bill rates and can be considered as tailor-made futures contracts (an OTC futures contract) without the associated constraints of brokerage, margins, standard dates and contract size. They retain the off-balance-sheet advantages of the futures market.

FRAs are chiefly used by professional market operators for trading in-house and hedging and to provide hedging products to investors, companies and government. An FRA enables borrowers and lenders to lock into future interest rates without exchanging principal amounts of the borrowing or loan. An FRA is struck between a client and a bank or investment bank, which fixes the interest rate to apply to an expected loan or deposit, for an agreed amount, term and date.

The bank or investment bank calculates the forward rate from an implied yield curve for the period specified. On the agreed future date the difference between the rate struck under the FRA and the prevailing market rate is settled between client and bank. Where the client has locked in a borrowing rate that proves to be lower than the bank-bill rate at the end of the agreed period, the bank pays the difference to the client, whose effective borrowing rate thus drops to the agreed forward rate; if, on the other hand, the rates set under the FRA prove to be higher than prevailing interest rates, the client pays the difference to the bank or investment bank, and raises its effective borrowing costs to that earlier agreed. Interbank FRAs in Australia are quoted to a maturity of one year, but longer maturities are available. Market practice is that the lender of an FRA is the *offer* and the borrower is the *bid*.

A borrower with an expected three-month borrowing requirement due to start in two months could use an FRA to protect against a possible rise in interest rates before the borrowing is drawn down. This borrower would hedge using a 'two-month against five-month' FRA—this means setting a rate today to apply in two months for a three-month borrowing. Likewise, a lender expecting surplus funds

Figure 13.1 Example of a forward-rate agreement

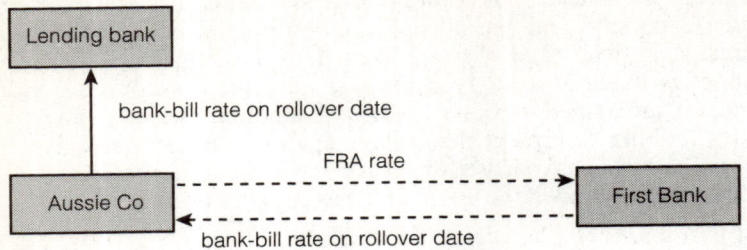

in two months that could be invested for six months could take a 'two-month against eight-month' FRA.

Example: *hedging a future borrowing*

Aussie Co Pty Ltd plans to draw down $10 million in 90-day bank bills in three months, and would like to secure a rate today for its future borrowings. Assume:

Bank bills (face value)	$10 million
Date 05/04/99	
FRA rate (starting 05/07/99 for 90 days)	5.7 per cent
Actual 90-day rate on 05/07/99	6.2 per cent

Sequence of events:

1 On 05/04/99 Aussie Co enters into an FRA with First Bank.
2 On 05/07/99 the 90-day bank-bill rate, as shown on Reuters page BBSW, is 6.2 per cent.
3 Because that is higher than the rate at which both parties entered into the FRA, that is, 5.7 per cent, First Bank must pay the difference to Aussie Co.
4 The settlement amount is equal to the difference between $10 million discounted at 5.7 per cent ($9 861 400.05) and $10 million discounted at 6.2 per cent ($9 849 425.23), that is, $11 974.82, and is paid by First Bank to Aussie Co.
5 If, on 05/07/99 the 90-day bank-bill rate shown on BBSW were 5 per cent, then the settlement amount would be equal to the difference between $10 million discounted at 5 per cent and $10 million discounted at 5.7 per cent, being $16 813.75 and would be paid by Aussie Co to First Bank. (NB: settlement is calculated on a discount, not yield, basis.)

Example: hedging a future investment

1 Aussie Co expects to receive $10 million in three months, which it will invest in a three-month bank bill or certificate of deposit.
2 To protect against a possible fall in interest rates over coming months, before the investment is put in place, Aussie Co sells an FRA, locking in today's interest rate for the future deposit.
3 First Bank is quoting a three-month against six-month FRA at 6–5.75 per cent and Aussie Co agrees to a contract rate of 5.75 per cent.
4 If, in three months, the settlement rate is 5 per cent, First Bank will settle in favour of Aussie Co and on FRA settlement date:
Aussie Co buys $10 million bank bills @ 5% (90 days) $9 878 213.80
Aussie Co has locked in $10 million @ 5.75% for 90 days on an FRA being $9 860 201.26
FRA settlement amount is $18 012.54
that is, Aussie Co will receive $18 012.54 on settlement of the FRA.

If, in three months, the settlement rate is 6.5 per cent, Aussie Co will settle in favour of First Bank and on FRA settlement date:

Aussie Co buys $10 million bank bills @ 6.5% (90 days) $9 842 254.28
Aussie Co has locked in $10 million @ 5.75% for 90 days on an FRA being $9 860 201.26
FRA settlement amount is $17 946.98
that is, Aussie Co will pay First Bank $17 946.98 on settlement of the FRA.

Advantages of FRAs

• FRAs are flexible whereas futures contracts are standardised in terms of amount and settlement date, and futures trading concentrates on calendar quarters. FRAs can be tailored to suit the requirements of each borrower or lender (within an ambit two-year period);
• credit risk is limited to the variation in interest rates and not to the full principal amount involved;
• FRAs are settled by exchanging amounts of cash and the principal amounts involved are not carried on the balance sheet for the period hedged;
• administration is simple—FRAs are not traded on an exchange so there is no demand for an initial deposit or margin calls, brokerage or clearing-house fees. Cashflows are therefore more

predictable and, with no margins to monitor, accounting costs are minimised;

- FRAs enable interest-rate risk to be hedged without making demands on current liquidity;
- FRAs are increasingly being settled under a master agreement;
- settlement of FRAs is against the bank-bill swap reference rate shown daily at 10.10 am on AAP Reuters page BBSW. The rate is a midrate, so neither side pays a spread.

Disadvantage

FRAs suffer from the disadvantage of not operating in a formal market, as do futures, and of carrying a credit risk in a way that futures contracts do not (since the risk in a futures contract is borne by the clearing house which is in turn protected by deposits and margins). Strip trading in futures contracts has become a popular rival to FRAs.

The next generation

> Except for the sovereign debt of the world's most developed countries, most debt has some degree of credit risk . . . an important concern for debt holders. Credit derivatives provide a mechanism for managing this risk.
>
> —*Chicago Fed Letter* The Federal Reserve Bank of Chicago, June 1998

Innovation in risk management continues, as evidenced by the emergence of twists such as pollution swaps, weather derivatives and credit derivatives. A potentially huge market has been forecast for credit derivatives, already widely used in the US, Europe and, more recently, in Asia. Launched in the US in 1992, credit derivatives are a form of OTC derivative which enable credit risk—the danger that loss could result from a borrower being unable or unwilling to repay—to be transferred and borne by a party better able to cope with it. Credit derivatives operate in the same way as interest-rate and currency swaps and options which offer methods to hedge or protect against movements in rates and currencies. They offer ways to replicate, transfer or hedge credit risk and, as with most OTC products, can be tailored to suit individual counterparties. Their application in Australia is growing and, as their market develops in size and liquidity, credit derivatives will change the way banks approach the management of credit risk.

Writing in *ASX Perspectives* in 1997, Harvey Crapp and Simon Gray, directors in PricewaterhouseCoopers Financial Services Group, commented:

Credit derivatives originated in New York in 1992 and the current market for them is dominated by London and New York. Market analysts are bullish about the prospects for growth in activity . . . Banks have been the traditional credit players and it is likely that initially they will be the main end-users of credit derivatives, but multinationals and fund managers, for example, may well perceive an increasing application for them. Typically, securities houses will play the role of repackagers and intermediaries, particularly as the volume and trading potential of credit derivatives expands.

Credit derivatives are available in several types—credit-default swaps, total-return swaps, credit-spread options and credit-linked notes. Of these, the two most actively used have been credit-default and total-return swaps.

Credit-default swaps are a form of insurance for lenders that they will get their money back even if a borrower defaults. The swaps are bilateral financial contracts which enable default risk to be transferred from one party to the other, with the hedging party paying a fee or premium in return for protection against a failure by a borrower to pay. Sometimes a loss threshold is stipulated which has to be reached before payment is triggered. Credit-default swaps are increasingly used by financial institutions to transfer credit risk. A variation, or secured form, of the credit-default swap is the *credit-linked note* where the party selling protection buys a note issued by the one buying protection and the reference asset is security, with the note redeemable at a value linked to that of the reference asset. Westpac Banking Corporation broke new ground in mid-1998 when it became the first Australian bank to issue credit-linked notes in the international markets, selling $US9 million of zero-coupon notes whose interest payments were linked to securities issued by a third party.

Total-return swaps enable the transfer of the full economic performance of an asset by replicating it off-balance-sheet in ways that capture credit and market risks. They can be used to reduce exposure to an asset that is held on the balance sheet while avoiding any impact on the balance sheet itself. The party buying protection receives periodic interest payments, set at a margin over a reference rate such as LIBOR or BBSW, and payments to compensate for a negative movement in the value of the asset when it is marked to market. In return, the seller of protection receives periodic payments composed of cashflows from the asset and payments for positive movements in the asset's value when it is marked to market.

Credit-spread options enable a hedger to gain protection against movement in the credit risk margin, which reflects the credit quality of an asset such as a loan.

Users of credit derivatives

For banks, credit risk is a major source of volatility in earnings. Traditionally banks have coped with this through loan loss provisions but increasingly they see credit derivatives as offering a less expensive method of managing credit risk. Banks also use credit derivatives to free up credit lines to particular sectors or industries or to reduce an exposure to keep within prudential limits or simply to make room for more lucrative business. Banks can reduce exposure to a borrower whose credit-rating is likely to be downgraded without hurting the borrower–lender relationship (in bankspeak, the transaction is 'relationship neutral'), or can reduce concentration in exposure to a specific industry, sector or country. Investment banks use credit derivatives to manage their portfolios of securities, especially those related to emerging markets or illiquid companies, while also fulfilling a role as intermediaries. Fund managers which have to invest in, say, a minimum of AA+ credits but are holding the paper of a company that is about to be downgraded to AA- can use credit derivatives to avoid breaching a trust deed. Portfolio managers can use credit derivatives to hedge or to diversify credit risk.

A comprehensive, up-to-date text on credit derivatives is *Credit Derivatives: Trading and Managing Credit and Default Risk*, edited by Satyajit Das, published by John Wiley & Sons. Das comments in the book:

> The application of credit derivatives is predicated on a shift in the *approach* to the management of credit risk. Traditionally, credit risk has been regarded as static in nature. The process of credit-risk management has focused on assessing credit risk and matching it with capital or provisions to cover expected losses from default. The principal management techniques have been diversification of the credit risk and the use of credit enhancement . . . In contrast, credit derivatives allow credit risk to be viewed as a disaggregated commodity, separate from other risks such as interest rate or currency risk, which is capable of being managed dynamically through hedging techniques previously associated with market risk.

14

Exchange-traded derivatives: futures

Derivatives in the form of futures contracts are not a new species of risk management, rather in the exotic and still-evolving world of derivatives, futures and options rank as 'mature' products. Futures and options traded on exchanges such as the Sydney Futures Exchange and Australian Stock Exchange Derivatives are used chiefly for risk management (hedging) but also for investment (trading), as well as for speculation (see chapter 15 for a discussion of exchange-traded options). Risk management enables those operating in markets to protect the value of their assets—bonds or shares—against changes in price and capital value. Traders and speculators use derivatives to make a profit; unlike the hedgers, they have no position in the underlying asset but use derivatives because they offer lower transaction costs and the chance for leverage, that is, to gain a large exposure to an underlying asset in return for a small initial outlay. Hedgers use futures to reduce risk; traders accept the 'unwanted' risk of hedgers and use futures to try to make a profit. A trader with a view in the physical market would also have a view in futures, so the deeper the physical market, the deeper the corresponding futures market is likely to be.

Background to futures trading

Futures markets have existed for centuries, initially based on rural commodities such as grains, beef or wool. Forward trading by written contract occurred in the sixth century BC in Greece; transactions took place, based on a form of forward delivery document, at European trade fairs in the Middle Ages. Futures contracts, in a form similar to today's contracts, developed in seventeenth-century

267

Japan. Markets in these instruments emerged in their present form in the US midway through the nineteenth century. The city of Chicago, in the midst of the grain and farming belt, evolved as a logical trading centre. The Chicago Board of Trade was established in 1848 and its business revolved around grain markets. The Chicago Mercantile Exchange started shortly after the Board of Trade, initially trading in butter and eggs and known as the Chicago Butter and Egg Board until a name-change in 1919. The early aim of both was to provide a forum where traders could take out some form of protection against fluctuations in the prices of the commodities they grew, sold or bought.

Financial futures are of far more recent origin, appearing as an outcome of the global economic upheavals of the 1970s when successive increases in the price of oil, fluctuating interest rates, rising inflation and the move from fixed to floating exchange rates focused attention on the need to protect against unforeseen shifts in interest rates and currencies and, more recently, share prices. Until then, futures markets had dealt in commodities such as corn, soybeans and pork-bellies, and in precious metals such as gold and silver. Given the uncertainties surrounding movements in interest rates and currencies, however, it seemed sensible to devise a method to hedge or protect against future unwelcome shifts that could rob a borrower or lender, exporter or importer, of profits in the same way that a bad season could have deprived a nineteenth-century grain farmer of his income. Currency futures started trading in Chicago in 1972 and the first interest-rate futures contract was introduced on the Chicago Board of Trade in 1976. This was the Government National Mortgage Association certificate (GNMA), popularly known as the Ginnie Mae. Long-term US treasury bonds and one-year treasury bills followed the Ginnie Mae, then the Chicago Board of Trade launched a 90-day commercial paper futures contract and the Mercantile Exchange brought out a 90-day treasury bill contract. Both proved popular and have been actively traded. Other futures exchanges have been established in the US and around the world. Among the most notable are the London International Financial Futures and Options Exchange (LIFFE), the Deutsche Terminbörse (DTB) and the Tokyo International Financial Futures Exchange (TIFFE).

The Sydney Futures Exchange (SFE), launched in 1960 as the Sydney Greasy Wool Futures Exchange, traded only wool until a cattle contract was introduced in 1975. A gold contract was launched in 1978 and in the following year the SFE was the first exchange outside the US to follow that country's lead in financial futures when it launched a 90-day bank-bill futures contract. Financial futures contracts are based on financial instruments, such as a

90-day bank bill of exchange or a government bond or a share-price index.

The Sydney Futures Exchange

Deregulation gave Australia's financial markets the potential to internationalise. Advances in technology made the move possible. The trend can be clearly identified in the development of the Sydney Futures Exchange, where Australian financial futures contracts are traded around the world and around the clock. A significant initiative was the introduction and expansion of SYCOM—the Sydney Computerised Market—launched in November 1989 as an after-hours automated screen-dealing system to enable trading in futures contracts during the hours when the exchange was closed. Continuing the move towards increased automation, the SFE announced in March 1998 that it had signed a contract with Computershare Limited, a leading information technology provider to the global securities markets, to install a Large Order Call Automated Market trading system (LOCAM). The new system is designed to enable SFE market participants to lodge large orders anonymously, with these orders then matched periodically throughout the day without disclosing their direction or size. The facility should reduce the costs associated with the disclosure of large orders in SFE's markets. The exchange viewed the move as an integral part of its automation strategy, complementing its established trading facilities and hopefully generating greater liquidity and international participation.

The Sydney Futures Exchange capitalised on the momentum for deregulation that prevailed during the 1980s, introducing a new class of members, called *locals* (individuals or companies who trade on their own account and not for clients), and exchange-traded options (ETOs) in May 1985 which increased the opportunities for arbitrage between the futures and physical markets. Many of the new techniques in futures trading flow from *basis trading*, which involves making the most of the difference between a futures market price and the present cash price for a commodity or instrument.

The Sydney Futures Exchange had diversified into financial futures in October 1979 when it launched an interest-rate futures contract based on 90-day bank bills of exchange. This was followed by a $US futures contract and then, in the early 1980s, successful contracts were launched based on the share price index and government bonds. Financial futures proved a boom industry of the 1980s as traders, speculators and hedgers tried to offset risk in an increasingly volatile and uncertain financial world. That is not to say, though, that every contract launched at the SFE proved an instant winner. Some contracts, such as those based on yen and sterling, and later the eurodollar and US treasury bond contract, did not attract sufficient volume to be maintained. Futures contracts that have come and gone on the SFE include boneless beef, silver, fat lambs, gold, US treasury bonds, semi-government futures and a range of currencies such as sterling, the $US, the yen and the eurodollar. Consistent star performers have been the Australian bank bill and commonwealth government bond futures contracts and the contract based on share-price index futures (SPI). Options, after a slow start, have also become a favourite.

Overall, interest-rate futures account for the lion's share of the SFE's business but the exchange has been working on expanding other product ranges, with a particular focus on energy-related contracts. In the 1990s, the SFE broadened its platform from a focus on financial futures to include a range of commodities. This entailed a revival of the wool futures contract—which had been the impetus for a futures exchange in Sydney in 1960—as well as developments in energy futures through a link initiated in September 1995 with the New York Mercantile Exchange (NYMEX) whose natural gas and crude oil contracts are world benchmarks in energy pricing.

Sydney Futures Exchange Clearing House (SFECH)

The clearing house stands at the centre of all futures transactions. The International Commodities Clearing House (ICCH), owned by a consortium of British banks, for many years provided clearing services for a number of exchanges around the world, including the SFE. In 1989 the contract between the ICCH and the SFE came under review and, following that, the SFE decided its members would benefit if the exchange developed its own clearing services and earned revenue from these, rather than pay for services provided by the UK-owned ICCH. The SFE would also administer a guarantee fund, financed by members' contributions, to replace the ICCH's global guarantee.

In June 1990 the SFE members endorsed the exchange's steering committee's earlier vote in favour of self-clearing and, after eighteen months of intense effort, SFECH began operating in December 1991, with a $100 million guarantee (increased to $150 million in January 1998), so that the SFE was henceforth responsible for clearing and guaranteeing its markets. All full members of the Sydney Futures Exchange must be members of SFECH. Associate members and other large participants in the SFE can also be accepted as members. All contracts traded on the SFE must be registered with SFECH, which maintains a continuous record of trading on both sides (buy and sell) of the futures markets.

The clearing house, although a wholly-owned subsidiary of the

SFE, has an identity separate from that of the futures exchange, with its own membership and board; its principal function is to provide a registration service for all contracts and to guarantee the performance of each contract to its members. The process of *novation* (a legal term for the procedure by which one party is substituted for another on one side of the contract), enables the clearing house to match bought and sold contracts, which provides flexibility for traders to open or close positions at any time.

Each clearing member's contractual obligations are to SFECH, not to the party from whom he or she is buying, or to whom he or she is selling; SFECH in fact becomes buyer to every seller, and seller to every buyer, so substantially reducing counterparty risk. SFECH decides the level of margin deposits on each contract and can vary those deposits, or call for additional deposits, daily to protect the market. A clearing member, though, in a volatile market can charge a client a higher amount than that stipulated by SFECH, whose deposit is regarded as a minimum. Interest is paid on these deposits, which are returned on settlement of the contract.

The impact of technology

Trading has traditionally been carried out by open outcry on the floor of most futures exchanges, including Sydney, as futures and option contracts are traded between exchange members on behalf of clients. However, as technology continues to make inroads into markets, an increasing number of exchanges, particularly those of medium rather than large size, switched to electronic, rather than floor, trading. Costs and economies of scale are generally cited as the reasons for the move. In the second half of the 1990s the momentum for screen-trading intensified. Even the larger exchanges in the northern hemisphere, such as the giants in Chicago and London, were investing substantial sums in improving after-hours screen-trading systems and major European exchanges such as MATIF in France and the continental European exchange EUREX (a combination of Germany's DTB, Switzerland's SOFFEX and others) embraced electronic trading systems.

The SFE announced in late 1997 that it would join the ranks of electronic trading floors and move to full global electronic trading. Across the Tasman, the New Zealand Futures and Options Exchange, whose business was acquired by the SFE in December 1991, has traded electronically since its inception in January 1985, largely because of the spread of brokers across two islands and several cities.

SYCOM: screen-trading at SFE

Automated trading has gained ground in exchanges around the world, in both stock exchanges and futures floors as more and more exchanges opt for the efficiency and cost-saving of electronic trading, even though that means sacrificing the 'smell of the ring' and the drama and emotion of floor trading.

Sydney Computerised Market (SYCOM) was introduced on the SFE in 1989 initially as an adjunct to floor trading and a useful back-up, should an emergency force the floor to close. Since then trading volumes have soared. SYCOM operates through personal computers linked to the SFE's mainframe computer. Trading hours, progressively extended over the years, were from 4.40 pm (ten minutes after the close of the Australian day's trading session) until 7 am (4 pm New York time) at the end of 1997 (occasionally longer, if an important overseas statistic is to be announced). The extension of the trading hours of SYCOM means that the SFE provides opportunities for trading for almost 24 hours daily. All major contracts listed by the SFE are traded on SYCOM through full members of the exchange. By the end of 1994 10 per cent of the SFE's turnover was traded on SYCOM and by early 1998 this had increased to more than 12 per cent. A significant advantage of SYCOM is that traders can react to events announced during the US or European market hours—for example, US trade or employment statistics—and so can control their positions while major world markets are open. Reflecting the relevance of this for private individual traders, one or two futures brokers opened 24-hour dealing facilities for individual traders.

In addition, the link between the SFE and NYMEX, through the two exchanges' electronic trading systems, the SFE's SYCOM and NYMEX's ACCESS, enables traders in Australia to trade NYMEX's commodity futures contracts during the US day, including the world oil benchmark, West Texas Intermediate, and gas, as well as COMEX's gold, silver and copper futures contracts following NYMEX's 1994 merger with the giant metals exchange. SYCOM has also developed as a platform for the SFE's launch of new products, for example, bond overnight options which, since 1993, have traded exclusively on SYCOM.

Trading sessions on the Sydney Futures Exchange vary in their starting and finishing times. The bank bills and bond contracts open at 8.30 am and run through until 4.30 pm, while the share price index futures contract and individual shares futures trade from 9.50 am until 4.15 pm). Commodity contracts trade on SYCOM

Table 14.1 SFE and SYCOM-traded contracts

Futures contracts	Introduced	Based on
90-day bank bills	October 1979	$A1 million bank-accepted bills of exchange
Share-price index	February 1983	$A value of 25 times the All-Ordinaries index
Treasury bonds	December 1984	$A100 000 face value of a 10-year notional treasury bond
	May 1988	$A100 000 face value of a three-year notional treasury bond
Wool	March 1995	2500 kgs clean weight merino combing wool
Wheat	March 1996	50 metric tonnes
Gold	September 1995 (through NYMEX)	COMEX 100 troy oz
Electricity	September 1997	500 Mwh of electrical energy
Individual share futures (ISFs)	1994	1000 company shares

Sydney Computerised Market (SYCOM)

90-day bank-accepted bill	January 1990
All-Ordinaries share price index	February 1990
Three-year treasury bond	February 1990
Ten-year treasury bond	November 1989
Overnight options on bonds	November 1993
Overnight options on SPI	February 1997

during the Sydney day and through the night. In mid-1998 the SFE traded the contracts shown in Table 14.1.

Wheat, wool and electricity futures trade on SYCOM during the Australian trading day and wheat and wool also trade on SYCOM overnight.

The SFE operates with four categories of members: full, associate, local and, since 1995, commodity trading advisers (CTAs). Full members, mostly banks and investment banks, are the only class whose representatives trade on behalf of clients as well as on the bank or investment bank's account. Associate members must deal through a full member. Local members can deal only for themselves and not on behalf of clients.

Recognising the growth potential of managed futures funds, which have seen explosive expansion in the US, the SFE created a

273

membership class for CTAs and, at the same time, joined the Managed Futures Association in the US, to boost its profile there and in Australia. In managed futures funds, professional advisers, managing their clients' assets on a discretionary basis, use futures markets as an investment tool. Their activity in SFE markets has increased as managers look for liquid futures and option contracts through which to spread their funds. The Asia-Pacific Managed Futures Association (APMFA), established in 1993 and representing 40 local and international members, is confident that managed futures will grow in Australia along the lines of their expansion in the US, where they are an established asset class with more than $US30 billion under management. Managed futures funds in Australia have a less well-developed profile but, if the US example is repeated, managed funds could grow significantly in this country. The performance of these funds, though, can only reflect the expertise of those managing them, so investors have to rely on their judgment. Managed funds can appear a fairly painless way to gain entry to futures trading but, as with all investments, are not risk-free.

Industry legislation

The Futures Industry Act regulating futures trading was replaced in 1991 by the Futures Industry Chapter (chapter 8) of the Corporations Act, administered by the Australian Securities Commission and known as the Futures Law. The futures industry is regulated by this and by the SFE's business rules. Derivatives traded on the Australian Stock Exchange's derivatives division (ASXD, see chapter 15) come under Chapter 7 of the Corporations Act. However, these distinctions could well disappear as the general intention is to harmonise chapters 7 and 8. The Futures Law imposes a number of obligations on futures brokers, such as maintaining clients' funds and other client property separately from the broker's own funds in a segregated account and adhering to strict rules concerning payments and withdrawals from these accounts. Documents covering clients' trading must be regularly prepared and provided to the clients, detailing each futures or option transaction, along with monthly statements. Brokers must keep comprehensive records of transactions dealt for themselves or on behalf of related companies. The law also stipulates that brokers must observe regulations prohibiting market manipulation and artificial price-making, false trading and market rigging.

All futures markets must be maintained on approved futures exchanges and all futures trading for clients must occur either on a local approved futures exchange or an overseas futures exchange that is specified in the regulations. Further, a futures market is defined as a market, exchange or other place at which, or a facility by means of which, futures contracts are regularly made. The Futures Law also tries to define a futures market by reference to features that distinguish futures trading from other forms of commodity trading, especially those involving forward trading. Under the Futures Law, a futures exchange must have ministerial approval.

The legislation required a further major revision of the SFE's articles and by-laws. It also obliged the SFE to establish a fidelity fund, to cover financial losses to clients resulting from defalcation or fraudulent misuse of money or other property. The fund would be available in a case where, say, an employee of an exchange member misused a client's money and the member was unable to reimburse the client. The fund would not be available to compensate for market losses or a member's negligence. The SFE's board could use its discretion in the case of a substantial financial shortfall caused by a major client default. The SFE contributed an initial $500 000 and members contributed by way of a levy on trades. The fidelity fund is administered by a management committee of the exchange.

The SFE's regulations reinforce many of the provisions of the legislation and provide a detailed code of conduct for members. The exchange's business rules impose additional obligations on members who deal with clients:

- full members must maintain minimum net tangible assets of $A1 million; full associate members must have $250 000 in net tangible assets and introducing broker associates $50 000;
- members must complete and lodge quarterly financial statements;
- members must execute a written client agreement with every client containing the minimum details as determined by the exchange;
- members must ensure that initial margins are called from clients regarding all futures and options positions;
- members must call for a variation margin payment from a client when that client's net debit margin exceeds 25 per cent of the total initial margin;
- where a margin call has not been satisfied by a client within five business days the member must 'top up' the client's segregated account by a deposit of its own funds.

The SFE's committee for inspection and audit, and its compliance and surveillance staff, are responsible for ensuring that the Futures Law and the SFE's business rules are followed. The SFE's business rules cover dispute arbitration to provide an impartial method of settling disputes between members, and between members and clients, where the parties are unable to resolve the matters. This offers a swifter and less expensive alternative to court proceedings.

As well as national legislation and its own expanded business rules, the SFE operates with its own in-house legal counsel and with an upgraded emphasis on compliance. Also, specific trading etiquette has been devised for SYCOM and new rules approved for the SFECH.

Futures contracts

A futures contract is a binding obligation, enforceable at law, requiring delivery of a specific quantity of a specific type of goods, at an agreed price, place and time. Every contract has a buyer and a seller. A futures contract can be terminated at any time before it is due for delivery by selling (if the trader were holding a bought or *long* contract), or buying (if the trader were holding a sold or *short* contract). Most futures contracts are closed out before delivery date; generally, only about 3 per cent of contracts run to physical delivery of the commodity or instrument on which the contract is based. Some contracts, such as the share price index and government bonds, are terminated by cash settlement and not physical delivery.

Futures markets' efficiency, from a cost point of view, was greatly enhanced by the guidelines on bank capital adequacy announced by the Reserve Bank in August 1988. The guidelines apply to items that are on the balance sheet and those that are off-balance-sheet, and take a risk-based approach to credit so that items are weighted according to categories of risk ranging from zero to 100 per cent. Futures contracts have been allocated a zero weighting because they fall under the category of 'instruments traded on futures and options exchanges that are subject to daily mark-to-market and margin payments'. On the other hand, forward transactions attract a risk category that reflects the credit status of the counterparty.

Financial futures contracts

Bank bill futures

The contract unit in the bank-accepted bill futures contract is $A1 million value of 90-day bank-accepted bills of exchange. Suitable stock for delivery can be either ten bank-accepted bills each of $A100 000 or one bill of $A1 million or the equivalent amounts in bank certificates of deposit (CDs). The bills or CDs must mature between 85 and 95 days from settlement date of the contract, and, if bills, must have the same drawer, acceptor and due date, and be endorsed by the seller (deliverer). The initial decision to base an interest-rate futures contract on bank bills reflected the dominant position of these instruments in the Australian financial markets. The subsequent decision to include bank certificates of deposit indicates the shift in favour of CDs (which rank *pari passu* with bills of exchange). Bank bills have long been popular because of the first-class credit status they carry and the protection they offer through legislation (the Bills of Exchange Act and a weight of legal precedent).

Bank bills are quoted in prices in futures trading, not in terms of yield as in the physical market. This puts them on the same basis for quoting as other futures contracts. The bank-bill futures price is calculated by deducting the yield from an index of 100: for example a yield of 7 per cent would translate into a price of 93.00 (100 less 7). Bank-bill futures prices therefore move in the same way as prices for other commodities traded; the seller looks for a higher price (lower yield), and the buyer looks for a lower price (higher yield). It is important to clarify whether a trader is referring to a yield or a price movement in bank-bill futures, as when one rises the other falls.

The minimum amount the price can move is 0.01 (one basis point) on the index; this is the same as 0.01 per cent in yield terms. (An exception is the bank-bill options contract where the minimum movement is 0.005 or a 'half-tick' which suits users better as it provides a more precise end-of-day settlement price and so more accurate variation margins.) The SFE provides a 'ready reckoner' guide for interest-rate contracts showing the dollar value of one basis point move at each yield level.

The contract months traded in bank-bill futures are the financial quarters—that is, June, September, December and March—out to five years. Trading stops for the immediate delivery month on the Thursday before the second Friday of that month: for example, in December 1997 trading in December bank-bill futures stopped at noon on Thursday 11 December for delivery on Friday 12 December.

As with other contracts, a minimum deposit is required on the bank-bill futures contract. The deposit level is set by SFECH, which pays interest to clearing members. The deposit varies in line with market movements. If the price of the commodity or instrument moves against a trader then margin calls (variation margins) can be made by the clearing house on all clearing members. They in turn call their clients for the funds. This is done to cover any risk associated with the movements in price. The additional funds requested by way of margin calls are a safeguard to ensure that sufficient funds would be available should a paper loss become a real loss. Once a paper loss is reversed the margin call is refunded.

Table 14.2 Ready reckoner guide

Yield level %	Dollar value of one basis-point move on 90-day bank bill contract	Dollar value of one basis-point move on a 3-year bond contract	Dollar value of a one basis-point move on a 10-year bond contract
4.00	24.18	31.78	113.25
5.00	24.06	30.76	103.67
6.00	23.95	29.77	94.97
7.00	23.83	28.83	87.10
8.00	23.71	27.91	79.95
9.00	23.60	27.03	73.46
10.00	23.49	26.18	67.57
11.00	23.37	25.37	62.20
12.00	23.26	24.58	57.33
13.00	23.15	23.82	52.89
14.00	23.04	23.09	48.84

Unlike the initial contract deposit, funds lodged through margin calls do not attract interest.

Government bond futures

Government or treasury bond futures contracts provide a method for bond-traders and investors to protect their investments against unwelcome movements in interest rates and thus in bond yields. Changing market patterns and preferences have resulted in a range of maturities being introduced and traded since the first bond contract opened early in 1984. Initially a two-year bond contract was thought the most suitable maturity but changes in the pattern of secondary-market trading resulted in increased activity in ten-year bonds—much of this due to overseas interest in these securities. The SFE responded with the launch, in December 1984, of the ten-year bond futures contract. A three-year government bond contract was added in 1988. The bond contracts are favoured by banks and superannuation fund managers.

Bond futures are quoted in a similar way to bank-bill futures, with yield per annum deducted from an index of 100, so that a bond yielding 8.5 per cent per annum would be quoted at a price of 91.50. The minimum price movement, or tick, is 0.005 per cent for the ten-year bond futures and 0.01 per cent for the three-year contract, with the dollar value of a 0.005 or 0.01 per cent change varying in line with interest rates, as shown in Table 14.2. The bond futures are not a deliverable contract; settlement of contracts still held at the end of the trading period takes place in cash. The cash-settlement price is calculated from the average of the buying and selling quotes provided by ten bond-dealers, brokers and banks, chosen at random on the last morning of trading. These random quotes are taken at three times during the morning session, at 9.45, 10.30 and 11.15 am and then averaged. The two highest and two lowest buying quotes, and the two highest and lowest selling quotes are omitted from the calculation.

Cash-settlement months are the financial-quarter months (March, June, September and December) out to six months. Trading stops at noon on the fifteenth day of the cash-settlement month (or the next day if the fifteenth is not a working day); this is in line with interest payments and redemptions of government bonds. The cash settlement takes place on the business day following the last day of trading.

Share-price index futures

This contract became a star performer within months of its introduction in February 1983 on to the Sydney Futures Exchange, at one stage overtaking bank-bill futures in volume, and has remained very popular with individual private traders as well as with institutions. Stock index futures had proved a winner in the US when they were introduced in February 1982 on the Chicago Mercantile Exchange. Subsequently Japan's Nikkei 225 index has been actively traded on both the Osaka Securities Exchange and on Singapore's SIMEX.

Share-price index (SPI) futures are useful for anyone—individual or institution—looking for protection against losses that could arise from price changes in the sharemarket. The contract also provides an illustration of expectations about share prices. Holding a SPI position is similar to holding a diversified portfolio of shares, but with SPI this exposure is obtained by purchasing (if the market is rising) or selling (if the market is falling) contracts.

The share-price index futures contract is based on the Australian Stock Exchange All-Ordinaries index, which is the accepted barometer of the Australian sharemarket. The All-Ordinaries index is calculated using the market prices of about 250 companies listed on the ASX. The market value of these companies adds up to about 90 per cent of the value of all shares listed in Australia. The index is calculated continuously through the trading day and is published daily at the close of trading. The All-Ordinaries index is purely a price index; dividends are not included so holding share-price index futures is not an exact substitute for holding shares. (The All-Ordinaries Accumulation index takes into account dividends paid by companies included in the index.) The sample of companies

279

used in the All-Ordinaries index is revised annually, on the first trading day in July.

The unit of the share-price index futures contract equals the All-Ordinaries index multiplied by $25: if the index were 2000, the contract value would be $50 000. Share-price index futures prices are quoted in the same way as the All-Ordinaries index. Every one-point movement in the index translates into a $25 gain or loss on each contract, so a trader or investor who has bought SPI and finds the market has risen by ten points has a paper profit of $250; conversely, a ten-point fall in the market signals a paper loss of $250.

The share-price index futures contract is another non-deliverable contract, with settlement taking place in cash. The price for cash settlement is the closing quote, taken to one decimal place, for the All-Ordinaries index on the last day of trading. Trading stops at 4.15 pm on the last business day of the cash-settlement month. Cash-settlement months are March, June, September and December, out to eighteen months.

Individual Share Futures (ISFs)

Individual Share Futures, traded on the SFE since May 1994, are futures contracts based on the shares of individual listed companies. ISFs are available on blue-chip companies such as BHP, MIM Holdings, National Australia Bank, News Corporation Ltd, Westpac Banking Corporation, Western Mining and Telstra. Each contract is based on 1000 shares of the underlying stock (although contract size can be altered to take account of capital reconstructions, for example, share splits, bonus issues, rights issues, although no adjustment is made for dividends). So if BHP shares are trading at $15, one BHP share futures contract would be worth $15 000. ISF prices are quoted like share prices; a minimum fluctuation of one cent is equivalent to $10. The considerable leverage available makes ISFs attractive to investors: for an initial margin (outlay, which changes constantly and can fluctuate between $200 and $800) a buyer has exposure to 1000 shares in a blue-chip stock. Profits or losses are credited or debited by SFECH to the account of the holder of the contract. However, as is generally the case in futures trading, most contracts are not held to expiry but cancelled by taking an equal and opposite position. Contract months are the same as those on ASX and expiry is the Thursday before the last Friday of the contract month. An advantage of share futures is that they can be traded at any time during the almost 24 hours that the SFE is open, which includes hours when ASX is closed; also, brokerage costs for trading in share futures are lower than those applying to sharetrading and it is easier to short-sell ISFs than conventional shares.

In March 1996 the SFE realised an ambition when it secured regulatory approval to have share futures contracts deliverable, with settlement effected by the physical delivery of share scrip through ASX's CHESS. Deliverable share futures better suit market-makers because they provide a more efficient hedge; it was always the view of the SFE that having a contract deliverable better cements the pricing relationship between the cash and futures markets; the potential for delivery encourages a greater convergence between cash and futures markets at the point when the contract expires.

Commodities traded on SFE

A reduction in government involvement in commodities markets so that prices move more in line with supply and demand prompted a revival of agricultural commodities on the SFE to provide a proven method of protection against adverse price movements.

Wool

Australia is the world's largest producer and exporter of wool, which is our third-largest export. The end of the Reserve Price Scheme for wool in 1991 left the Australian wool industry exposed to the vagaries of the wool price. In early 1995 the Sydney Futures Exchange reintroduced a deliverable wool futures contract. The move was of particular sentimental relevance for the SFE, which had begun life in 1960 as the Sydney Greasy Wool Futures Exchange.

Launched as a key plank in the 1990s revival of agricultural commodities trading on the SFE, the wool contract introduced in 1995 is based on 21-micron greasy wool. Options on the wool contract followed in February 1996. Two further wool contracts were launched in January 1998, adding to choice in managing wool price risk: a fine 19-micron wool and a broad 23-micron wool. These were provided to reduce the frequently high basis risk associated with hedging finer and broader wools using a 21-micron contract. The additional two contracts are cash-settled, whereas the earlier contract is deliverable.

The 21-micron wool contract allows delivery of wool that is finer or coarser by 1.5 microns, which carries a premium or a discount to par. Wool finer than 21 microns is in demand by fashion houses and sells at a premium, particularly in the Asian markets which demand 'cool' wool. A 21-micron wool contract was favoured by the wool-buyers, woolbrokers and the mills; Wool International, which owns the Australian wool stockpile, and the growers tended to favour 22-micron (the bulk of the stockpile is in 22–23 micron). In the SFE's view, setting the contract at 21 microns should enable most growers to hedge adequately; those most exposed to basis risk will be those growing, say, less than 19-micron or greater than 23-micron wool. Basis risk, the risk of divergence between prices in futures and prices in the physical market, is an integral element of futures trading, irrespective of the contract's base. Those in favour of a 22-micron standard point to the greater volatility in the finer wools.

Growers facing the greater basis risk can tailor their hedging requirements with a bank or woolbroker, execute an over-the-counter transaction with them and let the expert handle the risk. The following is an example of a simple hedge using wool futures.

Date	Cash	Futures
February	Plans to sell wool at auction in October	Sells October futures at 800 cents/kg
October	Sells wool at auction and receives 700 cents/kg	Buys October futures at 700 cents/kg

The grower has profited by 100 cents/kg from this futures transaction, bringing the total return to 800 cents/kg. Allowing, say, 2 cents/kg as futures brokerage, the grower netted 798 cents/kg. Prices in the cash market have fallen between February and October but by selling forward through futures a profit has been locked in. Had prices risen in the intervening period the profit made in the physical market would have offset (even outweighed) the costs of the hedge.

Wheat

In world terms, Australia is a small producer but a major exporter of wheat, which ranks among our top five exports. Wheat futures and options, the SFE's first grain contract, were listed in March 1996 to provide a facility for managing the price risk generated by fluctuations in world grain markets. Volumes in both were remarkable during 1997, with turnover in wheat futures showing an increase of 22 per cent and options doubling over the previous year's volumes. The trend was reinforced by SFE research during 1997 which showed that Australian wheat producers and consumers faced considerably larger price risk if they hedged their exposures on overseas rather than the local market because the Australian wheat price had moved from the prevailing US and international levels.

Electricity

Deregulation of the electricity market, and corporatisation and privatisation of the industry, have prompted growth in electricity-based derivatives to assist generators, retailers and end-users of electricity manage price risk. An over-the-counter electricity swaps market began operating in May 1996 and the SFE introduced electricity futures in September 1997.

A first step in the creation of a national electricity market in Australia was the establishment of a competitive wholesale market. An essential component in the national competitive market is a common electricity pool serving interconnected states where wholesale customers can buy the energy they require, spot, from the pool or under contract from a chosen supplier. This deregulation of the Australian electricity market is taking place progressively and is introducing an unprecedented element of competition into the industry. The development of the National Electricity Market (NEM) dates from 1991 when the Industry Commission delivered a report, *Energy Generation and Distribution*, which recommended a major overhaul of the electricity industry by breaking up existing utilities into generation, transmission and distribution, corporatising each entity and having them operate in a competitive market. A few years later, Victoria and New South Wales introduced state wholesale electricity markets and in 1997 these were linked to form the first step towards a national wholesale electricity market. Subsequently the link was extended so that the Australian Capital Territory, South Australia, Victoria and NSW are connected. With deregulation, corporatisation and privatisation, the price of electricity loses its certainty and risk-management becomes an issue for market participants such as the generators, which aim to sell electricity at the highest price possible, and the retailers whose aim is to buy and sell electricity at a margin to customers. Large-scale industrial users may also wish to manage their electricity costs more effectively.

To meet this demand, in September 1997 the SFE introduced two electricity futures contracts, one based on the NSW electricity pool price and the other on the Victorian electricity pool price. Participants in the electricity market can buy and sell futures contracts to reduce their risk of financial loss because of a change in the spot price of electricity; for example, an electricity generator could sell futures to hedge against a possible fall in price. The two contracts, each covering 500 megawatt hours of electricity, trade on SYCOM and are quoted for each month up to twelve months ahead. Minimum price fluctuation is five cents per megawatt hour. The contracts are cash-settled, with the settlement price calculated by averaging each half-hourly spot price over the calendar month, with the final settlement price rounded to the nearest cent, as adjusted by TransGrid in NSW and the Victorian Power Exchange and provided to the SFE. The SFE's initiatives closely followed the development of an over-the-counter electricity market in NSW and Victoria, with a handful of financial intermediaries establishing energy trading desks. Financial intermediaries do not have a natural exposure to the electricity market but identify a role in facilitating the trading of bilateral contracts between market participants and bringing together buyers and sellers.

The SFE's New Zealand subsidiary, the New Zealand Futures and Options Exchange (NZFOE), introduced electricity futures in 1996. The NZFOE's electricity contracts traded without interruption during the power crisis which gripped a section of Auckland early in 1998 and volumes in fact rose considerably. NZFOE members in Auckland relocated staff and redirected orders through offices in Wellington or Sydney, while NZFOE staff moved to premises outside the affected areas.

Example of a one-year hedge by a power generator

June 1: power generator wants to establish pricing for 5 per cent of its generating capacity for the ensuing twelve months. The generator produces 500 megawatts of continuous power with little risk of prolonged outages that might detract from its ability to produce power. The generator evaluates the strip of futures prices from June 1998 to May 1999 and its average is $25. The generator will dedicate 27.5 megawatts towards the $25 hedge which is roughly 19 800 megawatt hours for each month. The generator will need to sell an equivalent of 40 futures contracts each month, a total of 480 contracts for the twelve months, to meet its objectives. Prices are determined incrementally each month and the generator will be responsible for either closing out its position each month or going to delivery based on cash settlement. At the end of the twelve months the price had fallen by $2 to $23 so, cumulatively, the generator would be $480 000 better off because of the hedge it put in place.

Date	Electricity market	Futures market
June 1998	Generator anticipates average electricity price of $25 per MWh Generator anticipates revenue over the coming year of $5 940 000	Generator sells 480 contracts over 12 months at $25 per MWh
May 1999	Market had traded over the year at average price of $23 per MWh Total revenue (19 800 × 12 × 23) = $5 464 800	The price of the contracts falls to $23 (to reflect average price) Profit from contracts ($2 × 480 × 500) = $480 000

Total revenue	$5 464 800
Plus futures profit	$480 000
Total income	$5 944 800

Example of an industrial customer with short-term price risk

May 15: a distribution retailer has a customer about to increase production cycle for the month of June for 30 days. The customer indicates that it will need an additional 3000 MWh. The customer believes that there is a strong possibility that prices could increase. The prevailing market is trading at $25 for the June futures contract. The retailer provides the customer with a fixed price of $25 for the month of June and in doing so has $25 price risk for June in its books. The retailer can either hold the position and run the risk that prices could rise or transfer the risk by buying futures at $25 (that is, taking a long position). The futures contract size of 500 MWh indicates that the retailer would have to buy six futures contracts to cover the 3000 MWh of price risk for the month of June. By the end of June prices have risen to $26.50. The retailer is now obliged to sell electricity to the customer at $25, or $1.50 below the prevailing market price. The retailer would recoup the $1.50 through its futures position and at the same time has provided its customer with the service it wanted at no financial risk to itself.

Date	Electricity market	Futures market
May 15	Retailer anticipates electricity costs of $75 000 for June based on 3000 MWh	Retailer buys 6 June futures contracts at $25 per MWh
June	Market trades at $26.50 per MWh	The price of the futures contracts rises to $26.50 (reflecting changes in spot prices)
	Total cost of electricity for June $26.50 × 3000 = $79 500	Profit from contracts ($1.50 × 3000) = $4500

Retailer's total cost of electricity $79 500
Less profit on electricity futures $4 500
Effective cost $75 000 (or $25 per MWh)

NYMEX-linked contracts

The SFE's link with NYMEX (New York Mercantile Exchange) is a major plank in its growing commodities trading platform, in turn a key feature of ambitions to establish Sydney as a regional commodity trading hub. The first contract traded in the SFE's commodities platform was the West Texas Intermediate (WTI) crude oil contract, chosen for its economic importance to countries in the Asia–Pacific region, many of which are producers or refiners, or both, of crude oil. As with other futures contracts, a crude oil futures contract enables suppliers, users and traders in the commodity to protect themselves against the financial risk that prices might change by entering standardised agreements to buy or sell in the future.

The oil market centres mostly on the New York time-zone but some Australian intermediaries quote oil prices for clients and several banks run large energy books out of Singapore which would be coordinated with their bank's global book. The oil market quotes several different indexes. WTI crude oil, the world's most actively traded energy futures contract, is regarded as the benchmark indicator of world oil prices. Other oils quoted include Brent, sourced from the North Sea, quoted on London's International Petroleum Exchange, Tapis, bunker fuel, jet fuel and gasoil (similar to diesel oil). WTI and Tapis are the two main barometers for oil in the Australian/Asia–Pacific region and the development of Tapis swaps and options is of particular benefit to the Australasian markets. However, WTI and Tapis are quite separate markets which do not move in tandem; Tapis, less freely traded than WTI, is less of an indicator of world supply-and-demand factors than its more widely traded US counterpart. These features result in a price difference between the two of as much as $3 a barrel. There is a need for an exchange-traded product to cater for the heightened activity in oil and the frequently large basis risk between Tapis and WTI.

The Sydney Futures Exchange's trading link with NYMEX places NYMEX's WTI oil futures and option contracts in the Asia–Pacific time-zone and opens up a 24-hour market in oil. Under the terms of the agreement SFE members can trade NYMEX products based on heating oil, gasoline, natural gas and platinum, in addition to the benchmark WTI. Trades executed are cleared through NYMEX's clearing house. Also traded are gold, silver, copper and platinum on COMEX division of NYMEX

Products for managing oil-price risk include futures and the swaps and options covered in chapter 13. Futures offer exchange-traded contracts which enable a hedger to buy or sell a standardised product at a specified future date.

Using financial futures

Companies or individuals, unless classed as local members, must approach a broker or full member firm of a futures exchange to execute a trade. A full associate member firm or an introducing broker can also be approached; contracts placed through full associate members and introducing brokers are given to full members and brokerage is split.

Commodity futures markets were initially structured to accommodate those who traded in physical commodities—the *raison d'être* for those early exchanges in Chicago was to provide wheat farmers with a means of fixing forward delivery and price. A farmer or wheat merchant could spread purchases and sales of wheat throughout the year instead of being subjected to seasonal gluts or shortages which had a direct, and often adverse, effect on price. Futures exchanges, however, have expanded the range of commodities offered for trading. The quantity of traders they draw has also increased. People from many walks of life have begun to participate in futures trading so that it is no longer the territory of those involved with the underlying commodity markets. Futures trading is open to anyone who wants to take a view (have an informed opinion) on the course of prices for a commodity or financial instrument. People trade soybeans and pork-bellies on the Chicago exchanges but this does not mean they necessarily have a direct link with these commodities; sometimes they are speculating on the difference between the present and future prices.

Users of futures markets fall into three overlapping categories: producers or users of a commodity (who are essentially hedgers keen to minimise risk), speculators and arbitragers. The producers and users trade futures to hedge or protect against unfavourable movements in prices. The speculators may have no direct interest in a commodity but hope to profit by getting in on the right side of a market that looks temporarily out of kilter. Speculators and locals add to market depth; both contribute through their willingness to take on short-term positions which generate market activity. Speculators are attracted to a market if prices look out of line with the physical commodity in the 'real' world, suggesting an opportunity for profit. Their activity in response to such anomalies provides a self-correcting mechanism for the market. Speculators bring liquidity, thus enabling hedgers to effect transactions without pushing the markets unduly one way or another. The arbitragers aim to profit from anomalies between the physical and futures markets.

Market-users of interest-rate futures contracts fall roughly into the categories of producers/users (hedgers), and speculators. Banks and investment banks involved in the bill market use bank-bill futures to hedge their risk; likewise, banks and investment banks and other large holders of commonwealth bonds, including long-term investors such as superannuation fund managers, and debt-and-asset managers such as state-government authorities, use bond futures to hedge their liabilities. Finance companies and large corporations which hold and trade bills are also attracted to bank-bill futures. Overall, banks account for the bulk of activity in interest-rate products, followed by fund managers. Retail (individual) clients generally prefer share-price index futures, as they are more familiar with the sharemarket than, say, the bank-bill market, but some sophisticated retail investors do use the bank-bill and commonwealth bond contracts.

The futures markets offer the opportunity to moderate the effects of adverse movements in rates or prices. Successful use of financial futures can minimise risk—although there is no guarantee that risk can be totally eliminated. Total elimination of risk requires a perfect match between the physical and futures markets. This is not possible, and so gives rise to *basis risk* which can be defined as the difference in the correlation of prices between the physical and futures markets.

Even though contracts are rarely held for physical delivery, the banks which trade in, say, bank-bill futures have an edge over the individual speculator because, if they were to get caught on the 'wrong' side of the market, the bank has the financial capacity to hold the position to expiry and then give or take delivery of the underlying instrument or commodity. This is often not possible for an individual speculator.

However, individuals can participate in financial futures and with the right advice and proper risk management can make profits. Cardinal rules are: never trade futures with anything but risk capital (not with funds set aside for education expenses); cut losses and let profits run—tough in practice, because every trader is hopeful. And speculators are advised never to trade the spot month: that is left to the professionals, because of the risk of having to give or take delivery. This convention, however, is not applicable to contracts such as the SFE's SPI and bonds, which are cash-settled.

Hedging

Hedging is an insurance technique. The hedger is looking for protection against future price changes in the physical market. Hedging involves taking opposite and equal positions in the physical and futures markets, with the aim of preventing or minimising loss. The theory of hedging is to compensate in one market for potential losses in another.

A hedge can be either to buy or to sell—in market jargon it can be *long* (bought) or *short* (sold). In the case of a long hedge, a future buyer of securities, or lender of funds, buys futures contracts now to set a rate of return on a forward investment. In the case of a short hedge, a borrower or seller of securities would fix the cost of future borrowed funds or sale proceeds by selling, say, a bank-bill futures contract in anticipation of a higher yield (lower price) at the future date than the current futures contract price.

An investor or lender can use a long hedge to protect against a possible fall in interest rates. The hedger is able to fix the return on funds by purchasing futures contracts today for forward delivery. If rates drop, that is, prices rise, between the purchase date and delivery date of the futures contract, the resulting futures profit will go towards offsetting the drop in interest rates over the period, thus cushioning a loss of revenue.

A selling hedge is used to offset the effects of rising interest rates. A borrower of funds or seller of securities can sell a futures contract today, so that if interest rates move higher between the hedge date and delivery of the futures contract, then the value of the contract falls (rates up equals prices down) and the hedger makes a gain by buying back the contract at a lower price (higher yield). The profit on the futures transaction goes towards offsetting the rise in interest rates during the same period.

Hedging is a fairly basic trading technique. More sophisticated approaches have been developed to help companies and individuals protect their assets and liabilities from fluctuating currencies and interest rates. These methods involve financial futures options, cash-and-carry transactions, exchange-for-physical and straddles.

Cash-and-carry or cash-futures arbitrage

This type of arbitrage transaction enables a trader to gain advantage from a futures price that is not trading at fair value. The strategy involves a purchase of the spot physical commodity against a forward sale on the futures market. The physical commodity or instrument is then delivered to close out the futures contract. Cash-and-carry transactions are popular whenever pressure builds up on either the physical or futures markets, resulting in the yields on the two markets temporarily moving out of line. It is thus a form of arbitrage. An investor could take advantage of a differential by buying, say, a longer-term bill of exchange than is required, selling it forward on the futures market to achieve a fixed rate of return (from the date of purchase of the bill to the close-out date on the futures contract). This rate could be above the rate achievable through an outright purchase on the physical market.

For example, assume the rate in early July on a 150-day bank-accepted bill of exchange in the physical market is 5.5 per cent, while the rate on a 60-day bank-accepted bill is 5.25 per cent and September futures are trading at 94.6 (5.4 per cent yield). An investor with $10 million could buy a 60-day bank bill and receive a return of 5.25 per cent for the time the funds are invested. But by simultaneously buying a 150-day bank bill and selling a September futures contract the investor would fix a return of 5.58 per cent. This result would be achieved after 60 days when the bill is delivered, as a 90-day maturity, to fulfil the sold September futures contract.

Buy $10 million 150-day physical bank-accepted bills at 5.5 per cent = $9 778 968.52. Sell a September futures contract at 94.60 (5.4 per cent yield) = $9 868 598.93. The formula for calculating the net return for the equivalent future 60-day investment is:

$$= \frac{SP - PP - (C + I)}{PP + FD} \times \frac{36\ 500}{D}$$

Where SP = selling price
       PP = purchase price
        C = costs
        D = days held
       FD = futures deposit
        I = interest paid by the clearing house on the futures deposit

$$= \frac{9\ 868\ 598.93 - 9\ 778\ 968.52}{9\ 778\ 968.52} \times \frac{36\ 500}{60}$$
$$= \text{yield of 5.5757 (5.58) per cent}$$

(Costs, futures deposit and interest paid on the futures deposit have not been included in this transaction.)

The reverse situation applies with a borrower. A borrower draws down bank bills for a longer term than is really required, borrows against those bills in the physical market then buys the bills from the futures market so that the rate paid for cash is lower than would have been paid on discounting shorter bills. This is commonly known as *reverse cash-and-carry*.

Exchange for physical

This concept (EFP) was introduced to the Sydney Futures Exchange in 1981 in the form practised on US futures exchanges. EFPs facilitate switching. An EFP enables two parties, say, banks or investment banks, to agree the relative levels at which they will exchange a commodity or financial instrument, such as a common-wealth bond, with a related futures contract. An EFP is the only off-market transaction allowed by the SFE. It has come to be used mostly with bonds, to facilitate large portfolio adjustments and to trade spreads.

Financial instruments used in an EFP transaction can include bank bills of exchange, commercial paper or commonwealth, state or corporate bonds. EFP allows a wide range of financial transactions to be hedged. Once a differential between, say, a bank-accepted bill yield and the yield of the deliverable instrument has been agreed, the interest rate is fixed. The two parties involved swap securities at an agreed differential, with one side undertaking to supply the physical commodity. This is done by negotiating off-market simultaneous futures and physical transactions, with the futures leg then registered with the SFE. EFPs are attractive because they offer price certainty, delivery and flexibility in timing. A study commissioned by the SFE in 1997, carried out by the US-based Catalyst Institute, examined EFPs on the SFE and the Chicago Mercantile Exchange and concluded that EFP activity had not caused a decline in exchange trading, liquidity was not reduced and price volatility had not increased. The report even argued that EFPs could boost on-exchange business. It said: 'If the availability of EFP trading makes futures a more attractive risk-management tool, then more users might be attracted to the marketplace. Increases in futures volume and liquidity might follow.' The report emphasised that EFP trading needs transparency—if not, liquidity on exchanges could decline and levels of transactional risk and hedging costs increase. The SFE has addressed that by having screens reporting EFP prices within an hour of the exchange receiving them. EFP activity grew from 900 000 contracts in 1993 to 3.024 million in 1997 of which 2 million was in three-year government bond trading.

A popular use of EFPs is as a means of trading the interest-rate differential (or price spread) between the SFE's bond futures contracts and physical bonds traded in the market. In the following example, an EFP is used for bond switching.

Assume that a fixed-income dealer believes that the relative interest-rate differential between NSW TCorp 12.5 per cent 1 April 2001 bonds and commonwealth 12.5 per cent 15 March 2001 bonds will widen from 0.27 per cent to 0.35 per cent. The dealer can undertake a bond switch with an EFP by selling semi-government bonds and buying three-year bond futures as a proxy for commonwealth government bonds. The transactions are:

- 15 July 1999: The dealer sells $20 million NSWTC 12 per cent 1 April 2001 bonds at 7.89 per cent. The proceeds from this sale are then invested at the cash rate of 7.5 per cent. At the same time, the dealer buys, through an EFP, September 1999 three-year bond futures at 92.38 (7.62 per cent).
- 31 July 1999: The transactions are reversed, with an offsetting EFP and the NSWTC bonds bought at 8.27 per cent and futures sold at 92.08 (7.92 per cent).

Cash market: 15 July 1999
Sells $20 million of 12.5% NSWTC
   April 2001 bonds @ 7.89%
Value: $22 162 200
Invest $22 262 200 @ cash rate of
   7.5%

Futures market: 15 July 1999
Buys 120 Sep 99 3-year bond
   futures contracts @ 92.38 (7.62%)
Value: $13 386 195.60

31 July 1999
Buys $20 million 12.5% NSWTC 1
   April 2001 bonds @ 8.27%
Value: $22 115 200
Profit: $47 000
Interest on cash: $72 862.03

31 July 1999
Sells 120 Sep 99 3-year bond futures
   contracts @ 92.08 (7.92%)
Value: $13 284 948.00
Loss: $101 247.60

$$\frac{\$22\,162\,200 \times 7.5 \times 16}{36\,500}$$

Profit on physical: $47 000
Interest on cash: $72 862.03
Loss on futures: ($101 247.60)
Overall profit: $18 614.43

The dealer was able to make a profit of $18 614.43 because the price spread widened, as expected, by eight basis points (that is, the semi-government bonds weakened relative to commonwealth bonds). EFPs are highly suitable for trading spreads, giving both parties the certainty that each will receive the volume of contracts needed and a single market price for the futures transaction.

Arbitrage

Arbitragers enter a market to take advantage of discrepancies in prices resulting from temporary imbalances in supply or demand or time-lags in market response to an event or announcement. An arbitrager identifies an opportunity, comes in to buy or sell (buying if the price is low, selling if the price is high), thereby pushing up a low price or reducing a high price and so bringing prices back into equilibrium. To qualify as arbitrage, the process of simultaneous buying and selling has to involve two markets, such as cash and futures.

A cash-futures arbitrage would involve simultaneous transactions in two markets for securities which have similar pricing characteristics. When prices for futures contracts, allowing for the cost of carry, are greater than cash prices, an arbitrager buys the securities or commodities in the cash market and sells futures contracts (a long arbitrage). When prices for futures, allowing for the cost of carry, are less than those in the cash market, an arbitrager sells securities or commodities in the cash market and buys futures contracts (a short arbitrage). Arbitragers often do not hold a position for long; the position is closed as soon as the price relationship returns to normal, ending an arbitrager's interest.

Risks for an arbitrager are generally limited to a change in financing costs and the price risk associated with executing the various transactions involved.

Speculation

A speculator has the same objective as any market participant: to buy low and sell high. A speculator is not involved in the physical instrument or commodity traded but trades merely in anticipation of making a profit through a fairly high-risk strategy, while acknowledging that there is potential to make a loss. For example, a speculator might buy share-price index futures contracts in expectation of a price rise so that the position could later be closed by selling the contracts at a higher price for a profit:

October 10

Cash market	Futures market
No transaction	Speculator buys 10 December SPI
All-Ordinaries index at 2600.0	futures at market price of 2610,
	value $652 500 (ie, 65 250 × 10)

October 25

Cash market	Futures market
No transaction	Speculator sells 10 December SPI
All-Ordinaries index has risen to	futures at new market price of
2650.0	2660.0, value $665 000

Speculator's profit is $12 500, that is, $665 000.0 less $652 500.0, or 50 points × 10 contracts × $25 a point.

Profits to a speculator holding contracts that are increasing in value accumulate in the speculator's account with his or her futures broker; these profits result from the margin calls made daily to the party holding the opposite position to the speculator.

Spread trading

Spread trading involves simultaneously buying and selling two different futures contracts, with the trader hoping to anticipate correctly the likely change in the relative values of the two contracts. Spread trading can be *intermonth* (buying and selling different contract months of the same commodity) or *intercommodity* (using different commodities).

With an intermonth spread the objective is to buy the month

293

expected to increase in value and sell the month expected to fall. To be successful, the trader has to understand what influences the price differentials.

For example, a bank-bill trader may note that the differential between March and September bank-bill futures is 50 basis points. The trader believes that over the coming month longer-dated bill rates will rise relative to the shorter-dated bill rates and, consequently, the spread differential between the two contracts will widen to 100 basis points. To take advantage of this the trader decides to execute a spread trade by buying the March contract and simultaneously selling the September contract. Once the differential widens, the spread trade will be closed, crystallising a profit.

February 10 (spread 50 basis points)

Trader buys 50 March 90-day bank-bill futures at 95.00 (5%)	Trader sells 50 September 90-day bank-bill futures at 94.50 (5.5%)
Value: $49 391 069.01	Value: $49 330 990.68

March 10 (spread widens to 100 basis points)

Trader sells 50 March 90-day bank-bill futures at 94.00 (6%)	Trader buys 50 September 90-day bank-bill futures at 93.00 (7%)
Value: $49 271 058.32	Value: $49 151 629.41
Loss: $120 010.69	Profit: $179 361.27
Net profit on spread: $59 350.58	

The trader was therefore able to profit from the change in the spread differential. It was irrelevant whether interest rates rose or fell in absolute terms; the profitability of the trade was contingent on the change (in this case the widening) of the spread between the two contract months.

An intercommodity spread involves buying and selling different futures contracts to take advantage of the relative price changes between the two. A commonly used intercommodity spread is between the three-year and ten-year bond futures which is often used by bond dealers trading the shape of the yield curve.

15

Exchange-traded derivatives: options

Options traded on exchanges such as the Sydney Futures Exchange and the Australian Stock Exchange Derivatives branch (ASXD) are used chiefly for risk management (hedging) but also for investment (trading), as well as for speculation. Risk managers want to protect the value of their assets—bonds or shares—against changes in price and capital value. Traders and speculators use options to make a profit; unlike the hedgers, speculators have no position in the underlying asset but use options because these offer lower transaction costs and the chance for leverage, that is, to gain a large exposure to an underlying asset for a small initial outlay. Some of the following material is similar to that in the section explaining over-the-counter options (chapter 13) but is included here in the interests of those specifically concerned with exchange-traded instruments.

Types of options

Options are described as either *put* or *call*. A put option is an option to sell at a specific price; a call option gives the right to buy at a specific price, at any time between the purchase of an option and its expiry date. A *double option*—more commonly known as a straddle—combines a put and call option and gives the taker the right to sell or buy from the grantor of the option at a given strike price, at any time between the purchase of an option and its expiry date. A straddle is the simplest form of trading on the volatility of the market; it gives the taker the chance to make money no matter which way the market moves, providing the profit is sufficient to cover the cost of a double premium.

Options are defined as *in-the-money*, *at-the-money*, and *out-of-the-money*. A strike price is *in-the-money* if the option can be exercised at a profit at that time. A call is in-the-money when the futures price or prevailing market price is above the strike price of the option. *Out-of-the-money* is the opposite of in-the-money; a put is out-of-the-money if the futures or market price is above the strike price. An option is *at-the-money* if the current strike price is the same as the futures or market price.

Option traders talk of options having an *expiration* (rather than maturity) date—the point at which options expire or become worthless, if not exercised. In futures options, the traded month refers to the month of the underlying futures contract.

The option premium

The option *premium* is the price or cost of an option. From a buyer's point of view, the premium is similar to a one-off insurance premium. For the option writer or seller, the premium is the reward for taking the risk in granting/selling the right conveyed by the option. The grantor tries to set the premium as high as possible but is constrained by the supply from other grantors and demand from the takers. Supply and demand is a basic factor influencing the value of a premium. An anxious buyer and a small number of potential sellers ensures a high premium.

Another influence on the level of an option premium is the *intrinsic value*. This is the amount by which an option is in-the-money. By definition, an option that is out-of-the-money has no intrinsic value but it is often bought because, from a hedger's point of view, this is the ideal area to buy cheap protection. The premium asked for an out-of-the-money option varies depending on how far the strike price is from the futures price and how much time the option has until it expires. For example: in the bill market, futures may be trading at 95.00 and the 9525 put may be priced at 30 points (that is, 25 points of intrinsic value and five points of extrinsic or time value). The 9500 put, being 25 points less valuable, would be priced at only five points (that is, only having time value).

A deep in-the-money option costs more than an at-the-money option because it has more intrinsic value and is more likely to expire in-the-money, or be exercised. The further an option is out-of-the-money, the cheaper becomes its premium, because it is less likely to expire in-the-money or be exercised. Put premiums move in the opposite direction to call premiums. If a call option is in-the-money, then a put option is out-of-the-money.

Options dealers have to take into account the time to expiration of an option and the volatility of the underlying asset on which the option is based. The longer the life of an option, the longer the period the grantor has to carry a risk, so the grantor demands a higher premium. The more volatile the price of the underlying asset, the more risk the grantor is being asked to assume, so the grantor will want a higher reward, again forcing buyers to pay a higher premium. Volatile prices tend to increase the likelihood of an option being exercised, which further influences a grantor to demand a higher premium.

A number of complex formulas exist for valuing options. Most are derived from the Black-Scholes pricing model which highlighted the potential of options for limiting risk. It was developed in the early 1970s by two US economists, Fischer Black and Myron Scholes. Computers have assisted the proliferation of option-pricing formulas.

The valuation of option premiums is of most interest to the grantor or seller. Many ignore the calculations and make judgments about market forces, an approach that is loaded with risk. The hedger who takes or buys options generally merely takes a view about the cost of the premium and whether it is affordable as part of an overall hedging strategy. The more sophisticated hedger trades the market regularly, using options and futures, and structures trading strategies and monitors relative, not merely theoretical, values of premiums.

Financial futures options

Options are available on all financial contracts traded on the Sydney Futures Exchange. Introduced on 1 March 1982, these were the first such options to be traded anywhere in the world. Options have come to be traded in healthy volumes, in contrast to the poor reception they first received when they were less well understood. They are popular because they offer a low-risk or maximum-known-risk strategy (although this applies only to *bought* options, that is bought puts or bought calls).

Futures options are recommended as the best method of limiting risk and are particularly useful if a trader is working with a small amount of capital. An option is the *right* (without the obligation) to buy or sell at the strike (or exercise) price on or before a fixed future date. Options are the ultimate insurance for the option buyer, providing a cushion for a known cost and an unlimited potential for gain. The option seller has to take other factors into account and has the exact opposite risk/reward profile (that is, limited potential for gain, unlimited potential for loss). Options involve two parties: a taker (buyer) and a grantor (seller). The option taker pays a premium to the grantor of the option. The premium is negotiated by the parties to the trade in the same way as they would negotiate the price of the underlying SFE futures contract. But whereas a futures contract is a binding obligation which can only be terminated by closing out, an option taker is not compelled to exercise the option. If the taker does not exercise the option, his or her outlay is confined to the cost of the premium on the option, plus brokerage. The taker's commitment is therefore limited.

The option taker pays for the right to buy or sell a futures contract at an agreed strike price. If the market moves in the forecast direction, the taker exercises the option and trades the opposite way on the futures market to secure a profit. The grantor of an option takes the opposite view to the taker and is in a much riskier position. Grantors can be professional traders or large institutions or companies, familiar with the physical market of the commodity on which the option is based, as well as the futures market. The taker can exercise an option at the strike price at any time before expiry of the option, no matter what level the futures price reaches. To offset this risk, the grantor— who in any case receives a premium—may take a position in the futures market opposite to the option which has been granted.

Exchange-traded options (ETOs), introduced by the SFE in 1985, allow option-holders to trade out of their options if they so choose, giving them more flexibility and thus reducing risk. ETOs have been extremely successful in the US since they were introduced in October 1982 and have also boosted options activity on the SFE. The Philadelphia Stock Exchange is probably the most liquid market for trading foreign currency futures and options, especially on the $A. ETOs are not a phenomenon of the 1980s, however: ETOs were introduced on share contracts in 1973 on the Chicago Board Options Exchange and in 1979 on the European Options Exchange in Amsterdam. Currency options are a more recent development.

In mid-1998 the SFE traded:

Options	Introduced
90-day bank-accepted bills	May 1985
All-Ordinaries share-price index	June 1985
Ten-year treasury bonds	November 1985
Three-year treasury bonds	June 1988
Overnight 3-year and 10-year bond options	November 1993
Serial options*	April 1996
Overnight options on SPI	February 1997

* Serial options, available on three-year and ten-year government bond futures and share-price index futures, are effectively short-dated options which do not expire in the same month as the underlying futures contract. Two serial options are available at any time with the usual quarterly expiring option contract, for example, in July serial SPI options would be listed for expiry in July and August, based on a September futures contract. Serial options have the advantage of a lower-cost premium and offer the chance to use short-term strategies.

Options in practice

Speculation

A speculator, anticipating a fall in futures prices, could buy a put option which means he or she has a short (sold) position, at the option strike price, and knows that the outlay has been defined. For example, in April a speculator believes that interest rates have bottomed, so that interest-rate futures should have peaked in price, but has reservations about selling futures contracts outright because that would bring an exposure to unlimited loss if prices rose further. Instead of selling futures, the speculator could buy ten June put options on 90-day bank-bill futures, for a premium of, say, $250 per contract at a strike price of 96.00. If the options were in the money on the expiry date, that is, the price of June bank-bill futures was below the strike price of 96.00, the speculator would be assigned ten sold 90-day bank-bill futures contracts at 96.00. (NB: only in-the-money options are exercised, out-of-the-money options are left to expire worthless.) To realise the profit, the speculator would then close the position by buying ten June futures contracts. The following would result:

Options bought in April, ten puts June strike 96.00 (yield 4%), premium cost 10 × $250 = $2500

Exercised in June on the date of the option expiry

Speculator is automatically assigned ten sold June futures contracts at the price of 96.00 (yield 4%): value $9 902 333.15

Speculator buys ten June futures at 94.50 (yield 5.5%) to close the position

Value: $9 866 198.13

Profit: $36 135.02

Less outlay of $2500 (cost of premiums)

Net profit: $33 635.02

Hedging

A fund manager intending to buy bonds (at regular tender) in a couple of months runs a risk that bond prices might rise between now and when the funds for the purchase become available. To protect against this, the manager could set the purchase price now by buying call options on bond futures. The manager will be required to pay a premium for the options, which provide a hedge against a rise in the price of bonds. If bond prices fall, however, because interest rates have risen, the manager could abandon the call options and buy bonds at the lower price. The call option essentially puts a floor under the investment rate the manager will receive.

A borrower could also use options to hedge against rising interest rates by buying put options which put a cap on future interest cost. Again the option can be abandoned if lower market interest rates render the hedge unnecessary.

Long straddle

A long straddle is used when an option trader expects a big move in market prices but is uncertain about which direction the move might take. A long straddle comprises a long put and a long call, each with the same strike price and expiry date. The strategy works best when the market is close to the strike price for the two options. The strategy is profitable only at expiry when the futures market has moved substantially up or down. As the table below shows, at expiry, the September SPI futures contract must be above 2550 or below 2250 for a profit to be made on the option position, assuming a 2400 call and put were both bought at a premium of 75 points (that is, total cost of 150 points).

Long straddle

Maximum profit unlimited	Maximum loss sum of the two premiums 75 + 75 = 150	Break-even points at expiry
		1. strike price + sum of two premiums
		2. strike price − sum of two premiums
		1. 2400 + 150 = 2550
		2. 2400 − 150 = 2250

The largest possible loss on a long straddle is the sum of the two premiums, being in this example minus 150 points or $3750 and would be incurred if the futures price remained at its current price of 2400. The maximum profit that can be earned is unlimited. The long straddle would be profitable only if the futures price moved above or below the break-even points of 2550 or 2250.

The opposite of a long straddle is a short straddle, which involves selling both the 2400 put and the 2400 call in the expectation that the market will not move much from its present level. This allows the option seller to earn time premiums from the two options as these premiums decay. The maximum profit will be earned if, at maturity, the market is at, or close to, the exercise price of the two options. The maximum loss is unlimited, but losses would be incurred only if the market were to move substantially from its prevailing price of 2400.

ASXD: equity derivatives

In 1987, following the merger of regional stock exchanges into the Australian Stock Exchange (ASX), the exchange formed a new derivatives division (ASXD). The division has responsibility for equity options (which have been available on the stock exchange since 1976, a mere three years after options over shares had been launched in the futures capital, Chicago) and for developing a product range of equity derivatives. Widely used by retail and institutional investors, ASXD provides a market for trading put and call options on a selected list of actively traded equities. Call options, introduced with great success in 1976, were followed in 1982 by put options and in 1991 by warrants.

Equity options at ASXD are available in three types:

- those issued by companies (company generated), often referred to on overseas markets as warrants; these are issued over new shares so they increase issued capital and generate money for the underlying company;
- ASX warrants, issued by third parties and on overseas markets often referred to as sponsored or covered warrants; and
- exchange-traded options (ETOs) which are created between investors in the options market (the relevant company is not a party to the contract). ETOs deal in options over existing shares and so do not add to a company's share capital or generate income for the company.

Options Clearing House

The Options Clearing House (OCH) clears and registers contracts for ASX. An exception is warrants which, while traded on SEATS (Stock Exchange Automated Trading System) and cleared by CHESS (Clearing House Electronic Subregister System, a computerised subregister system of shareholdings), are issued by individual investment houses and held in corporate registries. OCH handles margining and risk management, and provides services whereby traders and investors can lodge collateral (securities, bank guarantees or financial instruments) as cover against margins on their positions.

OCH uses TIMS (Theoretical Intermarket Margining System), developed in 1986 by Options Clearing Corporation, Chicago, as the first risk-based margining system to be applied to exchange-traded options. TIMS takes into account the volatility, that is, size and frequency of price fluctuations, of the underlying security when calculating an investor's margin obligations. Generally, one margin call is made each day, but if the market moves violently up or down OCH may call for extra margin cover to be lodged (an intraday margin call) to take account of changes in the value of the underlying securities. TIMS breaks margins into two components:

- *premium margin*, being the market value of an investor's position at the close of business, calculated using closing market prices and equating to the amount the investor would need to liquidate a position; and
- *risk margin*, required to cover the potential change in the price of the option contract based on the maximum probable interday (or even intraday with extreme volatility) move in the price of the underlying security.

The total margin is the sum of the risk margin and the premium margin for a given position.

An option writer on ASXD can use collateral, such as share scrip, to cover open positions, or lodge a bank guarantee of a minimum of $25 000 to cover margins, or pledge fixed-interest securities through Austraclear Limited. Writers of options who do not wish to lodge collateral must lodge an initial deposit of at least $2000 with their clearing member; this is in addition to the margins levied by OCH on their positions. OCH calculates interest daily and pays interest on margins monthly, with the interest rate based on prevailing market rates.

Equity derivative products increased in popularity during the 1990s, reflecting the growing direct participation by Australian investors in the sharemarket and the higher investment in shares and consequent need for risk-protection by the burgeoning super fund managers. With superannuation assuming a higher and higher profile, the fund managers—and those individuals who have opted to run their own super funds—are under increasing pressure to perform. The major Australian institutions account for some 60 per cent of the users of equity derivatives, the rest being private individual investors. ASXD has responded to the growing needs of this sector by devising a range of equity risk-management products which includes options over shares, long-term exchange-traded options, flexible options, index options, low-exercise-price options and warrants.

Options over shares enable investors to gain a leveraged exposure to shares; that is, for a fairly small outlay they gain exposure to a substantial parcel of shares. ASXD offers American-style conventional put and call options representing 1000 underlying shares and with no adjustment made for dividends. They are available as standard options and spot options; the latter were introduced in 1991 as one-month 'spot' options over thirteen of the twenty-nine option stocks. Spot options offer protection over limited periods in return for a modest outlay. They are useful as a way of taking cover, say, around the time a company is making an important announcement, or some other factor is causing fluctuations in a stock (share) price, while avoiding the expense of covering a longer time value that might not be needed. Activity in spot options has been increasing to the point where in early 1998 it represented about 20 per cent of turnover on the ASXD options market.

Equity options, or options over listed shares, offer a right, but not an obligation, to buy or sell a given parcel of shares at a set price (the strike or exercise price) at a predetermined date. As with other options, an equity option can be an option to buy (a call) or to sell (a put); thus a call option gives the right, but not the obligation, to buy a stipulated number of shares at a specified price on or before a set date; a put option conveys the right, but not the obligation, to sell a stipulated number of shares at a specified price on or before a set date. The strike or exercise price of the option is the price at which the shares over which the option was written can be bought or sold, should the option holder decide to exercise.

The buyer (also known as taker) of an option pays a premium to the seller (writer or grantor) of the option. The premium represents the full extent of the buyer's potential loss. As with other options, equity options offer the chance for leverage, that is, taking a position in equities which is far larger than the initial outlay (the premium). The limited loss associated with buying (taking) options makes them very attractive to retail investors. An option buyer is in a secure position compared with an option seller. It is the option-holder's decision whether to exercise or not and if he or she decides to exercise his or her option to, say, buy the shares over which the option was written then the option seller has to find the shares. If the option-holder has an option to sell, and decides to exercise, then the option seller has to buy those shares to be sold according to the contract. An option seller (grantor or writer) has far greater exposure than an option buyer and would normally take steps to hedge his or her position. Reflecting their greater exposure, sellers of options are usually required to lodge security, through their clearing member, with the Options Clearing House. Investors buying and selling options on the ASXD options market deal through ASX member organisations which have been approved as clearing members under ASX business rules to enter into option contracts on behalf of clients.

Options are identified by type, for example, put or call, by the name of the underlying shares, expiry date of the options and their strike price—for example, BHP October 1600 calls selling for 90 cents a share. Option prices are quoted in price per share, for example, if Company A calls trade at 50 cents, the value of an option contract (generally over 1000 shares) would be $500. Compare buying a parcel of shares with buying options over shares. To buy 1000 Company A shares, if Company A is trading at $20 a share, a buyer would have to outlay $20 000. But taking an option to buy or sell 1000 Company A shares would involve a fraction of that cost while still bringing the option holder control over 1000 shares. An illustration:

- Company shares are $20. The options have a June 1999 expiry and interest rates are assumed to be 8 per cent and volatility at 20 per cent (that is, the price could move in a 20 per cent band around $20 over the life of the option). The strike price is $20. Based on one of the option-pricing models, Company A call options would be $1.53 and puts 96 cents, so buying calls would cost $1530 and buying puts $960 (plus commissions), outlays which would provide control over 1000 Company A shares worth $20 000.

The cost to the option buyer is the premium, which represents the intrinsic value and time value of the option, intrinsic value being the difference between the market value of the underlying shares and the expiry price of the option. On expiry of the option, the buyer can choose to exercise the option or allow it to lapse. There is no obligation to exercise. Whether a buyer chooses to exercise or not would depend on whether the option were in-the-money, at-the-money or out-of-the-money. For example, there would be no point in exercising a call option whose exercise price is above the prevailing market price for the underlying shares because the shares could be bought more cheaply on the market. The options would be left to lapse. Similarly, there is mileage in exercising put options only if their exercise price is above the market price for shares, enabling the option-holder to sell at a higher-than-market price.

As discussed in chapter 13, several factors influence the value of an option. In the case of an equity option these are:

- the share price;
- the time to expiry of the option;
- the option's exercise price;
- dividends that might be paid before the option expires;
- likely level of interest rates during the option's life;
- volatility of the share price during the option's life (refer chapter 13 for details regarding pricing an option).

Long-term exchange-traded options (LTOs), listed in 1991 over six of the twenty-nine option stocks, are standard options but with expiry dates from nine months to three years. They are generally American-style, with each contract covering 1000 shares, and are similar to the warrants issued by third parties which are also traded on ASXD. As LTO activity declined, ASXD instead introduced a rolling twelve-month cycle for the busiest stocks; in early 1998 these amounted to thirteen out of fifty-three stocks.

Flexible options, introduced in 1994, are a customised product. 'Flex options' are similar to an over-the-counter option in that the expiry date, exercise price, style (American or European) and underlying security can be tailored to suit the parties to the option contract—except that flex options are registered and margined, and cleared by the Options Clearing House (OCH) of ASXD. So they provide the benefits of the adaptability of an OTC with the security of an ETO. Flex options can be written for periods as short as overnight or as long as five years.

Index options are options over the overall movement in the market. The Twenty Leaders index option, launched in 1992, was the first of a series of index options introduced on ASXD. Lack of trading led to ASXD no longer listing new series of index options, although these may be revived at a future date.

LEPOs (low-exercise-price options) are extremely deep in-the-money call options covering 1000 shares and generally having an exercise price of one cent. These are European-style, that is, they can be exercised only on the last trading day before expiry. LEPOs are deliverable, not cash-settled. Because they are deep in-the-money options, the price of a LEPO moves very closely with that of the underlying share. Holding a LEPO is not the same as buying the underlying share because the holder does not receive dividends or have voting rights. However, by buying a LEPO an investor gains a leveraged exposure to share-price movements without the substantial outlay that would be necessary if he or she bought shares. Unlike conventional share option premiums, the premium on LEPOs is not paid in full but is margined so that a LEPO is a highly leveraged instrument similar in risk to a futures contract. This feature led to a dispute between the SFE and ASXD which culminated in a court challenge by the SFE. In March 1995 the court ruled in ASXD's favour and LEPOs began trading.

The following example (adapted from ASXD's *LEPO Explanatory Booklet*), compares the transactions in shares and LEPOs when the market moves against expectations and falls in value. Buying the shares would have resulted in a loss of $785 or 8.9 per cent on the amount invested, while the purchase of the LEPO resulted in a loss of $580 or 109 per cent of the capital invested—a higher

Example of a LEPO: compare buying 1000 Hopeful Mining Corporation (HMC) shares with buying June HMC LEPO

Date	Buy 1000 shares Purchase price = $9330		Buy a LEPO Premium = $9390 per contract or $9.39 per share	
24 May	Buy 1000 HMC @ $9.33	$9330	Risk margin (@ 5% of $9330)	$467 (pay)
	Commissions	$140	Commissions	$60 (pay)
	Stamp duty	$14	Stamp duty	—
	Total outlay	**$9484**	**Total initial outlay**	**$527 (pay)**
31 May	Share price @ $9.35		LEPO price $9.45	
			Risk margin (@ 5%) = $468 ($468 – $467)	$1 (pay)
			Mark-to-market margin ($9450 – $9390)	$60 (return)
			Daily settlement ($60 – 1)	$59 (return)
7 June	Share price @ $9.13		LEPO price @ $9.18	
			Risk margin (@ 5%) = $457 ($457 – $468)	$11 (return)
			Mark-to-market margin ($9180 – $9450)	$270 (pay)
			Daily settlement ($11 – $270)	$259 (pay)
14 June	Sell shares @ $8.90	$8900	Sell LEPO @ $8.93	
	Commissions	$134	Risk margin reversed	$457 (return)
	Stamp duty	$13	Mark-to-market reversed ($9180 – $9390)	$210 (return)
			LEPO gross loss ($8930 – $9390)	$460 (pay)
			Commissions	$60 (pay)
	Total income	$8753	Daily settlement ($457 + $210 – $460 – $60)	$147 (return)
	Total loss	**$731**	LEPO value 14 June	$8930
			less LEPO value 24 May	$9390
			less commissions (2 × $60)	$120
	Cost of funding	$54	No cost of funding	
	Adjusted loss	**$785**	**Total loss**	**$580**

percentage loss on the (small amount of) capital invested but a lower dollar amount than that lost on the shares.

Professional investors (large companies, superannuation fund managers and institutions whose business includes buying and selling shares and other investments) can benefit from the OCH's risk-based margining system, which takes into account all positions in a particular stock and calculates a margin based on the total position. Such offsets apply mostly to premium margins, although some offsets of risk margins are possible. Offsets, which help reduce the amount of premium margin payable, are explained in detail in ASXD's booklet on margins.

Warrants are similar to exchange-traded long-dated options issued by a third party, generally a large financial institution, and traded on the ASX's SEATS with settlements of purchases and sales processed by CHESS in the same way as it handles share transactions. Warrants are not cleared by ASX's Options Clearing House, nor does OCH margin them or novate positions. Warrants are covered by section eight of ASX's business rules. However, while ASXD provides facilities for financial institutions to list warrants on the market it does not guarantee these warrants, so the holder of a warrant is exposed to the creditworthiness and other risks associated with the issuer. ASXD defines a warrant as 'an option which is issued by a financial institution or other approved warrant issuer and traded on ASX share market. Warrants may be issued over assets or instruments such as shares in a particular company or companies, an index or a commodity.' Warrants, enormously popular in overseas markets, began trading on ASXD in 1991 and activity has reflected their increasing popularity, as evidenced by an almost five-fold increase in monthly turnover in 1997 compared with 1996.

Growth in the warrant market has been assisted by an expanding group of warrant issuers, spearheaded by Bankers Trust, Deutsche Bank and Macquarie Bank, which in turn led to warrants being issued over an increasing number of stocks and in a wider variety of types. Also, retail investors have become more aware of warrants, while at the same time overseas interest in Australian equities markets has grown.

Warrants are not standardised but can be tailored to various terms to suit the holder and can be written as put or call option contracts over shares, indices, currencies, commodities or securities. A call warrant gives the buyer the right, but not the obligation, to buy the underlying asset at a predetermined price on or possibly before a given date. A put warrant gives the buyer the right, but not the obligation, to sell the underlying security at a predetermined price, on or possibly before a given date. The warrant buyer pays the warrant seller for this right; the market price of a warrant is set by the forces of supply and demand, and so varies from day to day.

Warrants offer the flexibility of being either American or European in style and delivery can be in the form of cash or the underlying asset. Warrant issuers undertake to make a market in these instruments and this underpins their liquidity. The premium on a warrant is influenced by the same factors affecting option premiums, such as the prevailing price level and volatility of the underlying asset, the level of interest rates, exercise price and time to expiry. However, the premium can also be affected by the creditworthiness of the issuer, and adjustments for a bonus or rights issue or a dividend. Because warrants are to all intents long-dated options, they are more expensive than standard options because of the time value. Unlike exchange-traded options, though, warrants cannot be short sold; that is, if an investor wants to sell a warrant, he or she must first own one. If an investor owning a warrant decides to exercise then the warrant issuer has to sell the underlying asset at the exercise price (in the case of a call warrant) or, in the case of a put warrant, buy the underlying asset at the exercise price. In certain cases, such as the exercise of a cash-settled warrant, the warrant issuer may be obliged to make a cash payment instead. Warrant issuers do not have to make a margin payment to cover their obligations under the warrant. From the point of view of the warrant-holder, warrants (except low-exercise-price warrants, discussed below) offer considerable leverage as the investor gains an entry to the market in return for a small outlay.

Basket warrants cover shares from a group of different companies which might be in a common industry such as mining or banking. Basket warrants offer investors a chance to profit from the performance of a group of companies or from a particular industry.

Capital Plus warrants cover a basket of shares. These warrants are generally issued for around $1000 each, with the issuer guaranteeing at least this amount will revert to the warrant-holder when the warrant expires. Capital Plus warrants carry European-style exercise and the holder can choose to receive either the shares covered by the warrant or a cash payment. The warrants are issued for five years, with their value rising and falling in line with the value of the underlying shares; warrant-holders, who can sell their warrants at any time before expiry, are not entitled to dividends from these shares.

Fractional warrants are warrants issued to cover only a part, or fraction, of a share, so that the minimum holding of one marketable parcel of fractional warrants is a less expensive investment than buying ordinary share warrants.

Fully covered warrants are call warrants designed to reduce the risk associated with a particular warrant issue by requiring the issuer to place the underlying shares in, say, a trust, with the shares held to ensure that the issuer fulfils its obligations should the warrant buyer exercise his or her right to buy the underlying shares. As call warrants are issued, the issuer buys the necessary number of shares and places them in a trust or some other custodial arrangement.

Index warrants, based on the level of a share-price index, enable investors to take advantage of a movement in the overall market, or a sector of the market, rather than of an individual share price. Index warrants are generally cash-settled, with the payment calculated using a multiplier determined at the outset by the warrant issuer.

Instalment warrants are similar to conventional warrants except that the holder of an instalment warrant is entitled to any dividends, and possibly franking credits, that might be paid by the company over whose shares the warrants have been issued. The initial purchase cost of an instalment warrant can be higher than that of a conventional warrant.

Endowment warrants require payment of an initial premium of between 30 and 60 per cent of the prevailing share price, with the remainder of the share price covered for the term of the warrant by the expected dividend stream from the underlying shares. If, however, this proves insufficient, then the warrant-holder has to make up any gap when the warrant expires. Endowment warrants have a European-style exercise and are a longer-term 'buy and hold' investment; they differ from ordinary warrants in that they do not have a fixed exercise price and expiry date but an 'outstanding amount' which changes over time; in fact, it generally reduces as dividends paid by the underlying company are applied to the balance. In some cases franking credits also help reduce the outstanding amount.

Low-exercise-price warrants, as the name suggests, are warrants with a very low exercise price, usually of one cent. The buyer of a low-exercise-price warrant pays the full premium when buying the warrant and receives the underlying shares when the warrant expires. Low-exercise-price warrants appeal to overseas institutions because they offer the advantage of exposure to the stock without paying for franking credits which the foreign warrant-holder, which does not pay Australian tax, cannot use. These warrants generally have European-style exercise.

16

Dealing, settling and payments

A popular term among dealers for someone preoccupied with numbers and computers is a *rocket scientist*. This seems entirely appropriate, because at first glance a dealing room strikingly resembles a space agency control room, with large numbers of people gazing at banks of screens. Resemblance fades at the second glance, when it becomes apparent that while the operators' eyes are locked on to screens, their ears appear to be glued to telephones, and the room is filled with voices, a background hum punctuated by urgent cries, seemingly addressed to no-one in particular, of 'To the right' (the figure to right, or the offer figure, whereas 'to the left' would be the bid in an exchange rate of, say, 65.50/53) and 'Nineties' indicating 90-day bank-bills of exchange.

Welcome to the dealing room of the 21st century.

The plethora of electronic communications equipment and telephone activity reflects the reality that the instant receipt and dissemination of information is the lifeblood of dealing rooms everywhere—in Australia, Asia, the US and Europe. This need for the most up-to-date information is not new: the world's best-known electronic news and information service, Reuters, began in 1849 when its founder, Julius Reuter, realised the extent of the market for news and started a continental pigeon post. Technological change was swift. He forsook his birds for a telegraph office in London in 1851 and was soon transmitting international bulletins to newspapers around the world. What is new is the number and sophistication of the tools that today facilitate the flow of information.

The three chief sources of financial information are Reuters, Bridge Telerate and Bloomberg. A number of dealing rooms also have televisions continuously tuned to CNN and receive Reuters

Financial Television (RFTV) through their desk-top PCs which enables them to watch live broadcasts of the US Fed chairman addressing Congress or the RBA governor delivering a talk, instead of just reading headlines on-screen. Bloomberg is widely credited as providing the best historical data and to be the most user-friendly, if expensive, service, which leads many dealing rooms to operate with a limited number of terminals which are shared among staff. Dealers turn to Reuters as a source of extensive world-wide coverage. The umbilical connection to news sources is not interrupted when dealers are away from their desks; they carry small pagers which provide instant access to current prices as well as news stories that might break while they are out of the office.

The foreign-exchange markets use two Reuters systems—2001 and 2002. The Reuters 2001 is used to communicate with other dealers, onshore and offshore, as well as for agreeing transactions. Reuters 2002, which enables bids and offers to be matched electronically and provides hard-copy confirmation of a deal, and EBS (Electronic Broking Service) are foreign-exchange dealing systems. Participants display prices at which they are prepared to deal and if a buyer and seller's price corresponds a deal is done. The Reuters screen is divided into several windows which show prices in different products and markets. Information continuously flows in and out. While most financial markets dealing takes place by telephone, increasingly sophisticated screen systems are evolving and will continue to have an impact on dealing-room practices. The terms of a deal, whether in the domestic or foreign-exchange market, are printed in the back office (settlements area) where details are checked. The transaction is then confirmed and settlement takes place. Systems such as SWIFT (Society for Worldwide Interbank Financial Telecommunications) carry instructions for the exchange of astronomical numbers of dollars across the world each day. Estimates in 1998 suggested that the amount passing through the system each day totalled about $US6 trillion.

Telephone lines are the markets' arteries. Every day, all day, dealers talk by telephone—to other dealers in the professional markets, to clients whom they advise and to whom they quote prices. Much conversation is informal and sociable as dealers cultivate a 'feel' for the clients' business that will enable them to structure prices and products to suit particular requirements. Dealers talk to brokers who may be able to find an acceptable party for the other side of a deal. The role of voice brokers (brokers with whom a dealer communicates by telephone, not using a screen) has diminished but they are still in demand in some situations. For example, during a crisis such as the Asian financial markets' collapse in late 1997, a bank's credit department may decide that it does not wish the bank to be owed money, however briefly, by a particular organisation or group of organisations. Since a dealer can be hit on a price (have a price accepted) he or she has displayed on a screen by anyone who wishes to deal at that price, a situation can arise where the dealer is faced with the difficult prospect of having to decline a customer for credit reasons. A broker is able to substitute one counterparty for another without the dealer who initiated the transaction having to reveal his or her inability to deal, so avoiding embarrassing both parties. (All telephone conversations in a dealing room are tape-recorded as a precaution against a dispute arising over deal details, with the tapes generally retained for six months.)

The international financial markets and the dealers who form the front line are often portrayed as predators seeking quick opportunities for profit, preying on weak and ailing economies, attacking and withdrawing, leaving only wreckage behind. This image masks the reality that most activity in the Australian markets is directed towards forming relationships with clients and helping them to avoid, or at least manage, risks. In fact, risk management has become a major preoccupation in treasury operations. The overriding preoccupation, of course, remains the bottom line—that is, to make a profit. The hunters do exist and their activities attract much publicity, but the image of the circling shark is misleading. Dealers come from a variety of backgrounds but most are highly qualified, with finance or economics training. They are numerate and articulate individuals who interface with a client base that is also well-informed. The growing integration and proliferation of products means that they are often multi-skilled and flexible. Financial markets are global and the Australian markets a small but important sector in those vast markets; dealers need to understand the external factors which are often major influences on their markets.

A dealing room is no place for the faint-hearted. Dealers work long hours under high levels of stress. Competition for business is fierce. Mergers and acquisitions among banks and investment banks have resulted in a rationalisation in the industry and dealing teams have been downsized; however, the significant players in the market still have teams of between 50 and 100 dealers, sometimes more. Competition and intensified focus on costs and returns resulted in recruiting slowing in the late 1990s and, as a consequence, the average age of dealers increased slightly. Reflecting the increased dependence on technology, staff numbers in the settlements areas have also declined, even although the volume of transactions has increased enormously. Such is the demand for jobs in the financial markets, however, that it is not unusual for banks to receive applications from people offering to work for nothing just to get started.

Dealers in Australia must be accredited by AFMA (Australian

Financial Markets Association). They must have a thorough knowledge of products and participants in the market; they are also required to be aware of their obligations concerning compliance and legal and ethical issues. In recognition of the growing complexity and demands placed on staff in the settlements areas of banks, there is a move for a similar accreditation process for members of the Australian Treasury Operations Association (ATOA).

Dealing rooms are not uniform but they do conform to roughly similar structures. Most organisations have favoured a clear distinction between staff dedicated to marketing and those who are price-makers or distributors, but some prefer to subdivide their marketers by products or term, others by clients. Price-makers are responsible for a product or range of products, and are able to give quotes quickly to a marketer keen to respond to a client. For example, a corporate client may wish to invest surplus cash for a couple of weeks, so the client officer needs to know what a bank would be willing to pay for funds. Distributors focus on clients for whom they place debt securities such as notes or bonds. Nonetheless, even in companies which prefer to segregate products, there is a clear emphasis on communication between those talking to the same clients. Dealers need above all to be team players.

Each dealing room has a manager responsible for ensuring that the team is coordinated and the dealers motivated and satisfied. Given the growth in dealing activities and complexities involved— legal and ethical as well as financial—many organisations have appointed a manager for each section of a dealing room, with each manager reporting to a treasurer who has overall responsibility for the funding area. A typical financial markets division of a bank or investment bank would include sections covering funding and securities trading, origination and distribution, debt and capital markets products, foreign exchange, futures, structured finance and securitisation, equities, possibly metals and certainly economics and research.

While dealing rooms operate first and foremost as teams, some still have a place for dedicated (proprietary) traders whose task is to analyse different markets, onshore and offshore, searching for profit opportunities arising from anomalies, discrepancies or trends. However, large-scale speculative trading has, for the most part, disappeared. The withdrawal of the more entrepreneurial players in foreign exchange, and the misadventures of companies which suffered large losses through the activities of rogue traders, particularly in derivatives, has removed key participants. Speculation has not disappeared completely but it flourishes best with volatility which, in the domestic markets, diminished with the advent of low, stable interest rates.

Risk management

Dealers have to manage a range of risks—market, credit, settlement and delivery, financial, operational and legal risks. In response to the derivatives-related losses of the early 1990s, the Group of Thirty produced a comprehensive set of 24 recommendations for dealers and end-users covering the role of senior management, the need for dealers to mark their derivatives positions to market and the importance of stress-testing (marking a portfolio to market and then analysing the impact on its value of large price movements). In October 1995, after reckless trading by a dealer given excessive latitude had brought down the UK bank Barings Plc, the president of the New York Federal Reserve, William McDonough, summed up risk management as 'active oversight by directors and senior management; well-conceived risk measurement and reporting systems; comprehensive internal controls emphasising the clear separation of duties; and well-defined limits on risk taking'.

The growing emphasis on risk management takes different forms. For example, to minimise settlement and delivery risk, initiation of a deal is rigidly separated from its settlement and exposures are immediately and closely monitored. Increasingly, dealers input deals directly, that is, the dealer enters the deal details into a computer as the deal is done and the details flow through to the settlements area where they are checked and the deal processed. The deal, once entered, cannot be altered. Confirmation with the counterparty is often handled by the settlements staff. The direct input system enables limits to be constantly monitored; as each deal is done, the bank's exposure to the counterparty is immediately updated. If the limit is broken, the information is available straightaway to management as well as to the other dealers. Financial disasters such as the collapse of Barings have left a legacy of caution. In some organisations the separation between dealing and settlement is such that dealers are physically excluded from the settlements area. The concept of a 'middle office' has developed, falling between the dealers and the back office but liaising with each, particularly with settlement of a complex deal, and generally overseeing risk management, accounting and internal audit, and ensuring that customer and trading limits are observed. Financial markets have become very conscious of compliance and the need to operate within well-defined limits and controls.

As the markets have developed, increasingly complex instruments have evolved. Measuring the different elements of risk carried by these instruments can be extremely difficult. Dealers involved in this derivatives market may spend a significant part of their day analysing seemingly esoteric issues such as basis risk, correlation risk or theta risk. But all this apparent exotic and arcane calculation is built around a fairly predictable timetable, particularly in the domestic market, that is, the part of the market that focuses on business inside Australia.

The shape of the day

Dealers' days begin early, about 7.30 am. The start can be earlier for foreign-exchange traders and, since the introduction of real-time gross settlement (see chapter 4), for those responsible for a bank's liquidity management. Much of the first hour is taken up in checking overnight developments overseas, with the emphasis on the major US markets. Foreign-exchange dealers who have worked an overnight shift may hand over positions and pass on information gathered during their working hours. Dealers scan their screens for useful information and hold meetings and discussions among themselves to aid in formulating and setting strategies. There may be briefings from in-house economists and phone link-ups with interstate offices. It is not uncommon for economics teams and researchers to be a part of the dealing room and to participate in the early morning meetings. Those who follow charts may talk about trends they have identified. Overall, this early part of the day is spent assimilating information based on what happened during the Australian night but, more important, preparing for the hours ahead. The early-morning exchanges are likely to be fairly informal; other more formal but less frequent meetings take place where longer-term strategies are discussed. The morning meeting includes planning for short-term trading, considering what securities might be offered to clients out of portfolio, what tender panels might require bids and whether the RBA is holding a bond or treasury note tender. Most security transactions are executed by noon. Marketing and discussions with clients continue all day and in the afternoon trades are structured for settlement on the following day. For many senior operators in financial markets the day has no end but moves seamlessly through the 24-hour clock.

A fixed-income trader's day starts around 7.15 am with a quick review of what has occurred overnight in the major overseas markets. Traders would read faxes and electronic mail from overseas offices and clients, and consult their Reuters, Bridge Telerate and Bloomberg screens to capture the latest developments. Dealers begin talking to clients between 7.45 am and 8.30 am; they talk to issuers about asset and liabilities management, and examine their own domestic and overseas exposures. Bond futures opens at 8.30 am and the activity accelerates. Brokers start ringing around, and the day's quoting begins. Pressure points vary through the day depending, for example, on whether there is a bond tender or a major state government issue or an economic release in Australia or overseas. Trading opportunities can occur during 'thin' periods ahead of, or immediately following, a major announcement, such as the CPI, growth in average weekly earnings or national accounts figures. At times, such an announcement could spark a flurry of activity. The Sydney Futures Exchange's electronic trading system, SYCOM (Sydney Computerised Market, see chapter 14), extended the fixed-income trading day; futures trading on SYCOM opens at 4.40 pm, close to the end of the day-trading session at 4.30 pm and continues through the Australian night until 6 am (7 am during daylight saving). Potentially, then, fixed-income trading is a 24-hour market.

The day's trading session at the Sydney Futures Exchange starts at 8.30 am but futures brokers would have been in their offices much earlier, gathering information from their own sources and checking on deals done overnight on SYCOM. With the opening of trading at the SFE, the main activities of the day begin in the domestic financial markets. At 9.30 am the Reserve Bank announces the system cash figure on Reuters—that is, the total amount of liquidity that is available on that day. At the same time, the RBA informs the market of its planned dealing activity for the day. Dealers have until 10 am to respond. Between 10 am and 10.15 am the two Reuters screen pages BBSW and BBSY are updated. BBSW, originally established by a number of swap dealers who wanted a common bank-bill mid-rate, has come to be used for pricing a range of instruments. BBSY emerged as the issuers and buyers of bank paper realised they did not always price loans at a mid-rate; a number of banks put in a bid, mid and offer rate, with the highest and lowest of these removed and the remainder averaged. So BBSY shows the average bid, mid and offer rate for 30, 60, 90, 120, 150 and 180 days and the pricing of new issues and loans is based on these figures. At 10.30 am the Reserve Bank informs dealers whose bids or offers for stock have been successful. As 11 am approaches renegotiations are completed for call cash—that is, the money lent for the shortest term (overnight). This short-term cash may be lent at any time during the day but repayment must be requested or a new rate negotiated by 11 am. Treasury note tenders are held each Tuesday and bids have to be lodged electronically with the Reserve Bank by noon; likewise, with a bond tender, bids have to be with the central bank by noon.

Australian economic statistics relating to topics such as wages, economic growth, employment, the balance of trade, retail sales and inflation are released at 11.30 am and on days when data are expected this can produce an upsurge in activity, depending on the degree of correlation between expectations and reality. By midday the markets have generally settled. Futures trading closes between 12.30 pm and 2 pm. Most dealing rooms operate with a skeleton staff through the lunch break, mostly to interact with the Asian centres, undertake corporate trades and to note any political or economic announcement that might be made. The futures exchange's day-trading session finishes at 4.30 pm. Orders that have to be filled after this time are carried out on SYCOM and futures brokers can see a flurry of activity towards the end of trading when these are placed.

Real-time gross settlement (RTGS) has had an impact on the routine of the domestic market. The dealers responsible for the banks' liquidity and the settlements area have to be continuously aware of the flows in and out of their accounts at the RBA. In the early days of transition to the new system this monitoring absorbed a large part of the day's activities as people accustomed themselves to the changes. Between 7 am and 9 am banks settle transactions generated overnight by the clearing house (the net deferred funds that are the balances of all small transactions which take place between banks each day and those generated by ATM and EFTPOS activity). Should a bank have a final negative balance, it has until 8.45 am to rectify this by borrowing from another bank. A bank cannot undertake any transaction that involves spending funds unless it has sufficient funds in its exchange-settlement account. Banks' cash traders manage liquidity positions throughout the day; given that the cash rate sits within a narrow, Reserve Bank-determined band, the cash traders' role is to ensure there is adequate liquidity to support trading, not to finesse the overnight cash rate. At the other end of the day, after RTGS closes (4.30 pm Monday to Thursday and 5 pm on Friday) banks have 45 minutes in the 'closed settlement session' in which to fund any shortfall between themselves. Such a shortfall might occur if late SWIFT messages involve late payments. This activity lengthens the day for dealers responsible for a bank's liquidity and for those working in the back offices.

The foreign-exchange (forex) market has its own daily rhythm. Although the markets can deal 24 hours a day, they close at the weekend, so the official opening time each week, as designated by the ACI (Association Cambiste Internationale) which is the global forex association, is 5 am on Monday (Sydney time). Apart from this specific point the forex market revolves around the opening times of markets around the world. The high profile of the Australian dollar in world trading and investment, and the volume transacted in northern hemisphere markets overnight, means the day is constantly unfolding for Australian foreign-exchange traders. On reaching their desks their first task is to familiarise themselves, from as many sources as possible, with what happened in their absence.

Senior traders would have a video screen at home, so that they can track worldwide market intelligence—and rumours. The day that starts in Sydney and Melbourne has already begun in New Zealand and continues through to Tokyo, Hong Kong and Singapore then on to Bahrain, Europe (usually Frankfurt or Zurich), then London and New York and finally the US West Coast. The Asian markets are only a matter of hours behind Sydney; depending on the time of the year, the European markets open between 4 pm and 6 pm Australian time, and New York starts at midnight. In the larger organisations dealers work shifts and the desk is staffed around the clock. The evening shift starts at approximately 4.30 pm and hands over to the early shift about midnight. Departing dealers pass on open positions and client orders and discuss with arrivals any developments that may have occurred. Many non-Australian banks do not centre their foreign-exchange operations in Sydney; rather, they report to a 'hub' which may be Singapore, Hong Kong or Tokyo. These operations coordinate operations in currencies other than the Australian and New Zealand dollars.

The timetables described here only form the skeleton of an average day in the markets. But at any time, anywhere in the world, a politician or commentator may make a statement that dramatically and instantly shifts the currency up or down or changes expectations regarding short-term interest rates. In quiet periods the pressure points and deadlines may pass, if not quite unnoticed, at least with minimal impact. At other times a deadline or announcement could have an overwhelming effect on the day's activities. If, for example, an unexpectedly bad trade figure is reported at 11.30 am, the resulting furore can make all other considerations seem almost irrelevant. Pressure on the Australian dollar can result in considerable anxiety ahead of the opening of overseas markets. Financial markets, like every operation, have periods where activity slows but overall they remain areas of vitality and continual activity and challenge.

The back office (settlements)

The processes which take place within treasury operations (settlements area or back office) can be broadly characterised as recording, confirming and payment. Once completed in the dealing room, a transaction is passed to the back office for action.

The dealing room is responsible for producing bottom-line profit; the back office is responsible for preserving that profit. One of the essential differences in these responsibilities is that a dealer can use 'stop-loss' and 'stop-profit' tools to limit his or her potential profit or loss. The back office cannot. Performing its function requires clear understanding, adequate controls, an awareness of risks and, should an error occur, an ability to rectify it quickly. And the widespread use of technology, combined with the large volumes of funds traded and changes to settlement procedures, has placed growing weight and importance on the back-office support staff. They, together with the dealers on the trading desk, are responsible for the efficient and profitable operations of a treasury unit—the part of an organisation (bank, investment bank or company) that manages funding and interest-rate and exchange-rate risks.

The first function performed by the back office is recording. Automation enables dealers to record a trade by feeding its details into a computer system linked to the back office which ensures that all relevant data are correct and passes the deal details to Austraclear for payment and settlement. Any ambiguity or errors are returned by the back office to the dealer for clarification. Confirmation, once a deal has been correctly recorded, ensures that the two counterparties to a transaction have recorded identical details. This exchange of information can be handled by telephone, letter or through Austraclear. Where a transaction has been carried out using a Reuters or Telerate screen, a hard-copy print-out is accepted as firm evidence of the trade, provided all the necessary information is included. Confirmations are occasionally received on a facsimile machine; however, these are often treated with caution because fax messages can be faked. Where a broker has been used to execute a trade, he or she also confirms the trade to both parties; this is additional information and in the Australian market is considered as confirmation.

When a transaction matures the funds are transferred (and securities exchanged) according to the confirmation details and the deal settled. The methods used to effect funds transfer include:

- Austraclear, where both the sender and receiver acknowledge transfer;
- SWIFT (Society for Worldwide Interbank Financial Telecommunications), where authenticated messages are sent to authorise a debit of an account against payment to the beneficiary. SWIFT operates 24 hours a day as a means of transmitting foreign-exchange payment messages, although it is not part of any payment clearing system. The system provides for electronic transmission, rapidly and at low cost, of various messages from one member to another member or members, using a dedicated computer network with a high level of security and of global standardisation. SWIFT is a non-profit society, with headquarters in Brussels, Belgium, owned by its members, who must be involved in the transfer of international financial messages. Members number around 1500, representing 65 countries.

Most financial markets participants in Australia are members of SWIFT;

- EFT (electronic funds transfer);
- tested telex (authenticated messages between an account holder and banker) authorising the debit of an account against payment to the beneficiary; and
- cheque payments physically delivered to the beneficiary or the beneficiary's banker.

There is inevitably a risk that errors could be made during the process of recording, confirming and payment and any ensuing cost to a company—from covering overdraft cheques or unfavourable interest-rate movements—could be huge. It is therefore essential that back-office staff understand their role and are aware of the potential impact they carry for the company's overall position. To assist with settlements, the Australian market uses standardised documentation for the various products (these are covered in AFMA's guide to OTC documentation).

Austraclear

Financial markets settlements are handled by Austraclear's computerised settlement system, bringing a fast, efficient and secure method of settling security purchases and sales. Austraclear dramatically altered settlements for the Australian money market by eliminating the physical delivery of securities and providing a neutral settlement system for transactions and an electronic funds transfer mechanism for same-day settlement of cash transactions. Until the arrival of Austraclear, cheques and securities were collected and delivered by settlements clerks who spent their days hurrying around the city from dealer company to client or bank. Such individuals are now part of a colourful past.

Austraclear began operating in 1984, initially accepting promissory notes, bank bills, commercial bills and bank certificates of deposit, then including treasury notes, corporate and semi-government bonds, forward bill transactions and forward rate agreements (FRAs). It also worked with the Reserve Bank to develop RITS, an electronic system for settling government bonds. Austraclear was established with two objectives: to provide safe custody for money-market securities and to provide a clearing facility for cash and securities. A key benefit of the Austraclear system is that it enables the cash settlement side of a transaction to be completed on the same day, so a trader does not run the risk of giving good security and receiving a bad cheque; if a buyer cannot meet a commitment the security reverts to the seller.

Austraclear's head office is in Sydney but the computerised (real-time) system operates nationally. Austraclear did not change the pattern of trading but reduced the risk of human error in the settlement procedures. Given the speed with which settlements have to be carried out, and the frequency with which volumes of securities change hands each day, it is a tribute to those involved that few mishaps occurred during those years when cheques and securities were hand-delivered from client to client and bank to bank. Austraclear immobilises the securities in its vaults and electronically records changes in ownership or entitlement as they are traded or pledged as collateral. The speed and efficiency of settling through Austraclear has helped boost trading volumes in the market. Austraclear's daily turnover reflects market conditions and, in the first half of 1998, varied between $16 billion on a slow day and $20 billion in hectic trading.

One money-market practice that changed with the advent of Austraclear was the convention of endorsing bills of exchange when bought; the endorsements on the reverse side of a bill recorded the chain of ownership during the life of the bill and were evidence of the contingent liability of each endorser until it matured. The bills held in Austraclear are not physically endorsed but rank as if they were, with Austraclear holding the record of ownership. Austraclear checks the details of the securities it holds but does not underwrite the validity of these securities.

The membership of Austraclear represents the professional money market. Dealers in the professional market communicate with Austraclear through their own computer terminals, connected to the main Austraclear computer, and settlements staff input the details of securities to be switched. Large companies whose treasury operations virtually equate to small in-house banks may be members but most companies' turnover and activity would justify associate rather than full membership. Transactions between an Austraclear member and a non-member are handled outside the Austraclear system, and involve the old-style physical delivery of cheques and/or securities. Banks are involved with Austraclear both as members and as participating banks, providing cash clearance accounts for Austraclear members. The Reserve Bank is a party to the system as a participating bank to provide cash accounts for banks and others which hold accounts with the central bank.

Immobilising securities in computerised systems such as Austraclear, once seen as revolutionary, now appears to be no more than another stage in the search for the perfect settlements system. The Group of Thirty, a private-sector international group established to examine the efficiency of settlement systems, reported in 1989 that a number of countries had moved beyond immobilisation towards 'dematerialisation' of paper—eliminating the physical paper so that securities exist only as computer records. These securities are known as electronically recorded obligations transferable in computers, or EROTICs. A change to the Bills of Exchange Act would be necessary to achieve this in Australia with discount securities such as bills of exchange, promissory notes and certificates of deposit, because the Act defines the bill as an order 'in writing'. The practice of registering Australian government securities in the form of inscribed stock at the Reserve Bank, rather than holding them as bearer securities, is an early form of dematerialisation.

Future directions

In an effort to control cross-border settlement risk, a group of banks from the main OECD countries established Continuous Linked Settlement Services (CLSS) Ltd as a step towards a global clearing system. Impetus for CLSS came from a BIS study highlighting settlement risk in the trillion-dollar foreign-exchange markets. In 1998 CLSS was calling for new members and capital. Only countries with real-time gross settlement systems in place for domestic operations are eligible to join the system, which will operate through a New York-based clearer, the CLS bank, on a real-time gross settlement basis.

Industry associations: AFMA and ATOA

The expansion of financial markets, the growth in volumes of cash and securities they handle and the increasingly complex nature of some of the products developed have forced a maturity and formality among market participants. Where once dealing procedures were little more than market conventions passed on by word of mouth, they have come to be recorded as codes of behaviour that must be followed in the interests of the financial markets remaining, for the most part, self-regulatory. The development of the Australian Financial Markets Association (AFMA) is an example of how the financial markets have grown and adapted to new procedures. The establishment of the Australian Treasury Operations Association (ATOA) illustrates the increasing importance of ensuring the back office functions efficiently and is kept informed and up-to-date with new products.

AFMA began in the mid-1980s as little more than a luncheon club and grew into an industry organisation with a full-time executive director. The association developed in response to a need to formalise dealing procedures. It has set down dealing standards, market conventions and trading principles that have become firm rules. A key impetus in this was the spread of screen-trading. AFMA's predecessor, the bill dealers' group, met to define which bills were acceptable on the Reuters screen and to establish guidelines for trading. The group grew into the Screen Dealers' Association and expanded to cover issues besides bills. At the same time other market sectors launched their own representative groups, such as the Bond Dealers' Group and the Swaps Dealers' Association. A logical step was to combine into one association: AFMA. The association liaises regularly with other market bodies, regulators and government about market issues. AFMA established a code of conduct as a framework of reference for business behaviour and market practices, and also publishes a range of market-related information guides.

The Australian Treasury Operations Association (ATOA) began in 1987 to provide a way for those in the settlements area (back office) to be involved in changing market procedures and to keep track of new products. Financial deregulation and intensified competition brought increasing pressures to those in the back office. ATOA's objectives include developing and standardising treasury operating practices and procedures, providing a forum for discussion on treasury control and management, fostering training, liaising with local and international bodies on matters relating to treasury operations and providing information to members about developments and current issues.

ATOA's members include representatives from banks, investment banks, government bodies and finance companies (most of which are also members of AFMA). Like AFMA, ATOA supports further education for its members so that they are familiar with the arcane terminology often used in financial markets and understand products, procedures and the associated risk factors. Members of these associations attend the several courses offered by the Securities Institute of Australia which are relevant for the treasury environment.

Index